W9-ARA-297

The Origins of the Second World War

MAURICE BAUMONT

The Origins
of the
Second
World War

TRANSLATED BY SIMONE DE COUVREUR FERGUSON

NEW HAVEN AND LONDON, YALE UNIVERSITY PRESS, 1978

Published with assistance from the foundation established in memory of
Henry Weldon Barnes of the Class of 1882, Yale College.

Designed by Sally Harris
and set in Times Roman type.
Printed in the United States of America by
Vail-Ballou Press, Inc., Binghamton, N.Y.

Published in Great Britain, Europe, Africa, and Asia (except Japan) by
Yale University Press, Ltd., London. Distributed in Australia and New
Zealand by Book & Film Services, Artarmon, N.S.W., Australia; and in
Japan by Harper & Row, Publishers, Tokyo Office.

Library of Congress Cataloging in Publication Data

Baumont, Maurice.
  The origins of the Second World War.

  Translation of Les origines de la deuxième guerre mondiale.
  Bibliography: p.
  Includes index.
  1. World War, 1939-1945—Causes. I. Title.
D741.B2813   940.53'1   77-16652
ISBN 0-300-02215-8

10-31-78

Contents

Preface

I feel obliged to relate the circumstances in which this study of the origins of the Second World War was composed. I hope that readers will excuse me if certain personal details do not have a direct relationship to the work.

A graduate of the École Normale Supérieure with advanced degrees in history and geography, after the armistice of 1918, I had the privilege of working at the Bern embassy with such prestigious École Normale graduates as André François-Poncet and René Massigli.

From July 1919 to March 1927, I lived in Berlin, an excellent place for observation and study, with men very well informed on German affairs, such as Émile Haguenin, who died in 1924, and Oswald Hesnard. In 1922, in collaboration with a fellow graduate Marcel Berthelot, I wrote a book on postwar Germany, *Les lendemains de guerre et de révolution en Allemagne.* Our director at the École Normale, Ernest Lavisse, introduced the book to the public. We had attempted to distinguish, through a chaos stirred by violent upheavals, the indistinct and difficult birth of a new Germany.

From 1927 to 1940 at Geneva, I was a member of the International Secretariat of the League of Nations, which included such eminent thinkers as Jacques Rueff (until 1930) and Henri Bonnet (until 1932). I became friendly with remarkable men, of very diverse backgrounds and viewpoints: Joseph Avenol, Pierre Comert, Marcel Hoden, and others, to mention only the French. In such a milieu and in complete freedom of thought, we found ourselves in contact with the realities of international life.

Since 1946 I have been the "French editor-in-chief" of the German foreign ministry documents which were seized, in various hiding places in Thuringia and the Riesengebirge, by the American troops as they advanced into Germany. The American, English, and French governments decided to edit and publish these archives. They entrusted the task to historians, who were charged with the selection of "documents essential for understanding German foreign policy before and during the Second World War," and who were to be guided in their work only by scientific considerations.

The goal was to present a picture of the diplomatic activity of contemporary Germany "on the basis of the highest scientific objectivity," a formula which, far from being an empty phrase, defined a standard of conduct. The editors made their selection solely on this criterion. Their choice was not governed by political expediency; one cannot serve his country well by harming the truth.

Most of the mysteries about Hitler disappeared quickly, thanks to the historical treasures unearthed by the fortunes of war. In 1950, the great English historian Sir Lewis Namier told us that already Hitler was a "dead horse"; he felt that the essentials about him were known, although Weimar Germany remained somewhat enigmatic. On the Hitler years, 1933–39, countless details and testimonies from all quarters allowed truly reliable historical accounts.

Having earned a doctorate from the University of Paris with dissertations on German coal and heavy industry, *La grosse industrie allemande et le charbon* and *La grosse industrie allemande et le lignite,* I first taught economic geography at the Conservatoire National des Arts et Métiers, and then contemporary history at the Sorbonne.

For ten years I was a professor at the Institut Universitaire de Hautes Études Internationales in Geneva. Its founders, the Swiss William Rappard and the Frenchman Paul Mantoux, honored me with an invitation to this excellent meeting place of teachers and students from all countries. I cannot express too strongly my gratitude to the Institut in Geneva, and especially to its director, Jacques Freymond.

Introduction

To give a reasonably precise idea of the origins of the Second World War, we must recall briefly the nature of the Treaty of Versailles, which ended "the Great War." The war had created a terrifying upheaval and had brought upon that world which died in 1914 disorders from which we have not yet emerged.

Between 1815 and 1914 Europe, characterized by the stability of international relations, lived in a general atmosphere of work and progress. This stability was succeeded by an era of turbulence, interrupted in 1919 by a peace which lasted only twenty years, until, in 1939, the explosion of a second conflict ravaged the planet on a scale even more vast. Twice in twenty-five years Germany could stand accused of having tried to impose her rule throughout the universe. Do not these two disasters, hurled down upon mankind, form one single immense tragedy from 1914 to 1945, evoking the Thirty Years' War? In the seventeenth century as in the twentieth these Thirty Years' Wars, the first on a European scale, the second on a world scale, had as the principal actor a Germany in turmoil.

Regardless of the results of the treaty which would be concluded after 1918, the Great War entailed immense and grave consequences. In Europe it caused monetary inflation, social disorder, and a grand movement of matter and ideas; the Russian Revolution of 1917 would not facilitate a settlement rendered inevitably difficult by the number of countries that had been involved in this total war.

To what extent does the Second World War derive from the conditions surrounding the end of the First? The potential for a new war lay in the fact that the peace of 1919, "too strong for its weak points, too weak for its strengths," as Jacques Bainville said, had been accepted by the losers only with "a knife at their throats."

We will retrace briefly the different stages the European nations lived through from 1919 to 1932, the year, marking the opening of the Geneva

1

Disarmament Conference, which presented Germany with the possibility of winning her freedom to rearm, and France with the danger of losing her military dominance.

In January 1933 the rise to power of Adolf Hitler, the "man of the hour," suddenly cast the harshest of lights on Europe's tragic fate. The year 1933 drew the boundary between the two world wars.

From 1919 to 1933, thirteen years had passed. A truly international way of life had been born. Among most nations, a system of cooperation, courteous relations, and respect for law had developed. This was a fragile achievement, and the world economic crisis of 1929 had already struck it a disastrous blow. The illusion persisted that the pre-1914 state of things could be restored, and all responsibility for organization had been avoided; but there can be no sound organization without normal commitments.

To a great extent, the origins of the Second World War go back to the First World War. The second continued the first. A political and social phenomenon of supreme importance—Nazism—was added to this general and inevitable evolution. Nazism quickly ceased to have a strictly Germanic significance and became, with its indeterminate and shadowy aims, the principal international factor.

In his memoirs Harold Nicholson gives an account of a meeting he had with Monsignor Pacelli, who had lived in Munich for many years. Monsignor Pacelli saw in Nazism "a danger, a grave danger, perhaps a terrible danger." The future Pius XII perceived what was elemental and destructive in a movement of masses incessantly brought into action by two slogans: *Deutschland erwache, Juda verrecke*—"Germany awake" "Jews perish." The masses went blindly to Hitler, who promised them a popular community, free from struggle among classes or parties, as well as a social state built on national bases: work, bread, and peace.

Peace! When there are good reasons to believe that if Hitler had not been at the head of the German state the Second World War would not have taken place.

The question of the origins of the war cannot provoke such debate for the year 1939 as it does for the year 1914. In certain respects what the Central Powers then wanted more than anything was to maintain, even at the price of a European conflict, the Austro-Hungarian status quo, threatened by an unruly Serbian nationalism that was backed by a rash Russian diplomacy. In 1914 no great European interest, no great idea was at work. The whole complex of disputed questions was not very large. A peaceful settlement had already been found for Morocco; one could also have been found for the Balkans, where only frontier districts were being contested. Other agreements could have been reached. Worldwide questions, including a few heated issues—especially in the Near East—lent themselves better to bargaining than European questions. In Franz Kafka's famous aphorism of 1916, "This war was born of a frightful lack of imagination."

The tragedy of 1914 was the logical conclusion of the evolution of half a century. It can also be explained by an excess of economic power, the logical consequence of a dynamism intensified for decades by technical advances and, in many regions, by demographic increase. This dynamism, called imperialism since the 1880s, sought expression. At the core of states, special interests formed pressure groups through the persistent activity of leagues and associations. Colonial disputes burdened international relations.

Much simpler, the origins of the war of 1939 go back essentially to the insatiable appetites of Adolf Hitler. His goal had been to regain substantial military strength. Faced with all the questions Germany would try to settle to her advantage, he would use it fully, unconcerned by a possible global conflagration. The massive and uncontrollable rearmament of a power, soon freeing itself of all constraints and all obligations, created enormous risks for peace, less by the decision to revise the Treaty of Versailles than by an aggressive expansion sprung from the fierce will of one man, Hitler. So much destruction, so many deaths, rest on this man.

1

The Treaty of Versailles
and Its Enforcement

Most men believed that the armistice of November 11, 1918, had opened a universal era of felicity bringing the return of the Golden Age. There would be no more wars. The world that the great mass of fighters enthusiastically envisioned was a vast, generous dream of peace and freedom embracing all people.

The Allies had no doubt that their victory was a final victory; for them, it marked the triumph over violence. The carnage of war had killed war. No, we would never see that again! Men had lived through the last of wars.

The idealism of Wilson penetrated the popular heart; like that of Jean-Jacques Rousseau in times past, it wanted to believe in the basic natural goodness of man. It trusted in the people, in all the people, and they would all live in democracies. It dedicated itself to driving from humanity forever the scourge of battle.

The Peace Conference opened in Paris on January 12, 1919, and it claimed to give the world a new order. It had been carefully prepared. In every kind of meeting, committee, and commission, all questions had been discussed. In orgies of statistics and in piles of documents, reports, and dossiers had been accumulated by the zeal of a learned and persistent crowd of experts, diplomats, scholars, historians, geographers, jurists . . . who, from nation to nation, broke loose, confuting and finally negating one another.

The four hundred and forty paragraphs of the Treaty of Versailles, in itself a gigantic monument, were flanked by hundreds of paragraphs from the treaties Hitler called "the Parisian suburb treaties": Saint-Germain-en-Laye, signed with Austria at the château; Trianon, signed with Hungary in

5

the Grand Trianon; Neuilly, signed with Bulgaria in the city hall of Neuilly-sur-Seine; Sèvres, signed with Turkey in the National China Factory.

Far removed from the days of mercenary armies, modern wars became increasingly terrifying, causing armed nations to rise up one against the other, engaging entire populations and sustaining their bravery by a propaganda little concerned with sincerity. Bismarck, who was fond of aphorisms, said: "You never lie so much as before elections, after a hunt, and during a war." Propaganda pictured the war as a struggle between good and evil. What was at stake was something colossal. "Europeans are making war without realizing that it must end in peace," the great Chinese revolutionary Sun Yat-Sen said with Oriental wisdom to Count Sforza in 1915. Pro-war propaganda stirred passions, driving into the minds of people objectives that governments could not always translate into realities, and preventing large compromises.

It was, undoubtedly, not easy to restore peace in a world overturned by a long and bloody struggle. The ideal and the possible should not have been confused. Even among victors united by a common fight against a common enemy, it was not easy to come to compromises; yet the best peace treaties are compromises. Usually adjustments can be made among contending interests and it is possible for people of conflicting concerns to live in peace. But passions prevent compromises. In the fire of the "Great War," passions had been embittered. They affected particularly all questions dealing with security and reparations. They blotted out any sense of financial realities and political possibilities.

The "Big Three"

In 1919, for the first time in history, a general peace settlement was worked out by representatives of democratic states. Three powerful personalities—Clemenceau, Wilson, and Lloyd George—led the negotiations. Italy's representative, Orlando, who would be dismissed by June 1919 before the signing of the treaty, played only a secondary role.

The Big Three were impressive men. It would be unfair to compare them to their colorless successors. A glance at the notes taken by the interpreter Paul Mantoux, a scrupulous historian, is sufficient to make one realize that their conversations were on a high level, both morally and intellectually.

Far from being the malevolent mummy imagined by the pamphleteers, Clemenceau, during his conversations in the spring of 1919, appeared remarkable in his lucidity, his vigor, and his character. Several of his collaborators were exceptional: for example, André Tardieu, Louis Loucheur, and Philippe Berthelot.

Clemenceau's entire policy was guided by the German peril. In 1871 he had been a member of the National Assembly and, by voting against the Treaty of Frankfurt, he had put his name down among the 107 who protested. He was the only survivor of the group. "We have been conquered," he told the Senate in 1912. "We did not give in." For more than thirty years, he had been the Third Republic's foremost cabinet wrecker. He had brought down all the Third Republic's great leaders, Gambetta as well as Jules Ferry. As head of the government in October 1917, he had inspired new energy, crushed doubt, and revived confidence. Three words contained his program: "I make war," and he had made war like no one before him.

Was this remarkable war minister, seventy-eight years old in 1919, the ideal negotiator for peace? The bullet a wretched fanatic had left permanently embedded in one of his lungs on February 28, 1919, as well as two uninterrupted years in office, added to the weight of age. Nevertheless, he still had an extraordinary, dashing youthfulness, and a voice that never quivered. After the armistice his prestige was exceptional. Even such an implacable detractor as Keynes paid tribute to Clemenceau's great character, so well endowed for command: "Clemenceau thought of France as Pericles thought of Athens; he had one illusion, France, and one disillusion, humanity, including Frenchmen."

In spite of his "illusion, France," he was perfectly aware of the weaknesses of a country situated in the middle of Europe and suffering under deplorable demographic conditions. "We are not an island like England. . . . We are not surrounded by mountains and by the sea like Spain." He was very conscious of the power of the Anglo-Saxons. Was it not a fact that, in 1918, the United States had determined the outcome of the war and that during that conflict a very strong British army had fought on French soil?

The United States and Great Britain denied France a frontier on the Rhine, that is to say, a permanent occupation of the left bank by an Allied army, with one or more states independent of Germany, under the protection of the League of Nations. This was a project of Marshal Foch, who had the support of the president of the republic, Poincaré. To avoid it, Lloyd George had suggested that it be replaced by a joint guarantee of Great Britain and the United States against future German aggression. Englishmen and Americans would come to the aid of France with all their forces if German troops crossed the Rhine without League of Nations consent.

Eager to preserve the alliance that had made victory possible, Clemenceau dropped Foch's project in exchange for these promises, as well as for a temporary occupation by the Allies of the left bank of the Rhine. The bank was divided into three zones, one including Cologne, one Coblenz, and one Mainz. The first zone was to be evacuated after five years, the second after ten years, and the third after fifteen years. The occupation expenses were to be paid by Germany and an Interallied High Commission would keep watch over the local authorities in the occupied territories.

The resources of the United States, shown by the world conflict to be immeasurable, would protect from a new war an Old World freed from the inherent evils of the system of national politics and international rivalries. We had victory; we would have a real peace.

Lloyd George exerted a major influence on the destinies of England and the European continent. Cabinet minister without interruption after the Liberals took office in December 1905, he never stopped rising: minister for trade, then for finances; minister for munitions, then for war; finally, prime minister.

Lloyd George the Englishman! He should be called, rather, Lloyd George the Welshman. An astonishingly changeable Celtic liveliness, far removed from the English "wait and see" tradition, swept him along on floods of ideas. Although he was imbued with a messianic spirit, he trampled down doctrines and dogmas, except in matters concerning Wales.

Lloyd George the liberal! He should be called, rather, Lloyd George the radical. A self-made man, he had not been molded by the famous public schools and hardly resembled such liberal leaders as Gladstone, Grey, and Asquith.

His great moment had been the war. There he had shown a heroic determination filled with both energy and flexibility. According to Churchill, his greatest asset was his ability to forget the past and concentrate entirely on the new situation he had to master.

After December 1918, he addressed himself to those he had called "a nation of heroes" in one of his most famous speeches. The khaki elections ensured his government of an enormous majority of voters bent on getting the most from Germany by "squeezing until the pips squeak." Lloyd George claimed he was going to "turn out the pockets of the Germans," and have the Kaiser hanged. "God knows what I would have had to promise if the electoral campaign had kept on."

But he evolved very rapidly. At first he seemed to want to follow his policy of 1918: the "knock-out blow" for Germany. Then he thought of the British principle: "Don't kick a man when he is down." The Bolshevik revolution breaking out in Hungary on March 21, 1919, the radical tendencies appearing in the British trade unions, and the idea that the Germans could throw themselves into the arms of the Soviets persuaded him "not to bend the bow too far" in his obsessive fear that Germany would refuse to sign the peace treaty.

German Indignation

The Germans were indeed becoming indignant. When they had laid down their arms they had been promised a peace faithful to the spirit of Wilson's Fourteen Points. The whole peace settlement of 1919 had been debased by the conditions on which armistice had been granted to the Germans. It had been specified that the peace would be concluded on the basis of the "Fourteen Points" formulated by President Wilson on January 8, 1918. This basis was equivocal, since the Fourteen Points were general principles and had not yet been the object of a common interpretation. The losers denounced as an intolerable *Diktat* the "peace under duress" given them, a peace contrary to Wilson's principles.

Count von Brockdorff-Rantzau, the haughty leader of the German delegation, wrote to the Supreme Council presided over by Clemenceau: "Those who sign this treaty will sign the death sentence of millions of German men, women, and children."

In reality, the framework of the Treaty of Versailles was not at all unreasonable: the treaty was neither so badly made nor so ill fated as the famous British economist Keynes claimed. From the financial and economic standpoint it was perfectly workable, without condemning Germany to an inhuman standard of living. Nevertheless, it was spoiled by serious defects.

Why insert, with Article 231, a proclamation of German guilt, making the loser responsible, as the aggressor, for all the war damages incurred by the Allies? The loser would declare such an article insulting and, with infinite patience, try to show it untrue in order to demolish the whole treaty. The American experts wanted to make a moral treaty, weighed in the scales of justice, and to justify the reparations by putting them in harmony with Wilson's principles.

The Treaty of Versailles was unable to determine the total of these "reparations"—"war indemnities" were not to be spoken of. "That is the most difficult question of all," Lloyd George told Clemenceau and Wilson on March 24, 1919. "Our experts will never be able to agree." He refused to go beyond the limits of common sense and fall into extravagance. The enormous expenses of a modern war could not be covered any longer by a tribute, even of a fabulous sum, paid by the losers.

The Treaty of Versailles gave a Reparations Commission the task of determining the amount of the German debt before May 1, 1921. Why delay this determination of the debt after letting the Germans know they would have to work at least half a century to pay it off? Such a delay could only exacerbate the resentments of the loser and the discords among victors eager for the spoils. As Churchill wrote, "Reparations were a sad adventure, of idiotic complication."

With the treaties of 1919-20, the nationality principle became the public law of Europe and freed oppressed nationalities in Germany, in Austria-Hungary, and in the Ottoman Empire. But a nationality does not always correspond to a definite geographic area. There is often a discordance between nations as history has made them, and the geographic frame that shapes them. Sometimes they overflow that frame, sometimes they do not manage to fill it. The ethnic tangles left large German minorities in Poland and German and Hungarian minorities in Czechoslovakia, Rumania, and Yugoslavia. In 1919 people did not want to envision the transfer of populations, a cruel method the Treaty of Lausanne would inaugurate in 1923 between Turkey and Greece.

The treaties relied on "plebiscites" to determine the fate of minorities grouped in one area. In theory this system was perfect, but it excited national passions to an extreme, as became evident in 1921 in Upper Silesia.

Besides, some of these plebiscites would turn in favor of the losers. They would give an enormous German majority against Poland in the Marienwerder and Allenstein territories, a third of East Prussia. Germany would win over Denmark in central Schleswig; Austria over the Yugoslavs at Klagenfurt. In January 1935 the people of the Saar would return to Germany with a massive vote.

As a whole the treaties righted age-old wrongs: they brought freedom to millions of oppressed people who would never have been able to win it themselves. But with the mixture of peoples some injustices were inevitable. Real or imagined, these new inequities were lesser than the older ones; the number of Europeans forced to obey foreign governments was much smaller.

Finally, in the new Europe these national minorities, not as numerous as in 1913, were to benefit from protection and guarantees never considered before. Nevertheless the new injustices, precisely because they were new, were more striking than the old injustices to which people had become accustomed with the soothing effect of time.

The triumph of nationalities was tempered by the advent of an international organization intended to insure peace through the possibility of taking collective sanctions against "the aggressor." The Covenant of the League of Nations and the peace treaties formed an inseparable whole. But the League of Nations, responsible for the maintenance of peace, had no military force. Wilson had not wanted to replace national militarism with an "international militarism."

The Germans, neither won over nor permanently disabled by their victors, refused to accept the new order of things established by the Treaty of Versailles. They refused to admit that Germany should lose twenty-five thousand square miles and seven million people. They considered the Poles and the Czechs inferior races. They imagined that France would unify the Slavic nations, as Cardinal Richelieu had long ago grouped Sweden and the German princes against the House of Hapsburg. They did not accept the loss of their colonies.

They resigned themselves and accepted the treaty "with a knife at their throats" only after part of Germany had been militarily occupied and under the threat that still more important territories, such as the Ruhr, would be occupied.

In the Danube area, where Austria-Hungary disappeared, no economic confederation was imposed on the successor states. The "Balkanization" of Europe spread with the new frontiers, extended more than one-third in relation to those of 1914.

Of the three European continental empires, only Germany survived the storm. With Europe provisionally amputated from immense Russia and with the disappearance of the Hapsburg monarchy, an embittered Germany found herself more powerful than before 1914, in a Balkanized continent. From then on the nationalist movement, which had worked against the Hapsburg empire, worked for Germany. While her eastern neighbors formed only a series of small states, her unity emerged reinforced by the war, her territory no longer including Alsace-Lorraine, northern Schleswig, and the Polish provinces.

The American Secession

Signing the Treaty of Versailles in the Hall of Mirrors on June 28, 1919, Clemenceau was fully conscious of having established nothing definitive or perfect with a peace that could only be an Allied peace, since the war had been an Allied war. Such a war could not be followed by a separate peace. Nevertheless he felt that he had forged the best possible tool for France through his agreements with Wilson and Lloyd George.

The United States, drawn from its traditional isolationism and committed to a new system of world peace, had become one of the principal forces that would unite in Europe for peace, as they had for war. French security would be guaranteed against any threat, especially against the temporarily suspended German threat, for in the future the constant union of the democracies would rise against it.

The American secession upset any idea people had on the role the United States might play in maintaining the peace. America's power had become gigantic. She had returned to political isolation after her brief but decisive intervention in the war.

To understand this tragedy, one must know that President Wilson was far from enjoying the unanimous confidence of his own countrymen. People begrudged him the morbid inflexibility and the awkward stubbornness of a doctrinaire mind. His political capital was largely immobilized by the electoral situation. If in 1912 he had been elected to the White House, although he was a Democrat and the White House had been occupied by Republicans for sixteen years, it was only due to the split within the Republican party created by the conflict between Taft and Theodore Roosevelt. In 1916 he was reelected by a very narrow margin. In October and November 1918, the majority went to the Republicans at the elections for the return of the House of Representatives and one-third of the Senate. The Republican Theodore Roosevelt, who would die in 1919, bluntly mocked "the Fourteen Points, and the four supplementary points, and the five complementary points," and he denied that Wilson had any authority to speak in the name of the American people.

In 1919, for the first time, a president of the United States visited Europe officially. Wilson probably made an error when he came personally to Paris to negotiate this most complex of treaties, instead of remaining uncommitted while entrusting a delegation of Democrats and Republicans to represent the United States at the Peace Conference. His personal involvement considerably weakened his position. "Jupiter was coming down from Mount Olympus."

London and Paris refused to see that in the United States the Republican majority of Congress was opposed to the Democratic president, that the president was not an absolute monarch, and that, the more he involved himself in European politics, the more he became suspect to the isolationists.

Immediately after his return to the United States, Wilson launched a speaking campaign in favor of the Treaty of Versailles. "If by an inconceivable error," he declared on September 8, 1919, "America does not adopt a leading role in this new task undertaken in common, . . . if she lets down humanity, . . . the world will be frozen by such disillusionment that it will no longer have confidence in anything."

On September 26, making his thirty-first speech in favor of the treaty, Wilson suffered a sudden stroke that paralyzed his tongue. He was no longer able to defend his work personally. Europeans had believed that his signature and his word bound the millions of Americans he represented, but the old American ideology rose up against him.

After December 1919 Keynes, who represented the British Treasury at the Peace Conference and who would become Baron Keynes of Tilton, published *The Economic Consequences of the Peace,* an extremely successful book, especially in the Anglo-Saxon world. The book was precisely what the Americans needed to repudiate Wilson. The prejudices of isolationism and mercantilism were reinforced by the scientific statements and moral arguments of a brilliant polemicist. He taxed a "Carthaginian peace" with further condemnations. It had been "founded on hypocrisy"; it was "a challenge to justice, to mercy, and to common sense." He ridiculed the naiveté of Wilson, a "blind and deaf Don Quixote," duped by Lloyd George's clever trickery and terrorized by Clemenceau. Wilson, wrote Keynes, had finished by committing "an unheard-of treason," one of the most scandalous actions in civilized history.

In the United States a passionate and harsh campaign was unleashed for a return to neutrality and to the policy of Washington and Monroe, far from a depraved and deceitful Europe whose eternal disorders interfered with the vigorous movement of a young people swept up in a tremendous expansion. Enough of Wilson's universalism! The irreconcilable Senator William Borah denounced the Treaty of Versailles as "a crime born of blind vengeance and insatiable greed." Warren Harding, who would succeed Wilson in the White House, claimed that "with the League of Nations governing the world through special powers, the Republic will no longer play any part."

In November 1919, the Senate, judge and master of treaty ratification, was unable to rally the two-thirds majority constitutionally necessary for ratification, with thirty-five votes against it and forty-nine in favor.

Then came a tidal wave against Wilson. In the presidential elections of November 1920, the Democrats won only nine million votes, while more than sixteen million went to the Republicans.

It was not only the Treaty of Versailles that was rejected, but also the guarantee treaty offered to Clemenceau to make him renounce a permanent occupation of the Rhineland. The House of Commons had ratified the guarantee treaty unanimously; but, since Great Britain had given a joint signature with the United States, she was no longer bound because of the American withdrawal. The promised guarantees were void.

The French, abandoned, felt they had been tricked and shamefully duped. They had been refused the frontier necessary for their security. They denounced the treaty as an enormous fraud depriving them in a single blow of what they had gained by defeating Germany. Clemenceau, "the Father of Victory," was accused of "losing the victory." His prestige was so diminished that in January 1920 he was defeated in his attempt to become president of the Republic by Paul Deschanel, the scholarly presiding officer of the Chamber of Deputies.

It is a fact the French considered the Treaty of Versailles very inadequate. Marshal Foch confided that Clemenceau's policy had been "a calamity" and that Versailles was not a peace, but a mere armistice. The French thought that "the Old Tiger" had been "conned" by his allies.

France needed security; although victorious, she had suffered vital losses. Deprived of a million and a quarter men, with two million disabled soldiers, she had lost the flower of her youth. The birthrate would fall with the reduced generation of what would be called by military planners "the empty classes." Somber prospect, in comparison with a Germany confident in her demographic vigor and technical superiority.

After the victory France suffered a persistent anxiety. In her fear of a new German expansion she was devastated by an inferiority complex which provoked her passion for security.

Differences of Opinion between
France and Great Britain

The tragic American secession severely weakened the power of the 1919 treaties. To understand why the state of things established in 1919 did not last, it is necessary to consider also the differences of opinion arising after 1919 between Great Britain and France, the two dominant powers of a time when the United States was returning to isolationism, Russia was immersed in civil war and had ceased for several years to exist as a great power, Austria-Hungary had been totally destroyed, and Germany had just lost the war.

Right after the signing of the armistice, the English people undertook an almost total demobilization. After four years of fighting, they were overcome by an infinite weariness. They passionately demanded the abolition of war-time rules and restraints. They wanted to be free of conscription and, without even considering a Swiss-type militia, they insisted on returning to a small professional army. Without investigating the responsibilities the maintenance of European order would impose on the victors, the English were dedicated to disarmament. France alone kept a large army, well equipped with powerful arms. Therefore she alone remained strong. The sudden break in Franco-British military equality made France too strong, not by a French policy calculated to impose her dominance, but by the sudden desire of England, her ally, to give up her strength. Lloyd George saw the balance of power being jeopardized, with France reaching the peak of her prestige in Europe, where she was for a few years the only military great power, with a victorious General Staff under Marshal Foch.

From then on the powerful British idea of balance dominated the prime minister's mind. Impatient and a little jealous, dangerous as an enemy and not too reliable as a friend, he directed against France his game of balance of power. Very soon the battlefield comradeship disappeared. England broke away. To Clemenceau, who in 1921 blamed him rather harshly for it, Lloyd George replied: "Isn't that our traditional policy?" Indeed the famous and dreaded Palmerston had said: "We have no perpetual enemies and no perpetual friends; we have only perpetual interests."

Is it not true that, for the English, one of the most enduring diplomatic traditions is that an alliance loses its validity as soon as the war is won? In the age of aristocratic governments, these repudiations were masked by a chivalrous attitude toward the fallen enemy. Had such an attitude been declared in 1919, it would have been condemned as pro-German by English popular opinion, which as a whole was still violently anti-German. It was morally impossible at the time to refer publicly to the principle of European balance—a principle so vitally bound to British diplomacy. The prime minister therefore invoked no principle. The power of tradition was leading him away from France and toward Germany, but the tide of public opinion was then oriented away from Germany and toward France. He decided to follow one direction, while pretending to continue following the other.

The Treaty of Versailles had been Lloyd George's triumph. With unmatched agility and subtlety, he had secured the immediate settlement of England's concerns—the liquidation of German forces threatening English world supremacy: the war fleet, the merchant marine, the colonies. The English had almost nothing more to ask from a Germany now denuded of everything except her status as a continental power. This catered to their tendency to help the weak against the strong, a tendency prompted by their desire for balance.

However, through compromises on a series of important problems, Lloyd George had led Clemenceau into provisions that would expire: settling reparations, the Saar, military occupation, and demilitarization. He expected that, regarding all these delayed settlements, the English and the Americans would agree to serve as arbiters between France and Germany. The guarantor powers would feel obligated, even if they used diplomatic discretion, to give advice, to recommend moderation, to warn against any action that could spoil good relations. Franco-German relations would be subject to a constant arbitral surveillance by the Anglo-Saxon world.

After the American Senate left Lloyd George to face France alone, he followed the traditional line of British diplomacy with determination. Until October 1922, when he was abandoned by the Conservatives, he was France's adversary through years of diplomatic tournaments and confused activity. Lloyd George, who had allowed the mistakes contained in the Treaty of Versailles to be made, who had even participated in their making, launched a campaign of conferences, sometimes interallied, sometimes international, at which France was presented as a country that abused her power—the militaristic country par excellence. This campaign, which would earn him the fierce hatred of many Frenchmen, alternated with his efforts at seduction and with the lure he offered Briand, during the Cannes Conference in late 1921: he would promise France her security, but French policy would have to be put practically under British control.

In November 1918 England and France were united in peace as in war. A year later their divergent opinions were evident.

Knowing the events that followed, it is impossible not to regret bitterly the sudden dissolution of the close and firm Franco-British wartime bond and the dispersion of interallied organizations aiming to locate problems and study their solutions through a common effort.

The League of Nations represented a kind of coalition between two states, England and France, who in spite of their official solidarity did not make allowances for one another. Between the two countries, a strange relationship followed the alliance of war. Instead of a joint power held by two wartime allies, a sort of Franco-British duel began. The English and the French were opposed, not only over Germany, but more violently still over the Near East, where the Greek drama was unfolding. Mustafa Kemal's victories, sweeping away the Treaty of Sèvres (signed on August 10, 1920), were confirmed by the Treaty of Lausanne (signed on July 24, 1923).

"Identity of wills," which, Tolstoy said, "always rules the world," did not exist in 1919; it would quickly disintegrate even more. England and France haggled over the clauses of the peace treaty they had signed against the Germans, who, watchful spectators, had to await the outcome of this Franco-British duel. They slipped into dangerous illusions, bluntly shattered in January 1923 when Poincaré ordered the occupation of the Ruhr.

Germany, who was accused of trying everything to elude treaty provisions, saw the French as indicters and the English as defenders, and this contrariness tore asunder all of the enforcement organizations, from the Reparations Commission to military inspection. It opened a wide gap, enlarged by the stubborn effort of German propaganda, while in England the traditional feeling for defeated Germany reawakened, especially among businessmen.

Lloyd George, who had once demanded that the Kaiser be hanged, proposed a new mystique: the economic reconstruction of Europe through German recovery. This would remedy unemployment and save ailing British industry, which saw in the former enemy less a competitor than a customer. The German recovery was also tied to a generous settlement of the reparations issue, and that settlement depended on France. War debts intensified economic difficulties, distorted the foreign exchange system, and stirred up hatred between nations. Both moral and business sense demanded their gradual disappearance. The reparations issue, combined with the question of interallied debts—which the Americans treated as ordinary commercial debts, refusing to consider any reduction—upset the postwar years almost until the rise of Nazism.

For British as for French diplomacy, the fundamental problem was the German problem. It presented itself in totally different ways for each country. Paris, worried about preserving its victory, wanted to gain reparations while maintaining guarantees against German militarism.

As Alexandre Millerand, newly elected president of France, declared in his message to the Chamber and Senate during the summer of 1920: "The Treaty of Versailles, and the diplomatic instruments which accompanied and followed it, comprise the new charter of Europe and the world. Our diplomacy will ensure its strict execution."

France's whole diplomatic policy was finally sidetracked by reparations, which France, influenced by the disastrous slogan "Germany will pay," saw as the sole solution to her financial problems.

London, however, wanted to strengthen Germany in order to limit French dominance over the Continent. English opposition to French supremacy focused on reparations. In this problem, were not common sense and wisdom on England's side?

Effects of the Russian Revolution

The American secession and the Franco-British differences explain the instability of the Versailles settlement; but to these factors we must add the immense, mysterious void left by the Russian Revolution of October 1917.

Russia was not represented at Versailles. The treaties of 1919, supposedly diverting the threat of German oppression, needed Slavic cooperation to maintain the new order of things; but the Slavs' natural leader, Russia, was absent as a European force. Her intrigues shook Europe's foundations in 1919 and 1920 and established in Hungary and in Bavaria transient Communist governments, which threatened all of Germany and even Italy. As a boomerang, Fascism sprang from Italy. It would later bear a monstrous offspring: Nazism.

After a horrible civil war, the Soviet Union needed rest. The war against Poland, which had begun so well in April 1920, ended on August 15 outside Warsaw with the collapse of the Red Army. The Treaty of Riga, signed on March 12, 1921, gave the Poles a frontier ninety-four miles east of the line considered fair by the British foreign minister in 1919: the "Curzon line."

On March 16, 1921, Great Britain concluded a commercial agreement with the Soviet Union. From then on the Soviet factor carried much weight in international politics. Would the Soviets be allies of Germany, or allies against Germany? In 1919 they had hoped to turn Germany into a Communist country. The threats of "world proletarian revolution" faded. But even a non-Communist Germany had the same adversary as the Soviets: Poland, whose frontiers were considered illegitimate in Berlin and in Moscow.

On April 6, 1922, on the periphery of the international conference assembled by Lloyd George in Genoa for the restoration of world trade, a German-Soviet treaty was signed at Rapallo.

Reparations

Because Russia had taken a position against the Treaty of Versailles and the United States had rejected it, the peace settlement took place without the two states—the Soviet Union and the United States—on which destiny would impose the responsibility for establishing peace in 1945.

The peace quickly became unpopular and was violently opposed not only among the neutrals, but also among the powers that had signed at Versailles. It was castigated, particularly in Great Britain and in Italy, as the main cause of multiplying political and military problems.

The armistice of November 1918 had not brought peace to the entire planet; for years men continued fighting in several parts of Europe and, especially, of Asia. And everywhere a dangerous ferment increased the financial confusion.

Indeed the war had disrupted the economic system which had been the foundation of Europe's dominance. Ruined by the conflict, the Continent lived under a new regime of monetary inflation. The currencies of Central and Eastern Europe, except for the Czech, lost all value. The German mark fell to a billionth of its pre-1914 value. The unrestrained inflation, reaching its climax in 1923, caused frightful chaos. In many countries, this chaos seemed even gloomier than the war itself had been. The immeasurable social transformations it brought about made up a true revolution.

Under such conditions the reparations issue raised frightening difficulties. Soon the losers no longer wanted to pay, and the victors no longer used an iron will in order to collect. Since Poincaré had left the Elysée at the end of his presidential term in January 1920, he had not stopped demanding complete enforcement of the Treaty of Versailles, while criticizing its inadequacies. He denounced the concessions Aristide Briand made in 1921 when he returned to the prime ministry and the foreign ministry. Yet, unable to reach an amicable reparations settlement with Germany, Briand in March 1921 had Düsseldorf, Duisburg, and Ruhrort occupied, following the example of Millerand, who had had Frankfurt am Main occupied for several weeks in April 1920 when he also was prime minister and foreign minister.

On May 5, 1921, the Allied Conference in London notified Germany of the schedule for German debt payments, which had to be accepted within six days. After the resignation of a Fehrenbach cabinet, the Wirth cabinet reluctantly accepted the Allied conditions in order to avoid occupation of the Ruhr.

Conflicting points of view set the French and English against each other. The plague of foreign exchange depreciation was for France what the plague of unemployment was for England. Frenchmen knew nothing about the international monetary transfer system and the possible methods for payment. The regions devastated by Germany during the war were both a special monopoly for French business and a source of credits for Germany, credits manifestly exaggerated in French estimates.

In December 1921, the British ambassador Lord d'Abernon, the "Lord Protector of Germany," felt that the Germans, confronted with a possible occupation of the Ruhr, were giving in to fatalism. The occupation, they thought, would take place. Why make sacrifices to try to avoid the inevitable?

In January 1923 Poincaré, who had succeeded Briand the preceding year, sent French and Belgian troops into the Ruhr because Germany had not made all her scheduled coal and timber deliveries. He was convinced that "Germany, as a nation, would not resign herself to keeping her word except by force of necessity."

England protested this "invasion," considering it senseless; it created in England a negative feeling toward France, reinforced by the criticisms directed against Versailles.

In Germany, the government employees, the workers, and the railwaymen stopped working, showing the "passive resistance" the Reich organized in all the occupied territories. A Franco-Belgian administration for the railways was set up, and two towns were occupied in the state of Baden. The French found themselves forced to deport and imprison thousands of government employees, industrialists, and workers. Schlageter, who had been executed by the French military authorities for sabotage, became a national hero.

Meanwhile the mark's value was dropping with astonishing speed, and Germany was sinking into a monetary abyss. Chancellor Stresemann ordered the end of "passive resistance" on September 26, 1923.

Eager to avoid a complete break with Great Britain, Poincaré finally agreed in November to a meeting of experts chosen by the Reparations Commission to study Germany's capacity to pay.

As if intentionally, France had concentrated on herself all of Germany's resentments. The flaws in her reparations policy can be explained to a great extent by Germany's unwillingness to pay. If the sum total determined by the Reparations Commission in 1921—132 billion gold marks—was certainly very large, Germany systematically exaggerated its importance, hoping to obtain a constant reduction of the amount demanded, and in the end paid about 23 billion gold marks.

Faced with all these complications Italy, who felt that the peace treaties did not match the greatness of her victory, became a stage for grave events. From September 1919 to January 1921, Gabriele d'Annunzio occupied Fiume, which had been withheld from Italy. The general discontent and the disorders stirring the peninsula provoked a violent reaction: Fascism. In October 1922 Mussolini took over the government.

The Years of Hope, 1924-29

From 1924 to 1929 Europe lived through a few years of hope and illusion, in an atmosphere improved by currency stabilization and economic prosperity. Events seemed to be evolving in a reassuring way. It looked as if things were settling down and would continue to do so. The experts chosen by the Reparations Commission established the Dawes Plan in April 1924. It appeared to solve the reparations problem by planning annual payments of two and one-half billion gold marks for an indeterminate number of years. Two years later, the entire Ruhr region was liberated.

In June 1929 a new reparations plan, set up by the experts under the chairmanship of the American Owen Young, eliminated both foreign control in Germany and the Reparations Commission.

A protocol claiming to establish an indissoluble bond between "arbitration, security, and disarmament" had been signed at Geneva on October 2, 1924. It would never be enforced, owing to the opposition of the British Conservatives, who succeeded Labour at the head of the government.

Having begun with 2 seats in 1900, the Labour party went from 58 seats in December 1918 to 191 in 1923. Quite removed from Marxism, Labour was more concerned with practical results than with orthodoxy, as a consequence of the predominance of economic and social problems. In the future the struggle for power would continue between Labour and Conservatives, the Liberals being reduced to making up the balance of seats.

Generally the Conservatives were ahead, although Labour and Conservative cabinets alternated; the Labourite Ramsay MacDonald and the Conservative Stanley Baldwin were both remarkable in foreign policy for their conciliatory attitudes and eagerness to compromise. The Conservatives were defeated in December 1923 because of Baldwin's call for higher customs duties. In October 1924 the Conservatives won a smashing victory, but, unable to control unemployment, they lost the elections of May 1929, and Labour returned to power under Ramsay MacDonald.

However the situation grew worse when the world economic crisis began in October 1929. The Labour cabinet could not agree with the vigorous program for budget and salary cuts proposed by the chancellor of the Exchequer, Snowden. In August 1931, MacDonald set up a tripartite "National" cabinet with the Liberals, a handful of Labourites, and the Conservatives, whose leader, Baldwin, had agreed to serve under MacDonald. The elections of October 1931 brought the National government an enormous majority. This draconian step allowed Great Britain to solve her problems.

In France the Herriot ministry condemned the policy of isolation followed by Poincaré in 1922 and 1923 and set out to establish relations of mutual trust with London. In April 1925 Briand became foreign minister in a Painlevé cabinet. He remained foreign minister for seven years, until January 1932, through the whirlwind of succeeding cabinets, all very different: his own cabinets; Poincaré's "National Union" cabinets, aimed at stopping inflation, from July 1926 to June 1929; center cabinets or transient Radical cabinets.

Within the framework of a general structure to maintain peace, Briand worked toward a rapprochement with Germany. "It would be insane," he said, "to insist on eternal containment of a nation of sixty million people."

The Locarno treaties concluded in October 1925 promised France additional guarantees of security—Germany, Great Britain, and Italy guaranteed the territorial status quo of the German frontiers with France and Belgium. In September 1926 Germany joined the League of Nations, where Briand was triumphant, and the French minister tried to establish "the foundation for a policy of understanding," with Stresemann, at a luncheon in the village of Thoiry.

On August 27, 1928, the Kellogg-Briand Pact for the "universal renunciation of war" was signed in Paris. In September 1929 Briand advocated, like a thunderclap, a European federation.

Sincerely supported by the majority of the French associations of war veterans and civilian victims, the attempts at a Franco-German reconciliation were made possible by Stresemann, who like Briand directed the foreign policy of his country for seven years, trying to avert the worst. He was chancellor for only a hundred days, from August to November 1923, but he remained foreign minister until he died in October 1929. His death had disastrous consequences. He might have affected seriously the course of events which led to the Second World War. A patriotic German, he was not a man to throw himself lightheartedly into a new war. He was aware of the eminent risks of another war and of its consequences, necessarily catastrophic for Europe.

The Franco-German rapprochement was hindered by inevitable internal problems. In February 1925 Marshal Hindenburg was elected president of Germany, after the death of the Social Democrat Ebert. For a few years, however, this former military chief of Wilhelm II appeared as the bulwark of the republican regime, a regime he accepted only as a lesser evil.

In the name of the "Locarno spirit," Germany demanded urgently the evacuation of the occupied areas on the Rhine's left bank. In August 1929 France agreed in principle to an early evacuation and began work on the "Maginot line" fortifications.

The evacuation, finished in July 1930, was followed by nationalistic demonstrations. The German elections of September 1930 brought about the triumph of the Nazis, a triumph bitterly criticized in France by Briand. Briand also criticized the German proposal of March 1931 for a customs union with Austria—a proposal rejected by the opposition of France, Italy, and the Little Entente. In May 1931 Briand's presidential candidacy failed. He left the foreign ministry in January 1932 and died two months later.

During this relatively short period of prosperity, starting in 1924 and ending with the world economic crisis of 1929, currencies stabilized and the wounds of war healed. Europe rebuilt itself and the threats of upheavals diminished.

After Lenin—who had had a stroke in the summer of 1922—died at the age of fifty-three in January 1924, Joseph Stalin, secretary general of the Central Committee of the Russian Communist Party, gradually assumed the difficult succession. Having crushed Trotsky's faction, he enforced the prodigious efforts of the first Five Year Plan, begun in October 1928 and to be followed by other Five Year Plans. Starting in 1929, "the year of the great change," he also adopted Marxist orthodoxy in regards to agricultural collectivization, fighting bitterly against the prosperous peasants, the Kulaks.

He showed more realism and moderation in his foreign policy than had Trotsky, whom he labeled "the Clemenceau of comic opera." During these years, Russia was oriented mainly toward Asia, where German cooperation could not have the same importance it would have had in Europe, particularly against Poland. Stalin limited the propaganda effort directed toward bringing civil war to other countries and concentrated on Russia herself, with the desire to make of Russia an industrial and military power capable of facing external dangers.

2

The Disarmament Conference of 1932

The crash of the New York stock market in October 1929 generated massive unemployment and unleashed a terrible economic crisis throughout the world. Not one continent escaped the catastrophe. In Europe it had tragic consequences. It swept like a hurricane over Germany, afflicted to the point of despair, and brought National Socialism to power. The very unpopular deflationary measures taken by the German government, under Brüning, recruited millions of Nazis. Who knows if, without the economic crisis, the overwhelming drive of Hitlerism could not have been controlled. The rise of dictatorships followed the example of Fascism. Everything fell apart.

"As long as I am around, there will be no war," Aristide Briand had declared on September 11, 1930. When he died in March 1932, threats of war were appearing everywhere, but as yet there was no catastrophe. France was the richest and best armed nation in Europe. Her military predominance was reinforced by a financial predominance recognized even by the United States. At that time Frenchmen had no reason to fear the military outcome of a war. Surely the future was not reassuring. Germany, the French knew, would refuse to remain immobilized within her 1919 frontiers. She was preparing to exert control over her eastern neighbors, at least economically, as a prelude to the politics of "living space."

In front of Professor Oswald Hesnard, his fellow Breton and confidant in German matters, Briand said, pondering the future: "Life will not be much fun."[1]

However many obstacles had been raised on the road to war: the League

1. Maurice Baumont, *Briand: Diplomat und Idealist* (Göttingen: Musterschmidt, 1966).

of Nations, Locarno, the Kellogg-Briand Pact—treaties already concluded and treaties to be concluded. Seeds of new ideas had fallen on a Europe stirred by agitation of all kinds. Let the United States of Europe take shape and all men would be saved!

The United States of Europe never came to life, and Paul Claudel, poet and ambassador, wrote: "The day Europe took leave of its common sense, Briand took leave of life."

People speak of the "Roaring Twenties" as very changeable years when confusion gave way to illusion, but the real years of insanity began with the bewildering Nazi adventure. The years 1933–39 were in reality madder than the "twenties." Crowded with tragedies, they led to the chaos that burst forth in 1939.

In the origins of the Second World War, two of these years, 1935 and 1936, took on a major importance. During these two years, while the will of the masses was worn away, leaving them broken in spirit, the drama was played on every stage: London, Rome, Paris, Berlin, Geneva, Stresa. The story of the disintegration of the League of Nations and the rise of Hitler's supremacy is indivisible; no single part is comprehensible without the others. It is not easy to master such a terribly complex subject, with lines ceaselessly overlapping, intersecting, and changing.

Until 1935, internal relations centered on the Disarmament Conference opened in 1932 in Geneva—very different from the disarmament conferences that would follow the Second World War and run their course in total indifference. On February 2, 1932, this grand conference assembled sixty-four states, nearly all the nations of the world. Hailed with impressive petitions, accompanied by solemn religious services and earnest prayers, it resembled a great ecclesiastical council for disarmament. An object of religious fervor, disarmament was a good in itself, the guarantee and ransom of eternal peace.

In this year 1932, the universal economic crisis reached its highest point everywhere except in France. France would enter the depression later and emerge from it later; she was then at the peak of her prestige.

Public opinion seemed unanimous in maintaining that the seriousness of this crisis demanded overall solutions and the means of planning and discussing these solutions. But if this vague public opinion which was supreme in the League of Nations was sufficiently manifest to impose high-sounding declarations on the politicians, it was totally incoherent and lacked powerful leaders as well as the means for action. The weakness of democracies is well known—not to clash and not to act. Their passing governments had neither command of power, nor belief in power, nor the will to exert power. Witnesses and orators, they bent in the direction of the general current, without a rudder or a motor to go against it. Following them was a confused multitude of people unknowingly the prey of interest groups ranked according to wealth. Instead of serving as a guide, the press, often controlled by high finance, expressed only what had already been decided through schemes of profit and ambition. Sentences empty of any content were printed one after the other. On August 8, 1932, Secretary of State Henry Stimson recalled that the multilateral Kellogg-Briand Pact of August 27, 1928, had been founded on the strength of public opinion. He asserted that the firm intention of the American government was to make that strength effective, so that the pact of Paris would become a living force in the world; yet he spoke these words a year after the Japanese aggression in Manchuria, knowing well that neither the arms nor the intentions of his government had changed. Although the problem was to achieve a balance of power, it was thought possible to convince those who had power, as well as those who were eager to regain power, that words would be sufficient to ensure peace. The somber year 1932 was a year of elections for most nations. People had seldom found so many opportunities to express themselves. The result was an incoherent disarray. Inexperienced, mistrustful, or fearful politicians traded places and shifted positions. But they remained impotent shadows. Caught in this whirl of shadows, the states were never able to enter into a direct and thorough discussion of their relations. When, on January 30, 1933, there appeared an all-powerful dictator who alone was the German state, no comparable figure emerged to face him.

In this democratic whirlpool, the small states tried to oppose the big states. To maintain their hierarchical dominance, the big states invoked their responsibilities, but they carefully avoided transforming these responsibilities into real decisions.

Equal Rights

In order to maintain the peace settlement of 1919, accepted by the Germans only "with a knife at the throat," it was logically necessary to use force, a force superior to that of the Germans, who had never ceased being indignant about the Treaty of Versailles. To renounce force logically entailed renouncing the advantages acquired by force.

But the Treaty of Versailles was not a settlement like other settlements; it claimed to organize the future. "In any case," Clemenceau had said on September 25, 1919, "we have done something that . . . perhaps will be more important in history than the famous date of Mohammed II's entry into Constantinople. It is an event that will truly mark a new era."

The preamble to the section of the Treaty of Versailles that relates to the disarmament recognized that the disarmament imposed on Germany was only the first step in a general disarmament toward which the League of

Nations was to ensure progress: "In order to render possible the initiation of a general limitation of the armaments of all nations, Germany undertakes strictly to observe the military, naval, and air clauses which follow."

In a letter he sent on June 16, 1919, to Count von Brockdorff-Rantzau in the name of the Allied governments, Clemenceau completed the treaty by declaring that the German disarmament was only the beginning of the general disarmament that all nations would have to strive for, even the victorious.

For seven years, beginning in 1925, the Preparatory Commission for the Disarmament Conference negotiated in Geneva. Apart from the nations represented at the League of Nations, it included delegates from the United States, from Germany, after 1927 from the Soviet Union (which demanded overall disarmament), and after 1928 from Turkey. It held seven sessions. Studying the limitation and reduction of armaments with ponderous pretentiousness, the commission declared that the question was slowly ripening in the consciousness of peoples and governments.

In reality it was a long struggle sustained by France. Great Britain, Italy, the Soviet Union, and, naturally, Germany were opposing her, even during the post-Locarno euphoria. The German delegates led a vigorous offensive for French disarmament; no longer on the defensive, they now made demands and boldly recalled that the disarmament imposed on Germany in 1919 was only the beginning of general disarmament, a contractual obligation. World opinion had been mobilized to force disarmament—the abandonment of all military superiority—on France; yet France was entering on the period when her conscription system would no longer provide enough draftees, the demographic result of very low birth rates during the Great War.

In fact the Geneva discussions on disarmament were essentially a Franco-German dispute. Germany looked on herself as having equal rights with France. Either France should disarm, or Germany should rearm.

On January 25, 1931, the League of Nations Council decided that the international Disarmament Conference would meet at Geneva in a year. In May 1931, after having set February 2, 1932, as the opening date, it named as chairman Arthur Henderson, foreign minister in MacDonald's Labour cabinet.

Secretary of a major trade union after having been a machine fitter, Henderson had become a member of parliament in 1903 and had been a cabinet minister from 1915 to August 1917. He had then resigned because, while opposing the international socialist conference at Stockholm, he was in favor of deliberations among the workers' parties of the Allied countries. Interior minister in the first Labour cabinet of 1923–24, he was foreign minister in the second cabinet of 1929. With optimism and determination, he assumed the heavy task entrusted to him of presiding over the conference.

His loyalty and dedication made him an exceptionally good chairman; he knew how to lead a debate and how to impose the order so necessary in such discussions. His designation as head of a conference that represented a prestigious expansion of pacifism was one of the great pleasures of his life. With all his heart he hoped that through disarmament he would attach his name to peace. He and President Hoover had only one view in common: they both saw arms as the root of all evil. To defend peace, they dreamed of excluding force.

Henderson's joy did not last long. Three months later, feeling no friendship for Henderson following serious disputes within the Labour party, MacDonald formed a new coalition government that excluded him. No longer foreign minister, Henderson was thus deprived of the powerful means of action at a foreign minister's disposal.

From then on, more isolated than a representative from a small nation, Henderson visited the European capitals, where he was welcomed with respectful courtesy. He was received by Hitler, whose monologue depressed him. In 1934 he was awarded the Nobel Peace Prize. Soon his health was seriously undermined; until then his courage had dominated his illness.

In 1932 world opinion had been mobilized to force France to disarm; but, with the advent of Hitler in 1933, Germany's power to expand destroyed the anticipated equilibrium.

Far from abandoning the fashionable slogan, "peace through disarmament," men persisted in their frenzied pacifism. The mystique of disarmament, combined with faith in a universal peace, triumphed. For the British government, eager to mould itself to public opinion, disarmament was mainly aimed at restoring the balance of power. That restoration would be obtained through the League of Nations. No European settlement would be acceptable which had to rely on a superior force, that of France, to be maintained. Disarmament had to be accompanied by a revision of the peace treaties. A process of revision would eventually find a permanent basis for friendly understanding.

Little by little the sense of reality was lost. A strange confusion clouded people's minds. The Disarmament Conference, carried along by noble intentions, held as its main objective the dismantling of the only organized peacekeeping forces in Europe, those of France, while it granted a moral justification to the forces which had long been reorganizing in violation of the peace treaties. Under Hitler, these forces would again conspicuously regroup for aggression, in an unprecedented effort which would consume over sixty billion marks in the space of a few years.

What was expected of this international tournament? It was expected that France would agree to revise the section of the Treaty of Versailles dealing with disarmament and recognize Germany's right to rearm. Against whom would Germany arm? Obviously against France, whose policy and system for European peace would be threatened with destruction. Germany disarmed, facing a too well armed France: what an injustice! It was as if France had been indicted before a tribunal, the Disarmament Conference. She had to be forced to give up her military hegemony in order to restore the European balance by equalizing German and French armaments, thus eliminating all distinction between the victors and the vanquished of 1918.

An irresistible trend in Anglo-Saxon opinion became evident. On September 20, 1932, a delegation led by the archbishops of Canterbury and York, the head of the Methodist church, and the General of the Salvation Army was received at the Foreign Office by Prime Minister Ramsay MacDonald and the foreign minister, Sir John Simon. It expressed disappointment at the slowness of the Disarmament Conference's work. "The problems involved are of a moral, not a juridical, character. . . . The promises given at Versailles, by virtue of which the compulsory disarmament of Germany ought to constitute the first step toward general disarmament, have not been fulfilled. . . . The British government should formulate a definite disarmament policy, based on legal equality among all the League of Nations members."

In the name of the Labour party, Clement Attlee demanded the immediate abolition of the military clauses of the Treaty of Versailles. In this issue, France found herself morally isolated. Nevertheless it cannot be said that this isolation was caused by hostility against France; it was instead the result of a fundamental propensity of public opinion to see only the present and to rarely have any sense of the future.

Moreover, the French Left, thinking of the general elections of May 1932, had made disarmament part of its platform. Léon Blum assured everyone that "disarmament was the surest way to ward off danger."

With the world economic crisis culminating in 1932, the felicity of the Locarno period came to an end. How could people have maintained an optimistic serenity during the unrest of European bankruptcies and after the widespread commotion caused in September 1931 by the end of the fixed Sterling exchange rate. The principle of Lansbury, the Labour leader, reflected perfectly the almost unanimous British opinion: all nations should "disarm to the German level, as a first step toward total disarmament."

Tardieu, Herriot, Papen and
Schleicher, MacDonald

At that point everything, or nearly everything, seemed to depend on London. The National government had been in power since the summer of 1931. Prime Minister Ramsay MacDonald, a tall handsome man with horn-rimmed glasses and a full head of disorderly gray hair, was no longer the man he had been in the past. Hated by many of his former friends in the Labour party, he had become, as Lord Salter wrote, a tragic ghost. From the start of the conference, he declared himself in favor of the German position: equality of rights.

In 1932, on the eve of Hitler's rise, the general feeling in England was that France had to be disarmed. As a result, Germany would voluntarily limit her rearmament to the level of French armament. German rearmament was explained by France's unwillingness to disarm. In effect, England hoped that Germany would begin rearming. France, however, demanded that an effective security system be established before Germany could rearm.

With infinite persistence and in the midst of many hesitations, successive French delegations had presented plans for disarmament to the Preparatory Commission of the conference. These plans hardly went beyond a framework which made France seem to be promoting only her allies, by supporting the maintenance of a diplomatic structure necessary for her security. Invoking security, the very broad French proposals unfolded on a global scale with concentric spheres involving both quantitative and qualitative disarmament. They were believed to have a basis in astuteness: the ulterior motive of retaining overabundant military supplies. Ingenious efforts were lavished to protect these treasured supplies, which proved obsolete when the time came to use them. The General Staff counterbalanced the endless work of the commission with a persistent force of inertia, while Paul-Boncour delivered beautiful speeches to the commission in favor of "the organization of mutual assistance, determined in advance, coordinated in advance, capable of opposing aggression." He seriously tried to oppose German rearmament and cooperate with England, but he continued to fight German rearmament even when he could no longer count on British cooperation. At the commission and at the Disarmament Conference, the French tactics were inspired by the same defensive caution that gave birth to the Maginot line. The French delegation had only one thought: to merge its forces and its equipment in collective security plans inspired by its own anxiety over the fate of France. Instead of creating an offensive army, all these projects tended to bear witness to and accentuate the defensive nature of the French army.

In February 1932, André Tardieu claimed to be abandoning this tactic. After the death of Maginot on January 7, Laval had moved Tardieu from the agriculture ministry to the defense ministry when he formed a cabinet without Briand, taking the foreign ministry himself.

At the beginning of the conference, on February 5, Tardieu set forth in his opening speech a plan that indicated an entirely new policy. He claimed that he would guarantee security only by the application of the Covenant in

Europe, but of the whole Covenant as it had been written, and not the Covenant as it had been diminished by the respective interpretations of its principal provisions. The strengthening of the Covenant in Europe seemed advisable in view of the attitude taken by Japan, who was having her own way in the Far East; let disarmament be linked to the application of the Covenant in Europe! Tardieu, who had been the negotiator in 1919 of the double English and American guarantee, had no more faith in security from England. No more petitions would be sent to England on behalf of French safety. France would never again say to England: it is up to you to guarantee our security. Tardieu's argument was simple: disarmament was one of the Covenant's obligations. But this obligation could not be isolated. The Covenant had to be put into effect, the whole Covenant, said Tardieu. Article 16, in particular, was by its nature obligatory: if a member of the League of Nations resorted to war, he would be ipso facto considered to have committed an act of war against all members of the League—all commercial, financial, and personal relations with the nationals of that state had to be broken and naval and air strength used to enforce the obligations of the League. "An organized League of Nations is the only effective means of prevention and enforcement."

Tardieu's argument was new. Stresemann had shown his surprise when he heard Briand say that, all things considered, Article 16 was not obligatory.

Unfortunately this very clear position, which could have been fruitful, was hidden under Tardieu's heavy, crushing addition of proposals and elaborations—a complete superstructure sprung from an implacable but tactically mistaken logic. A French parliament can be seduced by the imposing architecture of an overall plan. Always slow to understand, the delegates of an international assembly are disconcerted by the amplitude and complexity of an arrangement that leads the listeners astray and loses them in details. It requires a great deal of patience to put simple ideas into their minds.

Tardieu, admirable for his sparkling logic, did not want to neglect any of the reasons that supported his argument. He was not a lawyer like Poincaré, but an orator always ready to display his dazzling mastery of a subject: "Tardieu the terrific," Léon Daudet bantered. During the war he had been successful with the Americans because they were less immune than the British to brilliant French speeches and, above all, because the Americans, at that time, did not want to accept the pressure and the pretentions of the British, who wanted to be the only intermediaries in Europe, the administrators and comptrollers of all the American loans.

In substance, the offer of February 1932 meant this: "Take the Covenant of the League of Nations seriously. Let it take effect! See what results it would have in Europe. And I will surrender the French war supplies to you." This materiel was like the gold reserve in the Bank of France, but it was depreciating faster than gold.

Tardieu's proposals had no results; they were not even honored with a general discussion at the conference. Litvinov observed sarcastically that an international army would run the risk of being exploited in "the interest of a state which would secure for itself a dominant position in the international organization, by alliances, ententes, and separate agreements."

Tardieu had many opponents, especially in his own country. He was discredited—his proposals were just a bluff. Did he believe in them himself? An international police force? He had few illusions on that point and his prime minister, Pierre Laval, had even fewer.

As defense minister in the Laval cabinet, Tardieu left Geneva for Paris, where he emerged as prime minister and foreign minister. He scarcely reappeared in Geneva; he did not want to be included in the MacDonald-Stimson discussions, and he did not substitute anything for them. His speech, filled with aggressive energy, had exhausted his desire for action.

In May 1932, Tardieu was succeeded by Herriot, who was convinced that the League of Nations could be effective only with the English entente. He was right. It is a pity that at that time British policy, highly Germanophile if not even Francophobe, seemed to reflect the opinion that the French represented the only European power capable of aggression. England was completely in agreement with the generally approved-of German argument: all states had agreed to disarm to approach the limits assigned to Germany; if they did not disarm, they would not meet their obligations and Germany would have the right to recover her freedom of action. She would not allow herself to be treated as a second-class nation. Time had done its work. It was impossible to rigorously enforce the disarmament of Germany alone—in theory at least—in the middle of an armed Europe. Germany had to carry out her rearmament under the cover of general disarmament.

All that the French had agreed to since Locarno counted for nothing. At Locarno they had accepted, on the same basis as the Germans, the double English and Italian guarantee. It is true that France, condemned to take a negative position, claimed to keep her other prerogatives in the ingenious, subtle game she played to avoid disarming, while pacts and conventions piled up.

In this futile series of efforts, France could have realized her inability to create collective security, and then tried to settle matters confidentially, with Germany alone. But, while the United States, Great Britain, and Italy abandoned their role of former allies and, as much as they could, used their freedom of action to negotiate with Germany, the axiom of the irreconcilability of France and Germany persisted. It was presumed that there could be no understanding between France and Germany. This situation lasted until 1933 when Hitler's rise to power brought the proof that an understanding was now inconceivable.

In these conditions, would it not have been better for France to deal directly with Weimar Germany? The *Reichswehr* respected the French army; it showed that respect by the cautious attitude of its generals in 1939. But, out of tactfulness, Paris refrained from acting alone in an attempt to reach a direct agreement.

The truth is that Paris felt unable to take any step without being very certain in advance of the reaction of the English Foreign Office. Not only did Paris want a close tie with England; it also showed an amicable docility in its subordination. Since the abandonment of the Ruhr policy, Paris had reached an almost total abdication in favor of London. It was continually announced that the French and the English governments were in complete agreement. In the case of the most harmless proceedings, the French wondered: what will London think of this? A real inhibition was at work in French politics. In 1932, would it not have been better to have direct talks with Germany than to sign the declaration of December 11 on the equality of rights to security?

Nevertheless, the idea of a direct agreement with Germany grew in certain French circles. France was not supported by Great Britain, who was herself supported by the United States. The French felt pressured by England and by Italy, who was even more favorable than England to the German position and its best advocate.

Why hold a world conference? The real problem was a Franco-German problem. France had kept her military equipment while Germany, disarmed according to the Versailles provisions, was asking for equality in armaments. France and Germany were the two main antagonists. In 1932, Germany was only allowed an army of 100,000 men, without heavy artillery, aircraft, or armor; France, however, had no condition limiting her armaments and she could deploy an army of about 360,000 men. Why not negotiate directly with Germany? Surely something would have to be given if anything was to be gained.

An opportunity had been offered by Chancellor von Papen, as we shall see, at Lausanne in July 1932. Herriot had not taken Papen seriously and had run up against a British veto. Then General von Schleicher, who had been *Reichswehr* minister under Papen and would later succeed him as chancellor, considered the possibility of an arrangement with France. Repeating one of Stresemann's sayings, he had airily characterized France's attitude in the question of disarmament as hypocritical; then he had taken the initiative of proposing direct talks. On July 28, 1932, Ambassador François-Poncet had drawn a very expressive portrait of Schleicher: "In spite of the ingenuity, the guile, the Machiavellianism of his intellect, (a man) extremely reckless . . . at once methodical and impulsive, obstinate and versatile . . . capable of the greatest concealment and of the most brutal frankness, and all with an underlying good humor, casualness, and cynicism that help him get out of the worst straits." Discovering in Schleicher a leader dangerous to the thousand-year Reich, Hitler decided to end his career on June 30, 1934, by assassination.

It seems obvious that in 1932 Franco-German negotiations would have led to nothing; it was symptomatic of the discrediting of the League of Nations.

The Declaration of December 11, 1932

During the summer of 1932, six months before Hitler came to power, the German delegation left the Disarmament Conference for a few weeks to bring pressure on the other delegations. On July 29, 1932, a communiqué was published: "Germany cannot give assurance that she will continue to participate in the work of the Disarmament Conference if the question of equal rights among nations is not settled."

On September 14, Neurath sent a note to Chairman Henderson: Germany would no longer take part in the conference if the principle of equal rights was not recognized. Herriot declared to the German chargé d'affaires that the situation was getting very serious. On October 3, 1932, at the Disarmament Conference, when Germany demanded equal rank with other nations through equality of armaments, this was approved unanimously by the English press. Édouard Herriot wrote:

> The verb "to disarm" is irregular in all languages. It has neither first person, nor present, nor past; it is conjugated above all in the future and in the second person. People do not say: "I am disarming," or "I have disarmed," but: "You will disarm."

At Gramat in the department of Lot, on September 25, 1932, Herriot had delivered a speech which left Germany indignant: "France . . . notices with bitterness that German popular opinion is not at all grateful for the sacrifices she consented to in evacuating the Rhineland before the deadline, in accepting the Young plan and then the Lausanne arrangements, in encouraging German trade by treaties . . . . France is worried about military measures which appear to be leading to another war."

On October 10 Ramsay MacDonald, bringing pressure to bear in an affectionate way, "as a man who confides in another and whose wish is always to keep the other's friendship and confidence," wrote to the French prime minister: "I do not believe that any one of us can uncompromisingly resist the German claim that it is necessary, in some measure, to reconsider the Treaty of Versailles. Suppose that you keep on replying no to her claims and that Germany says: 'Since we are not being freed willingly, we will appeal to the feelings of loyalty of our whole people, and we will free ourselves all alone, within reasonable limits,' what would you do?"

However, on October 18 Herriot confided to his colleagues that he was shocked to see England's insistence on disarmament of land forces. General Weygand, inspector-general of the army, declared: "The French army has reached a limit. . . . Any reduction would severely compromise its strength. . . . The army has converted to one-year conscript service; it has made a serious effort to reduce its size. We are confronted by a Germany which has always followed our concessions by new demands."

On October 18, Herriot concluded in front of his colleagues in the cabinet: "We are at a turning point in history. Until now, Germany has followed a negative policy, one of submission, although to be sure she was never resigned; now she is inaugurating a positive policy. Tomorrow it will be a policy of territorial demands with a propitious means of intimidation: her army. There lies the tragedy for the French government. Faced with such a state of things, the instinctive reaction is to say that we will not keep back a single man or a single cannon. . . . This solution is not satisfactory; for then Germany would declare herself legally authorized to rearm."

On December 11, 1932, in Geneva, Herriot, morally isolated, joined in a common declaration made by Great Britain, the United States, Italy, and Germany recognizing the principle of equal rights to armaments in a security system equal for all. Hitler, called to the chancellery six weeks later by President Hindenburg, hastened to make use of the concession just granted to Germany—equal rights—to secure for himself an enormous military force.

A decisive step, the German success of December 11, 1932, was by no means extolled in the German press. The nationalist Hugenberg's *Der Tag* regretted that Germany was returning to the Disarmament Conference. In a meeting with Stresemann in 1929, Briand blamed the Germans for being interested in a concession only when they did not obtain it. And in 1932, American undersecretary of state Castle said to Ambassador Paul Claudel: "Germany is like the barren wife in the Scriptures who never says: enough."

The "Five-Power Agreement" provided that Germany would acquire equality of armaments within the framework of a system of European security. For Germany, it was mainly a question of rearmament; for France, of security.

Let us consider for a moment the French meaning of the word "security."

Far from being new, this word is the oldest in the diplomatic vocabulary. It had been used again in the Covenant of the League of Nations: "The members of the League recognize that the maintenance of peace requires the reduction of national armaments to the lowest point consistent with national security, and the enforcement by common action of international obligations." Collective security has never been better defined than by the last part of that sentence. The Covenant of the League of Nations, far from being an ideological memorandum, was in fact a pact for common action, action by force when force was necessary. And among the principal obligations which had to be imposed to make a common action possible, the most important was that "the members of the League undertake to respect and preserve, against external aggression, the territorial integrity and existing political independence of all members of the League."

When a statute is written including such a binding provision, this provision can only come to life if the established authorities take it upon themselves to foresee and decree the laws and regulations essential to put it into effect. But from the start this obligation was considered a dead letter, and the lapse was accepted and publicly recorded.

The legalistic policy of France—an accumulation of pacts and arbitration conventions—also contributed to the weakening of the Covenant of the League of Nations, a covenant in which no one believed. Nothing could have replaced a policy founded on the Covenant, a flexible policy neither Machiavellian nor arbitrary.

3

The Lausanne Conference
(June–July 1932)

Near Cancellation of Reparations

"Men make history." This aphorism of the German historian Treitschke
retains its profound meaning, even in the century of economics. January 30,
1933, is one of the major turning points of the twentieth century. When, on
that day, Hitler was called to the chancellery by Marshal von Hindenburg,
the two questions that had never ceased to poison international relations
had almost been settled in their essentials: the question of reparations and
the question of armaments. The most hated clauses of the Treaty of Versailles were gradually disappearing.

President Hoover, faced with the violence of the financial crisis, declared
a general moratorium in June 1931. It suspended for a year all payments
of intergovernmental debts and reparations. The Lausanne Conference would
practically free Germany from the burden of reparations. Ramsay Mac-
Donald, chairman of the conference, took his role as honest political broker
very seriously; he spoke of "our French friends" and "our German friends."
Like Sir John Simon, he wanted to write off reparations.

Édouard Herriot, prime minister and foreign minister after May 1932,
realized that Germany could not pay for the moment; but things might
change, and one day she would be able to pay something.

The British suggested linking the abolition of reparations with a fifteen-
year political truce. Herriot observed that this would only mean one more
scrap of paper.

Chancellor since June 1932, Franz von Papen talked to Herriot about a military alliance; but Herriot told Sir John Simon: "The more I study the head of this cavalry officer, the more I admire his horse." On June 27, Papen confided to MacDonald that he had asked Herriot if a Franco-German alliance would better ensure France's security, but that Herriot had thought the idea premature.

On July 9, 1932, after laborious negotiations in a multitude of technical committees, the conference ended in a total elimination of reparations, masked by a sham promise of eventual payment. No one believed in this payment and it was never put into effect. In any case, Germany would not have to pay anything for three years, and long before that time limit expired Hitler was in power. The bonds Germany was supposed to issue for three billion gold marks were never marketed.

On July 11, 1932, the Führer declared that instead of the three billion marks just imposed on Germany, he would pay not even three. A German found it witty to send to Herriot a few banknotes from the time of inflation: "You ask for three billion marks, prime minister Herriot; here are one hundred billion, and let's speak no more of it."

France felt that at Lausanne she had agreed to "a formidable sacrifice" for the common good; she was annoyed to receive no thanks for it.

Interallied Debts

It was impossible to wipe the slate clean by canceling all war debts and reparations. The United States refused to relinquish the interallied debts. Congress was almost unanimous in remaining faithful to the resolution, voted in December 1931, which excluded canceling or reducing the debts. France was pictured as a fabulously rich nation, toward which the Americans had mistakenly been too generous. Selfish and greedy for hegemony, France, some people said, represented a greater danger to peace than had Germany in 1914. The United States, creditor of the creditors, did not want to be the victim of the consideration the Allies showed Germany. Let them reduce their military budget! Then they would be able to pay the United States even without reparations, declared President Hoover, whom Ambassador Claudel called "a victim of the most intense and the most widespread personal unpopularity that any statesman has managed to bring upon himself by four years of painstaking administration."

Consequently, the question of war debts to the United States remained in suspense. At the end of 1932, England resigned herself and made a payment. Herriot wanted to adopt the same attitude and keep up French payments. On this question he was defeated by an enormous majority in the Chamber in December 1932, three days after having accepted the declaration of the Disarmament Conference on equal rights. Four hundred and sixty-two deputies, against 187, felt that since America, through President Hoover's proposal, had eliminated any collection of money from Germany, it was logical to eliminate any payment intended for America.

In 1933 the debtor powers limited themselves to symbolic payments, which ended in 1934. Only Finland continued her payments, of little significance in any case. There was strong discontent in the United States and isolationism increased even more, although the Democrat Franklin Roosevelt, successor to a series of Republican presidents, had been elected in November 1932. Following the decisions made by Congress forbidding financial transactions with states that had not settled with America, Roosevelt recalled that the United States had never conceded the link between reparations and war debts.

The Lausanne Conference of June–July 1932 had given hope for a solution of the war debts problem and for a monetary and economic recovery. The monetary and economic conference convened in London on June 12, 1933, was supposed to find this solution. Amid the upsets and losses of the world economic crisis, this conference—oriented more toward the past than the future, aimed at a return of pre-1914 capitalism. With the New Deal hardly outlined by Roosevelt, the conference was dominated by the American economy, and it broke up on July 3 when the President disavowed the reestablishment of monetary stability in favor of economic recovery.

In taking up a position against the United States, France chose to stay on the gold standard. On her pedestal of precious metal, she was losing her export markets because of high prices and defending her internal markets by disorganized protective tariffs. Like a pernicious anemia, the budget deficit would ruin her public finances, her currency, and her credit. From the prosperous peaks of 1931, the Republic, carried along in a continuous fall, would slide into the valley of the depression, while the nations first hit by the crisis were climbing back up the slope. France began then to live with a sclerosis of currency and banking, with deflation, with a slowdown of production from fear of overproduction, and with a failure to replace industrial capital. She had been the dominant power on the European continent, but such situations are fleeting, and her successive governments were getting lost in the mazes of contradictory policies. She went from the peak of her power to the destruction of her prestige. It was like the sudden apparition of a hidden sickness. From the economic and financial standpoint, the weakening was general; from the diplomatic standpoint, the same weakening was apparent.

4

The Japanese Conflict (1932-33)

The League of Nations in the Far East.
Cooperation of the United States

Since February 2, 1932, the day the ministers assembled for world disarmament, the conference had disappointed its supporters. The Sino-Japanese
conflict had arisen on the eve of the conference, in the fall of 1931. The
Japanese complained that their interests were suffering from the anarchy
in China. They invaded Manchuria, where China had not really established
her authority. The Council of the League of Nations asked them to evacuate
it, but in vain. The Japanese intended to treat their claims in Manchuria as
a matter involving Japan and China exclusively. Having secured territorial
collateral, they meant to settle their difficulties with the Chinese under
favorable conditions.

There was no lack of precedents for an independent action by the great
powers in China. In 1926, did the English not land in Shanghai?

In 1931 the League of Nations did not succeed in reestablishing peace in
the Far East. Yet Briand's prestige was considerable; his duties as president
of the League of Nations Council made him the leader of the discussions on
that problem.

Moreover, the cooperation of the United States was assured—a quite
extraordinary fact thought to be a major success for the League of Nations.
In a message to the Council, the government in Washington had announced
its intention to take part in the settlement of the Far Eastern problem. But
the situation set in opposition two very different men, Sir John Simon and
Henry Stimson. Was Secretary of State Stimson willing to take a more radical
position than Hoover, his president? Did England contribute in making the

United States abandon the "Stimson doctrine," a refusal to recognize territorial changes brought about through the use of force?

Many Americans believed that the Japanese expansion would have been stopped in 1932 if Simon had accepted a proposal of economic sanctions made by Stimson. In reality this proposal had been very nebulous. It did not envisage a breach of commercial relations with Japan. The Americans did not want to understand that, without their active participation, the League of Nations could not act effectively in the Far East. Mutual recriminations only heightened the disrepute of the League of Nations in the United States.

The aggression in Manchuria opened an era of grave complications. Until then Great Britain had looked on the League of Nations as an instrument of conciliation, not as a means of security. Influenced by the Manchurian problem, the League members thought of creating a mechanism for organizing sanctions; this would make possible the League's action in 1935 in Ethiopia.

But would it have been wise to cut off international trade with Japan when the world economic crisis was at its height? And what could Great Britain have done while she was in the process of abandoning the gold standard and getting ready for a parliamentary election? Especially since the Washington Naval Treaty ensured Japanese supremacy in the Far East, and since British governments of every political nuance had all delayed the bringing into operation of the proposed Singapore naval base. In Great Britain the opposition to any anti-Japanese action would have been unanimous. The Labour party would have denounced an operation undertaken for the protection of imperialistic interests. Consequently, the National government limited itself to an embargo on arm shipments both to Japan and to China.

Japan's Resistance. Japan Leaves the
League of Nations in March 1933

Although the United States gave the League of Nations unexpected but limited help, Japan resisted. Invested with the duty of averting any blow to world peace, the League of Nations seemed powerless to put into effect any coercive measure, whatever it might be. The public concluded that if a similar conflict occurred in Europe, it would be vain to count on an organization so severely weakened, if not discredited. The people followed anxiously this test of the Covenant's effectiveness. The complete failure of the League of Nations in the Far East was the source of the strongest anxieties about the future. The timidity of the great powers was brought to light, and so was the weakness of the League of Nations; for what could the League accomplish without the great powers?

It is true that the defenders of the League of Nations asserted that a European conflict could not be likened to the Japanese conflict, which showed very special characteristics. What was in question was not the violation of the territory of a state exercising all of its rights over that territory. Before recognizing the Nanking government, the diplomats had tolerated Japan's strange activity in certain regions of China and had grown accustomed to a nearly separate Manchuria. The feelings of the Japanese were not to be hurt, their morale was not to be offended. The report of the League Investigating Commission in Geneva, without wanting to impose sanctions against Tokyo, declared that the imposed territorial modifications constituted a violation of the nine-power agreements of 1922 and of the Kellogg-Briand Pact of 1928.

Consequently, these modifications were not recognized—which was enough to bring it about that Japan resumed her freedom of action in March 1933 and withdrew from the League. That was a very serious act. Liberated from all fear, Japan's gains at China's expense had surpassed her initial hopes. Japan undertook vast conquests and founded a new state, Manchukuo—a situation recognized by Chiang Kai-shek when he made peace with Japan on May 31, 1933.

The Manchurian precedent had fateful consequences. Japan took the road to war. It would lead to the major conflict of 1937 in China, and ultimately to Pearl Harbor.

Would the League of Nations not be just as powerless in the face of a European aggressor?

5

Hitler and Disarmament

On December 11, 1932, five months after Lausanne and six weeks before the coming to power of National Socialism, France resigned herself and accepted the principle of equal rights for all powers in the armaments question. Since June 30, 1930, French troops had completely evacuated the German territory which according to the peace treaty they should have occupied until 1935. Of course, the means of applying the principle of equality of rights had not yet been defined and the now recognized principle of equality still had to be put into effect. But already Germany, strengthened by the promise of December 11, was able legally to rebuild an army.

In *Mein Kampf*, the French were called "the deadly, merciless enemies of the German people." However, when the Führer came to power there were no more French soldiers on German soil; there was no more German tribute to be paid to France; and France had recognized, theoretically, Germany's equal right to armaments—an equality, to be sure, that could only be realized in a system ensuring security for all nations, while ideas about security varied greatly from country to country. Rationally, it should have been possible to banish from people's minds and hearts the idea of a Franco-German armed conflict.

Hitler had retained as foreign minister Baron von Neurath, who had held that position under chancellors Papen and Schleicher. Sir John Simon was quite happy to see him keep the foreign ministry. Neurath was a diplomat from the old school, who had been ambassador in Rome and in London; of elegant appearance and pleasant to know, "he was only putty in the hands of Hitler."

Hitler, now chancellor, delivered reassuring speeches; but only because he felt vulnerable in the most dangerous period of his rearmament. In fact he

42

had adopted the most violent theories. It was impossible to discover the horizon behind this veil of threats and promises, of peaceful declarations and cynical maneuvers. Everything depended on the choice Hitler would make between a policy of moderation and a policy of force, tipping the balance in his own mind to the side of peace or to the side of war.

His frenzied ambitions would take advantage of the extreme agitation reigning in a Europe where the two levels of domestic and foreign policy were generally confused. Depending on the positions people took in their own countries toward Communism or toward Fascism, now spreading everywhere like spilled oil, they were for the Soviet Union or for Fascism abroad, in the same way as, in the sixteenth century, the *Ligueurs* of France sided with an ultra-Catholic Spain in their rage to annihilate the enemy and make their faith victorious.

The British Plan

Since February 2, 1932, when the prime ministers assembled to disarm the world, the Geneva Conference had poorly answered the petitions and prayers that had welcomed it. Hitler's first deeds since his coming to power in January 1933 had darkened an already dark future.

The very divided British government had warnings of the dangers already visible in 1932. It was an undeniable fact that Germany had never ceased openly violating the clauses of Versailles, and the activities of paramilitary organizations were obvious.

Was the British government waiting for France to be disarmed before it rearmed? Imperturbable despite the rise of Hitler, the British government persisted in the idea of arms limitation. They believed that it was in the common interest to keep Germany at the Disarmament Conference and not to push her into an isolated situation she would exploit in order to rearm.

The British government did not want to take part in a sort of encirclement of Germany intended to enclose her but instead to reach an agreement with her on the basis of the international cooperation she would show in accepting a limitation of her armaments.

Neurath's Program

When Hitler took power, the Geneva Conference was marking time. On March 10, 1933, MacDonald and Simon were in Paris. Prime Minister Daladier and Paul-Boncour, his foreign minister, expressed their fears prompted by Germany's paramilitary groups and by the beginning of her air force. They wanted to reinforce a front opposing Germany without acting directly against the

Reich. At Geneva, Beneš and Politis corroborated their fears. The French intelligence service had followed the progress of the secret rearmament, which remained very limited until the fall of 1932, and did not really start until November, under General von Schleicher. Georges Castellan's book, *Le réarmement clandestin du Reich, 1930-1935, vu par le Deuxième Bureau de l'État-major français,* gives the essential elements of the secret dossier referred to by the makers of French policy during the painstaking discussions on disarmament.

Until 1933 the German delegation had very skillfully exerted a persuasive influence by generally affecting moderate views and conciliatory attitudes. The German delegates had taken part in discussions concerning the transformation of permanent armies into militias—a transformation the Reich completely disapproved of. Would Hitler, in a situation so greatly modified by his presence and by his manic will, benefit from the gains of the last Weimar governments? He declared to his cabinet on February 8, 1933, that rearmament had to be reached within five years. It seems that until the end of September 1933 he searched for an agreement on disarmament based on the "Five-Power Declaration" of December 11, 1932. Such an agreement would have been established, within a relatively short time, an equality between Germany and France with respect to war-making potential.

Baron von Neurath neatly explained his program to the cabinet on April 7, 1933. Germany's goal—the revision of the Treaty of Versailles—had to be reached only by stages, so that her trials of strength would not meet with serious resistance.

First Germany had to obtain full equality of rights, especially in military matters. Granted in principle at Geneva on December 11, 1932, equality could only be realized after a period of five years during which Germany would have to strengthen her armaments. It was worthwhile for propaganda reasons to remain in the League of Nations.

Questions dealing with frontier changes should not be raised for the moment; these changes would be prepared for by actions undertaken in neighboring states on behalf of German minorities, with Wilson's principle of self-determination as a foundation.

Alsace-Lorraine should not be mentioned to avoid stirring up France, whose influence had greatly declined, but who remained the strongest military power in the world. She should be treated with caution and discretion. Czechoslovakia was France's best ally; nevertheless, it was possible to act upon the other members of the Little Entente: Rumania and Yugoslavia, especially in economic matters. Germany should support, although cautiously, the revisionist aspirations of Hungary, an ally of Germany by the nature of things. Indeed, as early as July 1933, Hungarian prime minister

Gömbös, overpowered by the Little Entente's hatred, rushed to Berlin in the hope of establishing a close cooperation with Germany, as Hungary had done with Italy and Austria.

The strong Franco-Italian clashes of interest in the Mediterranean were bringing Italy closer to the Germans. In order not to arouse Italy's hostility, Germany should not mention the question of Austro-German union.

The essential thing was to bring about a close collaboration with the British. But it was obvious that England would not, for the sake of Germany, endanger her good relations with France or with the United States, who would persist in its isolationism and not support Germany.

Despite contradictory ideologies, it was important to maintain good political and economic relations with the USSR.

As for Poland, she was the enemy of the Germans, who could not accept the loss of Danzig, the Polish Corridor, and Upper Silesia. It was useless to attempt a rapprochement with Warsaw. But that is exactly what Hitler was going to do, and with what success!

German Rearmament, Churchill, and Simon

On March 16, 1933, six weeks after Hitler became chancellor, Prime Minister Ramsay MacDonald submitted to the Disarmament Conference a vast plan intended to achieve, within five years, an equality of armaments between France and Germany: eight-month service for all Continental armies; equal strengths of two hundred thousand men maximum for France, Poland, Germany, and Italy—France having a right to two hundred thousand additional men for her overseas possessions and Italy to fifty thousand men; strictly limited armaments; destruction of all surplus armaments; prohibition of chemical warfare and aerial bombings, except for police operations in overseas territories.

Could such a system of military service be imposed on the League's member states? For Germany, it would have meant renouncing General von Seeckt's system, which made the professional *Reichswehr* the framework for the future grand army that could not yet be given armaments. The nucleus of a large army, the *Reichswehr* cared much more deeply about its own rearmament than about French disarmament. To establish equality between French and German war potentials, two methods were possible: to disarm France or to rearm Germany.

France was opposed to any heavy German rearmament—air force, tanks, heavy artillery—and demanded the transformation of the German professional army into a short-term, conscript army. She agreed to an increase in troop strength and in light armaments. But she refused to destroy her own heavy armaments before the establishment of a collective security system. Within the Reich, there were both advocates of the disarmament of France and advocates of the rearmament of Germany. These two solutions would, theoretically, produce the same result for Germany, but they did not offer the same possibilities for success.

Would Germany insist above all on the disarmament of other powers, claiming for herself only a limited rearmament? It was foreign minister von Neurath's impression, as it had been General von Schleicher's impression before, that if she did England and Italy might be able to convince France to destroy her heavy armaments. On the contrary, if Germany made large demands for rearmament it was certain that France, frightened, would not agree to the smallest destruction of her armaments.

However, the chief German delegate to the Disarmament Conference, Ambassador Nadolny, was a convinced supporter of the rearmament argument. His ideas were shared by General von Blomberg, who, having been commander at Königsberg, had become head of the German military delegation at Geneva and later Hitler's army minister. Hostile to Neurath, who fearing Nazi accusations of weakness was playing the strong man, Nadolny criticized the Nazis vigorously; but his boorish ways transformed the conversations into, in Eden's words, a "trial of strength."

Hitler's rise to power, bringing Blomberg to the head of the *Reichswehr* ministry, accentuated the differences of opinion between Neurath and Blomberg. Germany refused to transform her professional army into a conscript army. Hitler was repressing violent reactions against short-term military service. On March 15, Neurath, believing that he had obtained from Hitler important concessions to the French position, hastened to report them to Nadolny. But Blomberg sent contrary instructions to Schönheinz, his representative at Geneva, and he succeeded in making Hitler retract his concessions of March 15. Nevertheless, on May 8, during an interview, Blomberg had agreed in principle to the standardization of armies, because he wanted to facilitate the negotiations to be led by Eden in Geneva after May 9, in an attempt to break the conference deadlock.

However Blomberg took back with one hand what he had just granted with the other, when he informed state secretary von Bülow that a transformation of the *Reichswehr* would take at least twelve years and even longer, as the number of professional soldiers allowed decreased.

Great perplexity reigned in Berlin. The MacDonald plan, a series of complex chess moves, did not include any political considerations. Since Germany complained incessantly about the inequality of armaments, France was asked to destroy everything in her enormous war materiel which exceeded the contingents, calibers, and specifications adopted.

Because eloquent debates and negotiations aimed only at juridical formulas, the formulas themselves finally replaced reality. Committee after committee was created. With no practical results, they all floundered in minutely detailed discussions about the size of airplanes and the tonnage of ships.

It was known in London as well as in Paris that Germany was rearming. Baldwin admitted that since 1932 the government had felt danger. After having incorporated in its calculations to achieve balance the great undercurrent of enthusiasm for peaceful disarmament, the British government hesitated to admit that now the scales were tipping toward the other side, and that the application of equal rights no longer represented a work of justice aimed at peace. With the perspective of time and the lesson of events, it is difficult for us to understand that the British government did not dare to explain the necessity of rearming to its people, nor did it dare to justify the French position. After the assassination of Dollfuss, Baldwin himself said, on July 30, 1934: "Our frontier is on the Rhine." It is hard to conceive the extent to which ideas fluctuated among nearly irreconcilable contradictions. England, abiding by an archaic and strictly English concept of security, refused to commit herself. Throughout the Disarmament Conference, she did not dream of entering into an agreement other than the agreement of Locarno.

It is probable that the British government, fearing that England would be the only nation to remain disarmed, demanded total disarmament in the chimerical hope that, if France was disarmed, Germany would stop rearming.

In the opposition, Churchill had a clearer view of things. He labeled the Disarmament Conference a "solemn and prolonged farce," and in 1933 he began his great seven-year series of soliloquies on the untrustworthy and unreliable Hitler. Churchill was preaching in the wilderness when he invited MacDonald to "thank God for having the French army." It is true that at that moment, while engaged in his struggle to preserve intact the British positions in Egypt, in India, and on the road to India, Churchill was still very far from the idea of collective security. He wanted to base Great Britain's freedom of action outside Europe on French military supremacy within Europe.

In Hitler's coming to power, Churchill recognized very quickly the omen of a second world war. He tried in vain to open the eyes of his countrymen. Pathetically, he cried out that "the withdrawal of the conquered's complaints ought to precede the conqueror's disarmament." The successive Nazi acts of aggression would justify his predictions.

While French disarmament was still being demanded, he provoked incredulous laughter in Commons when he drew a picture of German armaments, although that picture was less gloomy than the reality.

Since the formation of a National coalition government, the Foreign Office was held by Sir John Simon. His feeling for nuances had made him an eminent lawyer, "a second Asquith," and his career had been distinguished by major arbitration settlements. This Liberal, son of a Protestant minister and opposed to violence, had during the war refused to impose conscription and, resigning from the Asquith ministry, had come to France to serve in the air force. Of ruddy complexion, Sir John Simon thought that a convention—even a bad one—interrupting the race for armaments was better than none at all. Founded on English trust in the power of public opinion, his illusion no doubt lay in believing that a limiting convention had a serious chance of slowing down German rearmament, when in reality it would only have consecrated Hitler's freedom. What would have been the result on Hitler of "inspection"? Reports bearing witness to Hitler's violations would only have confirmed what people saw and knew. France and England would then have brought the case before the League of Nations, but in reality they were ignoring the issue through their bilateral negotiations.

France's Difficult Position

France, exhausted by demographic decline, internal crises, and economic difficulties, was possessed by devastating psychological complexes. She suffered from accusations of militarism and imperialism. After 1919, and especially after the Ruhr occupation, she was accused of having aggressive plans. To these inferiority complexes was added a "security" complex already present when there was no longer a German military threat, and which had grown in 1919 when France's Anglo-Saxon allies had offered her guarantees only to withdraw them. Lulled by a false tranquillity, the country slept in an indolent indifference. After the shock of the Ruhr occupation, she seemed to have lost all sense of purpose. Never had there been a period more unfavorable for undergoing the trial of a new war, or even simply for exerting the energy needed for the maintenance of peace. In 1924, at the very moment when Stresemann was writing that France, victorious in 1918 and in 1923, had never been more powerful in Europe since the time of Napoleon I, the country lived in restlessness, anxiety, and dissatisfaction over the present, for all that she had twice overcome the Germans, and it was a dissatisfaction filled with apprehensions over the future. In 1932 this state of mind had dangerously worsened. The general impression was that in France everything had degenerated: the idea of the state, the feeling of public duty, the institutions. The French, confused and indecisive, gave way to incoherent whims and listlessness.

The situation was similar in Great Britain. Churchill declared in 1932:

"Great Britain has become weak, and the hour of weakness for Great Britain is the hour of danger for Europe." And Sir Robert Vansittart, called "Cassandra" by Baldwin, would write in 1948: "Our respective countries were not materially and morally ready to resist all infractions of the treaty by means of force. Starting from these premises, it could be concluded that a policy of flexibility would have cost us less than what the policy of determination finally made us lose. The fault in such reasoning would be to forget that the Germans were insatiable."

If France was to accept a disarmament convention, her need for security would first have to be satisfied. But all the world powers were pressuring France, who had been promised security in 1919, to sacrifice her armaments for the maintenance of peace while a disarmed Germany was rearming. They refused to be convinced that European peace would not be guaranteed by plans for equality of troops and armaments. Not one of the many suggestions for security advanced by the French delegation had been adopted. They had seemed too demanding. They had been heard so frequently over the years. Had they not become just a pretext to avoid disarming?

With the French army condemned to disarm, some members of the conference conceived of an ingenious plan to use the army as a European pattern and to impose it as a model on Germany. In spite of her distaste for conscription, the British delegation had accepted this system and had made the French service term the basis for its European plan. It is doubtful that Hitler ever intended to accept the standard of a Continental army—a defensive, short-term army—taken from the plan submitted to the conference by Herriot and Paul-Boncour. He knew that the mission of such an army, designed in large part to satisfy electoral needs, could only be to garrison the Maginot line.

It is indisputable that France was very ill inspired in adopting a strictly defensive military policy during the tumultuous interlude between the two wars, and especially in not making an effort a hundred times more serious toward the construction and massive use of armor and aircraft. Nevertheless, it seems that a study of this period does not allow us, in this case, to bring a draconian verdict on French diplomacy, at least until the deviation introduced, in practice if not in theory, by Pierre Laval's arrival at the foreign ministry in October 1934.

Assuredly Briand was at the foreign ministry when it was decided, under Poincaré's Union Nationale ministry, to build what would later be called the Maginot line. But this project, approved unanimously by the French people, did not necessarily preclude the use of offensive tactics if they appeared advisable. The defensive works of Vauban, "commissioner-general for fortifications," did not prevent the conquests of Louis XIV. If, during the thirties, the doctrines of the General Staff had turned more and more toward the defensive, they assumed full responsibility for it.

The famous remark "Away with cannons! Away with machine guns!" thrown out at Geneva in September 1926 when Germany entered the League of Nations, did not represent at all, coming from Briand, a promise to disarm France. It should be recalled that this "pacifist" had himself taken responsibility for introducing the legislative bill for the three-year military service in January 1913, when he was prime minister. "I could easily have broken my back with that little affair," he liked to repeat.

Foreign minister from 1925 to 1932, he did not become involved in military questions and he considered becoming even less involved since there was a great deal of friction between the Quai d'Orsay and the defense ministry, occupied by a succession of ministers who, except for Painlevé, looked with little favor upon his policy of international détente.

Above and beyond logic there is reality. Very often, events burst forth and run their course outside of what was believed to be the logic of things.

When the Locarno Pact was concluded in October 1925, bringing "a bit of collective security" to the area of the Rhine, vehement critics observed that nothing had been done for "the powderkegs of Eastern Europe." They suggested that the danger existed in the direction of the Vistula, not of the Rhine. But what would happen in reality? Hitler would begin by blowing up the obstacles piled up along the Rhine and, about thirty months after March 1936, he would attack the east; first Austria, then Czechoslovakia, finally Poland.

There is no doubt that the states who had military agreements with France were extremely troubled to see her devoted to a strictly defensive military policy, while the power of a Germany in arms was growing considerably.

If we want to see things as they really were, which is easier at the end of forty years or so, we must realize that until 1933 the peace of Europe was ensured by a French system: a policy of alliances interpreted as the guarantee of the overall status quo. The military hegemony of France, allowing the new or considerably expanded nations to organize themselves in full security, was exercised within the framework of the League of Nations, which gave it its legitimacy.

It must be said that a French supremacy in the twentieth century seemed rather surprising, somewhat abnormal—one might even say improper—to many people who considered France a survivor of the past, having lost her dominance in 1815, then again in 1870. The French policy of European peace, inaugurated in 1919, was threatened with annihilation by the Disarmament Conference, won over by the German argument of equal rights. Equal rights meant disarmament of France and rearmament of Germany.

Such was the direction of the movement which would continually grow after it began in 1932. On a graph, Germany traces a curve which starts from the defeats of 1918 and 1923, ascends, and, until 1940, gains more with each blow, without even experiencing a setback.

While France persisted in her obsession with security, the "minimum of security" ceaselessly shrank. Little by little it became limited to the very bounds of France, while concern for Eastern Europe faded more and more.

Finally, an agreement substantially reducing armaments was reached. It was to be carried out in two periods. In the first period, the European armies would be transformed into short-term conscript armies, with limited troop strength and an automatic, permanent inspection system; the major air forces would be reduced by half, in connection with an inspection system for civil aviation. In this first period, the states disarmed by the peace treaties would not undertake any qualitative increase of armaments.

During a second period, equipment exceeding qualitative limitations yet to be determined would be gradually eliminated; the former enemy states would then receive the armaments they did not possess, all under an effective, automatic, and permanent system of inspection.

Negotiations and Proposals

It has often been asked if the metallurgical industries, through their strong influence, had not contributed to the total failure of the Disarmament Conference. When the conference met at the beginning of 1932, the economic crisis was reaching its height, markets were closing, and unemployment was growing. Manufacture of armaments became the supreme hope. Freedom of manufacture should not be paralyzed by disarmament. In certain ways, rearmament represented a solution, at least in part, for the economic depression. A compensation, if not a cure. The publication of armament programs caused a universal rise in the stock market.

To protect powerful and undoubtedly very significant interests, the metallurgical industries could count on "the expert." As far as France was concerned, the experts took care to abandon nothing and engrossed themselves in their resistance to disarmament programs, even if these programs had no reality other than the fear they spread. Armament stocks were growing older. In trying to save them, to keep them, people wanted to forget that they were becoming obsolete. Everyone was protecting his routine like a cherished victory.

There is no doubt that the Disarmament Conference was truly demoralizing for the French General Staff, and that such demoralization was an important cause of the fatal weakness of 1940. The French army had already been weakened by the "spirit of the Maginot line," begun in 1929, and by its defensive system. The length of military service had been reduced from three years to eighteen months in 1923, and to twelve months in 1927. The General Staff, while jealously retaining its antiquated equipment, exerted itself not to move beyond a defensive framework. It always feared in the extreme the accusations of militarism cast from all sides, even within France. As an old adage says: no one can be right against the whole world.

The parliamentary committees were hostile, partly for political reasons, to Lieutenant-Colonel Charles de Gaulle's plan for a mechanized army. To build a mobile army, with a strong professional nucleus, with elite soldiers and combat-ready units, an army capable of deploying its entire force at the first clash and of mounting a crushing counteroffensive against any attack, seemed to endanger the republican system. Paul Reynaud, picking up de Gaulle's ideas, vainly urged the creation of a specialized armored corps.

Hitler adopted these ideas. In his own army, secretly swelling with national vigor, everything would be new, young, and strong: doctrines, methods, weapons, and officers trained to view offensive plans innovatively. Did Hitler really care about the destruction of so-called "offensive" heavy equipment which was imposed on France by the British disarmament plan, equipment now twenty years old and obsolete? His General Staff was hoping that France would keep this old equipment, especially artillery, as a pretext for Germany to manufacture new equipment. Germany demanded immediate equality of armaments—hence German rearmament and French disarmament—and as an additional demand Germany also asked for the destruction of the major part of old French equipment, while she acquired the right to confess that she had prototypes and to begin manufacturing them.

On May 11 Neurath declared publicly that Germany would rearm whatever the results of the conference. His statement created a certain agitation, even in Great Britain and in Italy. Lord Hailsham, British war minister, spoke of sanctions to be considered against Germany. Mussolini criticized the "ill-timed" speech. On May 16 Roosevelt sent a message to the Geneva Conference in support of the MacDonald plan for French reductions.

At the cabinet meeting of May 12, Hitler and Blomberg spoke of leaving the conference. Nadolny and Neurath agreed to advise him, out of caution, to remain at Geneva. Germany should not be isolated at a time when rumors of a preventive war to be launched by France and Poland were spreading.

As a result, on May 17 Hitler delivered an important speech to the *Reichstag*. It had great impact, notably in England where people believed that the MacDonald plan had been accepted as the basis for the agreement to be concluded. It was a complete success for Hitler, who appeared as a "new man." Chairman Henderson declared that such a speech gave proof that

Germany wanted to achieve equality of armaments, not by increasing her own armaments, but through the disarmament of others. Eden, who represented the British government at Geneva, and the American Norman Davis both felt that the speech was encouraging for the Disarmament Conference.

However Paul-Boncour did not accept the MacDonald plan, which included no provision for mutual assistance and no procedure for supervision of disarmament. He wanted to protest against the arming of the police and the SA, and he refrained only under English pressure. The system he accepted in July consisted in brief of: four years during which the reduction of troops would be carried out in accordance with the MacDonald plan; the reduction of armaments would become possible during a second period of four years. For eight years, therefore, there would be no German rearmament. An inspection committee would keep watch over German armaments.

The instructions given to Nadolny following the speech of May 17 agreed to the transformation of the German army into a conscript army, providing that the other nations destroyed their heavy weapons. In his speech, Hitler planned a transitional period of five years, a figure Blomberg had just accepted.

From then on, endless deliberations went on in Geneva, in London, and in Paris. Franco-British conferences followed one another, sometimes with the participation of the United States. Mussolini, who had never stopped supporting Germany's efforts to free herself from the obligations acquired through the peace treaties, suggested a compromise between the French and German arguments. On September 6 he presented his ten-point proposal. In these five-power conversations, the debate over disarmament ran aground. The French delegation could no longer find its usual supporters, notably the Little Entente. In fact, these negotiations already represented the temporary removal of the problem from the League of Nations. Mussolini informed the French that, if they remained intransigent, Germany would leave the conference and the League of Nations, to undertake unlimited rearmament; in any case she would rearm, either by agreement or of her own will. At the same time, Mussolini warned the Germans against a possible French occupation to acquire territorial collateral.

On September 15 Neurath declared that, if the armed powers continued to evade their obligation to disarm, Germany would "have the right and the duty to provide for equality and for her security, according to her own judgment and without hesitation." On September 21 he left for Geneva, where he saw Goebbels and had direct conversations with his English, Italian, and French colleagues.

In Paris on September 22, England, Italy, and the United States accepted a French proposal for a pause in the negotiations.

On September 23, Sir John Simon assured Neurath that the inflexibility of the French was weakening, but that they would not give their consent to measures for immediate disarmament. They persisted in their idea of two periods of four years: during the first period, no more arms would be produced; during the second period, disarmament would begin. Neurath replied that in any case Germany could not accept a unilateral inspection, and that from this day on she intended to have as many unprohibited arms as the other powers. She could not accept the convention that proposed two periods. At any rate, she wanted to know immediately which arms and what quantity of arms the other powers intended to retain during the second period.

In Berlin, the army and foreign ministries agreed to ask for quantitative equality of arms with France. But they interpreted the principle in different ways. The Wilhelmstrasse considered this equality to mean equality of armaments for each German and French unit; the French army having to be larger than the German army, France would therefore have more arms than Germany. On the other hand, the *Reichswehr* wanted the German army, taken as a whole and independently of its troop strength, to have the same armaments as the French army. Neurath criticized the unreasonable demands of the military; they went beyond the claims stated up to that point, and by their nature they were likely to create an explosion at the conference. Hitler agreed with the foreign minister.

On September 26, the Italians Aloisi and Suvich, who had spoken to the English and the French about disarmament, told Neurath that the French were ready to give assurances about the weapons they wanted to keep during the second period. For the first period, France would grant Germany two hundred thousand men and twice the arms she currently was allowed, but no aircraft. Neurath answered that Germany demanded to have all the arms not forbidden to the other powers.

Two days later, Neurath asked Paul-Boncour what assurances France was ready to give for disarmament. When Paul-Boncour answered evasively, Neurath declared that, in his opinion, it would be impossible to reach an agreement on this issue, and he suggested settling bilaterally the questions undecided between the two countries, through talks on security between military men or by some other means. Invoking his dossier on Germany's secret rearmament, Paul-Boncour replied that France's mistrust of National Socialist Germany was such that the talks suggested by Neurath could not succeed; nevertheless, he would discuss the matter with Daladier. Full of skepticism about the possibility of an agreement, Neurath noted that he considered any new meeting with Paul-Boncour useless.

On September 29, Massigli insisted on meeting with Weizsäcker. In the course of the week, the heads of the delegation had seen a great deal of each other; but had they weighed the extent of the concessions France was willing to make? During the second period, that is to say from the fifth to the eighth year, the French were ready to destroy all heavy arms exceeding the qualitative treaty provisions, including all the artillery above 155 mm. Why be so discreet in this matter? In the train leaving for Berlin, Weizsäcker reported the meeting to Neurath. The account of that meeting did not reach the foreign ministry until October 6, after the decision to break off negotiations had already been made.

As soon as he arrived in Berlin on September 30 Neurath met with Hitler, who rejected the plan for a break contemplated by his minister.

On October 4, the Wilhelmstrasse was informed by London that the English were preparing a new plan which would grant neither sanctions against France nor prototypes of forbidden arms to Germany. From then on, Hitler could free himself of promises made to MacDonald, who was modifying his plan under French pressure, and transfer his responsibilities to others. Irritated by the talks France, England, and the United States held without inviting Germany, he decided on October 4 to break off negotiations, in the course of a meeting with Blomberg. He had heard Nadolny's objections. Like Bülow, Nadolny was firmly opposed to a rupture with Geneva and thought a return to the MacDonald plan was possible: Italy and the United States would support it, and England would follow. Hitler bluntly dismissed a compromise suggested by one of the members of the German delegation, Baron von Rheinbaben.

Neurath was away from Berlin. The cabinet was not consulted, as it would not be in April 1935 and in March 1936 in the case of the major acts of brutality accomplished by Hitler in the field of foreign policy. According to Meissner, Hitler had not even consulted the president of Germany, who had expressed his apprehensions. Hitler reassured Hindenburg that he was not opposed in principle to the League of Nations. Germany remained theoretically in the League for two more years. These two years would allow for negotiations on disarmament and on the revision of the League of Nations. Hitler did not think that France would take countermeasures. She would cry out for a few days, and that would be all. Papen and Neurath supported Hitler before Hindenburg.

Germany Leaves the League of Nations and the Disarmament Conference (October 14, 1933)

On the morning of Saturday, October 14, 1933, Sir John Simon reported to the secretariat of the conference the results of the patient diplomatic campaign he had conducted during the summer. His exposé was remarkable for its lucidity and elegance—the gifts of this great lawyer so impressive in his analytical powers. To his audience, he gave the satisfying impression that an agreement had finally been reached, except for a few secondary difficulties yet to be resolved. He was convinced that Hitler had committed himself by a silence that represented accession.

The British plan, whose essential principles remained intact, was becoming a program for equalizing armaments over a period of several years.

In the first phase, the Continental armies would transform themselves to meet the same standard model: short-term service of equal length; troop strength and officer corps of the same proportions, under the same regulations. A permanent international commission would be created, which would in turn establish an inspection organization responsible for the faithful application of the convention.

In the second phase, following a program determined at the signing of the convention, the most heavily armed powers would reduce their armaments to meet the set limit. The so-called disarmed powers would then aspire to the same limits. This meant that the French government promised to destroy, under international inspection, the excess of its immense war materiel. The delegates of France, the United States, and Italy expressed their approval. Baron von Rheinbaben, who was the only German delegate present, placidly enunciated a few harmless generalities.

For a few hours, the Disarmament Conference was said to be and believed to be saved at last. All the imagination, all the effort had not been wasted. Brief was the illusion of those who found comfort in this thought.

Early in the afternoon, preceded by advance rumors, a telegram from the German foreign minister, Baron von Neurath, was handed to the chairman of the conference. In substance, it said that it was now clear that the Disarmament Conference would not reach its goal: general disarmament. It was equally clear that this failure was exclusively caused by the unwillingness of the heavily armed states to fulfill the contractual obligation to disarm. It thus proved impossible to satisfy the German claim to equality of rights, although this claim had been recognized and had been the condition under which the German government had agreed to participate again in the work of the conference. As a result, the German government found itself obliged to leave both the conference and the League of Nations.

No allusion was made in the telegram to the "system ensuring security for all," although, in the declaration of December 1932, this system was the condition for "the recognition of equality of rights." And yet the security requirements necessary to satisfy the French government before it would agree to destroy its war materiel (in due time, it is true) had become modest enough. The only requirements were a permanent disarmament commission, which did not yet exist, and inspection organizations to be devised by this future commission with Germany's consent. These organizations would be given, by common approval, the same rights as those exercised by the Allied commissions of 1920. Were these the only results of the perseverance of the French delegations since 1932?

Why did Hitler, instead of repudiating Versailles, leave the League of Nations? In issuing his challenge, he gauged it better than those who received it. More daring than he had ever been, he had just taken a risk that required all his courage.

He abjured the agreements solemnly made with the international community; he rejected its law, its obligations, its customs, its procedures. He made his own will the only law; if he succeeded, he would force his former colleagues to recognize it.

Inconceivable in the time of Stresemann and Brüning, did not such a rebellion run the risk of being checkmated by armed opposition? Hitler had evaluated the military risks of his supreme audacity; they could have been great. Armed opposition would have stopped him. Like a stunned athlete, he would have lost face before the crowds of his supporters.

For several more years, the forces available against him could still crush him. But who would be in a position to insist on and order their mobilization? His dossiers on individuals, and above all his psychic intuitions, far ahead of the General Staff's military statistics, gave him a vision of the frightened silhouettes his frantic will would dominate for six years.

He did not want to lose a moment. He felt compelled to act. For years, while pretending to be innocent and submissive to force and arguing as if she were completely disarmed, Germany had been secretly rearming. This fact could not be hidden any longer. The powerful expansion of the *Reichswehr* could no longer be kept a secret. It was well known in London as in Paris, where files of data were swelling: General Staff (forbidden by the Treaty of Versailles); militarized police in barracks, armed and trained; short-term enlistments in the *Reichswehr,* whose corps of noncommissioned officers (one noncommissioned officer for two soldiers) was proportionate to the troops being assembled by the paramilitary organizations; an air force; prototypes of forbidden arms; and a plan for industrial mobilization. It would not be difficult to give this secret rearmament a formidable scope.

Thanks to the influx of American capital between 1925 and 1929, on which payments of principal and interest had been interrupted by the world economic crisis, German industry—having received its share—had been equipped with splendid plant facilities and the most modern machine tools. This enormous "war potential"—an expression created by the French military experts who had not been able to have it accepted by their colleagues as part of the system for appraising armaments—was becoming active. Germany was growing into the most powerful arms factory in the world; it was giving jobs to millions of unemployed.

Another advantage of a long-range tactic was that the Covenant of the League of Nations formed the first and common element in all the treaties. By its very terms, it was the common source of all their obligations: "In order to promote international cooperation and to achieve international peace and security . . . , by the firm establishment of the understanding of international law as the actual rule of conduct among governments, and by the maintenance of justice and a scrupulous respect for all treaty obligations." All the regional alliances, in an attempt to compensate for the weaknesses of the League of Nations, included precise pledges against aggression; they were all part of the League of Nations' system and were under its authority. To leave so rudely this League of Nations, which Stresemann had entered under the terms of unwritten but formal commitments contracted at Locarno, was to free oneself from all obligations and to acquire full freedom of action all in one blow, while reducing all the juridical farrago to dust. It was also a bold revision of the Treaty of Versailles, the weightiest and simplest unilateral repudiation. If this provocation was accepted, could it be hoped that what remained of the treaty would have a better fate? Germany did not accept inspection, she had no obligations left; such was the situation created by the telegram of October 14.

At the same time the Machiavellian Hitler, gambling on the pacifistic feelings of Europe, was inaugurating a tactic that would be successful for him until 1939. After having violated his commitments, he would give the world a message filled with promises of peace, which in turn would be violated the next time. He would disavow his promises one by one, each time no more than the exasperated dupes would tolerate—the dupes being always ready to rejoice for having defended themselves so well and each time better prepared to give up still more. To crush people's wills, he would always use the same method, always with the same sure touch, of speaking on the sacrosanct "weekend." With each success his position grew firmer; each time he lured his adversaries with a hope which, each time, shattered them more.

Even before the chairman of the Disarmament Conference could make known the telegram he had just received, Hitler had obtained a dissolution of the *Reichstag* from Marshal Hindenburg, to allow the German people to be consulted through new elections and a referendum. A government manifesto, followed by a speech by Hitler, proclaimed loudly Germany's desire for peace, and, in an heroic gesture of liberation, her system for a peace free from the Geneva ideology so imbued with the prejudices of the Treaty of Versailles.

Hitler declared: "The German government and the German people re-nounce the use of force, which is unsuitable for the resolution of the dif-ferences existing in the community of European states. They declare themselves ready to destroy their arms, even to the last machine gun, and to demobilize even to the last soldier, if the other nations are prepared to do the same. They are ready to guarantee the peace of Europe for the longest possible period through Continental nonaggression pacts, to con-tribute to economic progress, to participate in the general restoration of European civilization. . . . [This is] no arms race, but only a security measure to guarantee the German nation tranquillity and freedom to continue its works of peace."

Then Hitler turned toward France, on whom he had just laid the responsi-bility for the failure of the Disarmament Conference, to make an appeal intended to stir her "noble sense of justice"; along with his love for peace, he affirmed his cordial esteem for M. Daladier. Had not the French prime minister shown a spirit of conciliation and understanding in a recent speech, in which he denied all desire to humiliate Germany? In the name of all Germans, Hitler pronounced himself in favor of a final reconciliation between France and Germany. What would two nations with an equally glorious past gain from new and bloody sacrifices? What a beautiful day it would be for mankind if they chose, once and for all, to exclude force from their common life! No one would dare demand the annihilation of millions of young men, simply for an undetermined readjustment of frontiers. After the restitution of the Saar to Germany, only a madman would contemplate the possibility of a war between the two nations.

For Hitler, the time had come for a policy of power. To leave the League of Nations was virtually to repudiate all treaties, no longer to acknowledge any law but that of force, and through force to impose his dominance. Six months earlier, Japan's withdrawal had shown the way. Coming after the Manchurian incident of September 1931, it had given the Japanese the chance to undertake vast conquests in China and to found the new state of Manchukuo.

As a solitary prophet, Churchill had declared on March 14, 1933: "The Germans ask for equality in armaments, and for equality in the organization of armies and fleets. And they have just told us: you cannot leave such a great nation in a position of inferiority; it must have what the others have. I have never agreed with this view. Nothing in this life is eternal; but as soon as Germany acquires an overall military equality with her neighbors, and while her own grievances are still unsatisfied and her frame of mind is still what we can now observe, we will surely see ourselves drawn into another European war sooner or later."

In the great unrest created by the German message of October 14, which stunned even the best informed circles, no one among the delegations present at Geneva was capable of giving such a reply. The next day, October 15, the members of the Disarmament Conference's organizational committee met for an exchange of views in the office of the chairman of the conference, Henderson.

He had not taken part in the negotiations among the five delegations; he had been kept away. Baron von Neurath's dispatch deprived him of the peace through disarmament to which he had hoped, in an act of faith, to attach his name. Peace, like a deathbed vision, slipped away from this sick man, who would die in October 1935.

Neurath's dispatch had to be answered. Henderson's response, briefly refuting the German allegations, ended with his regret that such a weighty decision had been made for reasons whose validity he could not accept.

At this moment of such obvious gravity, his listeners probably did not concentrate all their attention on the problem of the League of Nations. Some of them perhaps felt that their countries might find very attractive the image of peace offered by the Hitlerian diptych. Would it not be wise to enter into the so-called bilateral methods as soon as possible? Distress and uncertainty reigned.

Official ideas aside, vague whispers of preventive war were heard in the corridors. Given the state of world opinion, such words and such an idea caused a scandal. Democracies do not wage preventive wars. In the French Chamber, Georges Mandel thought himself obliged to repudiate carefully any idea of such a war, while denouncing with the rearmament of Germany "the policy of trading away our victory." Although hard to believe, was it absurd? What has happened since then would have justified the famous observation made by Montesquieu in *The Spirit of the Laws* (Book 10, Chapter 2): "Between societies, the right of self-defense sometimes brings about the necessity to attack, when a people sees that a long peace puts another people in a position to destroy it, and sees also that attack at such a moment is the only way to prevent this destruction."

Bold politicians would have spoken of undertaking not a preventive war, but a police operation. Hitler, in his rashness, could not have resisted it. What the world would have saved itself! After this first and incomparable audacity of October 1933, a series of violations would follow. To suppress each one, the stakes would go higher, rising to the point of threatening civilization itself with a catastrophe.

In the general uncertainty caused by a lack of clear vision and clear will, the true implication of Hitler's act was not understood: that it was the prelude to large-scale assaults. People wondered what could be done. End the Disarmament Conference and let everyone recover his freedom, or, on the contrary, let the conference continue as if nothing had happened. The majority leaned toward the second solution, including Paul-Boncour. But which plan should be followed? The conference had been convened in the name of the Covenant, and for the Germans there was no longer a Covenant. By leaving the League of Nations, they intended to nullify the negotiations outlined by Sir John Simon, which were taking place, within the framework of the League of Nations, among precisely the same governments to which the Germans were suggesting resuming negotiations outside the League of Nations. What elementary guarantees would be offered? The rearmament of Germany, a breach of her obligations, was a fact. By leaving the League of Nations, she repudiated a contractual system which she sought to ridicule and destroy. Could she be allowed to pose as a creditor, waiting for others to come and make proposals to right the wrongs she had suffered? In reality disarmament was no longer feasible if it was no longer possible to have confidence in contractual obligations.

The only logic came from Litvinov. Taking up the challenge, he suggested holding a conference to safeguard European peace. That was an ambitious venture. How could national security be defined as "compatible" with the reduction of armaments?

For years, in the war against war, the jurists had devoted innumerable texts and learned definitions to the aggressor. In the fall of 1933, the mask fell and the aggressor appeared in Europe. Having left the League of Nations, he was free from the whole legal web. People refused to judge his intentions by his actions. It is the weakness of democracies not to upset things.

The English remained speechless. For them the only substantial reality was still disarmament, a good in itself. The religious fervor for disarmament remained intact; Germany should not stand disarmed in the face of an over-armed France.

The abandonment of the League of Nations, which was the verbal nucleus of any policy and the means for a collective power, did not provoke any suitable reaction. It was decided that the Disarmament Conference would continue. This solution would have been acceptable if the conference had been able to reach unanimous decisions—for example, to make inquiries about German rearmament—and if the members of the League of Nations had not lost the desire to compel respect for their collective strength.

On November 12, in a referendum, 92 percent of the Germans who had the right to vote gave Hitler their confidence. In spite of the irregularities that had characterized the plebiscite, it was incontestable that the vast majority of the German people approved the policy of this disrupter of European order. The League of Nations was unpopular in the Reich.

Since Hitler had left the League of Nations, any commitment he might make would have to be sought outside the League. England stubbornly persisted in the negotiations, and the MacDonald plan seemed like a chess-board with moves still to be made. Although Germany was rearming and France—preoccupied, and immersed in a defensive and election-oriented concept of war—was disarming, the margin was still large. Who would have thought then that within three years, in a frightening leap, Germany would have totally erased France's superiority?

Already French security was vanishing. The General Staff hoarded an aging war materiel, just as the Bank of France hoarded the reserves of an inactive gold withdrawn from the economy.

Daladier's fall on October 23 caused some unrest in Germany among the pessimists. The unofficial missions given in Daladier's office to Fernand de Brinon, the first French journalist to be received by Hitler after he became chancellor, had made Daladier appear more inclined toward conciliation with Germany than the other statesmen. Daladier did not want to "break anything." With Daladier gone, could an invasion of Germany by the armies of France, Belgium, Poland, and Czechoslovakia take place? Although Blomberg was determined to resist, he believed that any resistance would be hopeless. Germany could rely neither on England nor on Mussolini, who had been displeased by the destruction of the Four-Power Pact. "Equal rights without any compensation?" asked the new French prime minister, Albert Sarraut, in the Chamber. "We say no!"

6

The Four-Power Pact (1933)

Fascism had been considered, until the great world economic crisis, a strictly Italian phenomenon; it was now gaining international importance. The "Four-Power Pact" had been for several years Mussolini's predominant thought, and he hoped to win a flattering position as arbiter. When he came to power in October 1922, he wanted the friendship of France, and he greatly respected Poincaré. He sent Italian engineers to the Ruhr; the French appeared strong. He interpreted the evacuation of the Ruhr as a sign of weakness; he had definitely been wrong about French hegemony. He was filled with disdain for their political inconsistency, and at the same time he was angered by the inflexibility of the positions they held in Europe.

The western powers had solicited Italy's participation in the Locarno treaty of 1925, although in 1921 they had kept her out of the Franco-British guarantee pact discussed at Cannes. Mussolini had crossed the Lago Maggiore in great haste to sign, at the last minute, the document which made him a guarantor of France. The Locarno agreements outlined a European entente among the great western powers, Italy included. They foreshadowed the "Four-Power Pact" binding the four great European powers: England, Germany, France, and Italy.

Little by little, Fascist Italy had taken a stand against France. She blamed France for the activities of the anti-Fascist émigrés, the ironic tone of the French newspapers, and the epithet of "costume-party Caesar" cast at Mussolini. The naval parity between Italy and France, established at the Washington Conference of 1921, increased the tension from time to time, a tension which could have been dispelled by a Mediterranean agreement. But Paris seemed confined within a pattern of relations hostile to Fascism. England, with her policy of balance of power, did nothing to reduce

63

the strain between the two countries. Mussolini never went to Geneva, which he denounced as "a gathering of gossips." For several years he was represented by Vittorio Scialoja, legal advisor to the monarchy, whose diplomatic shrewdness, skeptical wisdom, and smiling irony veiled with charm the matchless art of a Piedmontese jurist. After having been Nitti's foreign minister in 1919 and 1920, from 1921 to 1932 he accompanied the Italian delegation to the League of Nations, to which he astutely denied "a Praetorian right." He died in 1933 at the age of seventy-seven.

Sir Austen Chamberlain had given himself the task of ensuring good relations with Mussolini, whom he visited each year. After their first meeting, the vigorous Benito Mussolini had supposedly made a favorable impression on him: "It's Lady Chatterley's gamekeeper," he said, referring to the hero of D. H. Lawrence's novel.

At the height of his career in 1932, Mussolini found himself at a crossroads; he had always been a kind of Janus. Encouraged by a general apathy, he set friends and emisssaries to work everywhere. He appreciated informal conversations with foreigners, if they provided human contacts, and he knew how to listen and give the impression of a sustained interest. On the other hand, he had no respect for "professional" diplomats who, weighing their words and reticent, were expansive only to express their admiration; they could not have had any importance for him or any influence.

His personality, vigorous and domineering, calls to mind the tyrants of the fifteenth century. Violent, proud, touchy, very impressionable and spiteful, he brought arrogance and insult into international relations. It was as if, with a kind of childish candor, he held himself up as the model for a Nietzschean superman.

Everything he tried was a success. He believed in his omnipotence. His contempt for others exaggerated, in his own mind, the limits of his power. He thought that his projects were realizable once he had planned them. His passion was to imagine a heroic, grandiose Italy, now a truly great power after the humiliations of the Peace Conference in 1919. He felt such disdain for the European governments that he believed in the power of his arbitration. The weight of Italy, shifting to one side or to the other, appeared decisive to him. He stood back in a position of equilibrium. He did not want to go to war, he did not desire war, but he exaggerated the importance of his country and his person. He had such a conception of himself—reinforced by his panegyrists—and such an image of his country, that he dreamed of them and believed in them. Never disconcerted by life, he let his powerful imagination lead him into daydreams. His optimism made difficulties seem smaller; when, in time, he saw them, he knew how to adapt; but he became their prisoner when, in his flamboyant style, he had proclaimed his "will of granite," infallible for the Italians: "The Duce is always right."

Mussolini, Jouvenel, the Little Entente, and Poland

At Turin, in October 1932, Mussolini asserted that the collaboration of the four great powers—Germany, England, France, and Italy—would be necessary for European stability. A European directorate, excluding the Soviet Union, would become the supreme body for a revision of the treaties, which would be studied in a realistic frame of mind by the chancelleries. Such was the Duce's answer to Briand's European union plan.

On March 17, 1933, the very day Ramsay MacDonald arrived in Rome to present his disarmament plan, Mussolini handed him his project for the "Four-Power Pact." This suggested "a new policy" that would allow better opportunities for agreement and thus we could "save ourselves from the enormous costs of war." The English prime minister approved this proposal, which was favorable to a "reasonable revision" of the treaties.

The problem of Mussolini, with his perpetual changes of front—neutralist, then interventionist in 1915—and with his bitter jealousy, was a difficult one. Strangely susceptible to influence through vanity and pride, he pretended to be following a policy of balance between England, France, and Germany. Jealous of the French Third Republic's eastern alliances, he had been hostile to Briand's European system. He was decidedly anti-Yugoslav—aiming at the secession of Croatia—and resolutely favorable to Hungary. Beneš's Czechoslovakia took an anti-Italian position. In contrast to the static immobility of France, Mussolini declared himself for a revision of the treaties in favor of Austria, and above all in favor of Hungary, who supported him as opposed to the Little Entente and the Danubian Entente. Meanwhile, in Bulgaria, another opponent of the Little Entente, King Boris, had married a daughter of King Victor Emmanuel III.

Mussolini had too often referred to the sea once encircled by the Roman Empire as *mare nostrum* for his ultimate dreams to remain secret; but they could only be realized through a major conflict with England. It would have been, at that time, very imprudent to disturb things by such ill-timed prospects. In a new distribution of Europe, he wanted to give Italy her share in the Danube and the Balkans, a very large share increased beyond measure by his conceit. He wanted to push Germany back toward the north, toward the Baltic and beyond, and exclude France from Central Europe. With the Rhine as her frontier, France would take care of her colonies and retain a worthwhile share of territory.

It is a mistake to assign men an enduring value based only on their final accomplishments—which were disastrous in the case of Mussolini. This self-declared realist lived in an imaginary world, and his ideas, greeted by flattering whispers, often neglected the natural play of forces.

Sent to Rome in January 1933 as ambassador on a special mission for six months, Senator Henry de Jouvenel was able to win Mussolini's favor, although at first Mussolini had been in no hurry to summon him. When he was finally received, Mussolini asked him if he was enjoying Rome, and Jouvenel replied: "I am bored. I have waited so long to see you." He was converted to the "Four-Power Pact" on March 3, and he managed to win the support of Paul-Boncour and Daladier for the proposal, on condition that, through moderate modifications, everything would remain within the framework of the League of Nations.

Germany eagerly agreed with Mussolini, to whom she refused nothing. Hitler, whose moderation was being praised, hailed the pact as "a ray of light in the lives of the European people." In Paris people wondered if, thanks to this pact which could appear as a setting aside of the League of Nations, Germany would not win full freedom of action in Eastern Europe. But Mussolini feared Hitler's Germany and wanted to limit it rather than join it. He very much hoped to be the moving force in the directory he was planning.

He had, then, a precise sense of what could not be refused to Germany, and he knew where to stop. Hitler, in power only for a few months, was going to experience a period of caution like all newcomers who want to be established before running new risks; this situation was only temporary. Before Germany became too powerful, Mussolini, attempting a policy of balance, brought her into the "club of four" western powers which he had founded. Surrounded by three partners, Hitler would be less tempted to descend into disturbing deeds.

A Cool Reception in France

The "pact for agreement and cooperation" seemed to make an international détente possible. Henry de Jouvenel, whose premature death two years later deprived France of one of her most ingenious negotiators, saw in the pact the guarantee of "ten years of peace," and Paul-Boncour saw it as "the beginning of something great." Until then French diplomacy had stayed within the limits imposed by the rigorous prohibition of any reference to a revision of the treaties. In June 1933, France resigned herself to accepting the European directorship of the Four Powers. For ten years, the Four agreed to consult on all questions relating to them, to cooperate with all the powers within the framework of the League of Nations, to examine among themselves, before Geneva decisions, any proposal regarding the territorial integrity and independence of the states, the revision of treaties that became inapplicable, and the sanctions to be taken against the aggressor state.

This entente, even reduced to a minimum of essential questions, did not necessarily lead to tragic events. But in Paris there were many opponents to the "Four-Power Pact." A great-power directory, dominating Europe to the exclusion of the small powers, appeared to them as a negation of the settlement established in 1919. They argued that Mussolini sought to return to traditional diplomacy and to push aside the states aspiring to legal equality through the League of Nations. What equality could there be among four states, if two maintained a solid front of opinion while the other two were internally divided and suffused with all sorts of influences? Mussolini's project seemed to reveal the desire to ensure international acceptance of the two dictatorial regimes, Fascism and National Socialism, and at the same time the firm intention to keep Russia out of European affairs. He met with opposition from the small nations threatened with dependency, above all from the Little Entente, who feared to see her frontiers brought into question again.

Poland was deeply hurt not to be counted among the great powers. She was, noted her foreign minister, Colonel Beck, "a major power, and a country with self-respect." Beck blamed Beneš for accepting French concessions which he himself thought inadequate. This conciliation seemed "a treason" to him.

France hesitated a long time before adopting the proposal. To the last moment, Édouard Herriot, the most important man in French politics, urged Édouard Daladier, the prime minister, not to accept such a pact; the "war of the two Édouards" was at its height. As for Tardieu, he saw in the plan "the legalization of Germany's secret rearmament."

France's allies had no difficulty in convincing the Quai d'Orsay that such a pact would be dangerous and unacceptable, if not properly amended. Counterproposals followed one another. After laborious and subtle negotiations, the pact was enveloped by multiple reservations which did much to empty it of its content and make it almost a hollow shell.

Certainly the chances of success were reduced by the somewhat equivocal position taken by French policy. France strained to reassure her allies, who refused to let her accept the pact in full and asked for assurance that, in a European directorship, she would be only their mouthpiece. France promised that the application of Article 19 of the Covenant, providing for "the reconsideration by members of the League of treaties which had become inapplicable," now a dead letter, would be accepted only by a unanimous vote, including the votes of the interested parties. That removed all effectiveness from a compromise which might possibly have lent a slight element of stability to the vertigo of the period.

France no longer had an autonomous policy. Her horror of isolation made her seek out and call on friends that supported her. But alliances change into servitude. Her allies' idea of their interests largely determined the relations of France, not only with Germany, but also with Italy, from whom it was better to remain distant.

Nevertheless, at this unique and fleeting moment in the summer of 1933, who knows whether it might not have been possible, through the application of Article 19, to set in motion a gradual evolution which would have excluded a second world war? Being optimistic, one could imagine Czechoslovakia establishing a minorities policy with Hungary as well as with Germany—Czechoslovakia developing, with precautions and through careful steps, a federal system more or less on the Swiss model. One could—although it would be more difficult—imagine Poland agreeing to an extraterritorial route across the Corridor, leading to East Prussia, and perhaps even a greater flexibility in the political system of Danzig. Only Pilsudski would have had the strength and prestige to allow certain changes in the Polish frontiers; but he did not consider them. And, for the dream to take form, Hitler would have had to be other than he was.

Hitler could not be satisfied to nibble away at the peace treaties while adapting more or less to a few international limitations, for he was possessed by a violent nationalistic frenzy and a dark racial delirium. To suppose that the Hitler of 1933 had a sense of moderation and cautious common sense would be to have strange illusions.

The Pact Is Not Ratified

Initiated on June 7, 1933, the "pact for understanding and cooperation between the four western powers" was signed in Rome on July 15. It would never be ratified; it would simply evaporate four months later when the German withdrawal from the League of Nations removed the base on which it had been founded. "A hard decision," said Hitler.

7

The Polish-German Agreement of January 1934

Notwithstanding the considerable changes that had taken place in Europe, plans for a progressive equalization of military systems continued to follow one another. After Germany left the League of Nations, the question of disarmament was handled through diplomatic channels. The English transferred the disarmament negotiations from Geneva to Berlin, now the capital of Europe. Their desperate confidence was aimed at an honest and honorable contract. Berlin having become the center of the negotiations, Germany was asked what her intentions were. She suggested figures for the next stage of the discussions. At the same time, she offered bilateral plans to several countries—a negation of collective security.

Hitler wanted to start France on the road to bilateral negotiations. He suggested a nonaggression pact of ten years, on condition that France renounce the Saar before the plebiscite of 1935. The direct and indirect advances he made in the hope of reaching a two-power agreement, which would also affect the Rhineland demilitarization clauses, were rejected. General Weygand believed that forsaking the Saar would jeopardize French security.

On October 25, 1933, Weygand wrote to Daladier, the prime minister and defense minister: "It is of the utmost importance for the national defense to do everything possible to maintain the status quo in the Saar, and, if that is impossible, to do everything possible to make the old French Saar ethnically and emotionally French. . . . If the entire goal (the frontier of 1814, leaving in French territory the centers of Saarbrücken and Sarrelouis and the greater part of the mining district) cannot be obtained, even a partial success could be of the utmost advantage for our defense."

It was claimed that negotiating with Hitler would strengthen his power in Germany. Now his situation was precarious, people believed, for many officials gave his regime only a short time to live. However, the London *Times* of December 15 earnestly supported Hitler's proposal: "A statesman known for having always kept his word has solemnly promised never to make war against France."

Germany and Bilateral Agreements

France had refused; Poland accepted. Three days after the German plebiscite of November 11, 1933, a communiqué spoke of negotiations with Warsaw for a peaceful settlement of the problems existing between the two countries. Through a shrewd and daring tactic, Hitler skirted the main obstacle that German diplomacy was running into.

The Polish question had been the most difficult of all the questions facing the negotiators at Versailles. The antipathy of the Germans and the Poles to one another was obvious. It reached into the deepest past.

For the Germans, Poland was the first opponent to beat—the great and eternal enemy. The German military never missed a chance to disparage her. In November 1928, General Heye had told a French officer: "You will never get any German whatever to accept the existence of the Corridor, either now or later." "Poland," wrote General von Seeckt, "has been created exclusively to form a state to the east of Germany that will always be her enemy. . . . The frontiers between the two nations have been determined with a sadism that makes the two states mortal enemies."

Beginning in June 1925, a German-Polish commercial war had been going on. It had lasted for six years and had been very hard on Poland. Some German military men feared sudden attacks from the Poles, encouraged by their French allies. Until 1931, Poland was much stronger militarily than Germany. In the event of an act of aggression, the German General Staff planned to evacuate Silesia immediately. From time to time, rumors of a preventive war spread anxiety through Germany. Many of the German forces were deployed on the Polish frontier. They included the *Grenzschutz*, divisions camouflaged as frontier guards, which greatly worried the intelligence division of the French General Staff.

The coming to power of National Socialism excited German nationalism in Danzig. Poland reacted vigorously: she concentrated troops in the former East Prussia, and on March 6, 1933, she sent a battalion to sea and landed it by surprise, reinforcing the Polish garrison of the Westerplatte. Alleging that the danger was too pressing, Poland did not ask the consent of the League of Nations high commissioner, the Dane Rosting, before undertaking this energetic action in opposition to the agitation of the people of Danzig. In Danzig and in Berlin, the warning was understood. Geneva was deeply disturbed, especially the British, who saw the action as a threat to Germany and wondered whether Pilsudski had not made diplomatic soundings in preparation for a preventive war, or at least for the occupation of East Prussia. The League of Nations Council asked Poland to withdraw her reinforcements from the Westerplatte.

After France and Belgium had publicly denounced, on March 5, the illegal arming of the Prussian auxiliary police and the military preparations in the demilitarized zone, the British Foreign Office warned France against any occupation of German territory. Although the opposition to a preventive war was universal in France, on March 20 Mussolini gave notice to Germany of alarming French projects, probably in the attempt to win her over to the "Four-Power Pact." At the end of April 1933, the ambassador to Warsaw, Count Moltke, warned Berlin that the situation was serious.

Constant conflicts were rising over the German minorities in Poland, and over the eternally complex situation in Danzig. "The rheumatism of Europe," groaned Briand. Faced with a seemingly obdurate antagonism, the general belief had Hitler's ambitions turned toward the east, toward the Corridor and Danzig.

Unfriendly Relations between Poland and Germany

Through the agreement reached in January 1934 with Pilsudski, the axis of Hitler's projects toward the east was replaced by an axis toward the south. On his way to power Hitler—the Austrian—aimed first at Austria. On May 2, 1933, speaking to the Polish ambassador, Wysocki, he had expressed his desire to improve German-Polish relations. On May 20, Colonel Beck declared to Ambassador Moltke that he shared that desire.

Beck had taken charge of foreign affairs two months before Hitler's rise to power. With his devious ways, he was far from being a friend of France, and he was a determined enemy of the Czechs. In September 1933 in Geneva, at a luncheon meeting with Neurath and Goebbels—the German delegation to the League of Nations Assembly—he observed that "the frequent disputes arising between Poland and Germany oftern serve the purpose of interests that affect neither Germany nor Poland."

After Germany left Geneva in October 1933, creating a gap in German-Polish relations, Beck hoped for a direct understanding to guarantee good neighborly relations. Such an agreement would not be at all in contradiction with the French alliance, because of its strictly defensive nature. Like Pil-sudski, he took as a pattern the Austrian tradition. Hitler was an Austrian; the Prussians were confirmed enemies of the Poles. According to Beck, Hitler did not have a single Prussian among his close collaborators.

Hitler was a skillful opportunist. On November 15, he cordially received the new Polish ambassador to Berlin, Joseph Lipski. Poland's French ally was not informed of the negotiations with Hitler, which led rapidly to the declaration of January 24, 1934. This "declaration to renounce any use of force" amounted to a pact of friendship and nonaggression. The signatories asserted that their agreement did not in the least alter their prior obligations. They committed themselves, for a period of ten years, to negotiate without any intermediary on all problems dealing with their mutual relations and never to resort to the use of force against each other.

From then on, the pessimists who had worried when Germany left the League of Nations and the Disarmament Conference could feel reassured. Did not the treaty with Poland demonstrate Hitler's goodwill and the sincer-ity of his peaceful intentions? Through this treaty, Hitler had freed himself from any threat of encirclement. He wanted to be protected while he rearmed in preparation for his intervention in Austria and in Czechoslovakia. He had reversed Poland's attitude through conciliation, and the German-Polish détente gained strength.

However, this rapprochement was not popular in Poland and was made possible only by the existence of an authoritarian regime.

French foreign minister Vergennes had written in 1782: "Poland is used to viewing France as a nation ready to be her natural ally, and as a nation having no interest other than to make her happy." Poland, where Pilsudski had exercised his tenacious and rough authority since a bloody coup d'etat had brought him back to power in May 1926, tried harder each day to free herself from French influence. A Franco-Polish alliance, in sixteenth-century tradition, had been concluded in 1921, and a guarantee treaty had been signed between Poland and France on October 16, 1925, to take effect in the event of a German-Polish war. In 1934, with a blind and somewhat arrogant naiveté, many Poles thought they were dealing with the Germans as equals, and they tried to show, by their proud concern for independence, that they were strong enough to free themselves from the tutelage of France, who annoyed and irritated them by incessant references to a revision of frontiers, especially in the Corridor, under the pretext of lessening German-Polish misunderstanding. They wanted to set up a corridor within the Corridor, with railways under full German sovereignty. "Separating East Prussia from West Prussia was an absurdity, an imbecility," Herriot confided to the Belgian ambassador. "But," it was observed in Warsaw, "what is so extraordinary in this separation between Germany and East Prussia? Is Sicily not separated from Italy?"

The Poles had not forgotten Locarno, negotiated in 1925 without their participation, when Pilsudski had not yet returned to power. By guaranteeing the western frontiers, had Germany not given herself the green light for revisionist action in Eastern Europe, where the boundaries threatened to become precarious.

The Poles resented the Franco-Soviet nonaggression pact of November 1932, although they themselves signed a similar pact with the Soviets; they were displeased by any French rapprochement with Moscow. In 1930 they had been irritated by the early, rash evacuation of the Rhineland.

Pilsudski, with his clear eyes deep set below bushy eyebrows, and his drooping moustache, was dominated by a fierce desire for independence. In the past, he had been deported to Siberia and pursued by the tsar's police. Later, in Galicia, the "commander" had been the leader of secret societies in the "Polish military organization," and in 1914 he had thrown his Polish "volunteer legions" into the battle against Russia. He detested Russia even more since the Bolsheviks had taken power, for he recognized in Bolshevism a dynamism somewhat similar to what Islam had once had, and he saw Russian power being stirred by an imperialism of Marxist foundation. On July 25, 1932, he had, it is true, concluded a Polish-Soviet nonaggression pact, which had been ratified in December when Beck had already assumed his duties as foreign minister. Pilsudski used to say: "We cannot accept being put in a situation which would force us to sleep with our rifles; rifles should remain in depots for military mobilization." But his Russophobia did not change. His dream was to break up Russia, by establishing a vast Polish federation.

At the beginning of spring 1935, when Pilsudski received Eden as a passing tourist on his way to Moscow, he asked him if he planned to meet Stalin: "I do not compliment you on having a meeting with this bandit," he said. On May 10, 1935 (he died on May 12), he asked Beck: "Why is this simpleton Laval going to Moscow? Have you told him that it can lead to no good?"

He had been a prisoner of the Germans at Magdeburg from July 1917 to November 1918, and he could not be oblivious to their revisionist ambitions. But the Russian peril seemed more pressing to him than the German threat. Moreover, he had a certain feeling of brotherhood in arms for the Germans, and he respected greatly their military virtues.

He had no confidence in the League of Nations. Toward the English, who greatly distrusted Poland, he experienced the kind of feelings that Beck described to Eden on October 20, 1935: "For many years, England has followed a policy of spiteful teasing toward Poland in international affairs. We cannot hold a grudge against her. For a hundred and fifty years, she had forgotten that a Polish element existed; she did not reckon with it and treated it as a negligible quantity."

Pilsudski distrusted his French friends and questioned their status as an ally as well as their determination.

Colonel Beck

Colonel Joseph Beck was in charge of Polish foreign policy. In November 1932, at the age of thirty-eight, he replaced foreign minister August Zaleski, after having been his undersecretary for two years.

Born in Warsaw, he lived in Galicia where his parents settled and studied in Kracow and Vienna; in 1914 he had enlisted in Pilsudski's "legions." In 1917, when Pilsudski was imprisoned by the Germans and his "legions" dissolved, Beck had been transferred to a Hungarian regiment. In November 1918 he returned to Poland from the Ukraine. He had served on the General Staff and had been included in missions sent abroad, until in January 1922 he became military attaché in Paris. In the fall of 1923 the French, who criticized him for his excessive inquisitiveness and lack of flexibility, had him recalled.

He had attended the war college in Warsaw, and, as a colonel in the artillery, he had become personal secretary to the war minister, Marshal Pilsudski.

As foreign minister, he called for a policy of independence which, he declared in May 1936, would remain "outside the European chaos, thanks to the conclusion of agreements not dominated by any foreign agent." Pilsudski had set forth the principle that "one should never bow before anyone," and Beck criticized the Poles for being "too inclined to adopt a servile attitude." He wrote that the Beck system might or might not please, but that it inspired respect in the world.

Although the western powers became estranged from Germany after the rise of Hitler, the coming of Nazism shocked Warsaw much less. The Nazis' anti-Semitism was nothing to upset the Poles. Was it not an old tradition? Before Hitler, the Jews were thoroughly opposed to the Poles and in favor of the Germans. At the time of the plebiscite on Upper Silesia in 1921, they had voted as a bloc for Germany, against Poland. In April 1935, Szembek, an undersecretary in the foreign ministry, noted: "All the rumors circulating about preventive war always come from Jewish and Masonic circles." In April 1938, Ambassador Lipski promised Hitler a beautiful monument in Warsaw if he settled the Jewish problem.

In the nonaggression pact signed with Germany, Pilsudski and Beck saw the symbol of the autonomy of a great power—"of a very great power," added Barthou. They thought that the German change of policy was caused by the impression created by their own strength. Hitler had the satisfaction of having upset the old diplomatic game with his bilateral system; and the Polish government, eager for an independent policy, pretended in Geneva to be also a promoter of bilateralism.

Consequences of the German-Polish Agreement

Poland's entire diplomatic policy had been changed by the agreement of 1934. The French alliance had become a form of reassurance, maintained through speeches and used on occasion for loans. On September 13, 1934, in an attempt to prevent a possible intervention from the USSR, who was then entering the League of Nations, Beck denounced the minority agreements included in the Treaty of Versailles. Poland had completely freed herself from the authority of the League of Nations, and she refused from then on to cooperate with the international organization in all that concerned the rights of national minorities in Poland. France protested.

Warsaw achieved a remarkable virtuosity in abstaining and constant reticence. Poland invoked the bilateral nature of treaties and raised a watertight compartment, impermeable to discussion, by considering in every case the specifically Polish aspects. As a whole, Poland supported German policy, and she expressed herself through votes unfavorable to the French positions.

What, then, would have been the value for France of an alliance with a nation whose diplomacy created the precise situation which the alliance was meant to avoid? Poland—the ally of France—seemed to choose in favor of Germany, while retaining the French alliance that gave her more weight in her new relations with Berlin.

Through Hitler's wiliness in January 1934, Poland's relations with Germany appeared friendly until October 24, 1938, the day he set forth the demands from which the war emerged. Beck was quite satisfied with his policy of appeasement. Until he came to power, Poland had been constantly accused of endangering peace. He had an excessive trust in the word of the Nazis. In August 1935 he conducted diplomatic probes and then declared himself convinced of Hitler's sincerity. Overestimating to an extreme his country's position and considering German rearmament inevitable, he asserted that such rearmament did not frighten him.

During these six years, which led to a terrible catastrophe for mankind, France and Poland maintained strange relations. The French and the Poles remained united by an alliance promising aid and immediate assistance in the event of unprovoked German aggression. As a result of this alliance, France would go to war against Germany; and yet, until the hour of the event that triggered the alliance, France and Poland stood in opposing diplomatic camps.

8

The End of the Disarmament Conference (1934)

Up to this time the negotiations of the Disarmament Conference had been oriented toward a reduction by stages of existing armaments. To achieve equality of rights, a limited rearmament of the former enemy states was planned, but only in the distant future. From now on, the negotiators' aim was to replace this formula with one calling for the immediate rearmament of the former enemy states.

At the beginning of January 1934, Simon went to Rome, where he easily reached an agreement with Mussolini. In order to lessen the German objections and to hasten the moment when theoretical parity would be reached by the French and the German armies, the Conference proposed to raise their respective troop strengths to three hundred thousand men, by distinguishing between offensive armaments and defensive armaments—the defensive armaments becoming immediately unlimited.

On January 29, with Italian consent, London published a plan for the contractual limitation of armaments. This plan represented a compromise between the German argument and the French argument. It was much more favorable to Germany than to France; it combined an immediate disarmament of France and an immediate, but partial, rearmament of Germany. The plan aimed at a convention by which the most strongly armed powers— meaning France—would at once abandon certain types of armaments and would proceed to destroy materiel. Germany could immediately acquire artillery and many light tanks, but she could be equipped with military planes only after two years. The total equality of rights would be attained in ten years. For the moment, Germany would have the right to a conscript army of three hundred thousand men with modern arms, not counting the SA and the SS. Naval questions would be deferred to a naval conference to be held at the end of 1935. Colonial armies would be limited to fifty thousand men. Hitler emphasized the existence of these colonial armies and used them as an argument for maintaining the SS and the SA, whose military character he completely denied.

A system of international arbitration would be established, and non-aggression pacts would be instituted according to Hitler's proposals.

The British memorandum roused sharp discontent in Paris, where people saw it as a ratification of French disarmament and German rearmament. The French would definitely reject it during a visit from Eden. On February 14, a French note to Germany demanded an effective inspection system, as well as the disbandment of the SS and the SA.

Germany accepted the British plan as a basis for discussion, but she did not want to wait two years for aerial rearmament.

Eden left for Berlin, where the atmosphere appeared less negative than in Paris. On February 21, Hitler presented a definite proposal for French and German troop strengths: he wanted an army of three hundred thousand men; he left France five hundred thousand men. He wanted an air force equal to half the French air force. He offered to abandon all claim to artillery heavier than 150 mm and to content himself with six-ton tanks. He agreed to inspection of war materiel, as well as of the SS and the SA.

At the end of February, Eden easily came to an understanding with Mussolini, as Simon had done six weeks earlier.

Sir John Simon's Negotiations;
the French Note of April 17, 1934

On March 1 Eden presented Hitler's offer, considered relatively moderate, to the French ministers—including Barthou—who rejected it vigorously, while Belgium listened much more to London than to Paris.

With his biting tongue, Barthou blamed British policy for innocently rejecting strong measures and for making concession after concession to Hitler. The *Economist* spoke of "a return to the school of Poincaré" in 1934. But Barthou did not speak out of hatred for England; on the contrary, he felt a sincere friendship for "fluctuating England." He showed great independence from her, and refused to be convinced that peace would be guaranteed by scales of equality of troop strength and arms. He did all this without arousing the least doubt about his honesty—as would be the case with his successor Laval—but sometimes he was frightfully witty, according to Eden. Recalling a declaration made at Geneva on October 3, 1934, in which Barthou called Sir John Simon "my dear colleague and almost friend," Eden described the listeners as being either convulsed with laughter or frozen in horror. In April 1934, a perplexed French government had to choose among the possibilities resulting from the long negotiations at the Disarmament Conference.

The first possibility was that all states would disarm, as Henderson had vainly asked. The second, that France would disarm and Germany rearm, as many Englishmen wished. The third, that France would refuse to disarm and to accept, without guarantees for inspection, an immediate rearmament of Germany and a legalization of the rearmament already accomplished in violation of the treaties. This solution was supported by all those who felt that the shower of successive concessions granted Berlin would have catastrophic results, and that Nazi militarism had to be discouraged once and for all—the publication of the German budget showing excessive rearmament. The fourth possibility was that France would not disarm and that Germany would undertake a limited rearmament. This was the alternative chosen by England, Italy, and Belgium.

In his desire to reach an understanding with England, Barthou was converted by Ambassador François-Poncet, who pleaded for negotiations with Germany and for the benefits of an agreement, and he pronounced himself in favor of accepting this last formula. Flandin, future prime minister, and Laval, minister of colonies and soon to be foreign minister, were totally in favor of the acceptance of the plan, which was rejected by Prime Minister Doumergue, ministers without portfolio Tardieu and Herriot, defense minister Pétain, and General Weygand.

The note of April 17, 1934, rejected definitively the English proposals. After having been unanimously approved by the cabinet, it was handed to the British ambassador in Paris. This note had been carefully debated and was entirely different from the projects suggested at the Quai d'Orsay in the line of traditional diplomacy. Its brevity was found disturbing, and it was thought to have a bellicose tone. Doumergue had personally forced it on Barthou, who supported it only after he had tried to give it some practical conclusions. It defined a long-term foreign policy of fixed goals in an established direction. "The French government refuses to legalize German rearmament, which has made all negotiations useless. France will henceforth ensure her security by her own means."

What was the meaning of this sentence? It meant that France would follow her policy of collective security, but that she was determined to follow it while bringing in new forces. These new forces were the Soviets. If Hitler saw the Soviets as well as the western democracies in the opposite camp, he would not go to war; he could not go to war, because if he did he would be certain to lose.

The English did not want to commit themselves in the east. France would look to the east to ensure her own security, not to act against England; she would do so through a policy independent of British limitations, but not anti-British.

Was it a mistake to turn down the English program? Hitler, whose policy was not justified, was going to rearm as he pleased, without limits and without inspection. Would he have acted differently with an agreement? For him the problem had already been solved, Germany would rearm. Which international organization would have been able to oppose him?

The French note of April 17, not submissive enough, created a scandal in England. France was accused of having lost a great opportunity. According to Ambassador Phipps, Hitler's offer was the maximum that could be expected from him. Europe's spoilsport, Paris, had caused, through her obstruction, the failure of the Disarmament Conference, by pushing back Hitler's outstretched hand and by turning down the proposal of February 1934, which represented a frail and ultimate chance for agreement.

9

Barthou's "Grand Strategy"

The Sixth of February, 1934

Struck by the world economic crisis and dismantled by internal arguments, France had been cast adrift. She was losing her power, although financially she was still in control. The "gold bloc," which she led, survived the storm along with Switzerland, Italy, Holland, Belgium, and Poland. But the budgetary and monetary situation, restored by Poincaré in 1926, became critical again along with the intense political unrest, the end of reparations, the sharp anxieties created by Nazi Germany, and the world depression.

Mussolini's ideas penetrated France, so deeply divided into two camps that the Duce thought he would be able to recruit a pro-Italian faction. By picturing small investors as the victims of ruthless swindlers, restless, Fascist-structured "leagues" blossomed and exploited the financial scandal of the "Stavisky affair" against the parliamentary majority.

On February 6, 1934, Paris was close to civil war. While the Chamber of Deputies gave the Daladier cabinet a very strong majority, the crowd jammed into the Place de la Concorde to attack the Chamber at the Palais Bourbon.

Turbulent and confused, this day represented an aggressive demonstration that had no leader and led to no resolution, only police gunfire, sixteen dead, hundreds of wounded—a ghastly bolt of lightning flashing above a marsh. It was a symbolic day; the Daladier government lost confidence in itself and abdicated for fear of action; there was neither Jacobin boldness nor the steady lucidity which quiets disorder; the state was abandoned.

The Doumergue Ministry

In this time of anguish, the smiling Gaston Doumergue was snatched away from retirement in his country home in the Haute-Garonne, not far from Toulouse. He was welcomed as a savior. He was a man of wisdom and experience; but his talent had been one of astute patience calculated to wear out overly anxious political hopefuls. From 1926 to 1929, during a third of his term as president of the Republic, luck had given him the government of Raymond Poincaré, whose memory still cast a halo around him. Before and after Poincaré, he had known how to select as prime minister whoever seemed the best choice at the moment; when he left the presidency, the freedom of choice diminished.

Forming a "National Union" coalition cabinet, Gaston Doumergue surrounded himself with former prime ministers: André Tardieu, Édouard Herriot, Louis Barthou, Albert Sarraut, Pierre Laval. His ministry was the twenty-eighth since Clemenceau had left office in January 1920, the sixth since Hitler had come to power in January 1933.

Sordid weakness of a Republic too open to intrigues and personal ambition, but which worked rather smoothly when destiny called to power strong personalities—such dissimilar men as Waldeck-Rousseau, Clemenceau, Poincaré, or Briand. Abroad, the present cabinet-instability caused worry, astonishment, and at times denigration and scorn, for this dance of shadows was unique in Europe. Stalin and Mussolini seemed unremovable. In Czechoslovakia, Beneš was the oldest of all foreign ministers, and in Rumania Titulescu would only give in under the weight of German power in 1936. As for the British cabinet, it had never been overturned by the House of Commons; when the prime minister felt his majority weaken or break up, he asked the king to grant him a dissolution of Parliament and then called for new elections.

Politically France was weak. In July 1929, after the parliamentary ratification of the Young plan and of the 1926 agreements on interallied debts, Poincaré left the political stage because of serious illness. People thought that he would soon return to office, but he was stricken by a stroke from which he never recovered.

After November 1928, when the "Poincaré experiment" and its large Union Nationale majority came to an end, weak ministries followed one another at brief intervals:

Nine months of a Poincaré ministry without the Radicals.

Three months of an eleventh, and last, Briand ministry.

Three months of a first Tardieu ministry.

A few days of a Chautemps cabinet.

Ten months of a second Tardieu cabinet.

Two months of a Steeg ministry.

Ten months of a first Laval ministry, with Briand.

One month of a second Laval ministry, without Briand.

Four months of a third and final Tardieu ministry.

Political life became disjointed. The Chamber of Deputies, with a moderate majority, overturned Radical ministries, while the Senate, a Radical stronghold, crushed moderate ministries.

Then came the elections of May 1932, a clear success for the Left, which led to:

Seven months of a third Herriot ministry.

One month of a Paul-Boncour ministry.

Nine months of a first Daladier ministry.

One month of a first Albert Sarraut ministry.

Three months of a second Chautemps ministry.

One week of a second Daladier ministry.

The terrible crisis of February 6, 1934, a demi-revolution.

Fragments of a broken mirror, not one of the too numerous French cabinets reflected the unique, unchanging image of France, as it should have been traced every four years through general elections. Each of the provisional and successive overseers of the government had the Parliament approve a cabinet declaration, which was distinguished from past declarations by almost nothing and was written by men who often continued sitting around the same cabinet table even after their fall.

On the fringe of the national will, expressed more or less faithfully by universal suffrage, subtle influences penetrated the majority groups of each legislature and succeeded in reorganizing them into new majorities, different from the majority counted after the election, or even contrary to that majority. These too numerous governments cannot be compared to the vertebrae placed one after the other to form the backbone; for in this case the vertebrae did not harmoniously form the spine, but rather cut it up into sections.

A fast change of government is particularly unfortunate for foreign ministers, who have to establish a dialogue with foreign diplomats who are often more or less permanent.

Like Delcassé from 1898 to 1905, Briand had run the Quai d'Orsay for seven years, from 1925 to 1932. His disappearance was followed by a procession of transitory ministers, often totally different in doctrine, temperament, and methods. During the seven years which preceded the Second World War, the ministers were Pierre Laval, Tardieu, Herriot, Paul-Boncour, Louis Barthou, Pierre Laval again, Flandin, Yvon Delbos, Paul-Boncour again, and Georges Bonnet.

Each time a minister left office, the dialogue begun with the ambassadors ended, not to be continued, and all that remained were fragments of conversations to be pieced together. For diplomats and politicians who listen to a foreign policy chief are really less struck by his words than by his turns of thought, his reflexes, the nuances of his expression and his countenance, the meaning of his reactions—every sign betraying a will. And there are no true negotiations without a compromise between two wills.

The internal structure of the Third Republic was thus dangerously weakened. A slow decline in energy was taking place. The regime, out of breath, was reaching the point where it no longer knew what to do, what action to take.

In order to regain a foothold on this steep slope, the France of 1934 needed a wise but firm government, whose private resolutions and public decisions would be continued by the uninterrupted memory of its members and put into effect by their ongoing volition. France required that the successive candidates not be tempted every three months to upset the political game in order to lengthen the impressive hierarchy of former ministers and former prime ministers. Doumergue would be powerless to fulfill these wishes.

Louis Barthou and the "Grand Strategy"

Louis Barthou reappeared suddenly in Doumergue's ministry, succeeding Paul-Boncour as foreign minister.

Barthou was one of the survivors of a generation that had given a series of remarkable statesmen to the Third Republic: Poincaré, Briand, Millerand, Viviani, Caillaux, Leygues, Jonnart, not to mention Jaurès. This generation differed from the preceding one, that of Gambetta, Clemenceau (contemporaries, although the first died in 1882 and the second in 1929), Jules Ferry, Ribot, and Maurice Rouvier.

With resolute courage, Barthou had had the law for three-year military service voted in in 1913. As Chamber manager in 1919 for ratification of the Treaty of Versailles, which he wanted to see put into effect with "unrelenting strictness," and as chairman of the Reparations Commission from 1922 to 1924, he was very different from his friend "Raymond"—more complex than Poincaré, more flexible, more subtle, more a negotiator and less a pleader of legal briefs. As head of the French delegation at Genoa in 1922, he followed Poincaré's instructions faithfully; but in his incisive manner he did not try very hard to hide that his own intelligence—which excelled in making epigrams—was not bound by any discipline. Attracted since 1920 by the idea of contact with Russia, he recognized, through the dark cloud of the Bolshevik revolution, the renewal and rejuvenation of one of the major world powers after years of decay.

He had not played a very active role in the last ten years, but he had lived within the political and literary world. Passionately interested in music, one of the elder members of the French Academy, he wrote and took great delight in his fabulously opulent library filled with rare books and autographs.

He was now, thanks to Doumergue, closely tied to a task, and to this he brought the resources of his courage, his willpower, and his realistic and penetrating lucidity. *Quo vadis, Gallia?* Stresemann had asked in the past. A fervent patriot, Barthou did not want France to go to her doom. She had to recover the voice of her historical authority. It was not pessimism that could inspire action and the means to stand firm, but rather the resoluteness of a great country sure of her political path. The situation would be irremediably lost only if it were allowed to be lost.

During his seven months as foreign minister, Barthou launched, not only in words but also in deeds, a new policy aimed at meeting anticipated dangers. His work, his great work vanished with his assassination. Through a few decisive acts of firmness and confidence, he had traced the outlines of his work sharply enough to remain as a luminous figure before the historic collapse of 1935–36—two tragic years when the deterioration of willpower undermined the cohesion of all democracies. Soon, having been destroyed little by little, the Europe of Versailles was only a memory.

Through a policy of action related to the needs of the public welfare, Barthou intended to make France rise fearlessly from her languid inertia, attracting around her all those who expected her to take action and initiative in the world again. A pure patriotic flame gave youth as well as vigor to the seventy-year-old minister. History speaks of the "grand strategy" attributed by Sully to King Henry IV, assassinated in 1610. Louis Barthou, the king's fellow countryman from Béarne and, like him, assassinated, fostered even more than Henry IV a grand strategy to put an end to looming international catastrophes. His plan was to bring together France, Fascist Italy, and the Soviet Union. He believed that the stability of Central Europe had to be guaranteed to contain Hitler's Germany in a position of balance, without hegemony. This would be achieved through a method based on firmness. It was by this same virtue of firmness that as prime minister in 1913 he had succeeded, not without difficulty, in having the three-year military service law introduced and passed. Not only had he no fear of taking risks, but he had a feeling, even a taste for risk, and risks were necessary during the thirties for the protection of peace. And the worst happened: there was a lack of courage.

The Rapprochement with Mussolini

Barthou intended to reestablish a European balance of collective security. He saw Fascist Italy and Soviet Russia as two high cards against Hitler, two trumps. A common front had to be organized against Nazism, an imminent danger recognized and denounced by leaders almost everywhere.

Barthou aimed at the policy demanded in 1936 by Churchill, that prophet of doom, that storm petrel: "The grand alliance of all peace-loving nations against the aggressor, whoever he may be." For years, Churchill would never stop insisting on the effectiveness of the forces the League of Nations could unite to serve justice. The League would have found among her European members alone enough force against Hitler: "Never in history," he wrote, "could a war have been more easily avoided by acting on time, as that war which comes to destroy the whole earth. It could have been avoided without a single shot being fired. No one wished to hear me, and one by one all the nations were swallowed up in the vortex."

In choosing an international orientation, Barthou had hesitated at first, for he ran into obstacles. The Europe of 1934 no longer followed the trends of 1922. In Poland, were Pilsudski and Beck still the allies of France? They had discovered, in the nonaggression pact signed in January 1934 with Germany, the symbol of the autonomy of a great power, of a "very great power," Barthou stressed.

Barthou had then turned to the Soviet Union, and had convinced her to enter the League of Nations. An important change in the European situation was taking place.

Mussolini became quickly aware of it. This dynamism attracted him. France was resisting the pressures of the Disarmament Conference; she had freed herself by her note of April 17, 1934. Barthou's plans for Russia, his diplomatic visits in Europe and this new policy had made a great impression on Mussolini.

Moreover Mussolini knew of his attraction and the admiration he inspired among the masters of French diplomacy. Mussolini much preferred Barthou, who passed as a man of the Right, to his predecessors, men of the Left. One of them, Paul-Boncour, had called him a "costume-party Caesar."

The Clash between Hitler and Mussolini in Austria

Already Hitler's rise to power had reduced the strain in Franco-Italian relations, as the two countries faced a Germany quickly becoming too powerful.

Mussolini had judged that Germany would recover her rank and could not be denied rearmament. But Germany's determination and decisiveness had not been equal to her potential; after Hitler came to power, her capacity for daring and her determination grew frightfully.

In leaving the League of Nations, Germany had caused the end of the Four-Power Pact, thus touching Mussolini in his position as mediator, a position which brought him great international prestige.

In *Mein Kampf,* Hitler had dedicated to Mussolini the lavish eulogy of a disciple. What value could Mussolini have found in the compliments of an obscure, imprisoned agitator, at a time when men of the highest rank surrounded him with admiring flattery?

Since then Hitler had clashed with his master over Austria, his homeland and the country he wanted to bring into the great German Reich before any other; and Mussolini had been joined by men Hitler had once counted among his own. Hitler had not been too upset by these intrigues, inasmuch as they had not extended beyond the bounds of the opposing factions.

His Austrian policy was as clear as a whole as it was confused in detail. He had first hoped for a quick victory by the Austrian National Socialists, and he had given freedom of action to Theodore Habicht, one of their leaders; but, fearing Italian intervention, he tried to reach understanding with Vienna between September 1933 and January 1934.

But since 1932 Engelbert Dollfuss, the leader of the Catholic peasants and a man impervious to intellectual pan-Germanism, had been the elected chancellor. He had accepted Mussolini's support and had become his friend. Mussolini, blinded by his anti-Marxist passion, had prompted the armed suppression of the Austrian Socialist party—a party insufficiently conciliatory in internal policy but representing, with one-third of the Austrian population, the strongest anti-Nazi force. During this civil war, which had compromised Dollfuss in European leftist opinion, the German press could not take the Marxists' side; but, as soon as the fighting ended, it branded the Dollfuss regime a "regime of blood" in this mutilated Austria, who amid the miseries of her distress kept her optimism and the strength to smile.

On May 15, 1934, Dollfuss came to Rome, in the company of his extremely Germanophile Hungarian colleague, Gömbös. Together they gave their allegiance to Mussolini—Dollfuss with enthusiasm, Gömbös with a reserve inspired both by a passionately revisionist, Germanophile policy and by the desire to make Germany adhere to the Rome agreements. In spite of Hungarian reluctance, a Danubian coalition had been established by the Rome protocols of March 17, 1934. This coalition perhaps represented the future nucleus of a more powerful group; already it was a serious obstacle to any assault against Austrian independence, a fact which exasperated the Nazis of Austria.

Hitler, worried, wanted to evaluate the situation and suggested a visit to the Duce. On June 14, alone with Mussolini for a long time in a motorboat on the Venetian lagoon, he spoke; but there was no true dialogue. Hitler always avoided the equality of dialectic; any conversation was to lead only to the expression of his will, and to achieve this he had to first encircle, dominate, and fascinate his listener with a monologue which he prolonged as long as necessary. On that day, he had chosen the disagreeable idea of the superiority of the Nordic race as his introductory theme. He finally had to stop speaking. An exasperated Mussolini had remained unresponsive. With Hitler's plane on its way back to Berlin, Mussolini told his confidants of his ironic disdain for this "buffoon," pitiable in his rubber raincoat. The meeting between the Duce and the Führer had come close to being a "collision." The first was not at all sorry for the difficulties encountered by the second.

Sixteen days later, the frightening brutality of the German executions of June 30 surpassed all imaginable predictions. Fascist Italy had only seen one assassination, that of Matteotti, Mussolini's Socialist opponent. Was Hitler's dictatorship going to drown in blood? Mussolini wondered if the "butchery" of this Saint Bartholomew's Eve was the death knoll of the National Socialist regime. Hitler slaughtered at the same time his most dangerous enemies and those who had taken him as their leader only with the intention of forcing him to follow their wishes.

German-Italian relations were becoming much more tense, for Rome did not appreciate the racist delirium of the Nazis.

The Assassination of Dollfuss

Austrian Chancellor Dollfuss was assassinated in his chancellery on July 25, 1934, by ex-soldiers of the Austrian army, wearing its uniform. He was forty-two years old. Mussolini recognized without any doubt the hand of the man who had murdered his own followers on June 30. This assassination in Vienna was the first act of a revolution aimed at a German annexation of Austria. On the same day, Mussolini mobilized the Alpine troops which occupied positions in the Brenner Pass, ready to cross the frontier. He might not have shown such daring had he not known Barthou's plans.

He sent a telegram expressing his sympathy to the Austrian vice-chancellor, Prince Starhemberg, the leader of the *Heimwehr*—an armed, anti-Marxist organization—and the descendant of the hero of Vienna's resistance to the Turks in 1683, writing: "The independence of Austria is a principle for which Italy will never cease to do battle, with an ever-increasing resolve, and in circumstances far more serious. It will be defended fiercely."

In spite of the shock caused by the murder committed in the invaded chancellery, in spite of the shady complicity revealed by the organization of the assassination—Rintelen, German Ambassador to Rome, was expected to succeed Dollfuss—Mussolini's Austrian friends, encouraged by his mobilization, proved themselves capable of resistance. The Nazi uprising planned in Austria was rapidly and completely subdued, to the intense astonishment of Hitler, for whom this was a major defeat. The abortive takeover in Vienna was one of Hitler's rare blunders before 1939.

He hastily beat a retreat, forbidding the Austrian Nazis to take any action, and sending Papen to Vienna as ambassador and peacemaker. He had to wait four years before taking up these plans again, and not without apprehension; but when he did so Mussolini's international position had completely changed.

Right after the murder in Vienna, another tragic event took place, as if to restore and even reinforce Hitler's authority. On August 1, 1934, Hindenburg finally died. Hitler succeeded him. As early as August 2, officers and soldiers swore their loyalty to him. Head of state, head of the army, "Führer and chancellor of the Reich," he did not want to take the title of "president of the Reich," on the pretense that such a title was too closely tied to the person of Marshal von Hindenburg. Sanctioned by the plebiscite on August 19 with an enormous majority of more than 90 percent, Hitler ceased to be a mere soldier of fortune and became an absolute ruler, able to bring into step the whole society, which was cut off from all other forces. He could develop, as he wished, the powers of a dictatorship free of any law.

In the summer of 1934, the Italian press repeatedly and violently attacked Berlin. The *Völkischer Beobachter* having labeled as childish the Italian commentary on the events in Austria, the *Popolo di Roma* wrote: "It's agreed, Fascists are children. But what are the Nazis? Assassins and pederasts."

On September 6, Mussolini protested against "the barbaric hordes of the North. . . . Thirty centuries of history permit us to contemplate with some indulgence certain doctrines taught on the other side of the Alps by the descendants of people who were completely illiterate at the time when Caesar, Virgil, and Augustus flourished in Rome."

As Cardinal Pacelli pointed out to Ambassador Charles-Roux on October 28, 1932, "with a discreetly ironic tone," such oratorical outbursts were not to be taken literally. The cardinal, then secretary of state in the Vatican, remembered having been questioned by Stresemann the day following a withering speech given by Mussolini on the Tyrol. At that time, the cardinal had advised the German minister not to take these words too seriously; and, indeed, the Italian government quickly reestablished friendly ties with Berlin.

Mussolini in the Anti-German Camp

In July 1934, Mussolini was thus suddenly confronted by a crisis he had not anticipated a few weeks earlier when Hitler visited him in Venice. Although at the height of his prestige, he was not dazzled by the success of his mobilization on the Brenner. In any case his anxiety was acute. His policy was being threatened at its most sensitive point. It was becoming obvious that the Danube Basin would not remain outside of the next European conflict but would be at the center of it. Instead of staying free to throw her weight on the victorious side, Italy, directly involved, would be threatened with becoming the hostage to Hitler's policy; she would have to side against the Nazis. She would no longer be able on her own to protect Austria, the key to her independence. It was necessary to organize right now a common front against the Reich. Would not the western great powers eventually recognize the danger threatening Austria? Until this point, inspired by bitter jealousy, Mussolini's only plan had been to bring about the failure of all the western powers' plans, plans that had been inspired by precisely the same interest in the Danube Basin.

Hitler was creating an army and he would make war. Action was necessary, quick action. What Mussolini had done after the murder of the courageous little chancellor—so obstinate in his desire for independence—was prompted by Italy's vital interests. It was also in the interests of Europe, whose civilization would perish if the Nazi gangsters imposed their dominance.

The great crisis Mussolini had publicly predicted for the years "between 1935 and 1940" was arriving. He had always expected the revenge of a Germany risen from her defeat, but he had misjudged the time. He had calculated that the Italians would be able to take their share in a new distribution of Europe before Germany could direct and dictate the partition. But Hitler's schedule proved to be much tighter than his own. Instead of following the eastern axis in Danzig and in the Corridor, where he would have encountered the Franco-Polish alliance, this Austrian seemed to be interested only in Austria and in the Danubian Basin—the "living space" Mussolini thought essential to Italy if she was to retain the great power status she had reached after the war.

Mussolini saw, as in a vision, Hitler on his way toward hegemony. He had no doubt that the Führer, having suspended his momentum against Poland through the January 1934 agreement, would turn to Austria.

Since 1923 Mussolini had clashed in Central Europe with France, who opposed any territorial changes. Supported by France, the three states of the Little Entente, allied against Hungary and suspicious of Austria, wanted to maintain unchangeable frontiers. In his zeal to make his own policy and to have his own client states, Mussolini had caused the failure of all the plans for economic organization of the Danube Basin, the last plan having been suggested by Tardieu in March 1932. The British government had supported Tardieu's plan, but only halfheartedly, mostly to avoid displeasing Mussolini.

Mussolini could only accept his own plan and his own application of it. As early as 1928, he had won Hungary's friendship by declaring himself in favor of frontier revision in a resounding speech. Since 1930, he had acquired a foothold in Austria. When the Austrian Hitler, definitely concentrating on Austria, had set aside or postponed all action in the east by signing a pact with Poland in January 1934, Mussolini had felt the blow. He had immediately drawn up a pact for close political and economic cooperation with Austria and with Hungary. And then, the day after the demonstration in Rome in honor of Dollfuss, Hitler had struck.

Faced with a vision of Hitler's supremacy, Mussolini suddenly changed direction; he did not intend to walk alone along this new road. His boldness in mobilizing on the Brenner frontier had been less risky than it appeared. When he had announced with confidence and with some presumption that he was going to organize a front against Germany, he knew that the approach work had already been done by Louis Barthou. Rome was therefore open to the French foreign minister. At the beginning of October, Mussolini had expressed, with unusual cordiality, his desire to welcome him. He already foresaw "agreements, useful and fruitful for the two countries, in the interest of all of Europe." On October 6, he said to the workers of Milan: "An understanding between Italy and France will be useful and fruitful."

On the eve of a crisis beginning in Austria and threatening Italy's position as a great power, Italy had joined the anti-German camp. Italy needed the cooperation of France to carry on her ambitious policy in Central Europe.

When one recalls the plans Mussolini had at the time, one wonders sadly if it would not have been possible for a more skillful western diplomacy, free from anti-Fascist prejudices, to prevent Mussolini from reversing his position totally as he later did. The "costume-party Caesar," as Paul-Boncour had called him, was certainly unbearable, with all the violence, suspiciousness, and conceit of his spirit. Filled with contradictions, since 1914 he had been an enraged neutralist, then a frenzied internationalist, a revolutionary and international socialist, then an angered nationalist; but, even so . . . The dangers to French internal unity of the dislocation brought by contrary influences or loyalties—the influence of Fascist Italy on the

Right and the influence of Moscow on the extreme Left—would appear clearly in 1936, during and following the Popular Front elections.

The Rapprochement with Moscow

Because of the internal situation of a France so greatly divided, a policy favoring both Italy and Russia met the need for balance. Reaching an understanding with Mussolini meant soothing and reassuring the French Fascists mobilized by the Leagues. For otherwise France would encircle Germany by introducing Soviet influence into Europe, and it was impossible to imagine an adventure more disastrous for public order, at the exact moment when an energetic deflationary policy was about to be undertaken in France.

A moderate, a conservative like Barthou—in the past interior minister in Méline's conservatively oriented "cabinet of priests"—could not seriously be accused of tolerance toward Communism. Nazi Germany had to be kept under the threat of two fronts and a barrier of collective security had to be established against Hitler through a cautious but firm policy aimed at an understanding with two states independent of England: Italy and Russia, both anti-German at the time. The USSR was too much on the periphery; a strong structure had to be established for European peace. It was possible only with the full cooperation of Italy and France, each with her allies. Barthou felt that an agreement with Mussolini was natural and necessary to ensure full security in the east, by linking the USSR with the Little Entente, Austria, and Hungary.

While Hitler was struggling to make Berlin the center of Europe, his new policy toward Poland revealed a profound change to the Soviets, and confirmed their infinite mistrust; confronted with a very serious situation, they became the champions of maintenance of the existing territorial order. At the same time, Hitler's policy was for Mussolini the sign of a radical change in Hitler's line of direction, toward Austria and no longer toward the east. Two centers of opposition to Berlin thus took shape, one in Russia and one in Italy. In spite of their different ideologies, there was no practical opposition between them; Mussolini would only adopt his anti-Comintern language after 1936, when he turned toward Berlin.

Barthou energetically carried on the rapprochement with the Soviets, as Paul-Boncour had outlined it. A nonaggression pact with the USSR was concluded on November 29, 1932, by Herriot, and it was ratified unanimously by the Chamber on May 18, 1933. In July, Litvinov came to Paris, where he received a cordial welcome. In August, Herriot—who was no longer at the head of the government—had a brief stay in the USSR; in September, it was the turn of Pierre Cot, the aviation minister. German-Russian relations, which had been cordial for a long time, grew strangely cold. The time had passed when Stalin, in June 1930, declared France "the most aggressive and most militaristic country among all the most aggressive and militaristic countries in the world." The Soviets took *Mein Kampf* very seriously. In it was expressed the intention to expand in the east, not as a vague dream, but as a calculated project of colonization and division. A series of steps were taken in Germany against the USSR: newspapers were prohibited and searches were conducted in several Russian commercial organizations, in spite of their extraterritorial legal rights. The press used violent language against Russia, provoking official protests from Moscow.

Shortly after Germany left the League of Nations, Litvinov had proposed an alliance to France. Paul-Boncour had in mind only assistance limited to Europe, within the framework of the League of Nations. The League of Nations would undoubtedly have been reinforced if the USSR had entered it, but it was not advisable to shock England too much with a completely bilateral agreement, and anticommunist propaganda was very active, in England especially and also in France.

The Conflict between Nazi Germany and the Soviets

Germany intended to grab the advantages offered by her central position between west and east. When Stresemann decided to orient German policy toward the west, he concluded a treaty with the Soviets in Berlin on June 29, 1926, in order to pacify them. The treaty was good for five years and was extended in June 1931.

Since the "bomb of Rapallo," an active military collaboration had existed between the two countries. German officers were trained in Russian camps in the use of arms forbidden to Germany by the Treaty of Versailles: tanks, airplanes, and so forth.

On December 16, 1926, this military collaboration was denounced in the *Reichstag* by ex-chancellor Scheidemann: "Russia preaches world revolution, and at the same time she arms Germany. . . . These are not honest relations . . . enough of these dirty dealings."

But Russia did not plan to remain isolated in the face of a strong Germany. According to the ambassador to Moscow, Herbert von Dirksen, who had succeeded Brockdorff-Rantzau in 1929, Maksim Litvinov had been in favor of a policy of entente with France since the early summer of 1933. The German-Polish pact of January 1934 increased German-Soviet tension: would the pact transform Poland into a staging point for a German offensive against Russia, already threatened in the Far East by Japan?

In November 1933, the *Auswärtiges Amt* thought it timely to send as ambassador to Moscow, Rudolf Nadolny, who had been the German delegate at the Disarmament Conference and who was looked upon as an open supporter of Rapallo. Nadolny, wanting to maintain good relations with the USSR, had the German-Soviet neutrality pact of 1926 extended. But Hitler, who was fiercely anti-Russian, adopted an aggressive attitude toward Moscow. As early as May 1934 Nadolny resigned and left the diplomatic corps. During the following summer, the German mission was recalled from Russia. Trade between Germany and Russia declined, whereas between 1930 and 1933 it represented more than half of Soviet foreign trade.

The Soviets deplored Hitler's rise—even more so since General von Schleicher had the reputation of being pro-Russian. They did not fear Nazism in itself, and even if they did regret the terrible blows struck to German Communism, they carefully separated internal and foreign policy.

The reversal in German-Soviet relations incited by Hitler strengthened the Soviet rapprochement with France. The allies of the Third Republic found themselves scattered in contradictory positions.

Since January 1934 Poland had returned to a pro-German line. Barthou himself assessed the situation during his tour of Warsaw, Prague, Belgrade, and Bucharest. The way he was received in each city did not justify the conclusion of the note of April 17, 1934. Of the French alliance system, nothing remained but contradictions, and these contradictions could not be resolved by mere words. And so Barthou turned to the Soviet Union, where, on January 26 at the Communist Party congress, Stalin had expressed the idea that "rapprochement" with France against an increasingly stronger Germany was in the interest of the Soviets. Barthou was determined to call on Russian strength to counterbalance the growing German threat. If a coalition against him included the USSR and Italy, Hitler would not dare to take up arms against it. Despite English opposition, this was Russia's chance—she was reentering Europe. At the end of October 1933, the aggressor had appeared. Hitler freed himself of all legal entanglements by leaving the League of Nations. His purpose had to be interpreted by his actions and aggression to be discouraged through the reciprocal guarantee of the Continental powers.

Collective security is the law of an international organization intended to protect and impose peace. Barthou wanted to make the Nazis understand that collective security had not been destroyed by their withdrawal from the League of Nations at a time when, engaged in the most critical phase of rearmament, they were particularly vulnerable. He did not want to fall into the trap of bilateral pacts used by Hitler—alternating effusiveness, promises, and challenges—to successively isolate his neighbors and thus be free in his confrontation with each one. Men should not wait for Hitler to become the man of the hour. French diplomacy planned to conclude an "eastern pact" which would match the western pact of Locarno. The Russians wanted it also, in order to be free to act in the Far East.

England multiplied her reservations toward this pact meant to contain German expansion. She wanted to avoid what Germany would consider an encirclement, and she did not want to do anything that went beyond Locarno. Arthur Henderson spoke openly of an "encirclement of Germany through the eastern pact." All things considered, the English were opposed to a Franco-Russian rapprochement. On July 9 and 10, Barthou was in London to obtain from the English not their participation, but their indirect support, seeing that the same security would be guaranteed to Germany as to France and the USSR. The eastern pact would serve as the foundation for a future disarmament convention.

At first Mussolini showed hostility to an eastern Locarno, and Hitler— determined to expand his sphere of influence—rejected it totally. Under English influence, Mussolini accepted the pact, preferring it by far to a direct Franco-Soviet alliance.

Poland was not disposed to join the pact. In regard to the French alliance, Colonel Beck detested everything that might be interpreted as a sign of subordination. National pride refused to come under foreign "influences."

In April Barthou tried to convince Pilsudski that the Soviets should join the League of Nations. Being the first French foreign minister to visit Warsaw, and having, as war minister, taken part in concluding the alliance with Poland in 1921, Barthou was well regarded by the Poles; but since he had not been greeted at the station by Paul-Boncour when he arrived in Paris as foreign minister, Beck refused to meet Barthou at the Warsaw station. Beck had no doubt that Barthou, under the cover of military discussions, wanted to "smuggle in political ideas."

A French agreement with Russia would be added to the agreement with Poland. Barthou ran into a total refusal from Pilsudski, opposed to an alliance with the Soviets, to whom, in the final analysis, he preferred Germany. Like Germany, Poland was hostile to all pacts except the regional pacts concluded between neighbors. Did not the states, members of a pact, risk being dragged into events that did not concern them directly? Pilsudski did not want to become part of a pact which would include Lithuania and Czechoslovakia, two states on which he had territorial claims.

As Beck wrote, it was a matter of pushing the Eastern European countries into Russia's arms and of linking the entire group to French policy. A pseudo-coalition against Germany would be placed under French protection: "We would have had to guarantee the Czech frontiers. We had to play the thankless role of spoilsport. Our fundamental argument—that Germany should participate in this pact—represented for us a sine qua non for the maintenance of our policy of balance between our two great neighbors, Germany and Russia, and we knew that Germany would not participate in an eastern pact."

Barthou deplored Poland's somewhat equivocal position. During a luncheon in Geneva, he indulged in a bittersweet tirade, on a tone at once obsequious and sarcastic, which, as Eden observed, made Beck blush deeply: "And here are the great powers" —pause— "and Poland . . . We know, because we have been told, that Poland is a great power" —pause— "a very great power."

In September 1934, Poland showed herself to be thoroughly opposed to Soviet entry into the League of Nations.

France would give her guarantee of the status quo in Eastern Europe, while the USSR, for her part, would comply with the Locarno Rhine Pact of 1925. This would guarantee the frontiers of Austria and Czechoslovakia, which were particularly threatened. The "eastern Locarno" would have been a political shock to Hitler's system of bilateral treaties representing a free hand in the east for Germany.

On September 10, Germany officially rejected the eastern pact under the pretext that she was always denied equality of treatment. Ambassador Hoesch congratulated himself on this rejection, which prevented a Franco-Soviet alliance from being hidden by a display of League ideology. The Russians and the French would be forced to conclude their alliance openly, which would greatly displease many Frenchmen.

Poland coldly turned down the project. She multiplied reservations until they were equivalent to a rejection, and Finland and the Baltic States joined her. How could the aggressor be defined? All sorts of arbitrary interpretations were possible. What Poland feared most of all was to see Russian armies pass over and her land transformed into a battlefield, if for example the USSR intervened in Czechoslovakia's favor under the terms of the pact.

At the end of September, an overall agreement based on the "eastern Locarno" could be considered definitively dismissed. This failure did not upset Barthou. He had secured the alliance between France and Russia, joined by Czechoslovakia, a faithful ally of France. The Soviet Union had shown her goodwill by agreeing to a collective security pact.

On September 18, invited by twenty-eight nations at French initiative, the Soviet Union entered the same League of Nations which she had until then ridiculed, and obtained a permanent Council seat. Barthou introduced her to the League in perfectly clear terms: "Do not turn Russia back outside, into adventures, into the advocacy of a doctrine which you dislike. Accept her, since she comes on the conditions you yourselves have set."

Barthou believed Litvinov, who appeared a little like "the Stresemann of the 1930s," to be sincere in his policy; and his policy was sincere because it was the expression of Russian security and the manifestation of Soviet fears. Under the pressure of international necessities, it was a policy of balance. The USSR found herself caught between Germany and Japan. The lack of any Anglo-American action against Japan was evident. At least the barrier of a European coalition had to be opposed to Hitler's Germany. This was precisely what Barthou wanted: a strong coalition, a bloc. If it was strong enough, there would be no war. Hitler's Germany, surrounded for good, would not make war.

Russia's entry into the League of Nations, immediately after the withdrawal of Japan and Germany, brought an active contribution in favor of collective security, thanks to the freshness and vigor of a realistic point of view. Extremely worried by the Nazi threat, Litvinov was able to see the actual conditions which would characterize a European collective security—the law of an international organization whose prime mission was to protect and to impose peace. Everything depended essentially on the military cooperation that could be established between the western powers and the USSR. Her plans were the best evidence of what the League of Nations should have done to bring about the failure of Hitler's tyrannical projects. If the Litvinov-Barthou association had lasted, it could have prevented one of the greatest catastrophes ever to strike the world, bringing so much death, destruction, and misery.

Let us note that it was only a few months after France's terrible failure of March 1936 that the USSR joined the anti-Fascist crusade in Spain, and that Litvinov's policy would only be repudiated in 1939 by Stalin and Molotov, who were convinced of western weakness and thereafter linked to Hitler for the important partition of Poland and the Baltic States.

The Assassinations in Marseilles

The spectacular evolution of Soviet policy coincided with the reversal of Mussolini's policy toward France. Italy, who yesterday was almost an enemy, might become an ally; she was joining the anti-German camp.

Exploiting zealously these favorable circumstances, French diplomacy, under Barthou's eager and ambitious instigation, wanted to eliminate the serious causes of misunderstanding setting Italy against Yugoslavia. The relations between the two countries had been poor since their dispute over Trieste; the friendship between Italy and Hungary did not improve them. The Yugoslavs wanted to be protected by Germany against Magyar revisionism, which Mussolini supported. In May 1934, an important trade treaty was concluded between Germany and Yugoslavia. In Belgrade, as in Bucharest, people were not very much in favor of a rapprochement with the Soviets. Nevertheless, Barthou's visit to Belgrade and Bucharest at the end of July was a success.

Between Italy and France stood the wall of the Little Entente. How could Mussolini overstep it? He could break up the Little Entente by dismantling Yugoslavia, co-ruler of the Adriatic and unshakeable ally of France. It was a fact that this heterogeneous country was torn by centrifugal forces: by Croat and Macedonian separatists and by Hungarian, German, and Albanian minorities. King Alexander was trying to maintain unity through a violent dictatorship which carried out ninety-three executions in two years. But the Croats became irreconcilable and no longer wanted to bear Serb supremacy; it would suffice to cut them off.

In 1935 Mussolini discussed a Danubian entente with Prince Starhemberg, saying: "It would take a long time to achieve it. The Little Entente will oppose it; but in the near future, perhaps, common ties will reunite Austria, Hungary, and Croatia." And as his listener expressed his surprise, Mussolini continued: "I do not believe that Croatia will go on being part of Yugoslavia. I have very detailed information on what is happening in Croatia. The Croats are much more attracted to Vienna than to Belgrade. Serbia will meet with great difficulties there, perhaps very soon." The difficulties he knew so well were those being diligently prepared by the Ustachis, supporters of Croat independence who had taken refuge in Hungary and in Italy, where they were greatly helped, especially their leader Pavelić.

Some people have suspected that Mussolini knew what was being plotted among the Ustachis against Alexander, whom they had condemned to death. In a general way, Eden wrote in his memoirs, it was true. In his private diary, Baron Aloisi did not hide that he was shocked when he learned that terrorist activities had benefited from Fascist complicity.

Barthou needed the cooperation of Yugoslavia for the vast policy he had planned for Central Europe. He intended to reconcile King Alexander with Mussolini and to visit Rome after Alexander had been welcomed in France. The king's visit to the French Republic was, then, something more than an official state visit.

On October 9, at four o'clock in the afternoon, King Alexander arrived in Marseilles. Ten minutes later, he was assassinated by a Macedonian, a killer belonging to the Ustachis, who demanded Croatian independence. Barthou died with him, although he had not been their target. Against the assassination, so carefully organized, the police protection was scandalously inadequate; interior minister Albert Sarraut resigned.

Eden wrote in his memoirs that "these were the first shots of the Second

World War." Through an implacable act of fate, France was losing in one blow the leader in her new policy and one of her best allies.

There is every reason to think that Alexander would not have become involved with Hitler. Whoever the originators or the accomplices of this murder may have been, the results had to be just as disastrous for Italy as for France. Alexander's strength of character had given his country a clearly oriented policy. This sureness died with him. Germany won strong influence in certain circles of Yugoslavia, now without a leader.

Alexander's death in October 1934 struck France even harder than had the German-Polish pact at the beginning of the year. She was losing her two main allies: two blows which, relieving Hitler from worry, gave him freedom of action in the north and in the south.

Of Barthou, who died at seventy-two years of age to be followed into the grave six days later by his long-ailing friend Raymond Poincaré, Eden wrote: "France never again found so competent a minister. In 1935, he could have warned Rome, while there was still time." His method was one of firmness and trust, as energetic in deed as in word, and, in the Italo-Ethiopian conflict, he would not have played the equivocal role adopted by his successor.

After the tragedy in Marseilles, Mussolini was anxious to keep up appearances. In Rome he attended, in full uniform, the service held by the Yugoslav legation and the mass celebrated for the French embassy at Saint-Louis des Français.

At the League of Nations, Laval, worried that the dispute between Hungary and Yugoslavia might harm Franco-Italian relations, did all he could to cast a discreet veil over Italy's responsibility. The Magyar Kanya, a shrewd old diplomat with refined manners, did his best to help.

The Diplomatic Situation after Barthou's Death

At the time of Barthou's death in October 1934, what were the general outlines for European security traced by his policy, and what were their prospects?

In 1925 the Locarno Treaty had in fact limited for Great Britain the application of the League Covenant to the territory she had guaranteed; she had obstinately refused any extension of that territory.

To the east and south of Germany, Poland, Czechoslovakia, Rumania, and Yugoslavia were bound to France by treaties binding the signatories to apply the Covenant's provisions in case of aggression. This was a strange situation, made even more anomalous since Germany, having rejected all League obligations, refused to recognize any longer the League Council's authority. These commitments represented a heavy burden for France.

In the east, to help her allies if they were attacked, she agreed to take upon herself alone the obligations decreed by Article 16 of the Covenant for all the members of the League.

The Soviet Union, convinced by Barthou to enter the League of Nations, was ready to offer her neighbors a guarantee analogous to that given by England at Locarno.

Was Italy—also a guarantor of Locarno—going to extend her guarantee to the signatories of a Danubian pact in order to ensure Austria's security?

This vast undertaking, which would have been a chimerical dream in 1933, was well on the way. But very great difficulties still had to be overcome, psychological difficulties in particular. Between the potential associates, so many facts, suspicions, misunderstandings, and differences in political systems had raised immeasurable and frightful obstacles. Also Great Britain was hoping to reach an agreement with Germany on armaments. Finally, since January 1934 Poland had been shrouded in the illusions of the nonaggression pact spontaneously offered by Hitler—almost an alliance between great powers.

Everything depended on a combined action by Italy, the Soviet Union, and France; the latter remained the connection between England and the USSR—an infinitely delicate role. To dispel mistrust, France would have had to uphold and spread energy and confidence. Such a mission would have implied that her firmness, her willpower, and her sincerity could not be questioned.

Success could certainly not be assured. But in 1934, military power was still indisputably on France's side, and Germany remained at the mercy of that power. The final phase of Barthou's policy might have brought a lasting balance—lasting does not mean perpetual—if Hitler had been kept out of things. For Barthou, Russia's power and Italy's help counted only so far as they could be used against Hitler's Germany.

The year 1935, so successfully begun in Rome in January, would prove disastrous.

10

Pierre Laval's Policy

Louis Barthou, assassinated on October 9, 1934, had been replaced by Pierre Laval. On November 8, a Pierre-Étienne Flandin ministry succeeded the Doumergue government, which was powerless to reform political life and irremediably impaired. Laval, very different from Flandin, stayed at the foreign ministry. The two men were among the new opportunists supported by the business world, to which Albert Thibaudet, a discerning critic, applied the label of "post-war industrialism." Its limitation, wrote Thibaudet, was that "it automatically left the spiritual element, the realm of the ideal, to the opposing party." It had been obvious from 1930 to 1932, when Laval and Tardieu, leaning toward the center Right, had alternated as prime minister. In March 1930, Tardieu had organized a ministry with Laval as labor minister. In January 1931, Laval formed a government; he was interior minister, then for one month and one week foreign minister, while Tardieu was agriculture minister. In February 1932, Tardieu replaced Laval as prime minister and foreign minister. Laval quietly returned to the labor ministry. The Tardieu-Laval tandem seemed to make an unbeatable team. "A tandem bicycle!" exclaimed the presumptuous Tardieu; "Call it, rather, a velocipede: a big wheel and a little one."

After the leftist victory in the elections of May 1932, the industrialists had kept their influence. The uprising of February 6, 1934, had endangered the political system but not overturned it. In any case, is it certain that the industrialists, inspirers and backers of the right-wing Leagues, had really wanted the system to disappear? In a shaken Republic with a divided majority and a weak or accommodative government, did they not have access to offices and committees, and were they not in a position to control the state's power by guiding the economy to suit their own interests? Now Laval was going to carry out their policy.

Like Mussolini and Stalin, Laval was born in 1883—"a great vintage," he would say—in Châteldon, in the department of Puy-de-Dôme. As a youth, he would deliver meat for his father, a café owner and butcher, in a horse-drawn cart. He would also take the mail to the railroad station. Often the young coachman read, leaving the horse to find its own way. At sixteen, he was sent to Paris, where he stayed with a concierge, a friend of the family. He passed the secondary school and university entrance exams and became supervisor in a boarding school, where his syndicalist opinions frightened the headmaster. A member of the Socialist party, he founded an assistant teachers' union, with seven members; he told the minister of education that they numbered nearly a thousand. At the age of twenty-five, he held a law degree and was a member of the Paris bar. He handled cases sent to him by the most diverse clients, arguing everywhere and for all sorts of people. Finally, in May 1914, at thirty-one years of age, he was elected deputy of Aubervilliers, an extreme Left, "Red" suburb of Paris.

During the war, Laval stood with the extreme wing of the socialists who wanted peace. He declared victory impossible, defended the Zimmerwald and Kienthal conferences, criticized the president of the Republic as "Poincaré the Warmaker," and exalted "the great hope which has been born, the wind of peace which blows through our country." However, he won the confidence of Georges Mandel, Clemenceau's powerful and mysterious assistant, and kept him informed about the working class. When Clemenceau, "the tiger," formed his own government in November 1917, he wanted to give some ministries to socialists; Laval would have been an undersecretary. But the Socialist party refused to participate. Laval remained the messenger of an authoritarian government to the extreme Left, to which he advised moderation.

He lost the legislative elections of November 1919, where the "Bloc National" triumphed. However, as an "independent socialist" he was for more than twenty years starting in 1923 mayor of Aubervilliers, where the socialists had switched to Communism. In this working-class town, he manifested his active and effective loyalty. He was elected deputy at the legislative elections of May 1924. In 1925 and 1926, he was public works minister, then justice minister. In 1927, he became senator as part of the "National Republican Union" electoral coalition. From the Left, he was slowly slipping toward the Right. In 1930, he was labor minister; in 1931, prime minister, famous for the white tie he always wore, and for his savoir faire. His penchant for intrigue knew no bounds. He was nicknamed "Laval the lubricant," by men who said: "This is not a man, it is an oil can."

In the government Laval formed in January 1931, Briand remained at the foreign ministry. But Laval was growing tired of the irremovable foreign minister and he kept a tighter rein on him than Poincaré had ever done. In the presidential election of May 1931, he had ostentatiously voted for Briand, but he supported him only on the surface. In September 1931 he went with him to Berlin; in October, he went to the United States alone. He wanted to get rid of him, and, when Maginot died suddenly, he suggested that Briand resign. The governmental balance demanded his resignation, claimed Laval, since Maginot represented the Right and Briand the Left. Briand reacted vigorously: "Maginot is dead, that is his problem," and refused to be pressured into a political suicide. Laval then was forced to bring about the resignation of the whole cabinet. On January 8, 1932, ejecting Briand while asserting that he agreed with him on every issue, Laval formed another government with the same ministers but without Briand, naming himself as foreign minister. In February 1932, Laval's cabinet was overturned by the Senate, and Tardieu set up a government where he himself took charge of the foreign ministry, while Laval returned to the labor ministry.

The leftist victory of May 1932 kept Laval out of power until February 1934. During that semi-revolution, it seems that he was the first to think of Doumergue and to recommend him to the president of the Republic, Lebrun, as head of a government of pacification and unity. Under Doumergue, Laval became minister of colonies.

When Barthou died, Doumergue chose Laval as foreign minister, after having hesitated between two former prime ministers, Flandin and Laval, both members of the cabinet. Two other former prime ministers, Herriot and Tardieu, could not have been considered, because of the strong opposition each one had to the other's policy.

When he succeeded Barthou, Laval had already served as foreign minister, but only for a month and a week at the beginning of 1932—a mere training period. As foreign minister, he did not have to change trades. He knew how to negotiate on important international matters just as well as on simple matters. A lawyer, he had become influential and rich. In 1917, at the height of the war, he had moved from the very modest Rue du Faubourg Saint-Martin to the luxurious neighborhood of the Villa Saïd, Avenue du Bois. He handled important commercial suits or cases involving war damages—his specialty—or war benefits. As mayor of Aubervilliers, he avoided strikes by the municipal employees by granting them compensation to cover the rising cost of living—"a Louis XIV of the suburbs," said Anatole de Monzie ironically. As labor minister, he settled conflicts between employers and employees by speaking the language of management to the management and the language of workers to the workers, and by taking a little from management to give what was necessary to the workers, all the while shaking hands with everyone. He drew his inspiration from La Bruyère's portrait of the "plenipotentiary": "All his aims, all his maxims, all his subtleties in policy were directed toward a single end, which was to avoid being fooled himself and to fool others." He was not characterized by sincerity nor by clarity. He inspired confidence once, but not twice, in the English, in Mussolini, in Stalin, and in others.

The Marquis de Moustiers, foreign minister under the Second Empire, was asked one day where he had learned to be a diplomat. He answered: "I am from Franche-Comté and I know how to trade horses." Laval was attached by every fibre of his being to the soil of Auvergne; he spoke of it with sincere emotion, without pretense. Humble recollections from his childhood touched this countryman, who purchased the castle from his village. He felt the peasant's urge to own a piece of land. But, his enemies would ask, what accident had given him the face of a gypsy? He would live the adventurous life of a gypsy who knows no other profession but that of horse dealer. For him, everything was selling and bargaining with clever slyness. He went into nothing in depth. He had no background, no culture; his ignorance was of encyclopedic extent. But he had a very powerful and overly self-confident personality.

Laval arrived at the Quai d'Orsay in October 1934, and remained foreign minister for sixteen months, serving under prime ministers Doumergue and Flandin, in an ephemeral Bouisson cabinet and finally, in June 1935, in his own third cabinet.

He adopted Barthou's policy, with identical gestures, but opposite inspiration. Through underhand maneuvers, he presided over the side-tracking of Barthou's work. Belonging to a younger generation, he had not inherited the tradition of antagonism toward Germany. Deep down, he was opposed to that policy of firmness and action; but he had to appear to be continuing it. He had no intention of creating a large security zone in the east; he did not believe in it, but he had to give the impression that he did believe in it, that he was considering it. He wanted to accomplish conciliatory work: "No one is more resolved than I to bring about a rapprochement between nations." The essential point would be an understanding with Germany. "Chancellor Hitler," declared Laval on December 2, "asserts his wish for peace; we ask him to follow his words with deeds by cooperating in the policy which we are following in Eastern Europe." He tried to imitate Briand, although now he had to deal with Hitler's Germany. Very obstinate, he aimed at maintaining the peace at any price; convinced that Germany would eventually make war, he wanted to avoid French involvement. His hidden motive was, it seems, to make his cooperation more valuable to Berlin, through an understanding with Italy and with the USSR. This was an idle dream. Pushed on by his own impulses, Hitler, like a sleepwalker, was following a fanatic's path on which others could have no more influence than on the oribit of a planet; and Laval showed audacity only when making concessions.

The Rome Accords

To begin with, Laval thought it necessary to stifle discreetly the Barthou policy. A close understanding with Mussolini, sought after not to oppose Germany but to exploit Mussolini's symbolic value, would assure Laval of his influence over the sector of French public opinion which was controlled by the Fascist Leagues.

Laval then was not going to Rome only to visit a future ally in order to plan with him Europe's efforts against a common enemy, or to make it clear to Hitler, now engaged in the most critical phase of rearmament and extremely vulnerable, that collective security had not been destroyed. He was going to Rome mainly to visit the man so dear to his industrialist friends, the man who exerted such fascination on many in France. Beautiful maneuver of domestic politics: to bring back to France the friendship of a reconciled Mussolini. It was a personal accomplishment more than a labor of professional diplomacy: conversations without notes or minutes, without contradictions or indiscretions, except when they could serve to embarrass a bothersome interlocutor. From time to time, declarations and agreements would be published to glorify him and inspire confidence to France.

Shady hidden motives would thus soon undo the work of Barthou, for whom Russia's power and Italy's help counted only insofar as they could be opposed to Germany, in returning to France her freedom of action.

Laval arrived in Rome full of confidence. He had just done Mussolini a favor. At Geneva, thanks to Laval, the request of the Yugoslav government concerning the investigation of King Alexander's assassination had been directed exclusively toward Hungary—who went along with it—for having tolerated the preparations for the murder. No mention, no criticism had touched Italy, even slightly.

Laval was well received. He resembled so little the traditional French politicians, such as Poincaré, Herriot, and Paul-Boncour. Mussolini saw in him an anti-parliamentary type like himself, a man capable of quick decisions and secret agreements, a partner of the same temperament, a simplifier, fit to settle, through a few straightforward decisions, the endless negotiations which always stumble over the reservations of diplomats and bureaucrats. "Duce, you have written the most beautiful page in modern history!"

Within a few days, the thick undergrowth of disputable questions was clarified and the agreements signed. The colonial agreement was very simple. Italy received an island to the north of Jibuti and thirty miles of coastline, a share in the railway from Jibuti to Addis Ababa, and at the border of Libya and Equatorial Africa she received 54,000 square miles of land. A lunar desert, remarked Mussolini sarcastically. Laval pointed out the existence of two towns. Were they not barren oases, asked Mussolini. "Of course, they are not Rome or Aubervilliers," replied Laval.

In exchange, Italy gave up her trump card, a heavy claim on Tunisia. After a transitional period, the Italian community would be subject to the complete enforcement of French law and thus would lose her status as an extraterritorial colony.

The arguments and quibbles laboriously accumulated against France were eliminated in one stroke. At a point when the negotiations were running into difficulty, Mussolini, alone with Laval in a salon of the Farnese Palace, had suddenly, after midnight, ordered his delegates to accept the French formula.

Of the two sides of the scale, the side where the French had just placed their concessions was the lightest.

Other agreements created a Franco-Italian front: they recognized the obligation to respect the independence and integrity of states—a bilateral version of Article 10 of the League of Nations Covenant—and accordingly urged the individual states concerned to sign agreements not to intervene in each other's internal affairs through external agitation, propaganda, or attack against a political and social regime.

France and Italy proposed a "Danubian pact," aimed at guaranteeing the status quo in Austria and the Balkans.

Noting that no country could alter, through unilateral activity, its obligations concerning armament, France and Italy committed themselves to consult each other if such an eventuality arose. They recalled courteously the declaration of December 11, 1932, on the principle of equal rights. Following these preliminaries came the essential provision: "In consideration of the need to maintain the independence and integrity of Austria, the two governments agree as of now to consult with Austria about measures to be taken if that independence or that integrity is threatened. This consultation will then be extended by Italy and France to other nations, in order to assure themselves of their assistance."

When signing the agreements, Laval and Mussolini had asserted that they were not directed against anyone. In reality, the diplomatic style of the agreements was so strained that they could have been looked on as an alliance treaty. All the polite formalities were preserved, but Hitler could not be deceived. In the critical phase of his rearmament, he did not want to break relations with Italy nor did he want to give the impression that he saw a Franco-Italian front as a move against him. Never was patience so well rewarded at a later time.

However, the real significance of the Franco-Italian agreements was revealed by important unpublished military arrangements signed in May 1935. Both sides of the Franco-Italian border in the Alps were losing their military character, after having been garrisoned with troops for several years and strengthened with modernized fortifications. The two general staffs thus ensured their freedom to orient their mobilization apparatus in other directions.

France's military strength was considerably increased and the French Mediterranean transports to the African colonies would be carried on a free sea, and would no longer represent a war operation.

These military agreements were made public only in February 1945, during the trial of General Roatta in Rome. Laval spoke of them at length during his own trial in August 1945. In the event of German aggression in Austria, France would send two divisions to Italy. In the event of a military reoccupation of the Rhineland, several squadrons of aircraft would arrive from Italy.

The satisfaction the French General Staff felt at the signing of these agreements is understandable, and also the anxiety it later felt during the period of League sanctions on Italy. Italy had become an ally. General Gamelin and General Badoglio were exchanging visits. The situation had changed completely since the time in Geneva when Italy had supported the British plans for equalization of armaments, plans some tried to impose on France.

The Ethiopian Enigma

The Franco-Italian agreements were celebrated with a lavish reception at the Palazzo Veneto, Mussolini's official residence. Ambassador Pietro Quaroni notes in his memoirs the melancholy of the Ethiopian chargé d'affaires, lost in his own thoughts. A French diplomat, who did not want to miss the chance for a witty remark, observed: "He must feel as if he were on the menu."

It can scarcely be doubted that Laval had been told confidentially of Italy's plans for a military expedition in Ethiopia. The plans could not have surprised him. It has even been said that before leaving Paris he was already prepared to include them in the negotiations. Did he go beyond the official notes on economic withdrawal, after Mussolini asserted that "what mainly interested him in this settlement was to gain, in Ethiopia, a channel for the economic activity of an overpopulated Italy"? It is possible, but with the sneaky advice of a pal: be careful, don't upset things; see how well patience worked for the French in Morocco. Political influence would inevitably follow economic influence.

If the vast and complex body of the Rome agreements of January 1935 is assessed, is it possible to believe that the Italian concessions in Tunisia, recorded in a diplomatic agreement submitted for parliamentary ratification, had as compensation from Laval only an implied or verbal acquiescence, both personal and secret?

Mussolini was too aware of the fragility of French cabinets to attribute a lasting diplomatic value to a minister's nod of the head.

Some people wondered if Italy had feigned a commitment in Europe only to be free to act in Africa. This supposition must be categorically rejected. The fragility of Austria caused Mussolini true anguish. Through the Rome agreements he brought himself to reverse Italian policy toward France, not for the price of the whispered complicity of a transient French minister, but because the French became Italy's allies, on the eve of a crisis which threatened her status as a great European power.

After the signing in Rome, Virginio Gayda, spokesman for Mussolini, had not hidden the fact that Italy had no illusions about the value of the compensation she received in Africa. And yet, after three months of reflection, he wrote at the Stresa Conference, still unofficially giving Mussolini's views: "Many newspapers have described the French accords signed in Rome on January 7 as one of the most important events since Locarno. It is precisely from this overall European standpoint that Italy regards the accords." Were not these words the echo of Mussolini's satisfaction? His project of a common front against Germany was well under way.

It is possible that Laval did not understand the order of priorities in Mussolini's thought. Dictators do not like to reveal their anxieties—human weaknesses incompatible with the reputation for absolute assurance. If the new alliance was to be effective, French democracy had to welcome it with gratitude; it would, therefore, have been inopportune to show with what hope it was awaited by today's ally—yesterday's near enemy.

It is still true that, at that very moment, Mussolini passionately coveted Ethiopia. Once rearmed, Germany would not fail to claim her share of colonies. France and England, both with large colonial territory, would give their full attention to protecting their possessions. Would they not agree to have Ethiopia, the only unclaimed space in Africa, become German soil? Yet Ethiopia was the complement necessary for Italy to be a great power. She had to act fast to anticipate Germany's possible ambitions. Since 1932 General De Bono, the governor of Eritrea, had been receiving instructions about this major project.

As strange as it may seem, Mussolini's plans in the Danube Basin and in

Africa were closely linked in his own mind. This alleged realist lived in an imaginary world: his distorted vision reduced obstacles to a mirage of omnipotence. He was like a gambler engaged in a serious undertaking, one who could not resist the hope of enlarging his profits through a risky speculation.

Mussolini's great ambitions, sketched in solitude, in the silence of adulation, were closer to dreams than to reality; they neglected the normal interplay of forces. Mussolini's diplomatic activity was prodigious; he created a whole secret network of activities and agents in the Middle East, in Syria, Palestine, Iraq, and Egypt, and he tried to get a foothold in Yemen and in Saudi Arabia. Indeed, there stood the "complementary" territory of his dreams. For Italy to become a truly great power, proportionate to her leader, she would have to do more than assume the ambitions of the Hapsburg monarchy. A vast colonial empire would have to mark the map of Africa with her color. Mussolini wanted to join the scattered sections of Italian colonies and perhaps later replace England in Egypt. Ethiopia was necessary for him; he had planned to conquer it as early as 1925. Without Menelik's strong personality and Adowa's defeat, all of Ethiopia would have become an Italian protectorate forty years earlier.

Mussolini thus expanded to the extreme the scope of his pride; with a logic already projecting beyond the limits of reality, everything was thoroughly intertwined in his egocentric realm where obstacles became impalpable.

Everything contributed to Mussolini's dreams. In England, and mostly in France, an increasing number of admirers pledged their allegiance to the restorer of order. Like an echo, their adulation was reflected to Rome, where it swelled the drone of illusions surrounding the isolated speculator, giving more and more imaginary value to his plans.

If Laval had taken seriously the commitment he had just assumed concerning Austria, he would have been frightened to see France's new ally ready to scatter her forces in a faraway expedition instead of concentrating them in a joint undertaking. Could it be overlooked that a military confrontation in the Red Sea was incompatible with resistance to Hitler's plans, and that there was a contradiction between the African adventure and the European plans directed against Nazism? Instigating a strategic quarrel with Great Britain might bring serious consequences to the military arrangements to be studied by the Italian and French general staffs. Such a quarrel would make it difficult to convince Hitler that, in spite of his withdrawal from the League of Nations, he would still be kept in check by powerful forces of collective security. Mussolini's involvement in an African diversion would mean the end of Barthou's policy.

According to the logic of the agreements themselves, Laval's duty would have been to dissuade Mussolini. There was no lack of arguments. Let us not speak of the League of Nations Covenant; neither man believed in it. Mussolini would have seen Laval's scruples as an evasion. Moreover, did such obligations still exist in Mussolini's mind, since Japan and Germany had left Geneva?

However, other factors contrary to Mussolini's plans existed, less merely legal and more realistic.

The agreement on Austria stipulated that consultations planned in case of danger would be extended to include Great Britain. Was it wise to agree, without England's knowledge, to violate the tripartite agreement of 1906 guaranteeing the territorial integrity of Ethiopia? It is true that these colonial formulas have little value: in 1926, Austen Chamberlain had shown what concessions he could make to Italy. Not consulting France, he had established an arrangement not very consistent with the agreement of 1906, but at least it was not to allow the Italians to undertake a military expedition.

Laval had no such worries; he had just reached with ease agreements that would bear witness to his genius. They would be appreciated for their value in internal politics much more than for their diplomatic and military potential. The French, who rested their hopes on Mussolini, defender of order, would be happy. Later, if it became necessary to placate the left wing of a heterogeneous parliamentary coalition with some compensation, Laval would go to Moscow as though continuing Barthou's work.

It is easy to understand that Laval would never admit that he had given Mussolini carte blanche and that he had wanted to hide his adhesion like a shameful sin. On December 28, 1935, when the failure of their agreements was almost beyond remedy, he denied his adhesion in Parliament: "At the moment when I had just signed a friendship treaty with Italy, above all for the purpose of fulfilling hopes of Franco-Italian cooperation that had as its aim the organizing of collective security in Europe, I would have been foolish or blameworthy to encourage, or to provoke, an unknown undertaking in Ethiopia, precisely because it would deprive us of the presence and assistance of Italy in Europe."

Laval hoped to mask reality by arguing that he could not have committed such an absurdity. But for months the Italian press had boasted about the military enterprise in Ethiopia, making the preparations for it public. Neither in Rome in January, nor in Stresa, nor later, did Laval make any effort to dissuade Mussolini, to force him to choose between the colonial adventure and the European policy. Nothing would have been easier than to provoke an exchange of views in a private conversation. Was he already inspired by a secret policy?

On June 23, 1935, Mussolini told Eden that he and Laval were fully agreed that Italy would have a free hand in Ethiopia. As Eden recalled, "I interrupted him to say: 'Economically!'" To which Mussolini replied: "Having abandoned to France the future of a hundred thousand Italians in Tunisia, and having received in exchange a dozen palm trees in one spot, and in another a desert strip without even a single sheep, it was natural to infer that France was losing interest in Ethiopia." Eden acknowledged that Mussolini had indeed obtained only meager advantages on paper.

Men will never know the contents of the last conversation between Mussolini and Laval, on January 6, 1935, in the window alcove of a salon in the Farnese Palace. Eden's belief is that Laval's attitude was equivocal enough for Mussolini to try to take advantage of it. From then on, the Duce was convinced that he was assured of French support; having full freedom of action from the French side, he could move ahead and need not let himself be stopped by any possible British opposition—which, like Laval, he underestimated considerably. At Christmastime in 1935, he had French ambassador Chambrun say to the French prime minister: "Several times it was recognized that I had a 'free hand' in Ethiopia, with the exception of what was reserved for your explicitly specified rights." But he did not claim by any means that Laval had given his "agreement to the war which the following events made inevitable."

On January 23, 1936, before leaving office, Laval wrote Mussolini: "I may have used this common expression (a free hand) with the freedom of expression allowed by the friendly character of our conversation in the Farnese Palace on the evening of January 6. . . . I find it all the more unproductive to quibble over the meaning of these words, since your letter gives evidence on what is the essential point for me: that I never gave my agreement to the war which you felt obliged to undertake."

Talks in Geneva

On January 11, 1935, a few days after he left Rome, Laval arrived in Geneva to take part in the regular League Council session. He was awaited with intense curiosity. For a few days, ministers, diplomats, and journalists had lived as on an ocean liner, meeting repeatedly in the corridors of the League, in hotel lobbies, in bars, and in cafés—a general staff of international public opinion. In this atmosphere, dense with insight, discernment, and ingenuity, everything became invisible by enlargement, as if under a magnifying glass.

Laval was surrounded by his own cohorts, specialists in spreading his policy. With the exception of a few independent newspapers, his versions of events and his commentaries would provide the substance for the mass press.

Although not distinguished by an exceptional happening, this short session saw the formation of large clouds which would darken the sky in 1935 and 1936, two critical years for the destiny of France and Europe. A fog of ambiguity and confusion which blurred the vision of common sense.

In Rome Laval had just signed agreements which Barthou would have liked to have signed before concluding, as Laval did a few months later, a pact with the Soviets. The same acts, but were they performed with the same clarity as regards the objective, the same sincerity? Laval would have had to accept Barthou's conception of the danger threatening Europe, a danger arising from Hitler's Germany. Nothing in Laval's past, even in his most recent past, gave reason to believe this was the case. Thus uneasiness and curiosity emerged from different angles.

Barthou's policy had created unexpected and difficult problems for the British. It was the first initiative in more than ten years which did not represent a simple proposition offered for discussion and submitted to the League of Nations; instead it defined a self-sufficient program for action, a proposal for regional security, with the Soviet Union in the leading role. The entire British policy, defined and limited by the Locarno Treaty and now adapted to the situation created by the withdrawal of Germany from the League of Nations, was troubled by new uncertainties. Barthou had died and the Soviet Union had replaced Germany at the League of Nations. What would be the reaction of Mussolini, originator of the Four-Power Pact of June 1933 which excluded the Soviets from Europe? And what was the real significance of the very hastily concluded Rome agreements of January 1935?

In London, people knew that Laval, this master of quibbling, was very different from Barthou. British observers thought that Laval's attitude toward Germany, as it was manifested at the time of the Saar plebiscite of January 1935, had clearly revealed more haste than dignity. Feeling that the game was lost and acting accordingly, he seemed to worry mainly about gaining credit with Hitler for his personal desire to see the Saar returned to Germany.

He had been treated by the English with a courtesy which, perhaps, he did not appreciate enough. The British rightly felt that the Saar administration had been a credit to the governing commission, named by the League Council, whose English chairman had always shown a courageous impartiality. They had feared that, during the plebiscite, the local police, already completely subservient to tomorrow's masters, would be inadequate. Eden had arrived in Geneva with a proposal to entrust the maintenance of order to an international force, recruited and organized for that purpose. It would have been an interesting experiment. A few hours before the Council meeting, the British suggested to Laval that he introduce this proposal in the name of the French delegation. This suggestion was all the kinder since it had remained confidential and since Laval publicized it widely, for his own benefit.

The British delegation did not confuse Laval and Barthou, but it wondered about the real meaning of Mussolini's attitude. Did it mean a reversal of policy? Why such haste and why such satisfaction in concluding the agreement?

Italy's position in the Mediterranean was too important strategically for London not to follow carefully any change in her policy. The poor relations between France and Italy, as well as their naval rivalries, had been a very important factor in international policy since 1919. What would be the effects of the new good relations?

This strange metamorphosis was difficult to assess. The agreements of 1935 gave so little to Mussolini that some suspected them of being supplemented by secret clauses.

Such a major change should have been justified and explained in the interest of the French, who for the first time since 1924 were recovering, with initiative, the means of making their own independent policy. To define that policy did not mean to submit it for the approval of others, but to liberate it from suspicions and misunderstanding.

A certain unrest over the undetermined, the unknown, arose in the British subconscious. Was the new Franco-Italian intimacy dominated by Laval's approval of the conquest of Ethiopia? Did the unconcealed military dispositions, the preparations, and the embarkations not indicate this? What could the repercussions of an Italian conquest be in the Mediterranean, the Red Sea, Africa, and on the road to India? Would these agreements threaten Great Britain's naval supremacy in the Mediterranean? By January 1935, England increased her fleet in the *mare nostrum,* an indication of the cooling down of her relations with Italy.

However, as a whole British opinion was rather favorable to the Franco-Italian understanding. Against Germany, a friendly Italy was needed, and the Franco-Italian entente seemed to prepare an Anglo-Franco-Italian cooperation.

Litvinov and Titulescu were perplexed. Neither man could easily be duped. Litvinov, a veteran of all the disarmament discussions, had occupied since September 1934 the permanent seat of the Soviet Union in the League of Nations Council; he was its leading figure. Collective security never had a more determined and insightful advocate. Peace was indivisible, he had stated, which meant there would be no peace in the west if peace was not equally guaranteed in the east. In this, he was of one mind with Barthou. The too fragile Locarno front would break if a similar front did not hold in the east.

Nicholas Titulescu, strong man of the Little Entente, spoke for the Balkan

Entente, formed on February 9, 1934, by Rumania, Yugoslavia, Greece, and Turkey, with the strong encouragement of France and the USSR. It was formed to oppose the revisionist tendencies of Hungary and Bulgaria, which were backed by Hitler and Mussolini. Titulescu was aware of the role that Soviet Russia would be called upon to play on the international stage. But he had never lost touch with Italy, and he understood perfectly well the value of Mussolini's contribution to any Danubian stabilization.

Both Litvinov and Titulescu knew Laval. On the whole, they would have trusted Mussolini more, for his vital interests were at stake. What was the secret of the agreement between Laval and Mussolini? It could have been to make a negotiable offer and bargain directly with Hitler about the abandonment of the east. Such suspicions could not be dismissed. Barthou was no longer there to ensure caution in French policy. However, Litvinov and Titulescu had connections in Paris and powerful enough influence for Laval not to ignore it. Questioned and pressured, Laval promised that in his conversations with Germany he would not separate two closely tied questions: the adherence to the eastern and Danubian pacts, and the agreement on armaments.

From the first to the fourth of February, 1935, Flandin and Laval were in London to discuss the Franco-Italian agreements with England. Flandin was already known in London; he had impressive connections among those Englishmen already affected by persistent and subtle German propaganda. Lord Lothian, who had been Lloyd George's secretary, returning from Germany where he had seen Hitler, made his opinions public in the *Times* of February 1. English ruling circles had never been less inclined to join a league against Germany. In spite of everything about Germany which deeply offended the customs and upbringing of the British, she did claim to be the defender of order, that is to say, of the powerful interests which remain undivided by frontiers. In the city, the great cosmopolitan financial houses, related to or in partnership with the leaders of German trusts, asserted that they had never found more effective support than the support Germany was giving them now. As for public opinion, it was filled with a mystical passion for disarmament which influenced it in favor of a disarmed Germany and against a militaristic France.

But since 1934 France had been following a new, independent path: reconciliation with Italy, closer relations with the Soviet Union, plans for an eastern pact and a Danubian pact. Everything that had been set into motion by Barthou appeared on the way to realization. There was at work a force which could be neither ignored nor challenged. Consequently, the British let it be known that they saw with satisfaction the strengthening of the European balance of power through a powerful Franco-Italian scheme, having at its disposal sufficient military force to back its policy without having to ask Great Britain for more than a simple declaration of benevolent approval.

Ramsay MacDonald and John Simon were in conference with Flandin and Laval. Were their personal feelings as different as the policies they were trying to reconcile? Flandin, an Anglophile, felt perfectly at ease, but Laval could not adapt. Although he was shown much respect by the English, he felt rejected in spite of his social ascent; he could not endure the uneasiness very long. However, Flandin and Laval were not there to express their personal preferences. They had to return to Paris with a formal text confirming Laval's success in Rome.

His Majesty's government made no objections to the Rome agreements. It agreed to take part in the consultations caused by future threats to the independence and territorial integrity of Austria. It agreed to tie the abrogation of the disarmament clauses to a general settlement through which Germany would have to join in the Danubian and eastern pacts. It agreed to condemn any argument for unilateral repudiation of treaty obligations.

In addition, the British government contributed something of great importance for England in a field where she felt vulnerable: her air force was considered inferior to those of the Soviets, of France, of the United States, and of Italy. The British contribution consisted of a western air pact, whose signatories undertook to give the immediate assistance of their air forces to any among them who might be victim of an unprovoked air attack by any of the others. Italy, Germany, and Belgium would thus be asked to consider the possibility of negotiating without delay a pact aimed only at strengthening peace. In effect, this pact would be a Locarno of the air, but with a great difference: there were no longer any frontiers and no longer any distinction between the powers giving and those receiving guarantees. It would be a treaty of mutual assistance, protecting Great Britain as well as France. Sir John Simon wanted to discuss the news himself over the radio and insist on the point particularly sensitive for British opinion: the United Kingdom would enter into no commitment not already included in the Locarno Treaty. At a time when the development of the German air force was spreading fear, the air security of the British Isles would be ensured. Furthermore, such a collective pact would probably bring about an agreement on limitation, an agreement leading to parity.

This proposal, so natural and so reasonable, distorted the meaning of the London meetings, accentuating the imbalance between east and west, between the peace guaranteed by Locarno and the eastern instability. The new air pact was intended only for Western Europe. Still, the drafts brought from Rome and the British drafts were combined into a single communiqué, as if they formed a whole. The Italo-French formulas and the suggestions for a western air pact were listed one after the other. They all appeared linked, as indeed they had been meant to appear. It was thus suggested to the public at large that the entire communiqué had to be accepted or rejected as an indivisible whole.

Speaking to the Chamber on February 5, Flandin said nothing to dim such a resounding success. At most he admitted that, in order to accomplish the noble task of settling simultaneously disarmament and security, urgent reasons might demand proceeding by means of special conventions.

In reality it was a matter of, on the one hand, reinforcing the Locarno Pact, and, on the other hand, setting out adventurously in search of an eastern counterpart. Great Britain was firmly committed in the west; in the east, she persisted in contributing only her sympathy and good wishes.

Neither the Soviet Union nor the Little Entente could be satisfied with words alone. Would the French government not succumb to the ever-present temptation to get involved in negotiations with Germany? In the course of such negotiations, anything whose indivisible connection with the text of a communiqué was merely illusory would fall away like a sterile embellishment.

German Diplomacy

In 1935, Berlin led European diplomacy with a superior patience, moderation, and art. The segments of the circle Barthou had traced around Germany would fall, one after the other.

The German threat became dramatic. Hitler had triumphed on January 13, 1935, with the Saar plebiscite, which sealed the return of the Saar to Germany by 477,000 votes out of a total of 539,000. Such a large German majority made a tremendous impression. All things considered, a peoples' right to self-determination had been violated at Versailles, and the German wishes for revision now seemed justified.

French diplomacy had not used good judgment when it refused to renounce the plebiscite, as Germany, backed by Sir John Simon, asked at the end of 1933 and the beginning of 1934. How could the authors of the Versailles Treaty have claimed that the nationality of the Saar population was doubtful? The success of the plebiscite gave a greater freedom of action to Hitler, who declared that "only a madman would consider the possibility of a war with France." Recalling this phrase in his memoirs, Sir Robert Vansittart simply adds: "Now, Hitler was a madman." The settling of the Saar problem seemed to open an era of calm in Franco-German relations.

Engaged on the road to rearmament, the Führer no longer feared a preventive war, and, convinced of the infallibility of his gambles, he felt powerful enough to demand satisfaction of his claims. At the beginning of 1935, he seemed to believe that an agreement on armaments with Great Britain and France was possible. In the name of solidarity with the British government, French policy had discreetly distanced itself from the abrupt note of April 17, 1934. The shadow of Barthou was fading.

The Wilhelmstrasse seriously hoped to reach an understanding. The diplomatic corps, formed by Stresemann and not yet dominated by Ribbentrop's arrogant and brutal nature, conducted an extremely skillful campaign. Through a shrewd maneuver, it separated the two parts of the Franco-British communiqué sent to Berlin. That diplomatic document was not the coherent expression of two equally determined wills. One stroke was enough to separate them. As early as February 14, the German reply arrived in London; it distinguished between the two parts of the communiqué. It courteously acknowledged the first part—the Franco-Italian Treaty—as very interesting and requiring careful study, and reserved a most enthusiastic welcome for the second part; the settlement of such an air convention would mark a major step toward solidarity among the European states and toward the solution of many problems. But, in view of the vastness of the problems, why lose precious time by starting negotiations among so many parties? Would it not be better to clarify preliminary questions of principle first? The Germans thought the British government—as guarantor of Locarno and interpreter of the London conversations—perfectly suited for a preliminary exchange of views, and they invited the British ministers to come to Berlin on March 6.

The British accepted. German diplomacy therefore did not have to renounce its new principles of bilateral ethics or its free choice of partners.

A Soviet note let it be understood that the French had let themselves be fooled; Germany would now escape "encirclement," Barthou's concept of an eastern pact. The British ministers in Berlin were invited to continue their voyage from Berlin to Moscow.

London wanted to lessen the feeling that, since the indivisibility of the Franco-British communiqué had been broken, a direct negotiation with Berlin would bear only on the British proposals for an air pact. The coming meeting, said the English, would not single out one question by eliminating the others; on the contrary, it would occasion an exchange of views on all the points mentioned in the Franco-British declaration. London maintained that it followed clearly from the response of the German government that it intended also to undertake very extensive preliminary discussions.

Small but significant touches.

The speech given by Hitler on March 1, 1935, invoked optimism: "Let us hope that the return of the Saar to the Reich will definitely improve Franco-German relations" and that the two peoples will be able to "reach out to each other for the sake of the health of Europe." Optimism and hope soon disappeared.

While the British ministers prepared for their trip, scheduled for March 8 and 9, one of those unilateral repudiations which the French and the English had tried to prevent, suddenly took place. In London, the French and the English, using the terms of the Franco-Italian declaration, had announced solemnly that the three powers would consult immediately on how to meet such a unilateral action. Could a consultation result in resolve and action? The test was sudden and decisive.

The British government had decided before the conversations in Berlin that it was necessary to strengthen, before it was too late, a position that according to the experts was becoming dangerous. From 1920 to 1932, the labors of the Committee of Imperial Defense had been guided by one major principle: Great Britain would not risk becoming implicated in a major war. But the situation had changed since 1932; German rearmament could not be ignored. Baldwin would admit later that from 1932 to 1935 he had been informed of the danger. But, as long as the Disarmament Conference lasted, the pacifist currents in public opinion had such power that, if the government had announced that England had to rearm because Germany was rearming, the Conservative party would certainly have lost the elections. Such was Baldwin's confession.

The British defenses, in their precarious state, were much inferior to what the security of the empire demanded. To remain silent any longer meant to accept that their current level would be used as a basis for agreements, right from the beginning of the Berlin negotiations.

This deplorable situation would have continued indefinitely, if it had not been modified before the Berlin talks by planning the necessary measures. On March 4, a white paper was published in London. The white paper, giving the program for the new armaments expenditures and justifying them, cautiously indicated the concern caused by German military spending: the disturbing spirit which prevailed in Germany, especially among the young, was endangering peace. Great Britain was forced to modernize and increase her armaments. The white paper tried to demonstrate that unless there was an overall agreement, every country, even Great Britain, would be driven into an arms race.

It is difficult today to understand how far the British nation was led into error by her astonishing good faith. Far from awaiting the agreement of the other powers before rearming, Hitler had already taken such a lead that no fear of competition could stop him. His only worry now was to maintain and increase his lead. He knew well the state of British opinion; it was his best protection.

The white paper had hardly been published before the pacifist rebellion Baldwin had feared effectively covered the rear of the Nazi position, while the German press, unleashed, rejected with indignation "the slanders of the white paper." Labourites and Liberals violently blamed the government for violating the spirit of the League of Nations. Thirty years later, Eden would wonder what policy they would have followed, had they been in power in 1935. Would they have left England defenseless before Hitler's growing threat?

A Conservative faction also criticized the government vehemently. In the *Times* of March 11, Lord Lothian accused the white paper of using Hitler as a scapegoat and of making statements in the spirit of the *Diktat* of Versailles. The *Economist* called the white paper a "black paper." Some headlines from British papers offer striking examples of that criticism: Insult to Germany . . . , Repudiation of Whole Collective Security System . . . , Catastrophic Aggravation of Encirclement Fears for Germany . . . , Not the Voice of the British People . . . , Appease German Anger . . . , All the Fault of French Militarism, Insatiable Greed for Conquest, Rhineland Ambitions . . . , Threat Comes from France, British Government its Helot.

Thus spoke the men who, a few years later, would declare themselves irreconcilable enemies of Nazism. These waves of opinion left no trace once the storm calmed. Should they be erased from memory? They made a mark in this critical period, from 1935 to 1936, when Hitler's position could not have held out against a common thrust.

English opinion, so sincere that it appeared spontaneous, seemed possessed. For several years, long before Hitler, subtle German experts had been able to find the most generous, the most insular elements in the British soul. It is a futile effort to attempt to introduce foreign ideas among a people. The only possible way to act upon a people is through their national feelings, distorting or exaggerating natural feelings. The glorification of Locarno and the great waves of collective emotion related to the Disarmament Conference had imprinted strong images on the English consciousness: a disarmed Germany; hope for a world economic organization taking the initiative for a real peace; a bitterly militaristic France, hoarding all the gold on the planet and indifferent to the plague of unemployment; an England concerned about carrying out equitably her traditional mission of balance and peace.

The day following the publication of the white paper, France, worried over German armaments, decided to extend her military service to two years. The period of "the empty classes" was beginning. Frenchmen were asked to make an extra effort in order to compensate for the small number of young men and maintain the army's troop strength. The conscripts who would normally have been released were kept "provisionally" under the flag. The "two-year hitch" succeeded the "eighteen-month hitch," which had earlier replaced the one-year military service. No armament program was proposed. Let us note that this was the result of the state of mind induced in the French General Staff by its long defensive struggle during the Geneva disarmament discussions. France had been constantly criticized for her rich arsenals and powerful military materiel, which threatened peace. Every project and every plan at Geneva was aimed at reducing and destroying French armaments. These armaments had acquired such an inflated vlaue internationally that French military superiority was confirmed. No one seemed to suspect that the German armament plans would antiquate, at once, French arms and stocks, their distribution among the French army units, and the principles of their use.

Accidentally linked by their simultaneity, the English and French measures gave Hitler the most opportune chance to formulate, apparently in response to serious provocation, decisions he had made long before, which could no longer be realized under cover. His staging was excellent. On March 5, the British ministers he had invited to Berlin were informed that the Führer's throat required such care that he would not be able to receive them on the scheduled day. Diplomatic illness of course!

On Saturday, March 9, Goering notified the air attachés accredited in Berlin of the official organization of an air force. On Saturday, March 16, two months after the Saar's return to Germany, the "Law for the Building of the German Army" was published—a law the German ministers themselves learned about as a fait accompli. The one-year military service was established. It would be extended to two years in August 1936.

This represented clearly the formal abolition of the Treaty of Versailles military clauses. What would be the reaction of the English, the French, and the Italians, who had just declared any unilateral repudiation unacceptable and who had promised, if such a serious event took place, to consult each other immediately? The French and the Italians asked to meet at once. Mussolini defined his position by mobilizing, perhaps without any great illusions, two classes of conscripts. To a friend who had asked him if the western powers would allow Germany to rearm, he answered with a sardonic laugh and said: "In the democracies, will the parliaments agree to run the risk of a war because Germany manufactures too many cannon or aircraft? Besides, I don't think that England is very interested in European problems."

In the afternoon of Saturday, March 16, Neurath saw in succession the ambassadors of France, England, and Italy. He stated that Germany did not dream of attacking anyone and that she wished to live in peace with all nations.

Hitler put forward as pretexts Soviet armaments and the extension of military service passed in France despite leftist opposition.

Le Populaire, the official newspaper of the Socialist party, printed a special issue against the two-year service law. The Communists proclaimed: "Two-year service means war." On March 20, Léon Blum wrote: "Hitler has been able to justify Germany's rearmament to the German people because of the extension of military service in France."

In England and elsewhere, many politicians believed, in spite of Hitler's snubs, that the creation of the new German army amounted to a pressing invitation for general disarmament—as was stated in the *Daily Herald*. Faced with a systematic violation of the Versailles clauses, they could see only French disarmament as a countermeasure to German rearmament.

Hitler was convinced that there would be only "paper protests" from France and England.

He was struck by the forceful tone of the French note, which revealed plans of appealing to the League of Nations. The French government had also decided to send foreign minister Pierre Laval to Moscow, at Litvinov's invitation.

The English note was much more conciliatory. His Majesty's government also planned to appeal to the League of Nations, but, while protesting, it asked whether the German government was still disposed to receive the two ministers previously invited, "in the context of, and with a view toward, reaching the already determined objectives."

Hitler felt that Great Britain and France were not united. Suddenly the indignation betrayed by his bronchitis subsided. His throat improved and he announced that he would gladly meet with the English ministers, whose trip was set for March 25.

The British government had not consulted with France and Italy before replying to Berlin; mistrustful and angered, the two nations criticized an isolated act. It was "a gaffe," wrote Vansittart in his memoirs. England definitely wanted to play her hand alone. Eden would later admit that some British ministers, little inclined to join France and Italy, wanted to play the role of "honest brokers." Eden left for Paris, where the Italian Suvich joined him for a three-power talk. The French and the Italians had to be reassured that the forthcoming visit to Berlin was far from representing a British endorsement of German rearmament; it only aimed at gathering information.

Eden and Simon in Berlin

On March 25 and 26, Eden and Simon were in Berlin. Eden found Hitler definitely more authoritarian and less eager to please than the preceding year. He had seen him for the first time on February 20, 1934, calm, patient, and relatively conciliatory. "Hitler peacefully fixed upon me his slightly protuberant, greenish eyes," said Eden of that first meeting. This time, he was threatening in his hints and skillful in his evasions.

He declared that he would never have signed the Treaty of Versailles. He would rather have died, he exclaimed, fixing his gaze on Simon. Without the slightest smile, he recalled that once before Germany had been forced to violate a treaty—the treaty imposed by Napoleon on Prussia in 1806. On the eve of Waterloo, Wellington did not protest when the Prussian army arrived; yet Prussia had violated a treaty.

Hitler multiplied his complaints against the Treaty of Versailles, which had imposed on Germany a state of inferiority she never accepted. Eden, reminding him that Locarno had ended the idea of winners and losers, asked him whether the Locarno Pact could be separated from the Treaty of Versailles. Hitler maintained that Germany found herself in a position of inferiority on all points she had not rectified on her own. She was considered incapable of administering a colony, while Japan, who had withdrawn from the League of Nations, could administer the former German colonies.

In Berlin, the two English ministers were suddenly faced with something that had disappeared in Europe since the Ruhr evacuation: force, but this time a force unaffected by diplomatic or legal reasonings and indifferent to British prestige. Was this force already as firm as Hitler's self-assurance? For four years, confident in the fear he inspired, Hitler was able to take risks greater than his real means. The two British ministers saw him shatter the Franco-Italian plans like fragile illusions. He would never participate in an eastern pact. He also excluded a Danubian pact, but with more reserve and consideration for Mussolini. Ironically, he opposed any action in Austria by adopting the very formulas of the French and the Italians and using them in their most literal sense. He declared himself ready to conclude nonaggression pacts with his neighbors, even with Austria. Simon remarked that England wanted to maintain Austria's independence but without attaching as much importance to it as to Belgium's independence.

Hitler declared that he would complete his armament in total independence from France. All that Laval had brought from Rome to London was destroyed.

However, Hitler was much more receptive toward the proposal for an air pact. He saw in it a possibility deserving careful consideration. Air and sea constituted the domain of British security; he remained open to negotiations.

Simon asked Hitler what was the present size of the German air force. Hitler, without the slightest intonation of triumph in his voice, replied that parity with Great Britain had been reached. Eden thought that Hitler had exaggerated to make his power appear greater than it really was. In November 1936, in front of the Austrian foreign minister, Guido Schmidt, Hitler boasted that he had bluffed in order to intimidate the English ministers and lead them to conclude a naval agreement. In any event, the German air force would soon extend beyond parity with Great Britain.

A communiqué published by both the English and the Germans pointed out that "the ideas of the two parties have been completely examined in a most sincere and amicable fashion."

Hitler told his ministers that he had left the English in no doubt about his demands: an army of five hundred thousand men; air parity with Great Britain and also with France, whose air force was then the strongest; and a navy equivalent to 35 percent of the British navy.

The English ministers' visit in Berlin showed that it was impossible to hope for the conclusion of a general agreement on armaments. Simon himself, addressing Commons, spoke of "considerable differences of opinion which the Berlin talks have revealed." From then on, he judged Hitler correctly; he no longer had illusions about the man. In his diary he noted that Hitler was determined to follow his own path regarding disarmament, and that he did not dream of joining in collective security. He intended to reunite all Germans within the Reich, including the Austrians. Neverthless, a German delegation was invited to London to negotiate a naval agreement.

Eden, now on his way to Moscow, stopped in Warsaw. The Polish government was very self-satisfied. Two successive agreements—the first with the Soviet Union, the other with the Reich—had calmed all fears. Why disrupt that balance?

The agreement with Germany was particularly satisfying; nothing should be attempted which might compromise it. Already in 1934 Barthou had noticed the same attitudes.

As for the Soviet Union, she continued to believe firmly in collective security; only an armed coalition would stop Germany. Support from the Russians and the Italians might have limited Hitler's ambitions.

11

The Stresa Conference

Mussolini

From April 11 to April 14, 1935, the Stresa Conference—initiated by the Italians—was held on Lago Maggiore, in the exotic setting of the terraced gardens of the Isola Bella, wherein no one could enter except official delegates. Mussolini presided. The chameleon, wrote Vansittart, displayed his most vivid colors. Two Englishmen and two Frenchmen were at his side.

No one worried about the League of Nations. The real question was: would they form, against the German threat, the European front which Mussolini had attempted to organize since July 1934? The twin resolutions of Rome and London had already recorded a triple decision to look after Austria's independence and to oppose any future unilateral repudiation. Success seemed ensured.

But these were formulas, not men. The Englishmen and the Frenchmen surrounding Mussolini did not have the will to undertake any action, nor were they even aware that they ought to. Anthony Eden, physically taxed by his trip to Moscow, was unable to come with Prime Minister MacDonald, who was joined by the foreign secretary, Sir John Simon. They were both convinced that any project that Hitler would believe to be directed against him would inflame his irresistible fury against a threat of coalition. However they believed that a door remained ajar for Great Britain and wished that it not be closed.

They realized that since Hitler's plebiscite Germany was no longer that soft and fluid mass which, out of a traditional concern for European balance, they felt obliged to protect against French hegemony. Hitler had lost no opportunity to say or have someone say—to give assurance to English public opinion—that his attitude toward Great Britain had not changed. What he had written in *Mein Kampf* remained his lifelong conviction. Filled with respect for the British Empire, he only asked to stand by its side. Nazism considered the English as Nordic, as racial brothers.

In return, the English should now see Germany as she really was, see her true value: she was a great power which no longer resigned herself to the Versailles system. It was in the interest of all to erase the bad memories of the *Diktat.* In the future, there would be no more bondage to collective security, neither general nor regional. Germany would only agree to be bound by bilateral agreements. Hitler tried to persuade Great Britain to become the main link in his binary system. He had been successful with Poland. The old traditions of balance and arbitration, so dear to British diplomacy, could not have been dissolved by the Geneva methods of association. What would be the new European balance when the Soviet Union, now a member of the League of Nations, had regained the influence of the former Russian empire?

Since Barthou's death, moreover, the strict policy of balance of the Locarno Treaty was no longer unchangeable. France seemed to want to escape it. At the opening of the Stresa Conference, it had just been learned that the signing of a pact between France and the Soviet Union was imminent and that Laval was planning a visit to Moscow. Italy and Russia, two new trump cards which might open up a whole new game of European schemes.

Flandin and Laval, who did not care much for each other, had one thing in common: they would accept no risk of a war against Germany. In their opinion, any opposition to Hitler represented such a risk. After Rome and London, Stresa had to be a success for the government; in the series of statements outlining foreign policy, the conference which took place in the Borromean Islands would appear particularly brilliant.

But while Flandin gave much thought to his London friends, Laval, who certainly did not want to be anti-German, was already stirred by the Anglophobia which would inspire his actions—an Anglophobia he never dared to admit in the face of French opinion, and which, in November 1935, he sheepishly denied before Parliament. Was this Anglophobia artificially fostered by the intermediaries, emissaries and secret agents, whose company he preferred to that of the diplomats in his method of working through personal conversations? As Hitler had said to Rauschning: "The real work, the work which alone is of decisive importance, consists in becoming attached to important people, groups or parties, in foreign lands. . . . I create a zone of influence in a country. . . . In the coming war, I will reap the fruits of this underground labor."

MacDonald and Simon, Flandin and Laval

Perhaps Mussolini alone among all the ministers grouped under his presidency perceived in full clarity the reality of the German threat, now that Hitler, deferring any action in Poland, had turned toward Austria.

And his two allies, Austria and Hungary, drawn closer by the Rome protocols of March 1934, doubted that they and Italy alone could set up a strong enough barrier against Nazi Germany. They had tried to make Mussolini understand this and, with much reluctance, he himself had had to admit that it was so. King Alexander's death in October 1934 had not improved Italy's position in Yugoslavia; Germany was already taking advantage of it.

Three months after they were signed, the Franco-Italian agreements were submitted to the conference presided over by Mussolini. In London, they had been embellished by numerous additions; in the middle of these additions, the original text was almost intact, but it did not stand out. Lost in this composite whole, it no longer conveyed a simple, direct, and essential resolution. Could Hitler, so careful to measure others' wills, be fooled by it—in particular after his talks with the British ministers, who had rushed to Berlin immediately after the German repudiation of the agreements, and before the "immediate consultation," which had been postponed for a month, until the Stresa Conference?

His pride inflamed by the Brenner mobilization of July 1934, following the Dollfuss assassination, Mussolini felt very forceful toward Germany, and he wanted to reach an agreement with Great Britain and France regarding the precise limits on concessions to be made to Germany. If Germany violated one agreement after the other, she would attempt to absorb Austria, and that would mean war. He wanted to see how far the British ministers would go in their resistance to the Reich. Their trip to Berlin had made it clear that they did not wish to lose any chance of concluding with Germany the direct agreements whose foundations they were laying, and that they would not risk such agreements in a hazardous undertaking for collective security. They did not want to commit themselves to Austria, where they had no direct interests. On August 23, 1935, Lloyd George would even claim that MacDonald and Simon had committed an error in agreeing to support Mussolini over Austria, without demanding from him that he respect Ethiopian independence.

Before Stresa, Baldwin had declared: "It would have been preferable for us to remain out of it, but we are in Europe, whether we like it or not. Her dangers and her problems are ours." A few days before the Stresa Conference, an editorial in the London *Times* of April 4 hailed Hitler's declarations as "constructive suggestions," expressed great satisfaction in seeing the end of the Versailles mentality," and stated Great Britain's role, which ought to be a role of mediator. To the disappointment of the French, Sir John Simon had assured the House of Commons that the Conference would only have an exploratory character, which meant that no essential decision would be made without the Reich's agreement.

Mussolini therefore had very few illusions. The time when diplomatic notes could have contained Germany was past. Soon, when the formal protest, the only result of the "immediate consultation," was drawn up, Mussolini signed it with the same scorn Hitler assumed when he received it. Mussolini knew that in presence of the German threat, London preferred to negotiate directly with Berlin. He had just written in *Popolo d'Italia:* "No easy optimism. Stresa will not ensure peace. That depends on the missing parties: Germany, Russia, Poland. Stresa can only be a preliminary consultation. The only recourse for Italy is to maintain an army of six hundred thousand men, so long as there are clouds on the horizon."

Mussolini did not trust Flandin's and Laval's energy and noted the irresolution, the softness of the western democracies; they were not really planning to establish a common front against Germany, who, deferring all action against Poland, was threatening Austria and rearming frantically. Nothing could be done with the western democracies. Ready to capitulate, they had neither courage nor energy. Let a major war come, and they would be lucky not to be beaten to a pulp. What Vansittart called an "allergy to exertion" was common to both Great Britain and France.

Still, the French were not as irresolute as the English; but they did not dare make a move without England. Incited by the Italians, they had to convince the English of the need to act, lest England might come to think that France and Italy alone would be able to make Germany listen to reason. It was a good hand to play: France with the Little Entente and now the Soviet Union on one side; on the other, Italy with Austria and Hungary. The two temporary French ministers seated beside Mussolini did not carry much weight. In that year, 1935, they only did what the real masters of France wished. And these masters admired Mussolini and counted on him. Compared with the Marxism put into action by the Soviet Five-Year Plans, Mussolini, this creator of a realistic state without racism, reassured the restless. Why was France waiting to follow the Fascist example? A powerful press had already begun propaganda to place Mussolini in a position from which he would no longer have to negotiate; he would inspire.

A dangerous deviation. Mussolini no longer faced a cohesive, unassailable French state, which, supreme, could draw alliances to benefit her own national policy. He had gained in France important supporters who, to the disadvantage of French internal unity, would follow him without a word, even in measures most opposed to French interests. This reversal of relations—a dangerous game—would become one of the principal causes of the growing weakness of France vis-à-vis Germany. Moreover, the influential promoters of this admiration for Mussolini allowed it only for their domestic policy. As much as the English and for the same reasons, they were hostile to any struggle against Hitler.

This lengthy introspection over the Stresa Conference is not a useless digression, but an attempt to find its deepest meaning. For it was there that Barthou's projects, aimed at restoring a European balance of collective security, stumbled.

Mussolini's Energy; British Hesitations

After the Stresa Conference, new suspicions, new quarrels divided more deeply the three participants; only Hitler, careful observer, would benefit from it.

Mussolini had shown great willpower in the discussions. He felt the time had come to arm the Austrians, Hungarians, and Bulgarians, and for all to stand ready for action. This was a good occasion to reconcile and join the French and Italian forces. Barthou would have wanted to attempt such action, which seemed to have serious chances of success. But for men who wanted to avoid every risk of coalition, the supposed objections of the Little Entente offered an effective preliminary problem.

Sir John Simon had given an account of his talk with Hitler, whose own aversion to adhering to collective agreements extended to those negotiated without him. If this was the case, nothing could be accomplished at Stresa. Hitler, absent, dominated the conference.

The British minister contacted Berlin to consult Hitler on behalf of the conference. He asked Hitler's opinion on the signing of the agreements— almost his authorization. Would the eventual acceptance of an air pact by Berlin exclude all negotiations of mutual assistance among the other nations?

Hitler's answer was that, in principle, he disapproved of such agreements, which implied insulting suspicions about nations' respect of their voluntary obligations. However, he would not place on them any absolute condition.

Hitler was very careful to take into consideration the prestige of Mussolini, who had to be spared the failure of his conference. And perhaps he feared a coalition enough not to run the risk, however unlikely, of provoking it by an abrupt refusal.

The conference then agreed on a communiqué, which gathered, like a bouquet of faded flowers, the London proposals of February and expressed regret—Platonic regret—over the "unilateral German maneuvers." "Words, words, words!" wrote Vansittart.

The British ministers agreed to recognize, as a maximum, that the need to maintain Austria's integrity and independence ought to guide the joint policy of the three governments, who should declare themselves ready "to oppose by every appropriate means the unilateral repudiation of treaties; an action liable to endanger the peace of Europe." But they refused to commit themselves, although, in June, the Franco-Italian agreements actively urged by the two general staffs made provisions to send an Italian army corps into the Belfort region and a French army corps into the Trieste region in the event of conflict.

The British ministers were in agreement on an early meeting of a conference of all the governments included in the Rome protocols, for the purpose of concluding an agreement for Central Europe.

But when Ramsay MacDonald announced on May 2 that Italy was planning to convene such a conference, he made it quite clear that no new commitment would be made in this area, by specifying that His Majesty's government would only send an observer.

The French delegation proposed a memorandum on the German conscription law, to be submitted to the League of Nations Council, in an attempt to hide from public opinion the easy and resigned acceptance of a major violation of Part 5 of the Versailles Treaty. During the entire Disarmament Conference, the French government had indeed persisted in refusing a contractual abrogation, unless Germany agreed to both the conditions and the temporary regime prescribed by France.

To strengthen its declaration, the French delegation wanted to propose the application of sanctions in case of future treaty violations. However, the sanctions decreed by the pact were applicable only if a League member illegally resorted to war. Until now no one had dared to make use of them. To extend the sanctions to treaty violations would have required a unanimous vote by all League members, followed by the ratification of all governments involved. So it was just a bluff; the first attempt at a maneuver which would be renewed in 1936. Naturally the British ministers did not accept the French proposal. When the *Times* announced the refusal, it did not fail to explain it—and this six months before certain sanctions would be applied to Italy: "The whole question of economic retaliation is much more complicated than France seems to believe. Precipitously to adopt them, only to follow by withdrawing them if they have a boomerang effect, would only weaken the position of the powers wishing to employ them."

Let us note that, during its ordinary session, the League of Nations Council endorsed the resolution proposed by France, Great Britain, and Italy. On

April 17 the Council declared that, by violating Part 5 of the peace treaty, Germany had "failed in the duty" incumbent upon all members of the international community. The Council condemned the proclamation of Germany's military law as an attack on the peace treaty. It invited the interested governments to continue the negotiations begun in February, and it suggested a commission to propose measures to be taken in the future when a state endangered the peace by a unilateral repudiation of commitments. The German measures were accepted as a fait accompli; Hitler triumphed. He did not take seriously the warnings from Geneva, although they were unanimous except for Denmark's very cautious abstention.

The great powers were incapable of imposing respect for the treaties they had signed and of preventing their violation through their own means. In allowing itself to be reduced to a mere recording room where the great powers protested, the League of Nations Council accepted a substantial loss of its own authority.

For some time after the spring days spent at Lago Maggiore, people spoke of the "Stresa front," organized against the Nazi threat. It was well received in France, even by the Left, as "an additional barricade raised against the ambitions of Hitlerism."

Rather than a "front," it was a decorative frontispiece: three groups, going in three directions, stopped as their paths crossed and bowed courteously. There was no resolve to form in a common march toward a common goal.

What they had kept silent at Stresa, in regard to Ethiopia, became immediately much more important than what they had said.

This totally negative conference of Stresa was the last attempt to consolidate the weakest part of Europe, the region to the east and to the south of Germany. It was the only chance France, Italy, and the Soviet Union had to undertake a common task, the long and patient search for stable security and an economic organization. Great Britain, faithful to her unchanging policy since 1919, did not want to seize that chance. Moreover, she was not asked to take on new obligations but only to act in a favorable way: to stop her private negotiations with Hitler, which came to an end only with the declaration of war in September 1939.

Without anyone realizing it, it was at Stresa that Eastern Europe was abandoned; not giving it a collective framework was the equivalent of abandonment.

12

The Franco-Soviet Accord

Laval had found the Russian card in Barthou's hand, Barthou, his predecessor, who did not fail to see the unfortunately irreconcilable character of the contradictions opposing France and Hitler's Germany. Laval played that card haltingly; he played it badly; and, finally, he ripped it up.

The Protocol of December 1934

Poland and Germany had refused, with England's secret support, to take part in any pact for Eastern Europe which would have strengthened the security of France and her European allies. After the fruitless attempt, France had to be satisfied with the conclusion of a mutual assistance pact with the Soviet Union, whose political, economic, and military power was undeniable. Such an association was not dictated by present circumstances, but by the vital interests of France.

It seemed that Laval, prodded by Herriot, who was highly satisfied to see him "so happily transformed," had accepted Barthou's policy toward the Soviets. In Geneva, on December 5, 1934, Laval signed a protocol with Litvinov: the two powers agreed not to conclude any pact which might jeopardize the eastern pact.

The Franco-Soviet treaty was signed in Paris on May 2, 1935, by Laval and Ambassador Potemkin. The treaty referred to the Covenant: the two nations agreed to consult one another in the event of aggression by a European state and to discuss the measures to be taken against the aggressor, who would be recognized as an aggressor if he resorted to war in violation of Articles 12, 13, and 15 of the League of Nations Covenant. The two nations also agreed to any mutual assistance recommended by the League Council.

Barthou could not have hoped for better formulas. As he would have wished himself, the agreement was signed only in the expectation of a larger treaty among the eastern powers.

The Franco-Soviet pact had been expected, but it was still a great event. It seemed to satisfy the highest military authorities; it was to be supplemented by General Staff arrangements, without being followed by any secret military convention. Two weeks later, a similar treaty between the Soviet Union and the Czechoslovak Republic—quite favorable to a Franco-Soviet alliance—laid a second building block for a more extensive eastern treaty.

The reactions were immediate: acute Polish worries, a speech by Hitler, and a German legal memorandum intended to demonstrate the incompatibility between the Locarno Treaty and a new Franco-Russian alliance. Such times call for quick and forceful action; the treaty, excellent in itself, was less valuable for its legal content than for the political blow struck in the east against Hitler's system of bilateral treaties, a system signifying one thing: a free hand in the east for Germany.

Meanwhile Berlin, remaining calm and making use of reasonable and plausible arguments, was conducting an intensive diplomatic campaign.

Laval in Moscow

In the indeterminate events of history, chance is not the only ruler. It did however intervene while Laval was traveling to Moscow. When the French minister stopped in Warsaw to visit Beck, Pilsudski, who had had one obvious stroke if not several and had been ill for months, was dying.

From May 13 to May 15, Laval was received as a friend at the Kremlin. He was greatly impressed by Stalin and asked him to approve the defensive policy practiced in France. He proposed a communiqué which was instantly approved by Stalin: "Mr. Stalin understands and approves fully the policy of national defense undertaken by France to maintain armed forces adequate for her security."

When it was published in France, this sensational communiqué provoked enthusiasm and admiration for the subtle skillfulness of Laval, who thus triumphed over the objections of the extreme Left to the extension of military service. It astounded the Communists, whose allegiance to Moscow Laval had recognized, having obtained a formal change of party line from Stalin. Later it would be maintained that the consequences of this order to the French Communists were, with regard to the May elections of 1936, to reinforce their party by reassuring the electorate of their patriotism, and, especially, singularly to facilitate the formation of a Popular Front; the obstacles to an agreement with the Radicals had been removed. Since the Communists had become patriots and could no longer be accused of hindering the national defense, Édouard Daladier would raise his fist in company of Communist party leader Thorez, on July 14, 1935, at the impressive demonstration at the Bastille, although the "war between the two Édouards" was at its height among the divided Radicals (Édouard Herriot was then a minister in Laval's cabinet).

Laval in Kracow

After visiting the Kremlin, Laval went to Kracow to attend funeral services in the royal church of Wavel for Pilsudski, who had died on May 12. Goering was there, representing Hitler. He was often entrusted with such missions abroad, and he gave them all the weight of his personality. Laval and Goering met and spoke for several hours at the Hotel de France; "a moving conversation," Laval would later say. At the funeral services for King Alexander of Yugoslavia, Goering had already told the journalist Ward Price: "We deplore the abominable crime which so tragically ended the life of M. Barthou. Nonetheless, we cannot help but hope that his policy toward Germany will disappear along with him. We are confident that M. Laval will adopt a more conciliatory attitude toward us."

This time he would make the statement to Laval himself, probably with elaborations and arguments: Hitler's mistrust of collective security, the Bolshevik threat, the Communist thrust in France . . . Why choose Stalin over Hitler, who only wished for a good understanding with France? And why burn irremediably all bridges with Germany? Laval was already convinced that, for financial reasons, Germany would not be able to continue rearming for long.

The results of the Kracow meeting were immediate.

The Franco-Soviet treaty, at once ratified by Moscow, could also have been ratified without delay by the president of the Republic, Lebrun; since it included neither the yielding of territory nor economic provisions, it did not have to be submitted to Parliament. The French head of state could exchange ratifications immediately with the Russian head of state; his signature was sufficient.

Although Laval used Italian cooperation to the fullest, he did not want to bring pressure for ratification of the pact already concluded with the Soviets and ratified by them. He decided to submit it to Parliament for approval. Cleverly abandoned to the delays of passages from committee to committee, the pact was put on ice. It was urgent to wait, to seek shelter behind a parliamentary procedure useless in itself; perhaps an understanding with the Reich was possible. According to Vansittart, Laval's main objective when he signed the treaty with Moscow was to have Germany seek a rapprochement with France. After all, it seemed perhaps wiser not to ratify the pact at all. Its very sequestration was a sign of complacency and weakness, and it brought on Laval the unchangeable mistrust of the Soviets. In his *Histoire de la diplomatie,* Ambassador Potemkin blamed Laval's political allies for having done everything possible to give the pact a purely formal character and to avoid tying France automatically to the Soviets. He asserted that Laval wanted to annihilate the pact. In the French Communist paper *L'Humanité,* Gabriel Péri violently declared: We have to get rid of Laval.

French Doubts about Russia

If many Frenchmen of diverse political shadings declared themselves in favor of the pact, some influential groups campaigned against any alliance with the USSR. It seemed certain that Germany would go to the east to find her "living space"—Hitler never stopped proclaiming so. Between Germanism and Slavism there was unyielding antagonism. Let the Russian bear and the German wolf come to grips! Then we shall see, said the French. Attacked by the Right, the pact had been torn to pieces before being ratified; it was no more than "a scrap of paper." Some people claimed that the Russians wanted to cause the other nations to make war, to provoke a Franco-German conflagration and then to appear as a thief to reap the fruits of her intrigues. Laval said to his intimates: "The Soviets want a treaty to make war, and I to avoid it. Germany will make war, and I do not want my country dragged into it."

The Russians wanted the diplomatic pact to become a military alliance and intended to begin General Staff talks. But French military men were divided. The value of the Red Army's cooperation and aid was discussed extensively, although the strength of their air force was recognized. General Maurin, defense minister under Flandin and later under Sarraut, maintained that an alliance with the Soviets offered no military advantage. Weygand opposed it. General Schweisguth, chief of the military mission sent to the Russian maneuvers of September 1936, declared that the USSR hoped that the storm would break over France; a Franco-German war would make the Soviet Union the arbiter of the situation in the face of an exhausted Europe.

Devastating purges raged throughout the Soviet Union. Since 1934 these extremely violent "purges" had been fighting any "deviationism" with sinister trials, where the accused proclaimed their degradation and celebrated their executioners.

In 1937, the massive disappearance of high officers, including Tukhachevsky, who was considered the most likely wartime supreme commander, seemed to ruin the Red Army. Like the French, Hitler had no respect for the Red Army. Most of the military experts thought it would only be useful for defense, where Russian soldiers had always shown a courageous tenacity.

Colonel Jean Fabry, Laval's defense minister, was convinced that Russia wanted the war. According to him, Ambassador Potemkin had said: "Soviet Russia emerged from the last war, and a Soviet Europe will emerge from the next."

Stimulated by Hitler's propaganda, anti-Communist propaganda was raging. It divided public opinion in France as in England. It affected the vital interests of the financiers and the industrialists who controlled politics, and who suddenly became greatly worried by the widespread economic crisis and also by the relative success of the Soviet Five-Year Plans.

Deprived of any positive quality, the Soviet pact no longer counted among the tools of French diplomacy. On March 7, 1936, Hitler would use it as a pretext to send his troops into the Rhineland, when the French could not ask Russia for her cooperation.

13

The Anglo-German Naval Agreement

Baldwin, Prime Minister;
Sir Samuel Hoare, Foreign Minister

It was in June 1935 that the "Stresa front" was definitively dislocated by a fierce Anglophobia; a month earlier, the Franco-Russian treaty, in the process of being negotiated in Kracow, had been instantly rendered ineffectual. The policy of Lago Maggiore had been totally dismantled.

The Anglo-German naval agreement represented one of the first acts of the cabinet of which Stanley Baldwin became leader on June 7, 1935, though he had actually been the real prime minister since 1931. MacDonald's health and his increasingly vague and confused ideas no longer allowed him to bear the responsibilities of his position.

One of Baldwin's trusted supporters, the Conservative Samuel Hoare—who would become Lord Templewood—had replaced the Liberal Sir John Simon as head of the Foreign Office, leaving Simon to take the interior ministry. After three and a half years as foreign minister, Simon, an incomparable lawyer, was in favor neither with the opposition nor with influential Conservative circles, which reproached him for his constant indecision. His extremely mobile, brilliant, and analytical mind despised making decisions and always found, in nuances, an ingenious reason to avoid any action. More inclined to appeal to his colleagues to choose a policy than to defend his own, he could see so clearly any imperfection in a policy that he constantly hedged. An overly penetrating judgment and too fragile convictions provoked confusion.

The Labourite Zilliacus recognized the great sincerity in the government's desire to see the lion lie down with the lamb; but, he noted, the government was not too sure if the lamb ought to be outside the lion or inside it.

While minister for India, for which he had established a constitution, Hoare had gained a reputation for being astute but weak in his opinions, and Colonel Beck did not consider him Francophile. The naval agreement, "a gaff of the first rank" according to Vansittart, was explained by Hoare's haste and especially by the Admiralty's haste to make progress. The Foreign Office doubted that Hitler was planning to keep his commitments, but it still wanted to hold a piece of paper that would contain and delay him for a while. It was certainly a very small advantage, but better than nothing.

The Anglo-German Naval Agreement of June 18, 1935

Immediately after Stresa, Germany felt encircled and isolated. Ambassador François-Poncet noted a significant wavering in Berlin and observed that the Nazis had never been so "dispirited and discouraged." Hitler, impressed by the threat of the "Stresa front," seemed inclined to direct his policy, at least for the moment, toward a European understanding. On May 21 he delivered a conciliatory speech to the *Reichstag*—a speech labeled "constructive" by the British Labour party. He declared himself ready to participate in a system of collective cooperation in order to ensure European peace, to sign nonaggression pacts with each of the neighboring states, to ban the use of certain arms and the bombing of civilian populations. After the return of the Saar, he had no territorial claims to state against France.

Naturally he could reduce his armaments only if the other nations reduced theirs. He would join an air pact to supplement the Locarno Pact. He would agree to limit the German war fleet to 35 percent of the British fleet's tonnage—a ratio he had already suggested to London in November 1934.

Naval rivalry had been the main cause of the tension existing in Anglo-German relations before 1914. A German war fleet was a direct threat to England. Since the English ministers' visit to Berlin, exchanges on that question had never stopped.

On May 2, Prime Minister Ramsay MacDonald announced that the Anglo-German naval talks would soon begin. Ribbentrop, Hitler's special envoy, had arrived in London to inform the British of the conditions established for the definitive and permanent limitation of the German fleet: 35 percent of the British Commonwealth's surface fleet tonnage. For submarines, forbidden by the Treaty of Versailles, a ratio of 45 percent was allowed; it could be extended to 60 percent by agreement with Great Britain, with the assurance that, in the event of war, the Germans would not use submarines against merchant vessels; the submarine ratio could even rise to 100 percent if other powers upset, with their own building programs, the balance of naval forces throughout the world.

Germany, who was busy constructing a formidable war machine on land and in the air, could not even dream of immediately rebuilding a very large fleet. More flexible than in the days of Tirpitz, Germany knew it was in her interest to calm British anxiety; and, in any case, the freedom of action she had gained for several years by quadrupling her fleet allowed her to ensure her shipyards a high level of productivity.

All that remained was to transcribe Hitler's decisions into a technical treaty, to which the United States and Japan—signatories of the Washington Naval Treaty—would give their approval. Former chancellor and now ambassador Hans Luther claimed that, in the United States, the treaty was considered as opening the way to the abolition of world wars and a lasting peace.

On June 14, when the treaty was ready to be signed, London informed Paris and Rome. Would they agree to have Great Britain sign a naval treaty with Germany? On June 15 and 17 they answered negatively; nothing could be done without the agreement of all interested parties.

On June 18 the treaty was signed. The result was well worth the trouble taken by German diplomacy. In France and Italy, an anti-British storm erupted. It was certainly not spontaneous; it had been well prepared. But this explosion of discontent was significant only because it was swelled by a sincere indignation. Within only six weeks the fragile Stresa agreement had evaporated. The French and the Italians, ready to unite against Germany, had simultaneously been turned against the British government, now dealing separately with Berlin without consulting them. To mark the one hundred and twentieth anniversary of Waterloo, there was an outburst of indignation.

French Irritation; Eden in Paris

England's action represented more than a simple balancing maneuver. She had thrown overboard the naval clauses of the Versailles Treaty, without bothering to ask for the other signatories' consent. England became a link in Germany's chain of bilateral agreements, which opposed the chain of collective security Barthou had wanted to lay around Germany; the bilateral treaty of June 1935 represented an enormous success for Berlin.

Without any reference to the League of Nations, important clauses of the Treaty of Versailles had been purely and simply abolished, and German rearmament had been authorized, although the League of Nations was protesting against unilateral violations of the treaty and considering measures to be taken against them.

For Hitler, this was even a greater success than the pact of January 1934 which had diverted Poland from her alliance with France. According to Ribbentrop, whose prestige was enormously increased, Hitler declared: "This is the best day of my life." He had proof that the entente between Great Britain and France was weak. He would certainly run no risk in occupying the demilitarized Rhineland zone. From one month to the next, Germany's situation was completely reversed; the contrast was startling. The joy was total. All threat of encirclement had vanished. Germany, who already had an air force and an army, would soon have a fleet.

Now that England was in possession of a naval pact ensuring her a much better fleet ratio with Germany than in 1914, she was eager to reach an air pact. Such a pact, wrote German ambassador Hoesch on August 15, 1935, would erase the feelings of anxiety and fear now troubling the British masses. Sir Samuel Hoare, who had been aviation minister for seven years, was particularly insistent upon it. Was it not true to the policy symbolized by the naval agreement? But his hopes were disappointed. Germany was not eager to see the progress of negotiations toward an agreement which could not be strictly bilateral, in view of the modest position occupied then by the British and German air forces; the pact would have to be a collective pact. Germany declared that the Franco-Soviet agreement hindered the conclusion of an air pact.

The possibility of a Danubian pact quickly grew fainter. The Little Entente was irremediably divided. In Austria, Schuschnigg was weakening. The Germans' satisfaction was increased by the prospect of an Italo-Ethiopian war, which would keep Mussolini away from the Brenner frontier.

Laval immediately expressed the strongest indignation over the naval pact. He had not been too surprised. He did not become anti-British suddenly on that day. Among his closest friends was Fernand de Brinon, who had been received by Hitler and who, since he had publicized interviews in which Hitler offered his friendship to France, had become an informal emissary as well as a disseminator of anti-British animosity. The June 18 treaty gave Laval a plausible pretext to make this animosity explode. Without committing himself in a public speech, through his remarks and attitudes he encouraged a violently Anglophobe press which deeply disturbed the French. All the events which had taken place since 1919 unfortunately provided abundant material to be exploited. Experience had shown that it was impossible to be at once anti-German and anti-British, and that by agreeing to become anti-British one automatically stopped being anti-German. The

French did not really want to love the Germans under Hitler, but they were capable of hating the English, and their distaste for the English was easily transformed into Germanophile tendencies.

On July 3, 1935, the Polish undersecretary for foreign affairs, Szembek, remarked that France had never been as irritated as after the Anglo-German naval agreement. To smooth her feathers, England sent her "most seductive minister," Anthony Eden, who, instead of giving a barefaced denial, admitted with embarrassment that the British government had not acted as it should.

The English claimed that when faced with the failure of collective disarmament—a failure largely attributable to France—they had been forced to reach with Germany an agreement which, by limiting armaments in a sphere essential to their security, recognized their naval supremacy. Moreover they had not appreciated in the least the pact Laval had signed in Moscow on May 15, and their naval pact seemed to say that what is sauce for the goose is sauce for the gander. In both cases, the English pleaded their need for security.

In England, Soviet propaganda stirred much worry and anger. Eden observed that, compared to Communism, Hitlerism appeared the lesser evil to many Conservatives, even to some ministers, especially the oldest. The Labourites saw the Franco-Soviet pact as a threat to peace; this threat increased their desire for an understanding with Germany. Simon had even demanded that the application of the Franco-Soviet pact be subordinated to the Locarno Treaty; thus, if the *casus foederis* existed between France and the Soviets, the power of decision would rest with England and Italy.

Eden noted in his memoirs that two basic conceptions divided the cabinet: some, adopting a religious point of view, saw Communism as the Antichrist; others felt that one could eat with the devil, but doubted that he had anything good to offer. Nearly everyone in Great Britain believed that the Soviets' military power was very mediocre. Ambassador Hoesch, who had won the trusting friendship of the Prince of Wales, gave accounts of his confidences to Berlin. The Prince disapproved of the Germanophobia of the Foreign Office, where influential people understood fully France's need for security.

Russia's mistrust of England was increased by an agreement which considerably strengthened the German Baltic fleet.

Franco-British Differences over Yugoslavia

Laval was finally convinced of England's responsibility by an occurrence he considered extremely important. Yugoslav prime minister Yevtić was planning to come to Paris to erase the stains of the blood shed six months earlier in Marseilles before his own eyes. Everything was ready for the conclusion of a Franco-Yugoslav Mediterranean pact. On May 13, Yevtić expressed his desire to come to Paris in June. He was eager to strengthen the détente between his country and Italy. The news of his trip was to remain secret. On May 31, Laval informed him that he was expecting him for June 24 and 25; Yevtić would have lunch at the Élysée with the president of the Republic on June 24. The instructions Yevtić gave for his trip to Paris, now delayed by a few days, prove that he intended to direct the planning. On June 17, Laval made him informed that June 26 and 27 were suitable dates. The president of the Republic, Albert Lebrun, would receive Yevtić for lunch on June 27. On June 18, the chief of diplomatic protocol, M. de Fouquières, asked if Mrs. Yevtić would come to Paris, and who else would accompany the prime minister. On June 20, Yevtić accepted Lebrun's invitation; he would leave on June 24 and spend a few hours in Venice with the Italian undersecretary for foreign affairs, Suvich.

But on June 21, Yevtić expressed his regret at not being able to come to Paris. On June 23, Stojadinović replaced him at the head of the government, as foreign minister and prime minister. "At heart, he is not so well disposed toward us as Yevtić," observed the French minister, who pointed out in him "an excessive tolerance for everything German."

In Bucharest, Titulescu was troubled by this change in Yugoslav politics; he did not trust the unscrupulous financier Stojadinović. Germany, on the contrary, placed great hopes in him. Had he not studied in Germany? In the Vatican, his German sympathies were noted and the *Osservatore Romano* felt that Yevtić's departure might hurt Yugoslav friendship toward France. As for Stojadinović, he hastened to assure Laval of his "unblemished devotion to the great revolutionary and republican nation which is our friend and our ally." To the French minister and to the French press agency representative, he expressed a most ardent Francophilia and he promised "a close and constant cooperation" in all areas. In reality, he would soon draw Yugoslavia away from the Little Entente and bring it closer to Hitler.

This Yugoslav crisis, which took place when Ethiopia had become a burning issue, exasperated Laval. Although Titulescu attributed the crisis to a trip Goering had just made to Yugoslavia, Laval saw it as a nasty maneuver by England, to whom the Yugoslav regent, Prince Paul, refused nothing. Vansittart, who had seen the Prince at that time and received a book of poems from him, was the most Francophile of the Foreign Office diplomats. But he himself felt that it would be impossible to cooperate with Laval, of whom he said: "Lying is as natural for him as breathing."

Mussolini's Anger

Mussolini had been disappointed, then irritated by the results of Stresa. He alone had wanted to act against the German threat; he had met only with courteous indifference. More totally alone against Hitler than in July 1934, he felt that he had been deceived. The British press was attacking his African ambitions, which Ramsay MacDonald and Simon had ignored at Stresa. The signing of the separate treaty of June 18, coming so soon after Stresa's vain ritual condemning all unilateral repudiation of Versailles, provoked Mussolini's anger. For thirteen years he had fought in international conferences—with the backing of the English Admiralty—to gain parity with the French fleet in the Mediterranean; but suddenly, through England's own volition, Germany was not only freed of the legal bonds of Versailles but also acquired the right to a high naval tonnage.

Mussolini did not fall back so that he could choose his next move; instead, he adopted an attitude of defiance and threats. In his outbursts of violence, he became more a journalist than a head of government. He flared up with a spiteful energy; his polemics became his policies. His colonial expedition changed into a Roman struggle against foreign dominance in the Mediterranean. Neither Laval nor anyone else ventured to calm him. The more the anti-British demonstrations in France turned toward Fascism, the more his pride and his Roman rage were exacerbated. Around him, as around Laval, a few sly intimates carefully poisoned the wounds.

At Stresa Mussolini had been the direct adversary of Hitler, the only opponent capable of willpower and action; but never had the Germans lacked patience and respect for him. Hitler was biding his time, waiting for the day when Mussolini would be distracted from the European front. For the moment, because of his attraction to Africa, Mussolini was anti-English—a major step.

Meanwhile Germany was quietly continuing her military preparation. On June 26, 1935, compulsory labor service was introduced: for six months all young Germans had to take part in public works—roads, land improvement, construction, and so forth—and, at the same time, follow a physical exercise program—undertake military training. On October 15, 1935, the War Academy, expressly forbidden by the Treaty of Versailles, was solemnly opened in Hitler's presence. On November 7, 1935, 590,000 recruits began their service.

14

The Ethiopian Affair

Already the whole European situation was in an upheaval over the Ethiopian affair; in this troubled year, 1935, it served as a backdrop for international relations. As the German ambassador von Hassel wrote on June 21: "Italy's foreign policy is completely dominated by the Ethiopian question, to which every other international problem is so subordinated that relations between Italy and the European great powers are viewed in the perspective of those powers' attitudes toward Ethiopia."

The Ethiopian affair played a fundamental role in the origins of the Second World War. Acting as a poison for Europe, it lead to disastrous complications.

The kingdom of Ethiopia, encircled by Islamic states, had remained Christian and had lived on, slowly decaying. The Ethiopian chief, Menelik, had assembled the fragments of a medieval state, had conquered neighboring populations, and in 1896 had defeated the Italians, who had tried to impose their protectorate. By playing off the English, the French, and the Italians against one another, he alone had succeeded, in an almost entirely conquered Africa, in safeguarding his independence. In December 1906, his three neighbors had neutralized each other's ambitions by recognizing Ethiopia's territorial integrity; but they had divided Ethiopia into three zones of influence without worrying about Menelik's opinion. When he died in 1909, anarchy had reappeared, with feudal rivalries and rebellions led by the major chieftains, the *ras.*

After the First World War, a passionate press campaign had roused England against Ethiopian barbarism. Articles appearing at that time in the *Westminster Gazette* and in the magazine *West Africa* would fuel the Italian press in 1935.

In 1922, Sir Arthur Steel Maitland, New Zealand's delegate to the League of Nations, raised the question of slavery before the League Assembly. The Council was asked to gather information. An official English Document, *Correspondence Respecting Slavery in Abyssinia,* was the principal source of the report presented by the secretary general, Sir Eric Drummond. On July 5, 1923, the Council decided to continue the investigation.

The London press suggested that Ethiopia should be assisted in the planning of internal reforms and in the repression of slave traffic by an experienced administrator such as Lord Lugard, the real builder of Nigeria. In *West Africa,* Sir Sidney Oliver recommended an economic boycott which, if she resisted, would bend Ethiopia to England's will. In the House of Lords on July 30, 1923, the foreign minister, Lord Curzon, delivered harsh reproaches to the Ethiopian government.

Admission to the League

Suddenly, in October 1923, while the report on slavery was being submitted to the Assembly, *ras* Taffari, nephew of Menelik and regent, requested that Ethiopia be admitted to the League of Nations, creating a paradoxical situation. Having to choose between two contradictory solutions, the Assembly adopted the least plausible one: Ethiopia became a member of the League of Nations. Yet this state could not, at that time, meet any of the three conditions stipulated by the Covenant. Her frontiers were not defined; her government, unstable until then, did not exercise full authority; and, finally, Ethiopia could not give effective guarantees of her sincere intention to fulfill international obligations.

This decision, carried off by the French with the Italians' help and against British reservations, created extreme anomalies. Egypt was able to gain English support for her candidacy only in 1937. Several nations under League mandates had moral claims far superior to those of Ethiopia. When Iraq's turn came in 1932, the conditions established by the Mandate Commission for granting independence were much stricter than those used for Ethiopia. The League had given credit to *ras* Taffari and to his modernization projects.

What would henceforth be the fate of a country that was unable to find within itself the autonomous impulse to emerge in one leap from centuries of barbarism and chaos? Very ancient traditions posed a serious internal barrier to change. In granting it the title of member state, the League of Nations had done nothing to give it the means to reach the rank of a civilized state. Moreover, at this time the category of countries under mandate appeared rigorously defined by the strict terms of the Covenant, and the experiments in international development assistance, which would later be pursued in other countries, had not yet begun.

After her entry at Geneva, as before, Ethiopia remained surrounded by three signatories of the 1906 treaty. Their relations of mutual trust varied; in turn, each one restrained the others.

In 1919, invoking Article 13 of the treaty of April 26, 1913, Italy had asked Great Britain's good offices in backing her for the concession of a railroad linking Eritrea with the Somalian coast; this would pass to the west of Addis Ababa, across the zone, demarcated in 1906, where Italy had exclusive economic influence. In exchange, London could count on Italy's good offices for their construction of a road in the Italian zone, from the Sudan to Lake Tsana, and for raising dams for the waters of the lake regulating the Blue Nile. Six years passed before the Anglo-Italian understanding was concluded through notes exchanged in Rome in December 1925. The trusting relations, strengthened by Sir Austen Chamberlain, seemed to indicate that the arrangement would provide an opportunity for friendly cooperation.

The understanding was recorded in 1926 by a formal agreement. But the regent of Ethiopia informed the League members that this treaty, concluded without his participation, could not be imposed on him, and the two signatories yielded before his threat of appealing to the League of Nations Council.

The Italo-Ethiopian Treaty of 1928

On the recommendation of Great Britain, the Italian government had signed, in August 1928, a treaty of friendship and arbitration with Taffari, who in 1930 would adopt the name Haile Selassie (power of the Trinity) and the title of emperor. The treaty should have inaugurated a policy of respect and collaboration. It proved useless. A hatred of foreigners, deeply rooted in ancestral customs, brought against the Italians a hostile arrogance, which perpetuated the memory of Adowa, and an ineradicable suspicion that economic penetration was only a step toward military penetration. Mussolini came to think that, if Italy's prestige was not restored, any Italian advancement would become impossible in this African territory which, had it not been for Menelik, would have been under Rome's control forty years earlier.

Before 1914, no one would have been shocked by such calculations, and a war against Ethiopia would have been considered a colonial expedition similar to those undertaken in Africa since the last third of the nineteenth century.

Since that time, colonial administrations had developed only slowly. In these immense African territories where European governments exercised their sovereignty, the principles of the new public law of the League of Nations were less familiar than in the area of European and American international relations.

In 1928, without arousing protests from others, the British government was able to limit its adherence to the Kellogg-Briand Pact with one important reservation: "The integrity and well-being of certain regions of the globe have a special and vital importance for the peace and the security of Great Britain. Her Majesty's government has striven in the past to make it clearly understood that interference in these regions cannot be tolerated. Their protection against any attack is a part of the British Empire, of its own defense. The British government agrees to this new treaty, therefore, if it is clearly understood that it does not limit Great Britain's freedom of action in this regard."

Moreover, London never invoked this discretionary right, which, for unspecified areas, seemed inscribed in the margins of the League Covenant as a vestige of colonial-age traditions.

But with Italy's support Ethiopia had become a member of the League of Nations; she would, therefore, enjoy the rights and guarantees of the Covenant. Could Rome, who had insisted on having Ethiopia enter the League, now transform her into a colony? Such an undertaking seemed outdated and against international morality.

In his attempts to create a modern state, Haile Selassie had promulgated a constitution on July 16, 1931.

Were not the obligations of the Covenant, already so diminished in practice, supposed to remain the basis of international law, after the withdrawal of Japan and Germany? London had never blamed Mussolini for his Machiavellianism or for his much-flaunted mockery of "League ideology." He could not be treated worse than Hitler, who had freed himself of all international obligations by his own audacity, repudiating, one after the other, every clause of the Treaty.

What a strange and dramatic situation! Would Mussolini become the leader of an anti-Hitler coalition, or would his ambition lead him into a violation of the Covenant in Africa?

In August 1934, Mussolini spoke to Austrian chancellor Schuschnigg of an inevitable conflict with Ethiopia. At the end of the same year, he discussed it with Cerutti, his ambassador in Berlin: Germany, he said, would not be ready before 1938; it would take Italy one year to conquer Ethiopia, and after that she would again be at full strength on the Brenner frontier.

Mussolini had been anti-German in 1934, but his isolation at the Stresa Conference, where all his colleagues had done was to demonstrate verbally their support of Austria, had diverted him toward this extra-European distraction. Determined to settle old scores by avenging the humiliating defeat of Adowa, he gave no information on his plans and aspirations.

Conflict with Italy

Since the fall of 1933, Mussolini had been trying to find a pretext for a conflict; at the end of November 1934 he found it, in one of those incidents which occurred often on the poorly defined frontiers and which recently had cost the lives of several Frenchmen, among them the colonial adminis- trator Bernard.

At the oasis of Wal-Wal, between Ethiopia and Italian Somalia, a dispute arose which opposed the superior Italian forces and the Ethiopians, who fled leaving 110 dead behind; 60 Italians had fallen. The Wal-Wal incident marked the start of a great adventure that in the end would profit only Hitler. The Ethiopian affair had begun.

Italy demanded an indemnity of two hundred thousand dollars and the punishment of the culprits. The Ethiopian emperor offered to deposit two hundred thousand dollars with the League of Nations, while responsibility for the incident was being determined.

Another incident erupted, inside Ethiopian territory. At Geneva the dangers of the situation were recognized, and the Ethiopian delegates brought the dispute before the League of Nations for the Council agenda of January 1935. After semiofficial negotiations, the Ethiopian delegates agreed, through an exchange of letters, to postpone the discussion until the following Council session, in order to allow for preliminary direct negotiations. This arrange- ment had been reached through the mediation of Laval and Eden. Of the two men, it was clear that Laval, who had just signed a friendship pact in Rome, had been the more influential with the Italians. In Geneva Ambassa- dor Aloisi, Italy's Council member, presided over the steps decreed to ensure the freedom of the Saar plebiscite under the protection of an international armed force; he thus performed an important arbitration mission between France and Germany, all bringing to Mussolini the highest prestige.

The Ethiopian proposals were not accepted by Rome. On January 14, after two weeks of vain attempts, Sir Eric Drummond, former secretary-general of the League of Nations and now Lord Perth, British ambassador to Italy, succeeded in being received by Mussolini. The ambassador remarked that the Italian demands could compromise the emperor's position. Mussolini replied that he did not care in the least which emperor ruled Ethiopia. Faced with this rude rebuff, the ambassador concluded that the situation was not only serious, but threatening; Italy had to be informed that the Geneva talks would follow their course.

Hoping to delay League action while rushing his military preparations, Mussolini resigned himself to an apparent concession: Italy declared herself ready to continue settling the Wal-Wal incident.

In Rome, the ambassadors should have been more forceful, Eden would note in his memoirs. Count Charles de Chambrun was not the man to speak bluntly to Mussolini, and Lord Perth always seemed apologetic.

Since January 1935, the shipping of troops "for the protection of the African colonies" had been proceeding at a fast rate; the shipments were reported and the number of troops revealed, with ostentatious publicity. Large detachments had been marshaled in Eritrea and Somalia. Time passed and the situation grew worse. Negotiating without committing herself, Italy repeatedly postponed the date set for the conciliation procedure she had declared herself ready to apply. The reason was that a military intervention was impossible until the end of the rainy season at the end of September or the beginning of October. The Italian government thus prevented any effective assistance from being given to Ethiopia before it was too late.

League Litigation

On March 17 the Ethiopian government, confronted with the Italian military measures, requested the application of Article 15 of the Covenant: "If there should arise between members of the League any dispute likely to lead to a rupture, which is not submitted to arbitration *or judicial settlement* in accordance with Article 13, the members of the League agree that they will submit the matter to the Council. Any party to the dispute may effect such submission by giving notice of the existence of the dispute to the secretary-general, who will make all necessary arrangements for a full investigation and consideration thereof." The problem was thus put on the Council agenda for the April session.

However, the emperor's representatives accepted a second adjournment; they were convinced that France and England, who asked so insistently for the delay, did so only because they planned to intervene in Rome.

The Ethiopians themselves hesitated to open at the League of Nations a public debate, which might give England and France the occasion to seek some less favorable compromise. Once the dispute was more clearly defined, a solution would be found.

The debate finally took place during a special session lasting from May 20 to May 25. The only problem discussed was the organization of arbitration in the Wal-Wal incident, in accordance with the Italo-Ethiopian treaty of 1928. However, that particular incident had taken place long ago. From this moment, the entire problem of Italo-Ethiopian relations was raised, and whatever judgment the arbitrators might reach over Wal-Wal could no longer contribute to the solution of the problem.

The Council recalled the obligation undertaken by the two parties not to resort to the use of force. Since Mussolini was in no hurry, the emperor had to be patient.

This surface bandage could not have much value; with easy complacency, the Council agreed not to probe an infected wound. The state of mind reigning in Paris and London made any intervention from Geneva seem undesirable, unless it was absolutely inevitable. It would be accepted only as a last resort, "like a doctor's call in a harem, years ago," Secretary-General Joseph Avenol remarked.

Only France and Great Britain, who ruled the territories bordering Ethiopia, were fully aware of the complexity of the Ethiopian problem. Had they given Mussolini promises and encouragement? Did he intend to go beyond them? Did he want war? If such was the case, their responsibility toward the other members of the League would be heavy. These two nations, deeply involved in any potential war zone in Ethiopia, would then become accountable for the integrity and independence of Ethiopia, both as members of the League of Nations and as signatories of the agreement of 1906 which had established, between them and Italy, an unquestionable bond. If they closed their eyes to Mussolini's actions, the confidence they inspired and the prestige they enjoyed would be severely damaged.

But want did Mussolini really want? In January 1935, he did not yet want what he would want later. How dangerous is the game dictators play, when, in the isolation and total silence of adulation, no one dares advise them or contradict them? It is the monologue of a player who, to avoid losing his bluff, continues the game and doubles the stakes.

Even in May, Mussolini had not yet decided irrevocably to conquer all of Ethiopia. Only later would he be drawn into it; if he had not carried to their end the plans he was credited with, he would have appeared to retreat.

In May, did he want a limited military expedition which would restore Italy's reputation against the victors of Adowa? Or would he have settled for the prestige of some sort of mandate from the League of Nations? This seemed to be the interpretation given by the Italian statesmen in Geneva.

Marquis Theodoli, chairman of the Mandate Commission, who was constantly in touch with foreign affairs undersecretary Suvich, said repeatedly: "What can London do so that Mussolini is not forced to make war? How can Paris be of assistance in that task? Will not the arrangement of a mandate-type government be possible?"

These questions were asked also by General Badoglio's aide, General Visconti, who had commanded the Italian contingent in the Saar plebiscite, and who found in financial matters a reason or a pretext to come to Switzerland. In all the European nations, Germany included, the true military men were conspicuous by their wise caution. They refused to believe that Mussolini would undertake to conquer a harsh country, without roads, inhabited by a race of warriors and infested with scorpions. The examples of the Sudan and Morocco demonstrated the difficulties and delays of an African war. If Italy did engage in serious military operations in Ethiopia, she would run the risk of not being able any longer to oppose the absorption of Austria by Germany.

Silence at Stresa

In this strange affair, the gravest complications arose from the silence of the English, who asked no questions, and of Laval, who gave no information. Considering the primordial importance Mussolini attributed to his Austrian policy, it is difficult to believe that, if he had been forced to make a choice, he would not have tempered his passion for Africa, provided he could have done so without any public pressure and before it was too late. But can we say that the British and Laval would have been willing for the protection of Austria to take on themselves the precise obligations that alone would have put Mussolini in a position to make that choice? During this decisive three months when the Council, twice adjourned at the urging of France and England, had already received the Ethiopian complaint, no one committed the indiscretion of inquiring about the troops, whose departure was announced by the Italian press.

At Stresa, this silence remained unbroken. The military preparations and the threats they implied were not mentioned. The prime ministers and foreign ministers of Great Britain and France missed the chance to induce Mussolini to state his complaints, his hopes, and his projects, by backing him into a corner. Yet these three powers were the only signatories of the 1906 agreement, which, while recognizing Ethiopia's territorial integrity and independence with the formalities customary at that time, had divided the country into three spheres of influence.

The Italo-Ethiopian affair was on the agenda of the League Council. Mussolini, who had not declared publicly his intentions toward Ethiopia, expected to be questioned, and had come to Stresa accompanied by his experts in African affairs. Not a word was spoken, and when a little later Ramsay MacDonald was asked the reasons for that silence, he replied: "That question is irrelevant."

How could Mussolini, at the end of this imposing meeting of statesmen, not have believed that England's extraordinary silence represented a tacit approval, the discreet equivalent to Laval's knowing smile in Rome? Silence means consent.

In January 1935 the French foreign minister, who had been an associate and almost an ally of Mussolini in Rome, could hardly have ignored the Duce's plans for an operation whose military preparations had already been referred to with noisy publicity. Perhaps, as Mussolini's confidant, he had covertly recognized the legitimacy of Italy's claims on Ethiopia.

On November 11, 1935, when Litvinov was asked by Ambassador Schulenburg whether Laval knew where Ethiopia was, he answered: "His ignorance of geography astounds me."

It is hard to believe that Laval would not have mentioned the plans revealed by the Italian press, when he agreed to clauses that extended the Italian coastline on the Red Sea and granted Italy a share in the Ethiopian railway. De Bono would later write: "Laval's conversations in Rome gave us reason to hope that, if we acted in eastern Africa, we would not encounter any opposition from France."

As for the two British diplomats, the reasons for their silence at Stresa remain impenetrable. According to Eden, who was unable to go to Italy because of illness, they had agreed in London to question Mussolini about Ethiopia, where the situation had grown increasingly threatening since the fall of 1934. An expert on Ethiopian questions had accompanied them. Not one question was asked in the course of the conversation, devoted, it is true, to European issues.

It was an incredible act of discretion; or, as Eden would write, an extraordinary shortcoming. At the moment, no serious reproach was leveled at the ministers. People thought that their supreme caution, eager to spare Italy, served the cause of peace.

Later, particularly at the Labour party congress of October 1935, anger was unleashed at this silence, by then seen as an adherence to Mussolini's plans for conquest. Hugh Dalton would declare that, by not mentioning Ethiopia at the Stresa Conference, Sir John Simon and MacDonald had committed "one of the worst diplomatic crimes of the century."

At Stresa they had refused to discuss the Ethiopian affair, or even to hear it discussed. Many difficulties grow worse if they are kept hidden. Mussolini could hope that his ambitions would not be taken too seriously: the coast was clear.

The three-power conference at Stresa ended with a communiqué stressing the necessity of ensuring "the maintenance of peace within the framework of the League of Nations." With his own hand, Mussolini added the words: "in Europe." This significant addition made the French smile and left the English unmoved. Neither had the courage to speak frankly, to break through the reticences, the reservations, and the innuendos, although a clear explanation was the last possibility to preserve agreement among the western powers. For there existed a contradiction between the European policy of Stresa and the African adventure.

In England, no special feeling was displayed over the Italian preparations. Was the silence of Stresa a delusion? In any case, Mussolini had interpreted it as an implicit counterpart for the Stresa agreement. Mussolini knew that he was correctly informed of the tendencies of the city financiers and the views of the Foreign Office, since his intelligence services knew the secrets of the British embassy's safe. Italy's position did not cause excessive worries in London. The United Kingdom granted that Ethiopia had her faults; that she had not fulfilled all her international obligations of good neighborliness; that her government, unable to police her frontiers effectively and prevent incursions into neighboring states, had not put an end to slavery. Mussolini hoped to be able to rely on the enthusiastic support of the antislavery societies. In 1929 Lady Simon, the foreign minister's wife, had published a book on slavery, which described mainly the customs of Liberia, so close to those of Ethiopia. In international meetings, Italian journalists displayed the book and stressed its high moral import.

Mussolini was convinced that, in the end, England would give her approval and accept the annexation of Ethiopia, in exchange for the immense services Italy could render against Germany. In early May 1935, in Paris, Ciano assured Flandin that an Ethiopian operation would not encounter any difficulty from England.

Until then, the English had not found Mussolini very disquieting. With his usual offhand humor, Sir Robert Vansittart wrote that "at the beginning Mussolini was not an ass"; but, he added, "he could indeed act like an ass, and he finished by becoming one."

In the matter of disarmament—the major problem of the time—the Anglo-Saxon world contrasted the legalistic intransigence of Paris with the pacifist idealism of Italy, even of Fascist Italy. Rome thought that the bounds of joint policy formed by the three powers were such that Great Britain and especially France would refuse to break their solidarity with Italy in favor of Ethiopia.

Yet the policy of the two western powers was publicly founded on effective and total respect for the collective security system founded by the League Covenant. To allow the third power to commit a flagrant violation of the Covenant would be to shatter this policy.

After several diplomatic soundings in London, Ambassador Grandi had not told Mussolini of any sign of danger. A "Peace Ballot"—a chimerical project, people said—had been mentioned, as part of a campaign by Lord

Cecil and the League of Nations Union for collective security. But Baldwin had very recently added another declaration to the long list of declarations made by prior governments, who, in the name of British public opinion, had always declared themselves against any policy of sanctions.

Moreover, Mussolini did not take the League of Nations very seriously. His success in Corfu, twelve years earlier, had left him with a sarcastic disdain for the League. After several Italian officers commissioned to determine the Albanian frontiers had been assassinated in Greek territory, Mussolini had retaliated by bombing Corfu on Aguust 31, 1923, and then by occupying it. The League of Nations had intervened, but not very insistently. Mussolini had agreed to withdraw his troops and his fleet, in exchange for a Greek indemnity of fifty million lire as a "reparation." For a few weeks, Fascist Italy had felt isolated; but she had asserted her strength and forced Europe to yield.

In 1931, while his son-in-law Ciano was consul general in Shanghai, Mussolini had agreed to second the League's maneuvers in favor of China and against Japan. The result had been that Japan had successfully continued her aggression and then left the League of Nations. Japan had succeeded in the end, although she had not begun with as good a base in Manchuria as Italy had in Africa. The only important fact was the fait accompli; there had been a few temporary problems to tolerate, but Japan had won in complete security.

Meanwhile the English press was reporting on Italy's military preparations; were the Italians not preparing for war? The British cabinet itself had considered that possibility, but without alarm. At the end of January 1935, the cabinet had given an interministerial committee under the chairmanship of Sir John Maffey the task of studying the problem; a report was presented on June 18. The committee had concluded that there were no vital interests in Ethiopia which required British resistance to an Italian conquest. An independent Ethiopia was certainly preferable to an Italian Ethiopia, but the danger was distant, and it would be real only in the improbable eventuality of an Italo-Ethiopian war. This document immediately came into the hands of the Italian intelligence services. On February 20, 1936, Virginio Gayda published it in *Il Giornale d'Italia,* giving no indication that Italy had gone a long way toward realizing this "improbable" supposition. In any case, it was a mistake to draw any conclusion from these preparatory studies in which the government had asked a group of experts, who supposedly did not take the political point of view into account, to define every aspect of the problem with a view to future decisions.

What would these decisions be?

Until the beginning of May 1935, the general belief was that the Italians, still hesitant, would not embark on such an adventure. Fascism offered all sorts of economic and demographic reasons for the Ethiopian war, but such a war would be waged mainly to satisfy a need for prestige, and especially to erase the disaster of Adowa. It was clear that only an infinitesimal minority would profit from such conquests. Financial circles definitely opposed a hazardous undertaking. Filled with apprehension, they thought that only Laval would have enough influence on Mussolini to persuade him not to act. But Laval probably felt that his personal influence was a capital not to be wasted. If Mussolini wanted to fight his war, things could be arranged later—reasonably—at Ethiopia's expense. He refused to intervene, and he thought that he would be able to maintain his friendly and informal association with the Duce. After all, the fulfillment of Mussolini's African dreams would impress only the League of Nations—which had no importance—and Great Britain, who, as everyone knew, could protect her own interests. In Laval's mind, an anti-English tendency was developing.

Little by little, optimism faded everywhere, and the conviction grew that, during these decisive weeks, Mussolini was determined to make war, and that, as Drummond wrote, he was more capable of committing suicide than of yielding.

At the beginning of May, Ambassador Grandi told Simon that Mussolini was planning "a policy of major importance" for Ethiopia; he admitted that it involved the acquisition of territory.

On May 19 at Geneva, Aloisi expressed his surprise to Eden: people had accepted the Manchurian situation; why should Ethiopia raise such difficulties? Mussolini informed Drummond that he would put an end to the intolerable situation in Ethiopia; if he had to "resort to arms, in short, to go to war," he would do so, and he would send all the troops necessary to reach his goal.

The Eden-Mussolini Meeting

By the end of the spring, the Italo-Ethiopian affair had become an Italo-English problem. The Foreign Office was alarmed, finally convinced that "Musso" was definitely bent on war. Anthony Eden was dispatched to Rome. He arrived in the middle of the storm created by the publication of the Anglo-German naval treaty. Until then, Mussolini's visitors had been the prime minister or the foreign minister, and Lady Austen Chamberlain, a passionate admirer, who wore, ostentatiously, the Fascist party symbol. The arrival of the young minister for League affairs was rather a breach of tradition.

On June 23 and 25, Eden had talks with a very calm Mussolini. For several years, England had thought of offering the Ethiopians access to the sea; in exchange for the port of Zeila, she would have asked for a change of frontiers in favor of British Somaliland. To please the Italians, she would now demand from Ethiopia territorial concessions to Italy in the southern part of Ogaden, as well as economic opportunities. But Mussolini was opposed to the British proposals. If Ethiopia had access to the sea, she would be much stronger and would be able to import arms. The two Italian colonies would no longer share a common frontier. Ethiopia would broadcast her victory and think of England as a protector and benefactor, although England would have sacrificed only a minute part of her Empire, while Italy would gain very few territorial advantages. Sir Samuel Hoare, Sir John Simon's successor at the Foreign Office, had devised these ideas in an attempt to ward off a crisis in Anglo-Italian relations; apparently he had not "taken into account either the vital necessities of Italy or her national honor."

Mussolini then revealed his own policy to Eden. If he did not make war, he would be satisfied with the ceding of the territories conquered by Ethiopia during the last fifty years. The central plateau, which was surrounded by these territories not inhabited by Ethiopians, could remain under Ethiopian sovereignty. Italy would only ask for control over this "ancient Abyssinia" and would give it a charter similar to those of Egypt, Iraq, and Morocco. If Italy had to fight, she would occupy all of Ethiopia and wipe it off the map.

Great Britain, said Mussolini, should approve a solution in favor of Italy, a solution that would also serve her own interests. As for himself, he was determined to eliminate perpetual difficulties and to get revenge for the still humiliating and burdensome memory of Adowa, by settling the Ethiopian question once and for all. He had carefully weighed the consequences of his policy, which was now irrevocable.

Eden's visit in Rome did not occasion dramatic scenes, as some people have said; but it did banish all doubt about the intentions of Mussolini, who had the impression that Eden did not really know what he wanted. The publicity surrounding Eden's trip gave it results opposed to what had been expected from his mission, and the situation grew worse with his return from Rome.

On July 5, Hoare warned Grandi that it would be dangerous to let Mussolini believe that England was not serious about Eden's proposals.

The conflict between Italy and Ethiopia differed substantially from the conflict between Bolivia and Paraguay, which had worried the League since 1932. A great European power was implicated and it involved an area essential to the sea route between the Mediterranean and the Indian Ocean. France and England, as colonial neighbors of the two nations at war, would bear great responsibility toward the other members of the League of Nations. Great Britain, as guardian of the Suez Canal, would be faced with extremely weighty obligations.

According to Vansittart, "Musso knew he had nothing to fear from Laval, and he knew all too well our own indecisiveness."

The men who ruled over English policy were often slow in making decisions. They could always be forced to resign, or the cabinet could be reorganized. At the beginning of 1935, British policy toward Italy and Ethiopia had not definitively crystallized.

The Peace Ballot

The course of destiny was determined by a totally unexpected event; very few people understood its significance at the time. Long before there was any question of Italian aggression against Ethiopia, the extremely powerful "League of Nations Union," an organization of a million members, vigorously presided over by Lord Robert Cecil, had decided to poll the British people on their feelings toward the League of Nations. This referendum was first organized in the early fall of 1934, when the Ethiopian affair had not yet begun; the results of the poll were not publicized until June 27, 1935, when the Ethiopian crisis was at its height.

Lord Robert Cecil, an influential member of the high church and a typical Conservative, had declared in June 1934: "War is inevitable unless support for the League of Nations becomes real and not merely verbal."

Was the policy followed since 1920 by all British cabinets compatible with the effectiveness of the League of Nations? Was it possible to maintain peace, and at the same time refuse to assume any risks? While claiming to rely on the Covenant, London rejected and excluded any commitment to the organization of collective security, through an obstinate refusal that took refuge behind public opinion. Japan had thus been freed from any fear of consequences of the "Manchurian incident" and had peacefully left the League of Nations, a failure bitterly felt in Great Britain. A few months later, Hitler had followed the example given by Japan.

Despite all its efforts and its great popular support, the Union had been powerless to alter a policy it considered disastrous. The government and the diplomats viewed these interventions with scornful displeasure, as muddled and incompetent intrusions.

The League of Nations Union then decided to poll the British people on their attitude toward peace and war; this plebiscite was to be the Peace Ballot. "A paraphrase of the Covenant," as Cecil said. The churches threw themselves into the campaign. It was an independent undertaking, carefully organized, and conducted outside any party framework, by men of all political persuasions. Although this poll did not represent a weapon against the government, in the fall of 1934 Prime Minister Ramsay MacDonald, Foreign Minister Sir John Simon, and the first lord of the Admiralty had expressed the contemptuous ill humor it inspired in them.

Meanwhile the opposition, and especially the Labour party—an opponent of Fascism—were beginning to give stronger support to what they called a system of collective peace. The government ironically stressed the contradictory position of the Labour party, previously inspired by Lansbury's pacifism. If they wanted to apply the sanctions required by a collective security system, should they not be ready to make war? In any case, collective resistance was impracticable because the United States was not a member of the League of Nations, and Germany and Japan had withdrawn from it. On November 23, 1934, Baldwin voiced his surprise to see, in the Labour party, an increasing desire to support the collective security system: "I will never," he said, "approve the use of the Royal Navy to blockade any country, so long as I do not know what the United States will do."

Without being an open opposition campaign against the government, the Peace Ballot was a challenge to the official policy of every cabinet since 1920—including the two Labour cabinets.

Five questions were asked:

Should Great Britain remain a member of the League of Nations?

Are you in favor of a general reduction of armaments?

Should military aviation be abolished?

Should the sale of arms for private profit be forbidden?

The fifth question, through pure coincidence coming at the same time as the Ethiopian affair, would upset the whole of English foreign policy. It was thus worded:

In the case of aggression against a nation, should the other nations unite to impose sanctions upon the aggressor, of an (a) economic, (b) military nature?

Although the most optimistic had expected only 5,000,000, in fact 11,559,600 Englishmen voted. The outcome was: in the question of economic sanctions, 10,027,000 in favor and 635,000 opposed; in the question of military sanctions, 6,784,000 in favor and 2,350,000 opposed.

Lord Cecil announced the results of the referendum on June 27, 1935, to several thousand people gathered at the Albert Hall. The vote was now an article of faith. Neither the honesty of the count nor the sincerity and independence of the voters were questioned. No doubt could have weakened the authenticity of the results, which to the surprise of the ruling circles demonstrated the intensity of British feelings in favor of the League.

The League assumed a much greater importance for His Majesty's government. The power of this movement of popular opinion was such that it caused an almost instantaneous change in foreign policy.

With admirable self-control and an unfailing tactical sense of the present, the Conservative leadership became involved in the Peace Ballot, which seemed to contain great electoral possibilities. The Conservatives immediately monopolized the impressive results of the "peace plebiscite."

As a result, the Ethiopian conflict, a rather indifferent issue for the government, stirred a public swayed by ideology, and it advanced into the foreground, to the sharp displeasure of the Foreign Office. "Eleven and a half million votes! Not half understood what they were doing!" wrote Vansittart, who felt that the good faith of the British nation was being abused. To vote for the League of Nations was also to condemn Italy. This was a "blood ballot," lamented the isolationists.

The Peace Ballot, exploding so suddenly, was powerful enough to change radically the Conservatives' policy and make them invest their entire electoral capital in collective security. By capturing the League movement, the Conservatives had a magnificent opportunity to crush the pacifist Labour party. The Conservative party was becoming the collective security party.

People thought that Italy would go along submissively. And some cynics thought that if, after all, the League of Nations failed, they would no longer be plagued by endless appeals to that center of utopias. They constantly deplored the end of traditional diplomatic methods and wished to return to the classical diplomacy of ambassadors' talks.

After the Peace Ballot, it became impossible to repeat the formula invariably used by all British governments since 1920: to accept new risks and new commitments would be contrary to British public opinion. What was at stake was a reversal of official diplomacy, a radical change, the victory of a French idea. England had always refused to accept any collective and automatic obligation, and had persistently opposed the idea of collective security advocated by France since 1919. London had repeatedly stated its position: with respect to Articles 10 and 16 of the Covenant; with respect to the mutual assistance proposals; and before, during, and after the Disarmament Conference. Eden declared in March 1933 in Geneva: "As a nation on the edge of Europe and with large, varied, and widespread interests over the whole surface of the globe, the government of the United Kingdom cannot view the problem of collective security from the same standpoint as a Continental power." By taking part in the Locarno Treaty, England had done all she could and should do for the sake of peace in Europe. "The United Kingdom feels it essential to state clearly that it sees no possibility of extending its responsibilities by participating in a Continental plan," such as that outlined in the French proposal.

Until 1935, British public opinion had been hostile to collective security and sanctions. But by 1935 it was deeply stirred by the failure of 1931 in the Japanese problem, by the failure of 1933 at the World Economic Conference, and by the failure of 1932 to 1934 at the Disarmament Conference. It had also discovered Nazism. All that the British had previously dismissed, while the risks had been imaginary, they now accepted in the form of a real plebiscite and with dogmatic puritanism. This fascinating change dazzled the other nations; and it allowed the Conservatives to win the elections which Baldwin had set for November 15, 1935, right after the beginning of the Ethiopian war on October 7. Baldwin won with an overwhelming majority.

The skeptics found it regrettable that the Peace Ballot had not taken place a few years earlier, and that its influence had not changed the trend of official policy when there was still time. They stressed an unhappy coincidence: if a ground swell of indignation had roused the English nation against Italy, was it not partly because Ethiopia, being so close to the Suez Canal, was located on the route to India? England had always been aware of the supreme importance, for her sea route through the Empire, of the Red Sea and the Mediterranean, keys to world power.

In reality, the Labour party was sinking even deeper into contradiction by associating the imperturbable pacifism of Lansbury with the exigencies of collective security, which were plaguing the Foreign Office with irritating questions. Contradictions of this sort are not so unusual in opposition parties, where they are used as cumulative weapons for an offensive against the government; they only become real contradictions in the actions and responsibilities of governments.

By bringing into play over the Ethiopian question the great historical choices, the Peace Ballot simplified to an extreme the uncertainties of a terribly complex situation, tragically overshadowed by German rearmament. Under these conditions, the fate of the League of Nations should not have rested entirely on the outcome of Italo-Ethiopian relations, which became the sole determiner of world peace. Was this not an exaggeration? It hardly showed an accurate sense of proportion to get passionately involved in "saving the League of Nations" in Africa, while apparently losing all interest in its effective use for peace in Europe. The Italian mobilization on the Brenner frontier in 1934 should have been taken seriously; and it was no less important for world peace that Germany refused to accept the minimum of international obligations represented by the Covenant, and maintained without any legal limitation her free use of an enormous force which would be a threat in Europe, not in Africa. Why did Great Britain seem to show, to a dramatic extent, more interest in what could happen in Ethiopia, than in what could occur in the event of an illegal modification of Austria's international status (not to mention Memel), while she deliberately overlooked the Japanese penetration in China? The "realists" in 1935 said: whatever moral force and effectiveness the League of Nations might have should not be wasted on a map.

The conditions for effective use of collective security were not present in the Italo-Ethiopian situation; the position to be taken on the issue of peace should have been adapted to this particularly delicate situation.

A Divided England

Mussolini did not understand the importance that the League of Nations had assumed in British opinion. England became the champion of all the Geneva principles; Mussolini thought that England's attitude was only a shrewd pretext to hypocritically conceal from Italian ambitions a purely African policy, prompted by the British Empire's unwillingness to see Italy become a great power on the Black Continent.

The English resisted in the name of the League. Since it was the first time, they were not sincere, Mussolini thought. England acted as an enemy who strengthened Ethiopian resistance. The sacrosanct principles of the League of Nations influenced England's reactions only against Rome. In orgies of Anglophobia, some Italians claimed that the French initials for the League, "S.D.N.," stood for "sources du Nil," "sources of the Nile."

While proclaiming her absolute impartiality, Great Britain brought her fleet into the Mediterranean; this Mussolini said was a "covenient shortcut" for the English and not a vital artery, while for Italy it was life itself. The Italian campaign in Ethiopia represented a trial of strength between Italy and England. Why did England fail to denounce openly the Italian preparations and the threats that worried her? Why did she remain in the clouds of a supposedly disinterested ideology? An Anglo-Italian debate before the League of Nations Council could have expressed the real situation. A clearly defined problem of Anglo-Italian balance would have been stated before all. A clear position would have called for a clear decision.

The diplomatic situation grew more and more strained, while Germany was rearming rapidly, and Italy was undertaking a risky adventure. With what interest, with what care Hitler followed this African diversion.

Sir Samuel Hoare wrote in his memoirs: "To us, the dispatch of Italian troops to a remote corner of eastern Africa meant a threatening increase of Japanese forces in the Far East and of Nazi forces in the west." There were rumors that Mussolini would attack Malta. Hoare asserted that the members of the government, all opposed to war, rejected any idea of unilateral action against Italy. However, they were of "different minds." Lord Londonderry was in favor of isolation, and Eden, since his meeting with

Mussolini, had been the principal advocate of a collective action that would not only block Italy's ambitions but annihilate them. The "hard-liners" were with Eden. Neville Chamberlain, who was certainly not among these "hard-liners," still favored an immediate closing of the Suez Canal, which would have made any expedition against Ethiopia a disaster.

Since June, the Labourites—traditional opponents of Fascism—had demanded the closing of the Suez Canal. But, would this measure not lead to war with Italy? Article 1 of the international charter of October 29, 1888, governing the canal, declared unequivocally that passage would always be free and open to ships of all nations. The assistance of the British fleet would be necessary in order to close the canal. Although the small powers were enraged against the aggressor, they were safe, for Italy would not strike back at them. The ships of Lithuania, Chile, and even Sweden ran no risks. The British fleet alone would have to face an attack and Mussolini had certainly weighed, at least verbally, the possibilities of a war with England.

To Italy's surprise at seeing the British fleet assembled in the Mediterranean, Churchill replied proudly: "We have had supremacy in the Mediterranean since the War of the Spanish Succession, that is to say, for two hundred and thirty years, and we have never permitted anyone to dispute the right of our warships to move freely in that sea."

Nevertheless, Churchill was filled with apprehension over a possible conflict with Italy, as he confided to Hoare on August 25, while advising caution: "We must avoid the capital mistake of allowing diplomacy to move more swiftly than our naval preparations." And Hoare replied on August 27 that he was "especially sensitive" to such a danger. That danger alarmed Baldwin, who did not believe that the Home Fleet was powerful enough to oppose Italy without the assistance of the French fleet; he would later allude to his fears with the famous phrase: "My lips are sealed."

And Vansittart, noting that "many Englishmen believed that Italy could be taken by the collar with impunity," wrote in his memoirs: "I myself did not wish to take anyone by the collar." It was most important not to let the fleet run any risks, when England had practically no air force and no anti-aircraft defense; six years later, Japanese planes would sink the *Prince of Wales* and the *Repulse.* Vansittart was well aware of the choice that had to be made: on the one hand, Austria, and on the other, Ethiopia, where British interests were insubstantial. He proclaimed his respect for the League of Nations, but, he noted, one does not bet on a losing horse. He concluded: "Italians and Ethiopians were not going to fight each other over oil. Only for water, and there was not even very much of that. But somebody was thirsty."

There was total disunity in England. Lloyd George, who was actively involved and who still enjoyed the prestige of his wartime government, advocated "effective steps" against Italy. The *Daily Mail* claimed, however, that "Italy should be able to play in Ethiopia the role that Japan had played in Manchuria." Professor Gilbert Murray, "secular priest" of the League, said on May 23 that to give Italy a free hand was to tear up the Covenant: the state that attacked a single member of the League of Nations would set itself at war with all members.

A quarrel broke out within the Labour party over this issue. Ernest Bevin declared that he was getting tired of seeing the good conscience of George Lansbury exhibited from conference to conference. These sturdy trade union members did not have the temperament of pacifists, and their hatred for Fascism influenced the militant workers. At the Labour party congress in Brighton, just before the Ethiopian war began, 2,962,000 voted in favor of collective action, and 177,000 against. In October, Lansbury, whose authority had considerably weakened, resigned the leadership of the Labour party in the House of Commons, in favor of Major Clement Attlee, who had fought brilliantly in the war. On May 22, the latter had outlined his program before Commons: to "seek security not through rearmament, but through disarmament," with total abolition of national armaments and creation of an international police force which would remain at the disposal of the League of Nations.

Public Opinion in Italy

An anti-British press campaign was unleashed in Italy. In July, Mussolini began giving speeches filled with bellicose rage and interviews that spread a smell of gunpowder through the air. On August 28 he declared that England intended to "prevent Italy from restoring order in a vast country left in the most atrocious slavery and to the most primitive conditions of existence," and this when British interests were not even threatened.

In several countries, especially in Germany, people felt that the attitude of England in the Ethiopian affair was prompted by very different motives than those invoked in Geneva. England's hostility toward Germany was due to selfish African interests, which London was cleverly protecting by shifting responsibility on to others and by using the ideology of the League of Nations.

Already Curtius, Stresemann's successor as foreign minister, claimed that "Lake Geneva was full of crocodiles," for an Italian neighbor to the Sudan would displease England in the extreme.

Hesitation in France

While England was finally accepting the doctrines that had been the doctrines of France, she was seized with indignation and astonishment to see Paris, once an advocate of these doctrines, now depart from them through a striking change of policy, when it became a matter of enforcing collective security against Rome. Amid the outcries of anti-Fascists and the pastoral letters of bishops, she announced with much clamor that a decisive step toward collective security would be reached at Geneva and that the precedent about to be created today would be regularly applied tomorrow and in the future.

As for the French government, it was forced to condemn the Fascist aggression; but it wanted to believe that the issue was simply one of colonial aggression, such as the great powers had often practiced, and it did not want to make use of the League of Nations mechanisms, except in a conflict of its own choosing.

The complications involved in the Ethiopian affair quickly created a real opposition between Great Britain and France. France tried to hold England back and calm her. Sir Austen Chamberlain, a longtime friend of France, expressed his surprise in Commons over "the apparent hesitation and selfish concerns which seem to characterize French conduct in this [Ethiopian] affair."

It is easy to understand why Paris raised objections against English policy when England turned away from the German danger and toward Italy. From the beginning, these objections had not been formulated openly. How could England neglect the importance of Austria in Hitler's policy? After Stresa, the agreement between France and Italy had completely freed the "Alpine frontier" from military needs, and Mussolini seemed diverted from the German field of attraction and from an active policy of frontier revision. To save such an agreement would be to avoid a disaster in Central Europe. France, who had finished the Maginot line and who could count on only two English army divisions—"a bucket of water to extinguish a worldwide conflagration," Vansittart would write later—wanted and needed to be on good terms with Italy. An already too powerful Germany should not be strengthened by the annexation of Austria.

Paris persisted in believing, as long as possible, that conciliation with Mussolini was possible. Certainly, a deliberate and flagrant violation of the Covenant would be intolerable, but France refused to declare herself against Mussolini before he had taken action in violation of the pact. Was it absolutely certain that he had decided to go to war? Why did Great Britain act as if this was a certainty? Taking a hypothesis as a certainty seemed to be the best way of making it inevitable, and of putting Mussolini in a position from which he could no longer escape.

Laval had never been informed of the offer of the port of Zeila, an offer made by Eden to Mussolini; he was displeased. Why had England presented her own solution to Mussolini without first consulting France? If the British project were to be realized, France would undoubtedly have to declare Jibuti a free port, and the Jibuti railway accounted for a fifth of the expenditures in French Somalia.

England, who had not waited for the League of Nations Council to examine the Italo-Ethiopian conflict, presumed to defend the League, although she was acting outside of the League and its findings. She advocated an action founded on the Covenant and tried to organize it, in preparation for a possible violation of the Covenant. She thus seriously compromised any chances of settlement.

It was announced that Great Britain was studying ways to apply economic sanctions and that she was limiting herself to Italy alone. Even before any violation of the Covenant, consultations were held to consider such a violation. An agreement was being sought for a still unknown act. From then on, Italy found herself in the position of a nation who has to face a coalition willfully directed against her.

In his search for a realistic policy, Laval struggled to find a compromise; harassed by his worries, he was now well aware of his responsibilities. He wanted to perform a juggling trick: to respect the obligations of the League Covenant and, at the same time, to allow at least a partial absorption of Ethiopia, a member state, by Italy, another member state. He did not want to be forced to pronounce himself against Mussolini before any violation of the Covenant, and thus to lose all means of exerting his influence on him.

Mussolini, who had restrained Hitler in 1934, felt that he should be given some compensation: great-power status for Italy in Africa. Speaking to Eden on June 21, Laval emphasized the advantages to be gained by the emperor from an Italian protectorate over all of Ethiopia. His throne would be guaranteed against the *ras,* and he would retain complete legal sovereignty. His position would be similar to that of the sultan of Morocco. Laval pretended to maintain Ethiopia's integrity under Italian suzerainty. But Haile Selassie would certainly not accept such a solution; he would prefer to fight.

On July 4, Laval told English ambassador Sir George Clerk that he was opposed to anything that might endanger the harmony of Franco-Italian relations, and that he would use all of his intellectual faculties to find a solution. His hopes, the ambassador concluded, were founded only on some possible turn in the situation, just like the hopes of Micawber, the famous Dickens character trapped in his lazy optimism.

Laval, Eden wrote, lived from day to day. He refused to look any further. Future difficulties would straighten themselves out through future expedients. In his endless procrastination, he hoped against all evidence to find the means to negotiate a settlement before the application of sanctions.

In France the internal situation had been unstable since February 6, 1934. The division of the nation into two camps remained so strong that Mussolini had hoped to recruit an Italian faction in France. The very active Leagues, who claimed to be working toward the recovery of order and unity, had all sorts of ties to Fascism, which they passionately supported against English policy. The fact that the British government had conservative tendencies did not change the attitude of the Leagues. They felt no sympathy for the League of Nations, widely supported by the Left.

The government leaders, irresolute and confused, constantly wavered, making cabinet decisions very difficult. Laval would fight to the end before committing himself against Mussolini, and he would strive at any price to prevent the war from spreading. But the cabinet did not give him a blank check to act "in the best interests of France." Herriot, followed by all the Radical ministers and by center-right minister Georges Mandel, opposed Laval vigorously. Herriot was in favor of applying the Covenant, if necessary, and he added that "England had never known defeat." The moderates remained silent. A few right-wing ministers defended the Italian position, especially defense minister Fabry, because the General Staff's planners were complacently tallying up the number of Italian divisions which France could be assured of by an understanding with Rome.

It was over these disagreements that Laval fell from power. He was haunted by his concern to avoid war with Germany, and he thought that he could avoid it only by letting Italy act freely; he felt that Mussolini had a sort of right of conquest in Africa.

Laval was closer to Mussolini than to Eden, and he was becoming worried and irritated by Mussolini's actions and by the bellicose uproar he was indulging in. Although Mussolini lavished signs of his friendship for him, on July 19 Laval asked Chambrun to advise moderation: "We could neither encourage nor support an action inconsistent with the principles set forth in the procedures of the League of Nations." Mussolini replied by giving the ambassador an ultimatum: Italy would be against Germany or against France, and he asserted on August 13 that he would not hesitate to make war against England, who apparently felt that she could "push him into a defeat like that of Fashoda."

The French position regarding collective security was well known; it had not changed since 1920: to "put some teeth" into the League, to give it the means of coercion to enforce respect for League decisions, and to ensure the automatic application of sanctions by making any single act of force a violation of an indivisible peace. On July 11, 1924, Édouard Herriot had told the Senate: "Once the first building block falls, the entire edifice [of collective security] will tumble down all by itself."

In 1935 the very natural perplexity of French diplomacy was aggravated by the special role played by Laval, who was constantly evasive, lacked sincerity and clarity, took pleasure in ambiguities favorable to shady maneuvers, and allowed a confused anti-British campaign to be launched. Many Frenchmen, and not merely the least important, felt that the Ethiopian issue, with its Oriental-like complexities, had been exploited by perfidious Albion, determined to break up the Franco-Italian friendship. "Albion is more foolish than perfidious," exclaimed Vansittart. England was indeed foolish when, as with the Peace Ballot, she fell into the fits of insulting morality discussed by Macaulay.

Laval's eager servility toward Mussolini was degrading for France. He blamed the English for their policy of empty words at Geneva, where they engaged in Byzantine intrigues. He was convinced of England's impotence, since she had no army, a mediocre air force, and an aged fleet—this Home Fleet which was content cruising around Malta. England was just a paper tiger! Mussolini knew it, and so he would challenge her and she would not dare to suggest sanctions. On September 2, Laval told Eden: "I am a man of peace; I will never voluntarily enter upon a path that could extend the hostilities of Africa into Europe." Thinking of Hitler, Eden made him see that, if the sanctions were ineffective against Mussolini, they would be no more effective later against any other country. If the League of Nations did not function in the present, it could not be trusted in the future.

Hoare's Speech

On September 11, when the League Assembly met in Geneva, Hoare gave a resolute speech which was received enthusiastically in England, by Labour, the Liberals, and most of the Conservatives. It had been approved even by his oldest colleagues, including Baldwin and Neville Chamberlain. "The obligations of the Covenant remain . . . If this task is undertaken, it must be done collectively. If risks must be run for peace, everyone should run them. . . . His Majesty's government will be the first to fulfill the obligations of the Covenant."

The speech made an immense impression, and brought the League's self-confidence to a height, and with it the passion for Geneva. This British movement met a great need. The enthusiasm it raised was not anti-Italian; it was the joy of a united body which finally believed it had found leadership and with it a clearly defined policy, void of ambiguity. The depression which followed this happiness, rich with comforting hopes, was the failure of the League of Nations.

From Hoare's speech, which Aloisi labeled "the icing on the cake," it was generally concluded—this was the opinion, for example, of Belgian representative Hymans—that the British had truly decided to stop Mussolini, even if it meant the use of force; people were convinced that the British were not joking. The day following the speech, two large battle cruisers and a squadron of regular cruisers arrived in Gibraltar. The Home Fleet was focusing on the Mediterranean. Never before had this sea, now the center of universal attention, seen such a formidable fleet: nearly one hundred and forty ships. Goering, who was hunting in Poland with Prince Janus Radziwill, told him: "I would not like to be in the Duce's place."

While raging against Ethiopian barbarism, Mussolini maintained a totally negative attitude, and called "derisory" the proposals which did not offer "a minimum basis with respect to the rights and vital interests of Italy." He violently proclaimed the inequality of nations: those whose mission was historic, and the others. To claim that they were equal, as the Covenant did, was nonsensical. (In reality, equality meant only an equal right to live. An association of sovereign states can only be founded on each state's absolute power to veto. Without it, there would no longer be an association among states, but rather a federation of subordinate units. Equality exists only in this right to the veto for the protection of vital interests.)

Italy did not want her Council representative to have the same rank as the Ethiopian representative. She did not accept being treated on the same footing as Ethiopia in the League of Nations. This attitude was surely unacceptable, but it was a question of honor for Italy. On September 5, her delegates left the Council chamber, when Ethiopia started to answer their accusations.

Laval, who felt ill at ease after Hoare's speech, told him: "International morality is one thing, but the interests of a country are another." With morose cynicism, he resigned himself to assuming the League positions necessary to prevent the dismemberment of the French delegation, which included Herriot. If, in his speech to the Assembly on September 13, Laval promised to search for "proposals capable of satisfying the legitimate aspirations of Italy," he also affirmed his loyalty to collective security. He was congratulated by Hoare, but not by the Italian delegation. He found himself caught in stubborn contradictions which he could not resolve. This shallow realist could not conceive the depth of popular feelings. Because of the publicity given to Ethiopia's communications, she had been raised to the rank of a symbol, as had China in the past.

Laval was powerless against the two "guardian angels" at his side in Geneva: Paul-Boncour and the "Soviet Union's lieutenant," Herriot. Confronted with the increasing influence of anti-Fascist circles around Herriot, "poor Chambrun" fought valiantly. But what could have been done?

Some passionate friends of Italy demanded France's withdrawal from the League of Nations, as well as a total change in policy and a reversal of alliances.

Mussolini remained unmoved by England's attitude, by the resistance he sensed, even in Italy where people distrusted him, and by the anti-Fascist rage unleashed throughout the world. Universal opinion was against him; but, with bravado, he wagered all in the hope of winning all—his life and his regime.

On October 2, expressing the hope that Europe would not take "the road to catastrophe," Mussolini flattered Laval: "I refuse to believe that the generous people of France could join in sanctions against Italy. The five thousand Italian volunteers who fell on the soil of France in 1915 would shudder beneath the earth that covers them."

The Italo-Ethiopian War and Geneva Sanctions

At dawn on October 2, 1935, without a declaration of war, Italian troops entered Ethiopian territory, under the pretext of repelling an imminent attack. The emperor mobilized his nation. On October 7 the members of the Council, and on October 11 the members of the Assembly of the League of Nations, observed that Italy had resorted to war in violation of the Covenant. Economic sanctions were established, and a special committee organized restrictive measures: prohibition of exports to Italy, of arms, of ammunition and war materiel, and of a series of products—rubber, ore, draft animals, and so forth. There was also a prohibition of all direct and indirect loans and of bank and other credit. At the same time, the member states of the League of Nations would agree to boycott Italian goods. In order to obtain general consent, the committee restricted itself to relatively harmless measures. A few states—Albania, Austria, and Hungary—manifested their friendship for Italy by abstaining from the otherwise unanimous vote, to avoid participating in the measures decreed. For fifteen years, France had demanded automatic sanctions against the aggressor, and, thinking of Germany, had done everything possible to strengthen the practical application of the Covenant and of the legal obligations to assure its enforcement. Now she hesitated to take sanctions and exerted all her strength to keep them harmless. She refused to consider a naval blockade or the closing of the Suez Canal; she did not want to "inflame, envenom" a conflict which, at all costs, should be localized; real sanctions, she felt, would mean war in Europe.

Mussolini was engaged in a policy of bluffing, and little by little he bound himself to an attitude which became a set policy. With a somber feeling of fatality, he followed a dangerous path and continued on to a point of no return. On October 2, he declared: "To economic sanctions, we will oppose our discipline, our spirit of sacrifice . . . To military sanctions, we will respond with military measures. To acts of war, we will respond with acts of war. Proletarian and Fascist Italy, arise!"

The great majority of the Italian people were indignant at sanctions they found iniquitous, and an exalted patriotism was the response to the apparent provocation. Italy had to resist the pressure of the "fifty-two nations" leagued against the Italian action on "the front of conservatism, of selfishness, and of hypocrisy." In response to a government request for foreign exchange, golden wedding rings were turned in for steel rings. Even many anti-Fascists followed suit. From Belgium, the Italian socialist Labriola offered his assistance. Orlando threw himself into the action. "Burdened and satiated with solitude," Gabriele d'Annunzio wanted "to die for the cause of Mussolini, which is the cause of the invincible Latin spirit." With the benevolent neutrality of the Vatican, the clergy blessed the valiant troops entrusted with bringing the benefits of civilization and faith to a race sunk in barbarism.

Great Britain and France were strongly opposed: Great Britain, who wanted to divert Italy from Africa by force, demanded sanctions, which Hoare, in a cautious understatement, called "economic pressure," while France favored conciliation. Each nation mistrusted the other: England was convinced that France, with Laval's "pirouettes," was ready to sacrifice the League of Nations to Rome; and France was convinced that England wanted to use the League to crush Italy. In both countries, public opinion was shaken by the frightening menace of war. The debate between advocates of sanctions and advocates of conciliation allowed people to repose in their inertia.

A strong faction remained loyal to the League of Nations. Many of the small states, especially the Little Entente, urged firmness. "Just suppose," exclaimed an eloquent delegate from Haiti, "that one day we became the Ethiopia of some other power."

But, to many, even in England, anything was preferable to a war with Italy. It would be wrong to merely wait for the results of the League's action; everything should be tried in the interest of reaching an arrangement acceptable to Mussolini.

England, who did not want to risk a war at least for a few years, showed much hesitation. Arnold Toynbee has said, in reference to Baldwin, that people in power have often "been sparing with the truth," and Churchill wrote with crushing humor: "The prime minister declared that the sanctions would mean war; then he resolved not to make war; finally he decided to apply the sanctions." Eden conceded that if Baldwin led a fruitful policy in domestic affairs, "some sins of omission have been committed" in foreign affairs. On September 21, Chancellor of the Exchequer Neville Chamberlain expressed the hope of possibly "limiting hostilities" between Italy and Ethiopia, if it was impossible to prevent them; the British cabinet did not want to get too involved.

But what could have been attempted in Addis Ababa, when Mussolini, extremely sensitive where his prestige was concerned, refused any compromise and maintained his absolute ambition to control all of Ethiopia? All sorts of settlements were considered. The League of Nations searched ingeniously for methods and guarantees involving international assistance. Former secretary-general Drummond, now British ambassador to Rome, advocated, as early as July 15, some type of Italian protectorate over Ethiopia. Laval would back an Italian mandate over a large part of Ethiopia; it would incite Mussolini to negotiate. Ambassador Chambrun repeated a proposal which had supposedly originated from Japanese ambassador Sugimura, former undersecretary-general of the League of Nations: to give Italy a mandate over the so-called colonial territories of Ethiopia. Mussolini attributed similar suggestions to the chief secretary of state. Joseph Avenol, who succeeded Drummond as secretary-general of the League of Nations, still advocated, at the end of December 1935, the idea of a mandate of the three powers with territories bordering Ethiopia: Italy, France, and Great Britain. They would be trusted to divide the area for supervision while avoiding any direct interference in Amharic territories.

On October 15 Ambassador Clerk told Laval that, in the event of an Italian attack, England would rely absolutely on French assistance on land, on sea, and in the air. To the stupefaction of the ambassador, Laval made a reservation about naval support, since British naval forces in the Mediterranean were much larger and more numerous than usual. On October 18, he finally agreed to a general promise of military support: if a single English ship was attacked, the entire French fleet would join the Home Fleet.

In regard to the possible assistance of the French fleet, the French foreign ministry wanted to reach a Franco-British agreement which, far from limiting itself to the current issue, would foresee a Franco-British defensive alliance for the maintenance of peace in Europe, as well as for the strengthening of the British guarantee given at Locarno. France wanted this agreement because she was more committed on the Continent than England, through her agreements and treaties with the Little Entente, Poland, and the USSR.

The Hoare-Laval Agreement

Many influential Englishmen thought that Eden had gone too far in demanding sanctions against Italy, and they felt that he had placed himself too much in the lead. "He thrust himself into the role of the young Pitt before Napoleon," said Suvitch to the German ambassador.

In the eyes of many diplomats especially, the adventure of sanctions was a tragic mistake which had to be corrected as soon as possible. Now that the British elections were past, they wished for an arrangement which would ward off any risk of European war. Baldwin, who was always opposed to extreme measures, favored peace; this was also the feeling of the foreign minister, Sir Samuel Hoare. On December 5 he explained before Commons "the double line" followed by British policy: application of sanctions and efforts at conciliation. The minister, whose health was poor, had decided to spend Christmas resting in Switzerland; on the way, he would stop in Paris for a day, before continuing his trip to Switzerland on December 8. His timing seemed to indicate that no exceptional event had taken place. London had not thought that he would negotiate seriously with Laval. But a Hoare-Laval communiqué, published in Paris on December 9, announced that the two ministers had searched for a friendly settlement of the Italo-Ethiopian dispute, and that they had reached a "peace plan," about which the British government had not yet been informed: "After an agreement is obtained, the plan will be submitted to the governments involved, and to the League of Nations."

By offering a compromise through which the emperor would allow "a zone of economic expansion and settlement reserved for Italy," Hoare and Laval congratulated themselves on having averted the misfortunes that would follow; they hoped Italy would agree.

Their plan was revealed on December 13 by the Paris press. A secretary had given a copy of the plan to Pertinax, the editor of the *Echo de Paris* and the *Daily Telegraph*. The English believed that the leak had been planned by the Quai d'Orsay. It was not true; the leak infuriated Laval. Exasperated, Mussolini saw in the publication of the plan one of Laval's tricks to force him to accept it. He delivered fierce speeches against "the front of selfishness and hypocrisy."

The Hoare-Laval plan was not feasible. To ask the emperor to abandon half of Ethiopia's territory was a proposal that neither the emperor nor the

League of Nations could accept; even less England, where public opinion rose in indignation against "a shameful bargain." With this plan, the British government was abandoning the principles for which it had fought, six weeks earlier, during the "elections for the League"—elections the government had won. It had shamelessly deceived the voters. The "Paris plan" rewarded the aggressor. The government was taking the aggressor's side, said Attlee.

Meanwhile, in Switzerland, Hoare fell on the ice and broke his nose—a symbolic accident. Overcome by the hostility of British opinion, he resigned on December 18, to be replaced by Anthony Eden, who had the support of Baldwin and Sir Austen Chamberlain. Eden was invited by the cabinet to introduce the plan to the League Council, but without supporting it, simply as a basis for discussion. In Commons, Prime Minister Baldwin declared that the proposals of December 8 were "definitely buried."

Lord Halifax would later tell Eden that Hoare had made "an astounding error." King George V observed, in the presence of the new foreign minister, that it is impossible to run a train at full speed in one direction, then suddenly throw it into reverse, without expecting to derail it.

In London, people thought that the "sly and persuasive Laval" had cynically trapped Hoare "in the toils of a carefully woven net," as the *Times* wrote. By exerting unrestrained pressure on his victim, Laval got Hoare to accept the improvisation thrust upon him. Hoare, who feared that the British fleet would have to face the entire Italian fleet and air force alone for a few days, thought it necessary to "align oneself with the French"; he was encouraged in this idea by Sir Robert Vansittart, "more French than the French," according to Eden. After resigning, Hoare would declare: "When public opinion is a little less agitated . . . , some of my friends at least will think that there were better reasons for the line of conduct I followed than they think today."

Laval's Fall from Power

On the morrow of this resounding failure, Laval told Eden that he never had any luck negotiating with the English. His ministry did not survive the blow. The Right supported him only halfheartedly, when it did not actually attack him. Right-wing minister Georges Mandel drew away from him. The entire Left rose against him. Harassed by supporters of economic recovery through an increase in purchasing power, he had defeated them on November 29 by having his deflationary policies approved by a vote of 324 to 247. On December 6, the policy he was following to control the pro-Fascist Leagues won by a vote of 351 to 219; in this area, he had taken action, that is to say, he had maneuvered. On December 17, he succeeded in having the debate on foreign policy postponed, by a vote of 304 to 252. On December 28, he still succeeded in obtaining a vote of 304 to 261, even after the harsh criticism voiced against the wavering of his foreign policy, which was said to be so repelled by sanctions that it replaced them by rewards. Delbos blamed him for having "displeased everyone, without satisfying Italy." Léon Blum had accused him of having compromised France's security "by breaking up collective security," of having "created an atmosphere of war threats, either by allowing or by provoking the Italian threats," and of having "weakened the forces of peace in Europe."

Paul Reynaud had condemned the Hoare-Laval plan: "This is what we have been denouncing for fifteen years." A choice had to be made "between Italy, violator of the Covenant, and England, guardian of the Covenant." The ninety-ninth cabinet of the Third Republic, abandoned by Herriot and the other Radical ministers, collapsed on January 22, 1936, having lasted for seven months and eighteen days.

In England, the Ethiopian affair had provoked sharp discontent with France, weakened the supporters of an alliance with France, and increased the number of isolationists and people who wanted to reach some arrangement with Hitler. In Geneva, it was among the small powers that the most vigorous opposition to the Hoare-Laval plan was expressed. When the great powers decided to act without concern for their loyalty to the mission they had assumed, a mission in the interest of all—when, not taking the trouble to include the other nations in their preoccupation and their discussions, they tried to introduce their own plans as answers to collective needs—they discovered an unruly League of Nations; the mistrustful League refused to follow them in their hesitations, their retreats, their whims, their incoherences, and their inertia. Then the great powers yielded and let the League take responsibility for their helplessness. Double failure; they failed to rally the other League members—a loss of prestige—and they were unable to carry out the plans elaborated by their own diplomacy—another loss of prestige.

Difficulties of the Military Campaign

Flandin, who replaced Laval as foreign minister in Albert Sarraut's cabinet, was no more eager for sanctions against Italy than his predecessor. He behaved in a similar fashion, but was more discreet. Like Laval, he equivocated with "a self-confident cynicism," as Eden said. Like Laval, he asked for efforts at conciliation, when Mussolini could only have been satisfied with a total subjugation of Ethiopia. A long war was expected. The French, English, German, and other General Staffs believed that it would take the Italians several years to conquer Ethiopia. According to Badoglio, even the Italians spoke of six years. For a few months in 1935–36, Italy's military situation was fragile and uncertain. But the Ethiopians were poorly armed, ill supplied, and undernourished; there was discord among their leaders, whose radio messages were constantly intercepted by the Italians. The fight was unequal. Still, in this harsh land without roads, with mountains where unruly tribes stirred, the Ethiopians created difficult problems for their adversary, and through sheer heroism they contained him after the capture of Makalle and Adowa. At one critical moment, the Italian General Staff even considered evacuating the conquered territory and withdrawing to the former frontier.

Until the beginning of 1936, Germany had great doubts about Mussolini's fate, and felt that Italy's military situation in Ethiopia was very poor. German ruling circles were unanimous in predicting Mussolini's inevitable failure. On October 3, 1935, Ambassador von Hassell sent very pessimistic reports from Rome: the possibility of a military defeat would have the gravest consequences. Neurath, speaking as a friend of Italy, where he had been ambassador from 1922 to 1930, expressed to Attolico his personal feeling that it would be in Italy's best interest to end the Ethiopian operation as soon as possible, with an appropriate compromise. Attolico, who like many Italians disagreed with Mussolini, declared that he would inform him at once.

Beneš believed that this foreign adventure would undoubtedly fail and would, like the previous adventure of 1895–96, produce a backlash. Italy was growing weaker each day, and Mussolini along with her. On January 16, 1936, the French chargé d'affaires in Rome considered the expedition virtually lost, and on January 29 General Maurin, the defense minister, observed that an Italian defeat would inevitably be presented as a defeat of all colonial powers.

Mussolini had begun the campaign earlier than his military men had wished; he speeded up the operations to an accelerated pace. He did not want partial or successive efforts; he needed a fast victory, because of London, Geneva, and the sanctions. Gathering all his forces, he doubled the army, which by the end of the fighting reached a strength of four hundred thousand men. He replaced de Bono as commander of the army by an authentic and famous war leader, Badoglio. Shelling with hyperite rounds defeated the Ethiopians, who suffered losses a hundred times greater than those suffered by the Italians. A much more rapid and complete success than had been imagined justified Mussolini's audacity.

The Problem of an Oil Embargo

The problem of an oil embargo brought the opposition between the advocates of sanctions and the advocates of conciliation to its breaking point.

On November 6, 1935, a committee of eighteen, created at Geneva to apply Article 16 of the Covenant, declared itself in favor of the extension of sanctions to oil, as soon as that threat appeared effective. The committee was to meet again on November 28. Rome reacted violently. On November 22, Ambassador Cerutti informed Laval that Italy would consider France's adherence to oil sanctions as "a hostile act."

Laval had the meeting of the committee of eighteen delayed. On January 22, 1936, the committee decided to create a committee of experts on oil, for a meeting on February 3. But it seemed unlikely that this new committee would reach positive conclusions. Would Great Britain really want to impose oil sanctions? In any case, she had managed to shift the responsibility for default on to France. Mussolini's deathly fear of this sanction had to be exploited, as a powerful means of pressure and negotiation. An expert in bravado, Mussolini was an ardent gambler: "If you decide on this," he incessantly repeated, "it is an act of war." But he did not seriously talk of making war; he only threatened to leave the League of Nations. In reality, the danger of oil sanctions for Italy was much reduced by the increase in American imports. It seemed unlikely that these imports would decrease, since the United States wanted to maintain a rigid neutrality by rejecting the idea of discriminating between an aggressor state and a state that was the victim of aggression, and by maintaining between the two belligerents a balance theoretically equal, which prohibited Americans from going aboard either Italian ships, or Ethiopian ships . . . had the Ethiopians possessed any.

On March 2, the British government agreed that Great Britain would vote for oil sanctions if other members of the League of Nations did so too. Flandin showed strong indignation, claiming that Mussolini was not bluffing about the results of an oil embargo. On February 25, Mussolini had told the French government to weigh "the extraordinary seriousness" of the situation, and on February 27 he had assured Ambassador Chambrun that he was "still following the Stresa policy," that there was "absolutely nothing between himself and Germany." Flandin felt that Mussolini would be more likely to negotiate if he was freed from the threat of sanctions. That was also the opinion of Lord Perth.

Eden, to the contrary, would later judge that the war could have been delayed if more determination had been shown in enacting sanctions. It was an error to imagine Mussolini as being very powerful. In 1940, the Greeks were the first to knock him off his pedestal.

The Italian Victory

Vansittart remarked ironically that the experts were searching for a formula that would be acceptable by Mussolini, by the emperor, and by the League of Nations. The Italian victory made any further search useless.

Against all the military experts' predictions, the Italians triumphed before the rainy season. Confronted with repeated defeats since mid-February, and finally with total rout in April, the emperor made his way to Jibuti by May 1, and there embarked on an English vessel. Five days later, the capture of Addis Ababa confirmed the final success. For Mussolini, who had been living in almost unbearable tension, this was a triumphant relief. On May 5, he announced the restoration of peace to ecstatic crowds, "our peace, the Roman peace, which is expressed in this single, irrevocable, definitive statement: Italian Ethiopia."

On May 9, with all the prestige and exaltation of victory, he proclaimed the king of Italy as emperor of Ethiopia, and he bluntly declared that he had won the bet. Rome was becoming "the court of Philip II of Spain." On May 12, the Italian delegation announced that it would stop participating in the deliberations of the League Council if an Ethiopian delegation continued to be seated.

There was no doubt that, if Mussolini did not obtain recognition of Italy's annexation of Ethiopia, he would feel driven toward Germany and would join Hitler. He was ready to return to the League of Nations. Hitler himself had vaguely agreed to reenter the League. For Mussolini, to reenter the League meant not remaining alone to face Hitler, but resuming contacts with the democracies.

International opinion remained deeply divided. On April 30 and on May 5, faithful supporters of the League—especially the English—continued to demand the closing of the Suez Canal. They refused to see a small nation abandoned to the rule of the strongest.

Since there no longer existed an Ethiopian government, was there any reason to continue the sanctions against Italy? Many countries stopped applying sanctions and simply gave way. They should have been lifted as they had been imposed, collectively. On June 10, Neville Chamberlain, speaking from his habitual milieu in the City of London, expressed his deep anxieties. As chancellor of the Exchequer, he energetically pronounced himself in favor of the lifting of sanctions; an understanding with Mussolini had to be reached. Lloyd George called the ministers "cowards" since they were abandoning the sanctions.

Only on July 4 were the Geneva sanctions rescinded. Italy decked her streets with flags to celebrate, with the end of the "economic siege," the overwhelming "Abyssinian epic" which had made the entire world retreat.

Inexpiable resentments survived, however. Mussolini had considered France an ally. After having been seduced by Laval's realism, he now despised him for his wiliness. The apparent Franco-Italian intimacy had changed to hatred, and Italy's hatred of Great Britain made it difficult to restore the former state of good relations with that nation.

Churchill noted that an important spectator would draw from what was happening conclusions heavy with consequences. Hitler's power grew; he became the master; he alone was strong. In a world belonging to the violent, one should be on the side of the strongest. Mussolini gave way to the magnetism of strength. He was astounded by the spectacle of German strength, and he found himself seized beyond hope of return, subjugated by a master.

15

The Seventh of March, 1936

The League after the Ethiopian Affair

During the League of Nations' period of greatest strength, it seemed to be at the center of European policy, a means for contacts and collective conversations. In reality, it was only a stage, a setting, a meeting place. Everything appeared to take place in Geneva, but nearly nothing was done at the League.

Not only was everything settled through talks of the great powers "on the fringes of the Council," but these powers also governed the very activity of the League itself. They only let the League handle the "residual questions." Of course there was stronger and stronger competition to sit on the enlarged Council; but the Council remained inactive.

Generally attacked by the Right, the League of Nations became a rallying place and a sort of symbol for the leftist parties, who wanted to base their policy on a moral code. To the Left, the League appeared as the very foundation of foreign policy.

The League could certainly not become the only center for international transactions. The national diplomatic corps made sure that its sporadic activity did not impede their absolute freedom of speech and action.

Geneva lacked voices endowed with sufficient authority to raise a chorus of acclamation. Perhaps the League needed men with exceptional gifts, like those of Briand. Faced with a Hitler and a Mussolini, the League could only have functioned if it had been guided by men capable of bringing it to life and inspiring a wave of public support. Laval's tactics had undermined the League, already mortally wounded; even more so since his failure provided an alibi to the western great powers.

For four centuries, Europe had been the center of human growth. Her

177

emigrants, who had populated so many lands, still found in her the major achievement of their efforts. A great feeling of solidarity was binding them to the needs of the European peace specified in many treaties, but still unstable and disorganized. The peace of Europe was a good for the entire world.

From the beginning, it was clear that the extra-European nations were ready to contribute actively to the development of peace, but not to defend it by arms. Thus a major error was made by believing that the Covenant ought to be universally applied, while at the same time regretfully admitting that the League of Nations was not universal. As a result, its obligations were tacitly reduced in practice to their lowest common denominator, as it was commonly interpreted. Almost every clause of the Covenant which represented a use of force fell into disuse, leaving only the legal duties.

"Victors," wrote Clausewitz, "are always pacifists." Since 1919, France's foreign policy had been a policy of maintaining the status quo—for the victors and against the losers, in favor of those who had benefited from the treaties and against those who had suffered from them. To the advantage of the victors, Article 16 of the Covenant specified: "Should any member of the League resort to war . . . , it shall ipso facto be deemed to have committed an act of war against all other members of the League."

In regard to the losers, Article 10, another obligation of the Covenant, created a presumption of violation against any attempt at change: "The members of the League undertake to respect and preserve, as against external aggression, the territorial integrity and existing political independence of all members of the League."

Article 19 provided that "The Assembly may from time to time advise the reconsideration by members of the League of treaties which have become inapplicable." Every effort had been made to render this article useless, without ever attempting, under the pressure of legal difficulties, to give it a political reality.

Until 1933, the French system had assured peace throughout Europe. The hegemony of France had been that of peace. Since 1919, it had allowed the new or considerably expanded nations to organize themselves in full security. This hegemony was exercised within the framework of the League of Nations, which gave it its legitimacy: France's military obligations only became definitively binding by a vote of the Council. France, then, did not risk being automatically inveigled by the mistakes or maneuvers of her allies. The decision of the Council required France to fulfill her military obligations, and at the same time it required all League members to carry out the Covenant's obligations. The risks taken by the aggressor were high, even if these delegations were, in practice, reduced to economic sanctions. After Locarno, it seemed that this system was complete. The error was to believe that the system's intrinsic strength rendered useless all concessions to Germany, Austria, and Hungary, to reduce the disparity between their imposed disarmament and the unlimited military supremacy of France and her allies.

From this intransigence, Germany gained a moral profit, which weakened France's position during the Disarmament Conference.

Amid the misfortunes and ruses of the Ethiopian affair, a weakened France became suddenly a chosen target for Hitler, whose rise in the past three years has been overwhelming.

As we have seen, the Radical ministers in Laval's cabinet had resigned on January 22, 1936. Laval had fallen, and Albert Sarraut had formed a caretaker cabinet. Sarraut was a political leader of the second rank, a man who, in spite of his undeniable qualities as a statesman, would unjustly be remembered only as a high-sounding rhetorician. A cabinet he had organized at the end of October 1933 had lasted only a month. His second cabinet had from the very beginning an even more transitory character than was usually the case for Third Republic cabinets; the general elections would take place very shortly, at the end of April, and the electoral campaign had virtually begun.

Flandin, now foreign minister, seemed to be reversing Laval's policy, except in the Ethiopian affair. Within a few days, the atmosphere in Paris had greatly changed. People spoke less of Italy; they rediscovered the Little Entente, the Balkan Entente, and the USSR. Several heads of state and foreign ministers passed through Paris on their way to the funeral services for King George V of England, who had died on January 20, 1936.

The exchanges of views that Flandin undertook put him in direct contact with the problems of Central and Eastern Europe, and they made him aware of the importance these problems had for France's entire foreign policy. All these talks appeared, in a way, as a reaction against Laval. Flandin, very cautious, listened more than he spoke; he stressed the personal, therefore transitory character of his predecessor's policy. He emphasized the continuity of French policy, the system of collective security, and France's loyalty to her obligations wherever she had contracted them. He accepted, without flinching, the idea of an organization for mutual assistance in Central and Eastern Europe, without Italy, who was engrossed in the Ethiopian adventure and weakened by it. The Austrian government expressed its wish for a rapprochement with the Little Entente—a rapprochement strongly desired by the French. Prince Starhemberg gave definite assurances of the postponement, if not the burial, of the scheme to restore the Hapsburgs to the throne, a restoration strongly discouraged by London.

Litvinov had gone to the funeral services of George V. The welcome he received in London made a deep impression on him: was Great Britain no longer indignant at "the horrors of Bolshevism," and was she declaring herself in favor of friendship with Moscow? This attempt at an Anglo-Russian rapprochement had caused uneasiness and discontent in Berlin. Flandin had promised Litvinov to have the Franco-Soviet treaty ratified, assuring Litvinov that he would defend it himself in the Chamber against an increasingly hostile Right.

Paul-Boncour was minister without portfolio in the Sarraut cabinet. He had demanded that this title should be followed by the title of "permanent delegate to the League of Nations" in the formal cabinet list. Sarraut had not objected. Flandin had greeted this elaboration without enthusiasm.

Hitler's Plans

The French were wondering about Hitler's intentions. The sweet peacefulness they longed for after the agitation of February 6, 1934, was impossible with this fearsome sword of Damocles hanging over their heads. Hitler would undoubtedly take advantage of the disruptions caused by the Ethiopian crisis and do something; but what? Would he denounce the freely assumed Locarno agreements? Would he negotiate over the demilitarization of the Rhineland? Would he simply occupy the demilitarized zone?

Since the summer of 1935, the coming occupation of the Rhineland demilitarized zone had been predicted everywhere. Hitler was waiting for the opportunity. Germany did not consider the Rhineland status definitive; such a humiliation stained her honor. She could not allow for long a situation in which an essential part of Germany was left defenseless in the face of an eventual French invasion. Germany might create a fait accompli or she might proceed through friendly negotiations. As Goebbels said, the Führer acted not only with the strength of the lion, but also with the guile of the snake.

Hitler had never been more circumspect than during the months when Mussolini held the stage with Ethiopia, following a policy of exalting the grandeur of his regime and the new power of Fascist Italy. This was the dangerous period of Hitler's rearmament, when he was most vulnerable. The disruption of the League of Nations had put Mussolini in the forefront. Hitler was watching that disruption. It was in 1935 and 1936 that he would profit from it the most. He separated Great Britain from the resolutions of Rome, London, and Stresa, just as he had succeeded in crushing movements of opposition within the Nazi party with a deceitful and unscrupulous boldness. How naive were those who thought they could ridicule him by insulting his bluff! Certainly, he overreached and exceeded his capabilities; his will overreached and exceeded his actual power. But his was not just a reckless adventure. In 1935 and 1936, he was taking a risk. However, through an intuition enlightened by his own observation and by intelligence reports, he was certain that his adversaries would find the very reason he was giving them not to resist, thanks to the skillfulness of his tactics. He was himself suggesting pretexts for their retreat.

In moving tones he passed through spirals of peace. He was never more convincing in his desire for peace than when he had just torn up the clauses of the peace treaty: withdrawal from the League of Nations, reestablishment of conscription . . . He had understood that the most resolute audacity could only be gradual.

On December 13, 1935, he declared to the English ambassador that he was ready to negotiate with Great Britain and France for the limitation of armaments; but, in his opinion, such agreements could only be problematical as long as Russia was determined to increase her own armaments. And Moscow could not be included in a Western European agreement for arms limitation. He felt that it would be in the interest of England and France to agree to the abrogation of the provisions regarding the demilitarized zone.

In fact, Germany was preparing to abolish, through a unilateral maneuver, the whole of Part 5 of the Treaty of Versailles, which controlled her military status. Articles 42 and 43 forbade her to fortify the left bank of the Rhine and, on the right bank, a thirty-mile zone to the east of the river. They forbade her to maintain armed forces in these areas. Under the terms of Article 44, a violation of these provisions "in any manner whatever" would make other nations consider that Germany was "committing a hostile act," an act "calculated to disturb the peace of the world."

The Versailles prohibitions had been confirmed by the Treaty of Locarno, signed on October 16, 1925, after negotiations begun at Germany's request.

Germany had to proceed with caution. In a top-secret letter of May 27, 1935, army minister Blomberg asked the commander-in-chief of the army to avoid anything that could be interpreted as a violation of German military obligations in the demilitarized zone. He raised the issue again on November 19, after the foreign minister had emphasized the grave consequences that any negligence in that regard would have for Germany.

Uncertainty in France

However, there were rumors everywhere that Hitler was planning to abrogate the Rhineland provisions and resume "the watch on the Rhine." On October 20, 1935, General Gamelin informed the foreign ministry that repudiation of the Rhineland provisions should be expected "before the fall of 1936 at the latest," for the former military barracks were being emptied of their civilian inhabitants.

In the fall and winter of 1935, the military preparations in the Rhineland became obvious, in spite of the rigorous secrecy surrounding all plans for the reoccupation.

On January 17, 1936, the French consul at Cologne announced that, in principle, a reoccupation of the Rhineland had been decided: "Only the methods and the time seem to remain in question."

On January 18, the French General Staff informed the Supreme Military Committee that the reoccupation of the demilitarized zone should be expected "in the near future." An imminent reoccupation by the German army was expected, wrote the French consul in Düsseldorf on February 14.

In the last days preceding the reoccupation, Berlin tried to mislead everyone into believing that, "for the moment," no threatening initiative was planned.

However, in Belgium, in Switzerland, everywhere, people feared an act of force, and they feared even more the reaction it would bring from the French. In Warsaw, Colonel Beck indicated "serious pessimism over the possibility of maintaining the Rhineland zone"; the situation would immediately become very serious.

In January 1936, the French military attaché in Berlin felt that "the reoccupation of the right bank of the Rhine can hardly be delayed beyond 1937." The year 1936 would not end without some initiative being taken by the German government in that area. "There can be no doubt," he noted again on January 15, "that the demilitarized zone will be reoccupied by Germany; only the date remains uncertain."

In the European chancelleries, this eventuality was one of the main subjects of the discussions, which were carried on in a fatalistic tone. A good many people claimed to be informed of the imminence of a German action. Chamber deputy Bénazet spoke of it to foreign minister Flandin, who shrugged his shoulders and said: "It doesn't mean anything; don't worry about it."

In reality, the foreign ministry had no illusions; too many warnings prevented it from following an ostrich-like policy, burying its head in the sand.

On March 3, Ambassador François-Poncet wrote that 1936 had to be the year of the abolition or the attenuation of the clause providing for demilitarization of the left bank of the Rhine; it would be completely futile to have the slightest illusion in that regard.

On February 6, Vandervelde, leader of the Belgian Socialist party, told the French ambassador in Brussels that it would be "difficult to maintain forever this clause . . . so offensive to a great nation, because of its unilateral nature."

On February 12, Belgian cabinet minister Hymans said to the same ambassador: "Could we resort to an armed response? Would we succeed in mobilizing the armies and the civilian population under such conditions? I myself doubt that very much, at least so far as Belgium and England are concerned."

Similarly, many Germans felt that London would not oppose the introduction of German garrison troops into the demilitarized zone. They were given this impression by the English press.

The French were trying, with powerful words, to counteract this tendency. On January 13, François-Poncet told German undersecretary of foreign affairs, von Bülow, that a violation of the Rhineland provisions would immediately provoke "a most serious situation," and that Germany should have no illusions.

On February 22, a note from foreign minister Flandin to all French diplomatic representatives asked them to indicate clearly in their conversations that "the French government will not permit the treaty provisions to be infringed by a unilateral repudiation."

But the government did not really know what to think. On February 14, Flandin informed the defense minister, General Maurin, that, according to rumors spreading in Berlin and printed in the *Morning Post,* the British government would not object to a limited reoccupation of the demilitarized zone; but that the French ambassadors in Berlin and London had informed him that this rumor was without foundation, and that Baron von Neurath had assured Eden that Germany had no intention of violating the Locarno agreements. "Nevertheless, by spreading the opinion that London would accept a violation of the demilitarization clauses, the German press is preparing for the eventual opening of a discussion which . . . the German *Auswärtiges Amt* will try to begin, if the outcome of these developments offers an occasion, for the purpose of obtaining a limitation of the Locarno provisions for the Rhineland zone."

People did not believe that Hitler would act as violently as he did. On February 17, General Maurin wrote to foreign minister Flandin: "You have asked me for my opinion on the possibility that France would eventually accept a more liberal interpretation of the Rhineland provisions, in the event that Germany should take the initiative for negotiations over the Rhineland. Such negotiations appear to me . . . something to be avoided. . . . Experience has shown that Germany would not be grateful to us for the concessions we had given her, and that she would demand further concessions as soon as she had obtained these ones. The opening of a breach in the Rhineland provisions . . . could bring closer and closer this remilitarization we want to avoid at all costs.

"Those are the views of the war ministry on negotiations which ought to be strictly limited to maintaining the provisions of the Peace Treaty and the Locarno Pact, if they cannot be avoided altogether."

What could have been done against what Hitler was preparing to do? No countermeasure to this declared and anticipated challenge was seriously being considered. Everything was conceived in defensive terms, within the theoretical framework outlined by the League principle of collective security, as well as by agreements for cooperation with the guarantors of Locarno.

France was totally oriented to defensive plans and did not dream of launching an attack on Hitler if he made a move.

On January 14, the political relations section of the Quai d'Orsay, becoming aware of the consistency of the rumors reported on a remilitarization of the Rhineland, advised the government to "begin exchanges with the British government in order to decide on a policy to be followed when the event should occur."

On February 14, the British military attaché, Lieutenant-Colonel Beaumont-Nesbitt, asked Captain Petitbon of the French General Staff: "What do you intend to do, alone or with us, if the Germans occupy the left bank of the Rhine?"

At the meeting of the French General Staff on February 19, General Gamelin "thought that Germany could not be prevented indefinitely from doing whatever she wished within her own frontiers." When the effects of the "empty classes" on French troop strength would no longer be felt, "after 1942, the risks imposed on France by [German] recovery of this freedom of action would be considerably diminished."

The general refused to consider the idea that "France alone could occupy the demilitarized zone," and he noted that "England did not seem inclined to take the necessary measures in time."

Later, on March 28, he wondered "what might be the outcome of a conflict limited to France and Germany," for he believed that from the standpoint of "war potential" Germany had "a clear superiority in population and industrial power; her war industry . . . could reach full output at once," and he concluded: "Certainly it would be illusory to expect decisive successes against Germany without the support of a coalition."

On February 24, the French foreign ministry noticed that no mention was made at the defense ministry of measures to be taken by France to intimidate her adversary. When questioned, the General Staff replied with lengthy evasions, and only grew angry when questioned again for a more precise answer.

"No plan," Eden would write, "existed to seize, for example, the strategic points in the zone." Coercive measures were wanted that could be applied without striking a single blow.

At the funeral services for George V in London, Neurath, who had remained inconspicuous, had simply repeated his criticism of the collective security system and glorified the advantages of bilateral agreements.

Flandin had questioned the major English cabinet ministers on the attitude the United Kingdom would take in the event of a German reoccupation of the left bank of the Rhine. Prime Minister Baldwin had replied with a question: he wished to know what position the French government was planning to adopt.

On February 27, the French cabinet considered the issue. General Maurin, who had been kept as defense minister by the new Sarraut cabinet, felt that only strictly defensive measures could be adopted without mobilization of three classes of army reserves and of all the frontier residents. They would occupy the defensive lines from which a forward move could then be attempted.

Thus France was not planning a spontaneous response, as was stipulated in Article 2 of the Locarno Treaty, to a flagrant violation of the provisions for the demilitarized zone. She would only undertake an act of force previously authorized by the signatories of Locarno and by the League of Nations Council.

The Treaty of Locarno had precisely defined the attitude to be adopted by the signatory powers in the event of a violation of the Rhineland provisions. The matter would be brought immediately before the League Council. Any violation would be reported without delay to the signatory powers, since each one had committed herself to "give immediately, in such a case, its assistance to the power against which the act in question was directed." In the event of a flagrant violation, immediate assistance would be given to the power against which the violation was directed, without awaiting the Council's deliberations.

On February 27, Flandin told the Belgian ambassador that, in the event of a German violation of the articles regarding the demilitarized Rhineland, "the French government would not take any independent action; it would only act in agreement with the other signatories of Locarno."

On March 5 Flandin confirmed this statement to Eden.

The Seventh of March

Hitler, who had been extremely irritated by the Franco-Soviet agreement, incessantly and violently denounced the Bolsheviks as the enemies of the human race. Strengthened by the anti-Communist propaganda which was spreading throughout the world, Germany cherished the idea that she formed a bulwark against Bolshevism, and that her supreme mission would be one day to lead a crusade for the extermination of that plague.

Hitler had claimed that the Franco-Soviet pact, into which "an element of legal insecurity" had been artfully introduced, was incompatible with Locarno; for it was specified in a supplementary protocol that, in the event of an international conflict, the two contracting parties would try to remain within the framework of the League stipulations and would ask the Council for a decision. But if the Council was unable to decide unanimously that one of the two powers had been the victim of aggression, and if, consequently, the Council did not order the sanctions provided for that eventuality, France and the USSR reserved the right to take joint measures on their own. They would thus have the means to take offensive action, even without the League Council's approval; they would themselves decide whether there had been an act of aggression.

For Hitler, this provision to "complete and extend the pact" represented a contradiction to the letter and spirit of Locarno; it weakened Germany's security. The Wilhelmstrasse blamed France for "introducing within the collective principles of the Covenant a series of special alliances which, in reality, have warped the spirit of the Covenant."

On February 20, 1936, in the presence of Neurath, Ribbentrop, and Ulrich von Hassell,[1] Hitler declared that it was now time to exploit the Franco-Soviet pact; a series of attractive offers would prevent any talk of German aggression. Hassell expressed the idea that even so, "95 percent of the French and many of the English would be conscious of the threat represented by the occupation." Hitler merely replied that he would strike as soon as the pact had been ratified by the French Chamber. Neurath and Hassell unsuccessfully suggested waiting for ratification by the French Senate as well, so as to have "firm ground beneath their feet."

On March 2, Blomberg gave military directives for the occupation, and on March 5 he set the date of execution for March 7.

On February 22, Hassell informed Mussolini, "confidentially" and at Hitler's request, of Hitler's views. The Duce thought that the Franco-Soviet pact was dangerous, but did not directly involve Italy. France was leaning more and more toward the Left, and in the future she would have Léon Blum as "an uncrowned king"; she would ratify the pact in the end, replied Mussolini.

Hassell observed that the matter could then lead to weighty decisions by Hitler, who would not allow such a violation of Locarno without reacting; and the Führer made his decisions alone. "In the event that Germany reacts before ratification, I can conclude from what the Duce told me that Italy would not join the Locarno powers, if they did decide to act. Twice the Duce confirmed the correctness of my interpretation." Mussolini had declared that Stresa was "dead and buried," which did not prevent him from

---

1. Hassell, the son-in-law of Admiral von Tirpitz, participated in the well-known assassination plot of 1944 against Hitler and was executed on September 8, 1944.

reassuring Flandin, on March 1, that he would stay "within the lines of the Stresa policy"; at the same time, Ambassador de Chambrun was asserting that "the bases of French friendship remained untouched."

Mussolini kept on with this farce through the following weeks. On April 18 he assured Chambrun once more that he would continue, as in the past, "to be ready to intervene with all his forces for the defense of the Danubian front against a German threat," and he agreed that it was necessary to re-establish "the Stresa front."

On April 28, the French military attaché in Rome felt that he could state: "Mussolini remains perfectly determined to guarantee the maintenance of the status quo in Austria." On May 7, speaking to the French ambassador in very friendly terms, he reminded him of the ties between France and Italy: "Let us take care of Europe," he said, although the collapse of Franco-Italian relations had already begun.

Hitler had thought of responding to the Franco-Soviet pact by denouncing Locarno. Neurath advised a caution indispensable at a moment when Germany was restoring her military power.

Speaking to the *Reichstag* on May 21, 1935, Hitler contented himself with declaring that Germany would respect the Locarno agreement as long as the other powers would.

On May 25, a note of protest was sent to the signatory powers of Locarno. Berlin then voiced shock at the apparent ease with which Frenchmen and Englishmen considered as probable a violation of the Locarno agreement by Germany. Berlin found it irritating that there should be any question of talks between the French and English General Staffs. The Wilhelmstrasse constantly repeated that Germany had no intention of questioning the existence of the 1925 agreement.

Hitler would have been happy to prevent ratification of the Franco-Soviet pact; it would have been a first-rate success for him. Hoping to influence the French Chamber against ratification of the treaty, already under debate since February 11, 1936, he granted the French journalist Bertrand de Jouvenel an interview which showed a very conciliatory attitude toward France, with appeals for harmony among nations and warnings against a dangerous Russia. But the interview was not published until February 28, the day after the Chamber had ratified the Franco-Soviet pact by a large majority—333 votes in favor, 164 opposed, and 100 abstentions—despite a note from General Weygand circulated through the lobbies: "Not consulted as inspector-general of the army, opposed as a French citizen." The pact would be ratified by the Senate in April, following the crisis of March 7.

The Franco-Soviet pact was no longer an obstacle for Hitler, but rather an excuse. On March 2, he told François-Poncet that the threat represented by the pact was all the more serious since the Soviet army, according to M. Herriot, was already extremely powerful, and since the French elections might bring pro-Russian men to power in the near future.

Hitler's plan was to use the ratification of the Franco-Soviet pact as a pretext to occupy the demilitarized Rhineland zone.

In the morning of March 7, between 10 and 11 o'clock, Neurath received in succession the ambassadors of Great Britain, France, and Italy. He handed them a seven-page memorandum, which was being delivered at the exact same time to the British, French, and Italian foreign ministries. The first part of the memorandum consisted of a denunciation of the Locarno Treaty; the second offered negotiations for the conclusion of a new pact founded on equality of rights.

Hitler had made the decision to reoccupy the Rhineland during one of his stays in Bavaria, where he liked to ponder his great decisions. He tried to appease Blomberg and several other cabinet ministers by assuring them that "countermeasures" would be taken in the event that the planned operation was not carried out peacefully, as expected. What were these countermeasures? If the French reacted with an armed intervention, the German troops would withdraw and refuse to fight.

But Hitler was sure that France would not act, although he did hesitate until the last moment. A few hours before the German troop movement, which began at dawn, he asked whether the troop transports could still be stopped. After the event, he told Colonel Hossbach that he would wait ten years before exposing himself again to such nervous tension. He was aware of the risk he was taking.

But the reoccupation of the demilitarized zone was a refreshing and joyful march. The troops, parading in the euphoria of a triumph free of danger, were welcomed by the enthusiastic cheers of towns decked with flags and flowers.

What the French Government Could Do

In the memoirs written in serene reflection by a man who certainly deserved, in every respect, sympathetic regard, Eden admits that the need to "call Hitler to order, if necessary by force," could no longer be disputed. This was the last chance to stop the dictator.

With this thundering act of force, the prelude to flagrant attacks, the time had come for France finally to set limits to Hitler's ambitions. "It is difficult to imagine," wrote Ambassador François-Poncet, "that the French government would accept this fait accompli . . . without a strong reaction."

Only out of its own willpower would the French government have found the power to enforce the rights acquired in 1919. It had to weigh the risk and the effort involved. The cabinet declared that the German provocation was a hostile act which required a military reaction by the signatories of Locarno. The cabinet's duty was to act without procrastination, as its means then allowed, and, in such a clear case, to take a commanding initiative, while informing the Locarno guarantors: England, Belgium, and Italy, each one of which was justified in intervening without waiting for a decision from the League of Nations Council. The French government could consider itself in a state of legitimate self-defense as a result of the "hostile act" committed against France. While laying the matter before the League Council, France was free to act immediately through military means. A clear and categorical affirmation of an immediate countermeasure was needed. France knew her rights; it was up to the others to judge their own obligations.

Czechoslovakia announced that she would adopt the same attitude as France, and Yugoslavia expressed her firm intention to put her army at France's disposal, if circumstances required.

According to Polish undersecretary Szembek, after February 4 foreign minister Beck, struck by French worries over the Rhineland, thought it useful to study the state of Polish obligation toward France, in the event of a reoccupation of the demilitarized Rhineland. It seemed to him "that we have not assumed any obligation in that matter as a result of our alliance."

On February 26, Beck confirmed that "such an interpretation, that there is no *casus foederis* for us here, could probably be made." But on March 2 the legal advisor of the ministry concluded after having studied the texts: "We would be forced to march against Germany."

In the afternoon of March 7, Szembek noted, foreign minister Beck received French ambassador Léon Noël. "It is serious this time," said Beck, stating that he was "ready to enter into any necessary talks with the French government on the subject of the situation created by today's German action." He considered, added Szembek, that with this declaration he had made an important gesture toward France.

On March 10, Beck reconsidered the issue. He told his undersecretary: "Poland will fulfill her obligations toward France, resulting from the Franco-Polish agreements, but only when the *casus foederis* occurs. The Locarno Pact has never had the sympathy of Polish public opinion, which felt that it undermined the European balance of power to our disadvantage."

He felt real hatred for Flandin, this "contemptible individual who lacked the most elementary courtesy. . . . This buffoon claimed to give us lessons, when French diplomacy had just given the proof of its own incompetence." On the contrary, he had great respect for Paul-Boncour, despite his "doctrinaire attachment to the League of Nations," and he found Delbos "upright, honest, and likeable."

The French cabinet met on the morning of Sunday, March 8. In the evening, Prime Minister Sarraut spoke on the radio, giving a speech which was not just firm, but virulent, and which he declared to be the opinion of a unanimous cabinet. No negotiation was possible with a nation who broke her word at will. "There will be no more peace in Europe, there will be no more international relations if this method becomes common." The Locarno powers would be warned. "We are not willing to let Strasbourg be placed once again under German guns," declared Sarraut; a phrase which became famous, and was seen as pure bravado—verbal fireworks!

Francois-Poncet noted the next day that in Berlin people thought: "Once the first reactions of anger and indignation have passed, France will see that she does not have the total support of Great Britain and will not push things to war."

In Paris, very few ministers wanted to act, only Sarraut, Paul-Boncour, and Mandel. At the foreign ministry, Flandin, who was physically so imposing, wanted to do something, but what? He was overwhelmed with confusion. If Eden is to be believed, Flandin accepted the British point of view when he was alone with a British delegate; in a conference session, he took the opposite position.

The government decided to put into action the procedure provided by Locarno: to lay the matter before the League Council and to consult with the Locarno signatories. The eventuality of military action by France, even acting in isolation, was not excluded. There was talk of crossing the Rhine and occupying Kehl or Saarbrücken. Was France really thinking of reentering the Saar, when fourteen months earlier the Saarlanders had declared themselves in favor of returning to Germany by an overwhelming majority? France, wrote Eden, would have put herself in the wrong.

A military conference was supposed to be held on March 10. General Maurin did not intend to settle for just words. It would be ridiculous to mobilize the two most recent classes of reservists—this could be done without a parliamentary vote—only to leave them without the support of reserves and logistical services. A partial mobilization would not suffice.

If territorial collateral was to be gained, general mobilization had to be undertaken. General mobilization, only six weeks before the elections? Such measures seemed out of proportion for the occupation of an area beyond the French frontier as a bargaining counter. General Maurin, the most defensive-minded of all the generals, refused to take part in a vague adventure which would take him beyond the Maginot line. If you put your finger in the gears, he felt, your whole arm might get caught. He could not take such risks. What was most important was to reinforce the Maginot line.

General Gamelin too was in favor of waiting. He considered that mobilization was necessary for France to enter the Rhineland zone; to enter the Rhineland zone would be to start the war.

Lieutenant-Colonel de Villelume, liaison officer between the General Staff and the foreign ministry, observed that occupation of German territory would lead to a total war, at a time when the French army was in no condition to face the German army, and that, under the Locarno Treaty, the benefits of English help were extremely problematical.

Long after the event, and knowing what followed, one wonders how it was possible that Paris did not act. But there is a tendency to naively simplify the situation. It is wrong to imagine that the soldiers dispatched as "the symbol of German sovereignty" would have scattered like rabbits at the first sight of a French soldier. Was a German reaction impossible? People spoke of the German air force. Was Germany, at that time, really incapable of making war?

Without believing Gamelin's claim that the German General Staff could deploy 295,000 men in the Rhineland, it is certain that the French troops were not impressive in number, and that the English troops—assuming that they came at all—only numbered 70,000 men. At this time of "empty classes," the French military leaders refrained from telling Prime Minister Sarraut to go ahead. At the Nuremberg trials, Keitel and Jodl would minimize the German forces to ridicule the French General Staff.

General Gamelin could certainly not be accused of being too rash, and his minister, General Maurin, was even less daring, not to mention air minister Marcel Déat. What was most important for him was for France not to appear as the aggressor; an act of force should not be undertaken without the League's approval.

As for Piétri, the navy minister, he pointed out to Sarraut on March 12 that "the expression 'military sanctions,' borrowed from the terminology of the Covenant, could allow for a different and milder sense of the word 'war' only in the case of action by a strong state against a much weaker state." The situation in Germany in 1920 or 1923 had shown what were, or could have been, military sanctions without total war: occupation of the Ruhr, plans for the occupation of Hamburg, and plans for the occupation of Helgoland. "Today, this sort of semiwar or punitive war is no longer at issue. Any military action can lead to total war. Thus it is important, in undertaking such an action, to be ready for all eventualities."

The ministers drew back in the face of the extent of the measures to be taken and the complications and difficulties they raised. They alluded to the French franc, which ought to be protected. Eden was right when he wrote that "the French government was not sufficiently supported by French public opinion to be able to use force effectively." And he concluded that "public opinion and the government have shown as much timidity as indecisiveness."

A fundamentally pacifistic state of mind made it seem that a collective action was infinitely more important than a motion by France alone. The task was too great for a nation to act in isolation. An isolated military action would be considered bellicose. No adventures, no bravado!

The days had long passed when Briand, in March 1921, had been accused of weakness by the conservative "sky-blue Chamber," although he was speaking of "grabbing Germany by the collar." And the time had long passed when Poincaré thought it wise to seize "industrial areas as territorial collateral."

"The occupation of areas as security guarantees can lead to war," declared Gamelin on March 28. And he added that it was "illusory to expect decisive results against the Reich without the support of a coalition." The ministers abandoned any solution that included the use of force, even limited force, and they were really not angered to see that the English and the Belgians—not to mention the Italians—did not go along with their halfhearted proposals.

As long as Hitler was rearming, he was disarming France through a skillful exercise of will. France was resigned beforehand to the surrender toward which he was pushing her. The French had not been able to maintain their reserves of strength and determination, nor to follow a tactic of preservation of energy, in case of aggression. They did not feel able to react or to act alone against Hitler. They were experiencing a loss of potential, a sort of physiological weakening, an abdication. The conviction that international order had to be maintained against Nazi Germany gave way to a fatalistic skepticism. Lost advantages should be given up for good! Why dramatize the disappearance of one of the inequalities stipulated by the Versailles *Diktat?* France should resign herself and accept German power. Hitler had won. Fortunately if the demilitarized zone no longer existed, there was still the Maginot line. France kept her universally recognized defensive military strength, and Hitler did not dream of attacking her national territory.

British Policy

When instead of acting alone the bewildered French turned to their allies, they were all in favor of preserving peace.

On March 7, Eden hastened to tell the French ambassador that "owing to the seriousness of these circumstances, it would be desirable that no action leading to an unalterable obligation in the future should be undertaken before the interested governments had been able to consult one another."

On March 9, while denouncing before Commons the definite violation of an international agreement, he noted that it was necessary to remain calm: "There is fortunately no reason to suppose that the German action represents a hostile threat." The denunciation of the treaty, said French ambassador Corbin, did not seem to give him any concern, but rather the unavowed relief which follows a long-feared misfortune. His attitude was that of a man who wonders what advantages can be drawn from a new situation, not what barriers should be raised against the hostile threat.

On March 10, the signatories of Locarno met at the Quai d'Orsay. Flandin strove to gain their adhesion to a program for common action which could extend as far as military measures. He was not supported by Belgian prime minister Van Zeeland, whose major concern was to maintain unity among Hitler's adversaries. Since Flandin's proposals did get accepted, thus establishing a common front, acceptance of the fait accompli began: "Nothing should be done with regard to Germany which might create a danger of war."

Flandin went to London, to "act in the best interests of France." According to Georges Bonnet, who was also a member of the Sarraut cabinet, Baldwin categorically declared to Flandin that "Great Britain cannot accept the risk of a war." Flandin supposedly replied that France was ready to assume on her own all the burdens and risks of an intervention; all she asked from the English was freedom of action. But she was asked to delay; her hands were tied. It was not a matter of mere reticence, but of actual resistance. Flandin asserted: "We would have had a break with Great Britain had we persevered in our wishes." On the other hand, Paul-Boncour was convinced that if France made a move England would follow; this was also the opinion of the head of the political relations section, René Massigli. But the French ministers had been struck by the categorical attitude of London, which at that time did not want to create any difficulties with Germany.

The Locarno Treaty made it an obligation for England, as well as for Belgium and Italy, to oppose an invasion of the demilitarized zone. But Italy, out of spite over Ethiopia, showed no interest in the Locarno system, and it was clear that British opinion could not conceive fighting to keep German troops out of Cologne, Essen, Mainz, Aix-la-Chapelle, Trier, and Saarbrücken. The English were guarantors; from the beginning they acted as mediators instead. The treaty referred to sanctions. England, who in 1935 had taken the lead in imposing sanctions on Italy, took the lead in 1936 in *not* imposing sanctions on Germany, using the need to pacify Europe as a justification. In London, the violation of the Locarno agreements was not considered as serious as the Italian aggression against Ethiopia.

This frame of mind dominated the talks among the Locarno powers. Even among those who condemned the German action, a lazy optimism tended to think that perhaps this new crisis might be beneficial in the end, by accelerating the dissolution of the past and by allowing the beginning of a new Europe founded on a "constructive policy." With placid homilies, the *Times* hailed "an opportunity to rebuild" the Continent.

On March 9, Prime Minister Baldwin, who two years earlier had proclaimed that "the frontier of England is on the Rhine," declared to Commons that his greatest wish was "to continue to try to join France and Germany in bonds of friendship with ourselves."

On March 12, with diplomatic concern for equilibrium, Eden gave "the assurance that in this work of reconstruction, especially in organizing the security of Western Europe, His Majesty's government will make its full contribution."

The British intention to repudiate a strict interpretation of Locarno was certain beforehand. But Hitler had skillfully suggested all sorts of enticing lures.

Hitler's Speeches and Proposals

Two hours after the western powers had been informed of the German reoccupation of the Saar, the Führer spoke before an ecstatic *Reichstag*. He would not yield to any force that would try to prevent him from restoring the honor of his people. But at the same time he committed himself to fight for the establishment of an entente among the European nations, especially with Germany's western neighbors. He spoke of Europe as a family, of the western peoples as the children of a common civilization. Germany, he continued, no longer had territorial claims in Europe, and she would never break the peace. The *Reichstag* was dissolved; on March 29, the German people would be able, through elections, to express their judgment on Hitler's policy.

With an artful technique which had already proved effective in October 1933 and in April 1935, Hitler combined each of his blows with offers carefully calculated to tempt his victim. While striking, he offered peace. Without really making up for the blow, the glitter of such offers made it more difficult to strike back.

Through an avalanche of speeches, he continually affirmed his desire for peace with France; it was necessary to "bury the hatchet for good."

In England, Eden noted in his memoirs, there was not "one man in a thousand ready to pay with his life by participating in a French action against the reoccupation of the Rhineland. . . . no one in England was ready to do so, literally no one."

The Labour party explicitly condemned, as contrary to the spirit of collective security, not only the plans for the eastern and Danubian pacts, but also the Stresa resolutions and the Franco-Soviet pact.

Germany, the English felt, was perfectly justified, morally, in rejecting the presumptuous French claims. Ambassador von Hoesch found, "even at the highest social levels," strong reactions against France's "blackmail," against a French policy which was too legalistic and carried immeasurable risks; a policy for which the English had no desire to go to war again.

Edward VIII, a close friend of Hoesch, "played a very prominent role in avoiding a conflict." He would not hear of war, nor would the city financiers, "despite Jewish influence." They all wanted to believe that everything would take care of itself.

However, Hoesch did wonder whether Sir Austen Chamberlain—had he succeeded Hoare at the Foreign Office—would not have convinced the French to react militarily. As a signer of Locarno, Sir Austen claimed that England was unquestionably committed to go immediately to the aid of France. But Austen Chamberlain, who was now dying, was isolated in his efforts to remain on the best possible terms with the French, and, if England wished to reach an understanding with Germany, to do it only with their support. "In reoccupying the Rhineland, the Germans were only going into their own backyard," said Lord Lothian; he was suspected by the French of secretly giving information to Ribbentrop and advising Hitler, who thus possessed major trump cards in London. Sixteen years after the war, it was perfectly normal for Germany to act as she wished on her own territory. The zone she was reoccupying militarily had undoubtedly been placed under her own sovereignty; it could not have remained demilitarized indefinitely.

A blow had been aimed, not at French territory, but only at the Treaty of Versailles, in which no one believed any longer.

In the cabinet, Kingsley Wood advised the Foreign Office to think less about France; the time had come to attempt to reach an understanding with Germany. Lord Halifax recommended good relations with the Nazi leaders.

Would the way open for an understanding between England and Germany, with all the consequences it could have for Europe, and for a change in the balance of British alliances? Already newspaper cartoonists were drawing Albion, the tall, bony woman, curled up in Hitler's arms. Some impassioned Englishmen, inclined to exaggerate and to provoke, accused France of having been ready to accept control of the Mediterranean by Mussolini, whom they supported—an issue which displaced that of German hegemony. The French Republic encountered much hostility in London. The British made her fully responsible for the Ethiopian failure, and resented her for it. They were losing patience, and they intended to pay very little attention to France's opinions and fears, in their plans for a reconciliation with Germany.

Unquestionably, on March 7 solemn obligations had been violated. In a show of moral indignation, France was almost accused of complicity in this violation.

Deliberations in Paris

If France had marched in spite of London's reluctance, would it not have been almost impossible for the United Kingdom to abandon her? That question has often been asked. It is impossible to measure the force of the impact that results from a determined will.

"I doubt," wrote Eden, "that world opinion would have approved such a French action in 1936." He was right; France would not have received much sympathy. She would have been accused of repeating the Ruhr invasion, condemned by Pope Pius XI. But times had changed. Only the blind could still ignore Hitler's threat to all of European civilization. On March 16, 1936, the same Pius XI confided to French ambassador Charles-Roux: "If you had immediately moved two hundred thousand men into the zone reoccupied by the Germans, you would have done everyone a great service." "I replied," said Charles-Roux, "that if we had not done so, it was only out of our desire for peace." "Yes," he said, "and that was to your credit; and besides, no doubt you had judged that you would not be followed by the English, still less the Italians. But, I repeat: had you done so, you would have done everyone a great service." "A thoroughly unexpected opinion from a man whom Maurras calls a Germanophile," adds Charles-Roux.

In March 1936, a French military action would have been deplored; but, if it had been conducted with force and limited to the Rhineland, it would have commanded respect.

It is likely, wrote Eden, that there would have been some combat; but would it have exposed France to the risks of a major war? In any case, an intervention followed by military and political success would have reversed the situation, by ruining Hitler's authority and prestige—especially in his army—and by demonstrating how dangerous his policy really was.

Confronted with the immensity of the danger, most Frenchmen, still believing in an easy peace, did not understand the benefits of risk. "This essentially pacifist nation," continued Eden, "realized that in this situation pacifism was insufficient, and it sought for a means of action that would gain the approval of world opinion but would not risk war: no such means existed."

Completely unknown fifteen years earlier, the man in the brown shirt now held the peace of the entire world in his own hands. In Germany, he controlled a monstrous power. Under the blow of Saturday, March 7, the French hesitated; they were lost. Under the sway of destiny, they would be led to war and defeat.

Meeting of the League of Nations

The secretary-general of the League of Nations, Joseph Avenol, had been officially notified of the affair by the French government. The formal confirmation of a violation of the Versailles and Locarno treaties rested on the Council.

The signatory powers of the Locarno Treaty—except for Germany—met in Paris. Eden, with the vigorous help of Van Zeeland, tried to calm the French: they would all deal with Hitler by diplomatic means. The League Council, convened for March 14, would meet in London, at England's invitation—at the explicit and joint request of Eden and Flandin.

Pope Pius XI laughingly told Ambassador Charles-Roux: "If Aesop were still alive, he would have material for a good fable: the cat who invites the mice to dinner." The idea that the English excelled at manipulating the League of Nations was widespread in Italy, and Pius XI was struck by the return of England to the role of mediator and arbiter, for which she always had a real inclination.

The issue of collective security was not brought up in the League discussions. Long conversations and negotiations were held in private, away from the Council, whose members waited, inactive. Negotiations of weakness!

Flandin "asked the Council to confirm the violation by Germany of Article 43 of the Versailles Treaty, and to invite the secretary-general of the League to officially notify the signatory powers of the Locarno Treaty, in accordance with Article 4 of that treaty. This notification would put the guarantor powers in a position to fulfill their obligations of assistance.

"The Council would also examine how it could personally support this action with recommendations to the members of the League."

What this proposal intended to make understood, discreetly, without daring to say it openly, concerned the study of sanctions against Germany.

But Germany had not violated the Covenant itself. What had been violated was, first, the Treaty of Versailles, and then the treaty concluded at Locarno between a few members of the League. The Council's notification to the signatory powers was the only intervention possible. The Council had no role other than to say: your military operations (if you undertake them) are legal. That statement represented a legal justification for operations that could be undertaken, but which no one intended to undertake.

The accused could not be condemned without first being heard. A German delegation, to be led by Ribbentrop, was invited for March 19. It was specified that, before the League Council, the representatives of Germany would be placed on an equal footing with those of France.

On March 19, after Ribbentrop had given the political and legal reasons for Germany's attitude, the Council—including Italy, but with the abstention of Chile and the absence of Equador—resolved that the German government had infringed Article 43 of the Treaty of Versailles. The Council then informed the guarantors of Locarno, leaving them free to take whatever measures they judged appropriate. The powers who had not signed the Locarno Treaty could condemn Germany, but they were under no obligation to act against her; they pronounced themselves, as did the Locarno powers, opposed to any possibility of war.

The verification of a violation of the Treaty of Versailles—a verification carried out without conviction—encountered no difficulty. It could have been pronounced on the very first day. It was the simple verification of a public and obvious fact. Far from encouraging the resistance of totalitarian states, the League had been reduced to the condition of a registry office for accomplished deeds.

A laughable sentence and a confession of impotence, the condemnation—or, more precisely, the "moral reproach"—inflicted on Hitler for the events of March 7, 1936, did not trouble him any more than the condemnation he had encountered for April 17, 1935. He was being encouraged to persevere in his methods. France had not progressed but still seemed ready to believe in anything.

Having returned from his expedition to the League meeting, Flandin spoke to the Chamber on March 20: "After days burdened with anxiety, the government brings you the consolidation of the peace. Faithful to the provisions of the Treaty, the government brought the problem before the Council. Negotiations continued night and day. . . . Yesterday they resulted in the formal confirmation, reached unanimously by the Council of the League of Nations, of the violation by Germany of Article 43 of the Treaty of Versailles and of the Treaty of Locarno."

For French public opinion, nearly unanimous in demanding peace above all, the violent collapse of March 1936 was dulled by these safe words: peace was assured. These words were only an illusion.

The economic sanctions the French wanted imposed on Germany did not find the same support as those imposed on Italy in the past. Even the Scandinavians declared themselves neutral. The example—certainly not very encouraging—of the sanctions that had failed against Italy was invoked, in order to avoid having to impose sanctions on Germany. With respect to a market as important as Germany, such sanctions would be very costly to those who observed them.

Flandin suggested prohibiting German ships from entering the ports of the Locarno powers; the idea was not accepted. A blockade of German ports! A boarding of German ships! This would mean war!

Flandin was vaguely considering financial sanctions. The experts emphasized Germany's economic problems, depicting Germany as a brazen giant with feet of clay; they stressed the conflict between the financial expert Schacht and the Nazi leaders. They spoke of Germany's already shaky finances, of her precarious balance of payments, of the expedients she had to use for her daily existence. Nothing was done.

Several of the European members of the League of Nations took refuge in a neutrality in which they still believed—an illusory refuge.

To remain in the League was to bet on Anglo-French strength. Yet some of these powers deeply resented the Anglo-French weakness, which they blamed for the collapse of the League of Nations. Mussolini's victory had certainly dealt a disastrous blow to the principle of collective security; but then it was not Europe that was at stake, but an underdeveloped African state. The way it had been treated was scandalous, but the practical considerations and the high political dealings involved could not be overlooked.

In March 1936, what was at stake was the Treaty of Locarno, the cornerstone of the entire diplomatic structure of Western Europe. If France and England did not react forcefully when their own vital interests were at issue, if they did not have the strength to protect their own security, what support could their allies and the neutral states expect from them? A deep pessimism was spreading.

Between April 17, 1934, and March 7, 1936, the situation in Europe had completely changed, passing from a state of balance, which contained Germany, to the supremacy, the hegemony of Hitler; and this in less than two brief years. In 1934 he had been at the mercy of outside forces; with calculated moves, he had passed through the most critical period of his rearmament. He had broken up the elements assembled to maintain balance.

Although France still seemed to hold her rank as the first military power in the world, she had proven incapable of imposing respect. By yielding to Hitler, she had rendered her military alliances worthless. By the end of 1936, the bias of neutrality was destroying the only framework for coalition that Hitler had really feared. Even in 1937, when Hitler pretended not to refuse an invitation to reenter the League of Nations, he included the condition that all the League's powers of coercion should be abolished.

France no longer enjoyed the means of assistance formerly granted by the application of the Covenant's collective obligations. That system vanished, the paper barriers were torn up, and the pacts against war disappeared. There was total chaos. This represented the triumph of the Nazi methods of domination, through the isolation or intimidation of neighbor states, one after the other, by means of so-called bilateral understandings.

Belgium was now concerned only with the defense of her own territory. On July 20, 1936, the foreign minister, Paul-Henri Spaak, stated that he intended to follow "an exclusively and completely Belgian foreign policy." On October 14, King Leopold III repeated his minister's words and announced suddenly "an exclusively and completely Belgian policy." "Since when," asked Eden, "have kings been tossing bombs in public squares?"

The Franco-Belgian military agreement of September 7, 1920, was abandoned. To lessen the impression that the Belgian policy of friendship toward the French, who were confronted with the fait accompli, had been seriously weakened by a brusque return to neutrality, and to appease their apprehensions, Brussels kindly stressed its determination to make a considerable effort to defend Belgium's frontiers, and to maintain the contacts between the two general staffs.

The Plebiscite of March 29

Amid the cheers of enthusiastic crowds, the plebiscite of March 29, 1936, showed that 98 percent of the forty-five million German voters approved of a foreign policy that broke the bonds of the *Diktat* and reaped a series of impressive victories, without leading to war. The Weimar Republic too had aspired toward the results gained in 1936, and the Reich could only rejoice in seeing the end of the limitations imposed by Versailles. The reservations some Germans, particularly diplomats and generals, had about Hitler's policy, arose from a fear of engaging in perilous adventures, whose difficulties were pointed out, weighed, and exaggerated.

Hitler was proud of having been correct in his evaluation of the international situation and in his bold predictions. He knew that he no longer had to fear the League of Nations, and that France would not dare to stop him by force. A feverish rearmament was taking place. The creation of a new *Wehrmacht* in March 1935 and the remilitarization of the Rhineland in March 1936 amounted to the destruction of Versailles, except for the territorial provisions. Germany had recovered full military sovereignty; she no longer had to fear a preventive war. The German army quickly gained an enormous superiority in actual fact over the French army, now reduced to a strictly defensive role. Hitler felt powerful enough to seize by force what would be refused to him in friendly negotiations. The way was open for the acts of aggression that would begin in 1938.

Hitler's finance minister, Schwerin-Krosigk, insists on this point in his memoirs. In March 1936, the lack of reaction that followed Hitler's decision to reoccupy the Rhineland, and his easy victory, convinced him of the weakness of the western powers, and encouraged him to undertake the most daring ventures.

After having felt humiliated, Germany became more immoderately arrogant than if she had been victorious in 1918. Freed from the balancing force of Hapsburg Austria and from the restraints of a constitution, administrative regulations, and civilized conventions, Hitler's power would lead Germany to madness.

Discussions among France, England, and Belgium

Eden declared on March 19, and he repeated it on July 23, that "if France and Belgium were made the objects of unprovoked attack, Great Britain would come to their aid."

To compensate to a certain extent for the weakening in security suffered by France and Belgium, to avoid a repudiation of the 1925 commitments, but mostly to "cheer up" France, as Eden said, by giving her an obvious concession, England announced a closer cooperation between general staffs. Would it not be more effective than the demilitarization of the Rhineland, now a dead issue? The Francophile Vansittart hoped for "the consolidation of a closer understanding between the three Locarno powers. . . . Contacts between the general staffs would be decisive proof of the tightening of the connections between them." But Sir John Simon opposed it. British opinion feared that the General Staff talks would lead to alliances, which might automatically draw England into international complications on the Continent and ensure the French of her military aid. Lloyd George warned against the approaching danger for the United Kingdom of a military alliance with France. He passionately denounced France's intransigency and declared her largely responsible for the existing situation, which she created by her persistent refusal to disarm.

However an agreement reached in London on March 19, 1936, between the French, English, and Belgian governments directed the general staffs to make contact and to prepare the technical means necessary for the fulfillment of their obligations in the event of unprovoked German aggression.

Talks were held in mid-April. The French hoped that they would lead to an automatic Franco-British alliance, which they thought would be the only means of keeping Germany in check. But as early as April 1 Eden indicated that the General Staff talks would be limited to the period of the negotiations with Germany for the conclusion of a new Locarno Pact, and that they could not bring about "any promise of a political nature or any obligation with regard to the organizaion of national defense." Only if this effort to reach reconciliation with Germany failed, would measures to "address a new situation" be considered.

It was asserted that, as a result of the London talks which culminated in the agreement of March 19, the Locarno commitments would be "provisionally" maintained. The signatories of Locarno had given themselves the task of revising the Treaty, if Germany accepted certain preliminary conditions. In anticipation of a possible German refusal, the General Staff conversations were to begin among the other parties for the purpose of preparing a common defense. Italy withdrew. Only France, England, and Belgium remained.

The talks held in London on April 15 and 16 among the English, Belgian, and French general staffs, had no substantial result. However, it was decided that if German troops crossed their own frontier to carry out an unprovoked act of aggression, and if the British government then decided to come to the aid of France, the English General Staff could send two infantry divisions to France.

The British government did not want to undertake any precise obligation, but it did begin to rearm vigorously.

The talks among the Locarno powers, who had abandoned any idea of coercing Germany, ended with a few proposals intended to allow the opening of serious negotiations. Hitler accepted practically none of these proposals. He simply answered that he was ready to conclude a new treaty founded on equal rights.

On March 31 he presented a "peace plan." He proposed to France and Belgium the establishment of demilitarized zones on both sides of the German frontier—a proposition that was a real spoof, since, if taken seriously, it would mean the destruction of the Maginot line, which was not yet counterbalanced by the Siegfried line.

Hitler wanted to conclude nonaggression pacts for a period of twenty-five years with France and Belgium, and also with Holland. These treaties, like Locarno, would be guaranteed by Great Britain and Italy. The offer made to Europe of twenty-five years of peace would marvelously replace Locarno, on a basis of perfect equality of rights. Hitler declared himself ready to negotiate similar pacts not only with Poland, but also with Czechoslovakia. He also declared himself ready to conclude an air pact, forbidding the bombing of cities situated more than twelve miles behind the front lines. For the sake of "humanizing war," gas and incendiary shells would be forbidden. Germany was prepared to negotiate nonaggression pacts with all her neighbors and to join the League of Nations; finally, she was ready for the most extended economic discussions.

Were these offers by Hitler an example of high comedy? Or was he sincere . . . in his own way? He would sometimes tell his intimates that he was determined to reach his objectives through peaceful means alone: to begin with, the absorption of Austria and the Sudeten Germans, as well as a reasonable settlement for Danzig and the Polish Corridor.

In search of a new security agreement which would replace the Locarno Treaty, the statesmen responsible for British policy had adopted a "wait and see" policy; they agreed to consider Hitler's proposals, hoping to reach a three-power understanding. They told the French that they did not want to miss any chance for agreement and that all Hitler's offers had to be carefully explored; the Labour opposition vigorously announced itself to be of the same opinion.

The French answered the German plan in their note of April 7. Attempting vainly, as they had since 1919, to give effective powers to the League of Nations, they spoke of regional treaties, of nonaggression pacts with mutual assistance under the Geneva system, and of an international force under League command in the event of treaty violations.

By virtue of a decision the Locarno powers made on April 10 at Geneva to probe the German government, on May 6 England asked Germany for precise details, in a lengthy questionnaire published by the newspapers. It created ill-feelings in Germany because it revealed the "doubts held by the government in London as to the good faith, loyalty, seriousness, and peaceful character of the Reich's political intentions."

Hitler, who had been asked to respect "the existing territorial and political status quo of Europe," was angered by this "schoolmaster's tone" and gave no reply.

Exchanges of memoranda, concerning only proposals, not preliminary conditions for general negotiations, continued without the slightest progress being made toward the preparation of a treaty to replace the Locarno Pact.

The Failure of the League and of the French System

Hitler had won without having to fight. He had acquired the privilege of daring all. Collective security could no longer be taken seriously; the failure, already apparent after 1932 with Japan, was striking in 1936 with Germany.

The League, Litvinov had said, had to become conscious of the seriousness of the task it was entrusted with. A default in that sphere would cause the worst dangers for those who still believed in it. Litvinov had vehemently denounced the German action and, refuting the criticisms of the Franco-

Soviet pact, had demonstrated the emptiness of Hitler's proposals of March 7. He concluded: "We cannot include among collective measures of security a collective capitulation to the aggressor, a collective acceptance of a bonus given to the aggressor, through the adoption of plans . . . advantageous to the aggressor. The resolutions of such a League would only be laughed at. Why have a League of Nations of that sort?"

People everywhere denounced the failure of the League. This gave alibis to both Paris and London; the failures of Paris, of London, or of both, were labeled failures of the League of Nations. There was disdain for the League assemblies, which dragged on in a futile buzz of speeches. They had practically ceased to represent a political community.

Nevertheless, many small nations remained tied to what survived of the League; there they exchanged information and worries. In a situation that saved them from isolation, some independent publicity could be raised against the powerful offensives of totalitarian propaganda.

Since the challenge of March 7, 1936, the entire structure of 1919 had been collapsing; the edifice of Versailles was now just a historical memory. It was a terrible blow to French policy and also to British policy—although this would only become apparent later. The "gathering storm" was absolutely certain after March 1936. French prestige was fatally injured.

The French system had been, for fifteen years, the backbone of Europe and had oriented the status quo in favor of those who had benefited from the treaties, and against those who had lost the war; but now it had disappeared. It had rested on the firm determination to maintain the Covenant, to respect and enforce respect for its obligations; this determination no longer existed. The Ethiopian affair had shaken the foundations of the system; the Covenant's obligations were falling into disuse. Moreover, France could no longer marshal the force necessary to impose respect for her own will. Until 1935, she had had a much superior military strength, on account of German military inequality, and because the left bank of the Rhine gave her an offensive base which ensured her freedom of maneuver.

After March 7, 1936, France's allies could no longer ignore the fact that she was losing any strategic base of offensive maneuver in the Rhineland and in Westphalia, Germany's major industrial center. Hereafter, a war could no longer begin on the Rhineland frontier, which would soon be protected by the fortification of the Siegfried line. On April 30, 1936, at a meeting of General Staff leaders, General Gamelin philosophically declared that "if the Germans build fortifications in the Rhineland, and if, in addition, the German army does not advance into Holland or Belgium, the French army would find it impossible to invade Germany. Germany could stop the French army with rather a small number of troops; she would then be able to act against Czechoslovakia, Poland . . . In that case, a maneuver of the same type as the Salonica operation—but perhaps of far greater dimensions—would be necessary."

Although until 1936 France had the most powerful army, Germany, who had just recovered equality of military rights, eliminated France's base for offensive maneuver and thus won effective superiority. The French note of April 17, 1934—"France will henceforth ensure her security through her own resources"—seemed a cruel mockery.

From then on, France no longer possessed the determination of a great power able to decide its political line. She no longer had her own foreign policy. She submissively followed in the wake of Great Britain, on whom she would have to rely more and more against an ever more threatening German attack.

16

The Rome-Berlin Axis and the Anti-Comintern Pact

Two Ominous Years: March 1936–March 1938

For Europe the two years that followed March 7, 1936, stand out as a sultry calm, a foreshadowing of the great storms to come. In the military and economic fields, that time was actively used by Germany, where rearmament was at its height. German youth was being given military training before being called to the colors of a nation that had been transformed into a gigantic war factory. Lessons were learned from the practical experiences of the German air force during the Spanish Civil War.

It was calculated that in 1937 armaments absorbed only about a fifth of the total product of the metallurgical industry, whose exports had not been perceptibly reduced. Everything changed in 1938; the speed of rearming, especially in aircraft and tanks, surpassed all expectations. The excellence of these results was evident in the Spanish war. Since September 1938, Germany had speeded up war preparations much more energetically than France. This situation continued during the strange period of the "phony war," until May 1940.

In September 1936, a four-year plan was begun to totally exploit all German resources. The economy was put at the service of war preparations, under a rigorous system in which the state controlled private initiative.

During this same year, 1936, the Nazi regime achieved a definite internal stabilization. On June 2 Himmler became commander of all the German police forces, which from then on were independent and omnipotent within the SS state.

In August 1936, for ten days, the Olympic Games provided the occasion for an astonishing parade of force, discipline, and order. It was an immense moral success for Germany, then building the Siegfried line and proclaiming herself devoted to an understanding among nations for twenty-five years of peace.

On January 30, 1937, four years after he had come to power, Hitler told the *Reichstag:* "The period of surprises is over. Peace is our supreme goal."

International policy was no longer mainly concerned with Germany, but rather with the settlement of the Ethiopian affair and the Spanish Civil War. In the same speech of January 30 Hitler proclaimed: "I solemnly remove Germany's signature from the declaration extorted from a weak government against its better judgment: that Germany is responsible for the war."

This formula, which in the 1920s would have created a scandal, raised no protests. The foreign press simply observed that German responsibility, recognized in the peace treaty, could not be eliminated through a unilateral declaration.

The coronation of George VI in England and the World's Fair in Paris in 1937 did not give Europe periods of truce. While he advocated peace, Hitler proclaimed "national dynamism" in his sonorous voice. Going from audacity to audacity, he would overcome all obstacles through a brutality mixed with shrewdness, dissimulation, and cynicism. He asserted as a truism that "success is the sole judge of right and wrong."

The Rome-Berlin Axis

Hitler was laying the foundations of his alliances: he drew closer to Italy and Japan. With the League of Nations reduced to powerlessness, Hitler would have been forced to respect the peace only if he had seen both Italy and the Soviet Union among his adversaries.

But now the Ethiopian affair had thrown Mussolini back on to the German side. He directed his anger toward the League of Nations, "an assembly of austere swindlers . . . a Holy Alliance of plutocratic nations, formed to exploit the greater part of the world." On November 11, 1937, he left the League. His vindictive impatience had forged "the Rome-Berlin Axis" in November 1936. He wanted to be on the side of power, the only decisive attraction for him. Flattering himself that he was the supreme judge of war and peace, he began to eliminate the basic caution that had kept him, until then, within the bounds of a reasonable and realistic moderation, despite his ambitious blustering.

When Mussolini visited Berlin in September 1937, he was dazzled by Germany. He became Hitler's ally, in a way his prisoner, as Hitler's power brilliantly asserted itself. Mussolini was celebrated as "an epoch-making phenomenon" (*sekuläre Erscheinung*), but he saw himself in reality cast into the background with the rank of "brilliant second."

Following the example of the German diplomats and military men of the old school, Hitler was not interested in the Mediterranean. It was in the Mediterranean that Mussolini sought compensation for what he was about to lose in Central Europe.

Moreover Hitler wanted passionately to reach an alliance with Mussolini, whom he admired for his victorious struggle against Marxism. It was obvious that the crossing of the Italians to Germany's side considerably reinforced German nationalism and bellicosity. In fact, German propaganda had moved more slowly than Italian propaganda—that is to say, than Mussolini. The Duce wrote personally for the newspapers, and Fascist Italy had not been slowed down by the moderating forces imposed on the most extreme Nazis by the multiplicity of people and influences. Mussolini attempted to make Germany move more quickly toward the intimidation she could exert more forcefully over Europe now that Fascist Italy had united with Germany and in November 1937, joined the Anti-Comintern Pact.

The Anti-Comintern Pact

Violently anti-Bolshevik, Hitler was also Russophobe—a feeling that was natural for an Austrian, but contrary to the traditional eastern orientation of Prussian officers. Hitler put an end to the military cooperation which had been established since the Rapallo Treaty.

In its audacity, Nazism claimed the divine mission of fighting Bolshevism. From the Rapallo Treaty of April 1922 and the Treaty of Berlin which confirmed Rapallo in April 1926, Germany moved to the Anti-Comintern Pact, directed against the Communist International—in fact against the Soviet Union—and signed with Japan in Berlin on November 25, 1936.

This pact, open to all nations and intended to combat all the activities of the Communist International, assumed the form of an ideological entente. Through a secret agreement, Germany and Japan committed themselves to fighting the attempts of Communism to expand through war. In the event of an unprovoked attack or threat of attack by the USSR, the signatories would consult each other and observe a benevolent neutrality toward each other. Neither of them would conclude with the USSR a political treaty contrary to the spirit of the anti-Comintern agreement, without the prior approval of its partner.

It was obvious that the pact marked a break with the Soviets, who were then thrown into a dangerous crisis. It was to a large extent a crisis of economic growth, but so serious that it became the beginning of a paralysis; and even a regime of terror, with its bloody "purges," could not put an end to it. The Anti-Comintern Pact provoked great concern in Moscow.

The Spanish Civil War facilitated the rapprochement between Italy and Germany. The Anti-Comintern Pact had been planned by Ribbentrop even before the onset of the Spanish Civil War, and it was vigorously urged forward by the unofficial diplomacy of his *Stab,* despite vague opposition by official German diplomacy. On November 6, 1937, Italy joined the German-Japanese Anti-Comintern Pact. The Berlin-Rome-Tokyo triangle established a friendly cooperation in diplomatic issues. "Three powers in the world," Eden declared, "who recognize only one factor: brute force."

The Japanese at that time considered the pact to be aimed exclusively at the Soviet Union. They refused to confront the united naval forces of the Anglo-Saxon powers, for they believed that, should there be war with England, the United States would intervene.

Events in the Far East

In studying the origins of the Second World War, it would be a mistake to ignore the importance of events in the Far East. Germany drew great benefits from them. Old-fashioned diplomats like Neurath did not want to orient their policy unilaterally toward Japan and against China, where Germany had important economic and cultural interests. Ribbentrop adopted the opposite policy, for he was a fanatical believer in Japan's military power. On April 29, 1939, he explained his views to Count Teleki, prime minister of Hungary: "Today the situation is totally different from what it was during the Great War, when Japan was an ally of the Entente." He claimed that the power ratio of the Japanese and American fleets was three to one.

After 1935, prompted by her military men, Japan resumed her expansion in China, where a war begain in July 1937, although a state of war had not been formally declared. The "Chinese incident" followed the "Manchurian incident" of 1931. The Chinese put up strong resistance. In November 1937, the signatory powers of the Washington Naval Treaty of 1922 limited themselves to recording Japan's violation of the treaty agreements.

In October 1938, Japan controlled nearly half of China, including the wealthiest provinces and the ports; but the occupied areas were theaters of incessant guerilla warfare.

Hitler's long and feverish anti-Communist propaganda campaign would not keep him from concluding in August 1939, through his Machiavellian opportunism, the German-Soviet Pact.

17

The Appeasement Policy of Neville Chamberlain

Neville Chamberlain, Prime Minister

After a twenty-six-year reign, King George V died in January 1936. The Prince of Wales, who then became Edward VIII, abdicated at the end of the few months during which the French crisis of March 1936 ran its course.

After the coronation of George VI, brother and successor of Edward VIII, Baldwin resigned as prime minister, in May 1937. Neville Chamberlain, who had been chancellor of the Exchequer for the past six years and was now sixty-eight years old, succeeded him as prime minister.

Chamberlain was born in Birmingham, where he had been lord mayor from 1911 to 1916, and in 1917 he had become conscription minister in a cabinet just created by Lloyd George. His half brother, Austen Chamberlain, had won him this position with the help of Lord Curzon, and especially of Lord Milner. He remained minister for only seven months, having failed totally in a task which, according to Lloyd George, required exceptional talents. He never again wanted to work with Lloyd George. He became a member of Parliament only when he was about fifty. In 1931, he was named chancellor of the Exchequer.

Neville Chamberlain, who had come from a provincial business milieu, now found himself at the center of the dazzling financial oligarchy of the City, recently shaken by the devaluation of the pound. As finance minister, he was successful during this difficult period. Since the fiscal and customs policy was then international, he was initiated into foreign relations. His

210

views were those of his milieu. Very isolationist, Chamberlain was convinced
that British prestige was unshakable; he had no doubt whatever on that
point. A vast armament program was strengthening British prestige as well
as fighting the economic crisis in the most effective way. All sectors of
business were stimulated by it: the stock market, primary materials, price
levels, and so on. This return to prosperity was not to be compromised by
the risks and adventures of war. In 1935, England had been humiliated because she was not armed; now she would be strong, and never again be
humiliated.

When Neville Chamberlain took over the prime ministership, he noted: "I
will be more interested than Stanley Baldwin in foreign affairs." Marvelously
sensitive to what the British people thought, Baldwin had directed England
toward an enlightened conservatism, which attempted to eliminate class
hatred. After the general strike of 1926, he had rejected any idea of reprisals.
He had good judgment in foreign policy. On July 30, 1934, five days after
the assassination of Dollfuss, he declared: "Our frontier is on the Rhine."
He had never had any illusion about dictators: "We have," he would say,
"two maniacs in Europe; something fatal is bound to happen." But, too
legalistic and too passive, he refused to embark on a policy fraught with
unmeasured risks.

Chamberlain too had a very dispassionate opinion of Hitler, for whom
he felt no personal sympathy: Hitler was a "thoroughly dishonest" character.

Chamberlain had been struck by the weakness of France, who, on March 7,
1936, could only yield before Germany. He had been alarmed by the Popular
Front's triumph in the elections of May 1936, and he feared a too powerful
Soviet influence in a divided France constantly in a state of cabinet crisis.

He felt little respect for the inconsistent governments, formed every four to
six months, which rushed to London for recognition and sovereign investiture
in foreign affairs. An extreme pessimist, in January 1938 he deplored "the
public danger" constituted by the hopeless weakness of France, "incapable
of having a government last for more than nine months," and with governments themselves incapable of "keeping a secret longer than a half hour."
The prime minister was surrounded by an atmosphere of hostility toward
France, and every argument that could further weaken his trust in France
was used to influence him: political divisions, failure to execute air force
rearmament programs, and so on. How could anyone have confidence in a
country with such an exiguous air force? In such political chaos, was not
Communism to be feared?

Many Englishmen considered France a first class "honorary" power. She
was becoming "the sick lady of Europe," according to the Francophile

Vansittart, faced with a Germany where there was "one people, one nation, one leader."

After the remilitarization of the Rhineland, and after the loss of Italian friendship, France's authority was nearly crushed. Her stock in international dealings had fallen terribly since March 1936, while England's stock had gone up tremendously because of British rearmament. France had lost her own diplomatic system, which had been profoundly dislocated by Hitler's will. Of her past positions, now undermined and dismantled, almost nothing remained. Her ruined foreign policy became just a supplement—although still a powerful one—to the English diplomatic system. It is true that no one questioned her defensive military force, with the Maginot line, and Stalin told Ribbentrop on the night of August 23, 1939: "In my opinion, the French army, all the same, deserves respect." The British army was weak; but Stalin expressed the idea that, despite its military weakness, "England will make war with astuteness and tenacity."

The French no longer played an important role in international politics. Following in the wake of British policy, they avoided independent initiatives, all the more since the initiative of April 17, 1934, was now considered an irresponsible, impulsive act. They let England take action: toward Spain, Italy, Czechoslovakia, and Poland. They obeyed. They would obey and yield in Munich in September 1938, and declare war in September 1939.

The Policy of Appeasement

England, who was regaining her armaments and, with prosperity, her national pride, was now in a position to follow a policy of waiting and attrition.

After all, Hitler and Mussolini guaranteed a capitalist order; that was a great deal. Russian propaganda caused much worry and anger. German expansion protected Europe against the Bolshevik threat. England herself had nothing to fear for her integrity. Everyone respected her—Hitler more than anyone. His agents in England repeated what he himself had professed in *Mein Kampf:* an alliance with England was for him the necessary condition for any new order.

England, armed and strong, could display understanding and goodwill and could reach an understanding with both Hitler and Mussolini through a policy of appeasement. Of course, these dictators wanted some satisfactions: but it seemed unreasonable to uphold the absurd arrangements of the Versailles Treaty and to persist in imposing them by force and keep German minorities in heterogeneous states. This abnormal situation defied common sense and ignited centers of conflagration. In a Europe threatened by the disturbance of Communism, Chamberlain—the incarnation of appeasement—was ready to undertake a radical revision of the 1919 treaties. Following the old balance of power policy, he would consent, in his realism, to make large concessions to satisfy Hitler's claims, on condition that these claims would be achieved with "decency," through peaceful means. The concessions England would make had to be "reasonable." She could, she had to, reach an understanding with Hitler and with Mussolini.

Most of the "appeasers" had no conception of Hitler's haunting visions of unlimited power. Filled with circumspection, they did not feel what was frightful in his racial hatreds, what was criminal in the brutality of his despotism.

At the *Times,* Geoffrey Dawson and Barington Ward were active "appeasers." For some years, the real center of the government of the British nation was in the oligarchic milieu of the Astors.

As chancellor of the Exchequer, Chamberlain had been invited to and received at the great country houses. Like beautiful luxury hotels, they offered him the most comfortable hospitality and the simplicity of the English country weekend. With a discreet informality, the other guests left him with the impression that he was there to rest. Some guests had been invited especially for him. In this milieu, the only legitimate international was that of capitalism. What mattered was to revive the world economy and financial cooperation: these were the most serious problems.

Chamberlain felt no sympathy for Nazism, and he hoped that Hitler would be stopped in time. He believed that once Germany reached the limits he had set to Hitler's ambitions, she would go no further. Hitler would not dare go beyond these limits. A serious misjudgment! The man in the brown shirt was convinced that England would never resort to the *ultima ratio*—the use of force—and that she wanted peace at any price. Before his crowds of followers, who one day would fear his recklessness and the next be exalted by his triumph and strengthened by his audacity, Hitler knew no limit.

Chamberlain's realistic policy was backed by the great majority of his ministers: Sir John Simon, Sir Samuel Hoare, Lord Halifax, and others.

His "realism" encountered some opposition at the Foreign Office, where France had some good friends who had often opposed the clearly Francophobe Treasury in the reparations issue. Sir Eric Phipps, now ambassador to Berlin and soon to be ambassador to Paris, felt "a religious horror of the Nazi regime"; he pictured Hitler as an abnormal being who could not be trusted, and he found very amusing a comparison Hitler had dared to make between the SS and the SA, on the one hand, and the Salvation Army, on the other.

Since 1935, foreign minister Anthony Eden had been considered "an uncompromising enemy of Fascism"; now, accused by Chamberlain of destroying his attempts at conciliation with Mussolini, Eden was forced to resign on February 20, 1938. In the presence of the ironic Italian ambassador, Grandi, they faced one another "like two cocks about to fight." Sir Robert Vansittart, His Majesty's chief diplomatic advisor, also had to resign: Chamberlain considered him a fanatical Germanophobe.

Sir Horace Wilson, His Majesty's chief economic advisor, became the prime minister's closest collaborator.

Chamberlain thus wanted a policy of entente with the totalitarian states. He was determined to do anything to keep England from extremely dangerous risks. A provincial puritan whose narrow soul was enclosed in coils of craftiness, Neville Chamberlain had an exalted sense of British respectability, and also the deep-seated pacifism of a businessman. He had the greatest confidence in himself, as well as in England. But amidst the Astors, in the oligarchic milieu in which he was immersed, emissaries brought in illusions and left with what was supposedly very reliable information on anti-Communism. Ambassador Grandi was mistaken in attributing decisive power to such groups.

The prime minister's feelings for France were not based on love, and even less on admiration. He did not think, as his half brother Sir Austen Chamberlain had in the past, that "one loves France as one loves a woman." France had an army which was part of British armaments. Nevertheless, the prime minister could not allow England's own freedom of action to be limited by the French.

Until the last day of the League of Nations' collective life—that is, until 1936—the forces of order in Europe were sufficient to protect Europe against tyranny. In 1934, at the very moment when Germany decided to free herself from the League in order to later destroy it, Russia entered it as a permanent Council member. Alone in the *chassé-croisé* of the Council, England and France had remained at the center of the League from the beginning to the end. By themselves until 1934, and with the support of the Soviet Union during the following years, they could have deployed forces sufficient to stop Germany. They lacked only determination and a sense of adventure. Their role was to be leaders; they still believed that it was a role of arbiters.

In the Franco-British association, the stock of France had lowered drastically since March 1936 in relation to that of England. People did not trust the effectiveness of the resistance France would oppose to German-Italian initiatives. France doubted herself and began planning a "withdrawal to the French Empire" in foreign affairs.

The British, on the contrary, enjoyed the prestige of their rearmament expenditures, of the publicity surrounding them, and also of the beneficial effects they had on economic recovery. But what value was there in tons of steel without one strong spirit?

The truth is that France had already lost three-quarters of her authority. The Germans and Italians had realized the extent of her collapse. The nonintervention that would be proclaimed in the Spanish situation was a farce. The English failed to understand that they were themselves, though to a lesser degree, affected by the same factors.

18

Changes in Germany: February 1938

In the German chancellery on the afternoon of November 5, 1937, Hitler announced to Goering, Neurath, war minister Marshal von Blomberg, and army chief of staff General von Fritsch that German rearmament was now completed and that he had decided to ensure Germany "more space" in Europe. That space had to be taken by force. His plans were clearly outlined: absorption of Austria, destruction of Czechoslovakia, and settlement of the Polish question. He did not desire war, but he accepted it. He had decided to achieve his program in one way or another, *so oder so.*

The aggressive plans Hitler revealed on that day brought reservations from Neurath, Blomberg, and Fritsch. The generals did not want Germany to confront both England and France.

On the Eve of Aggresssion

February 4, 1938—three months after this meeting which Colonel Hossbach recorded in his minutes—became a date that symbolized the change taking place in the balance of forces at the heart of the Third Reich. Marshal von Blomberg, who had recently married below his class, and General von Fritsch, who was accused of having homosexual tendencies, were retired along with a dozen rebellious generals who were criticizing a foreign policy that provoked the Russians and was reckless in Spain. The Führer himself assumed command of the armed forces and placed at their head officers sympathetic to Nazism; from then on, they would be under the thumb of the National Socialist party.

A few days later, the president of the *Reichsbank,* Schacht, who distrusted Hitler's venturesome projects, was replaced as minister for economic affairs by the National Socialist Funk. And finally, Ribbentrop, ambassador to London since 1936, succeeded Baron von Neurath as foreign minister.

Ponderous, impassive, phlegmatic, and shrewd, the Württemberger Konstantin von Neurath had good sense, but no imagination. Since he had as his undersecretary his own son-in-law, Mackensen, a witty remark circulated in Berlin, attributed like so many others to Ambassador François-Poncet: "At the Wilhelmstrasse you can find the Father and the Son, if not the Holy Spirit." Neurath restrained Hitler in his dangerous adventures, but not very much. He wanted an agreement with England, and England asked for nothing more. He was hostile to Russia, but discreetly.

As long as Baron von Neurath more or less controlled the foreign ministry, German diplomacy devoted itself to improving the Reich's position, without war but by every means other than war. Germany encouraged the efforts undertaken to undermine Austrian independence and took pride in the difficulties of Great Britain, and even more of the Soviets, in the Far East, and also in the difficulties of Great Britain, and even more of France, in the Mediterranean. Germany profited from a favorable set of circumstances: having few interests in the Mediterranean and in the Far East, she could weave astutely the web in which the prey would soon fall. And following the path drawn by Baron von Neurath with such artful deceit, she was moving toward dominance in Eastern Europe.

Neurath's departure was a surprise. He had just turned sixty-five and, for his birthday, had received the most cordial congratulations from Hitler, who respected him and listened to him, although he seldom followed his moderate advice. Neurath's fall was due mostly to Goering and Goebbels, who criticized his passivity—Goebbels asking for nothing better than to become foreign minister himself—and also to Himmler, as friend and supporter of Ribbentrop. Neurath was appointed "premier of the secret cabinet," an honor no more substantial than the appointment of Fritsch as commander of a regiment.

Ribbentrop

After March 1938, the German foreign ministry was run by Joachim von Ribbentrop, industrious but poorly gifted, very incompetent in a group of such extraordinary competence, very sensitive to questions of protocol, arrogant, ardent in conflicts over jurisdiction and authority. He wanted to give the impression that he was a statesman with profound thoughts. He spoke French and English very well, and Hitler considered him to be an expert on England. He had been an officer during the war and had assisted General von Seeckt in matters of the armistice. According to his colleague, finance minister Schwerin von Krosigkh, he was still wondering in 1930 whether to run for the *Reichstag* as a Center or as a Democratic candidate. In 1932 he had been a newcomer to the Nazi party. In April 1934, he was appointed special commissioner for disarmament issues. Hitler sometimes called him "his Bismarck," but he often declared that he was a zero, *eine Niete*. Hitler kept him because he did not want to admit past mistakes, and because he did not like new faces.

Eden wrote of Ribbentrop—in the past a vendor of champagne and the son-in-law of Henkell, the major German champagne producer—that he was essentially a traveling salesman: "His ideas about policy and diplomacy never reached higher than this level; his weakness, tragic for his country, resulted from his inability to understand." He was impervious to any point of view other than his own.

The change in German policy occurred at the precise moment when in London Neville Chamberlain, with his policy of appeasement, was ready to offer major concessions to Germany.

The greatest talent of Ribbentrop—that "first parrot of the Third Reich" in the words of Goering, who despised him, as did Goebbels—was to formulate in diplomatic terms exactly what Hitler wanted to hear and to confirm, in the traditional language of diplomacy, Hitler's famous "intuitions." The only man who might have been able to open Hitler's eyes instead flattered the agitator, entrenced in a frightening pan-Germanism that was not only brutal but beastly, the agitator who, in his reckless and childish feeling of omnipotence, would decide, on "the throw of the dice," matters whose infinite consequences depended upon his yes or no.

Germany's strength had become immense. If Germany had had as leader a diplomat of genius such as Bismarck, with his astute harshness and the caution he showed in his dangerous glory, he would have been able to use her strength to its fullest; or even Stresemann, who had given back to a disarmed Germany her position as a great power, and who too wanted a revision of the Treaty of Versailles, but without throwing Germany into an adventure with unforeseeable consequences.

German Diplomacy

While showing extreme caution and taking great care to cover themselves before leaders who were difficult to deal with, the German diplomats were aware of their responsibilities. They indicated the possible baneful repercussions of the different decisions of their government. Conscientious and diligent, they gave accurate information on the whole, and the clarity of the advice provided by some of the diplomats was remarkable—whether given by Diego von Bergen at the Vatican, or by Herbert von Dirksen in London. Undersecretary von Bülow, himself quite removed from Nazism, would say to von Dirksen to comfort him: "Here, as everywhere else, you cannot cook without water." In Washington, Hans Heinrich Dieckhoff never concealed that Germany had rapidly found herself confronted by a formidable coalition, and in Moscow Count Friedrich Werner von der Schulenburg[1] was a great ambassador.

Deep in his heart, Hitler despised diplomats; he looked on them all as men often without energy and always without frankness. He had them watched by Nazi emissaries. The diplomats increased their warnings; did these warnings ever reach Hitler, the only man truly responsible? They did, but Hitler paid no attention; he disdained the processes and ways of traditional diplomacy. In the days of Bismarck, or even of Wilhelm II or of Stresemann, the reports of the Wilhelmstrasse had a major importance: they gave direction and produced decisions; now the diplomats continued their routine in vain. In the event of an international crisis, the diplomats would no longer be in control, now that there was Hitler. Sometimes diplomacy was only used to better deceive foreigners.

Hitler was much more influenced by the reports of the so-called "intelligence" services than by diplomatic dispatches. The Italian historian Mario Toscano has very rightly stressed the incalculable influence exercised over dictators by information consisting essentially of the intercepted and deciphered secret documents of foreign powers. Are dictators particularly impressionable? Obsessed by their prestige, convinced of their genius, and accustomed to having their clairvoyance admiringly praised, they are deeply hurt by the harsh judgments passed behind their backs by their adversaries. Reading the flattery they should ignore, they react impulsively. They feel personal anger for the offensive and bittersweet remarks no one dares make to their faces—remarks reported to them by the secret services, which enjoy unlimited funds.

The war of espionage and counterespionage which preceded and accompanied the second world conflagration appears to have surpassed in reality all that has been written in fiction. The undersecretary of the Wilhelmstrasse, Baron Ernst von Weizsäcker, does not conceal in his memoirs that the intelligence service, the *Forschungsamt,* deciphered a good half of the dispatches of the Berlin diplomatic corps. If, among the English codes, the very most secret was not known, the Italian, Polish, and many other codes had been broken. Some governments had no secrets but open secrets, and

---

1. Schulenburg participated in the assassination plot of 1944 against Hitler and was executed on November 10, 1944.

it was discovered that in several capitals—in Rome in 1935 as in Ankara in 1943—that embassy safes were the easiest things in the world to open. The most confidential orders would arrive regularly each morning on the desk of a dictator, a fascinated reader.

In Germany diplomacy moved more slowly and more cautiously than press and propaganda. Smooth-tongued, it glided into the breach that was always threatening to open between England and France.

Hitler's Tactics

Other factors worked in Hitler's favor: his adversaries' weakness and discord, and the passionate nationalism of the Germans living beyond the Reich's limits—this nationalism created a moral position unfavorable to the powers who wanted to oppose absorption by Germany. As long as Hitler emphasized the principles of nationality and self-determination of peoples and used them as reasons for his actions, it was difficult for the western powers to justify intervention.

Events, spurred on by Hitler's dynamism, hurried along their course. With unscrupulous daring, the Führer freed himself of all international obligations by repudiating treaty clauses one after the other, shaking off all constraints, and building alliances with Japan and Italy.

But he understood that the boldest audacity had to proceed in stages. His progression was astutely calculated, each step individually not important enough or not dramatic enough to make anyone accept the risks of a real war. He unfailingly affirmed his desire for peace. The cleverness of his game gave his opponents reasons for not resisting and suggested pretexts for retreat.

Chamberlain's most cordial gestures of consideration could not satisfy Hitler. He would switch over to overt aggression: the absorption of Austria; the dismemberment, followed by the occupation, of Czechoslovakia; the war against Poland. In Germany it was not only the Nazis and the believers in the prewar regime who desired a revision of the Treaty of Versailles. Most of the opponents of National Socialism approved of Hitler's foreign policy, as long as it was crowned with success. In order to dominate Europe, he was determined to launch a war, but he did not want a world war like that of 1914–18; he intended to limit himself to a series of small conflicts.

Since 1919 German policy had relied, to a large extent, on the attitude of England, who had been delighted to see Germany disappear as a naval power. That reaction corresponded entirely to the ideas Hitler had expressed in *Mein Kampf* advocating an Anglo-German alliance. He was overjoyed at the conclusion, in 1935, of the naval pact with England.

The arrival of Ribbentrop at the foreign ministry as successor of the Anglophile Neurath marked a serious turning point in German policy. Ribbentrop's conversations as ambassador to London had given him the conviction that "since the abdication of Edward VIII," Germany would have to fight the English to make her "vital interests" triumph.

Public opinion, supreme in Great Britain, was shocked by the excesses of Nazism. It deviated from its Germanophilia. The English people probably felt that the treatment of Protestants, Catholics, and Jews in Germany was the business of the Germans; but so much cruelty, so much barbarism, made any agreement with Germany difficult. In such a situation, how could foreign policy be separated from domestic policy?

At the same time, the changes in the social structure of Germany tended to alienate her from England, by reducing the importance of the old traditional ruling classes in favor of the Nazi party leaders who were largely drawn from the middle classes and from the lesser bourgeoisie.

The Visit of Lord Halifax

Lord Halifax's visit to Germany on November 19, 1937, was a striking indication of England's appeasement policy. A former viceroy of India, Lord Halifax was now lord president of the cabinet; three months later, he would succeed Eden at the Foreign Office. He enjoyed the confidence of Chamberlain, and the prime minister held great hopes for this visit; Eden, on the contrary, was displeased by it. Tall, grave, reserved, ascetic-looking, with a paralyzed hand always gloved in black, Lord Halifax enjoyed fox hunting: he would be called, in jest, "Lord Hallalifax." He had been invited by Goering to visit an international hunting exhibition in Berlin; from Berlin, he went to Berchtesgaden to see Hitler.

This visit has been compared to Haldane's visit to Berlin in 1912. But they were very different in nature. Haldane, then war minister, had left for Germany with a precise program for negotiations on naval and diplomatic questions with the kaiser, Chancellor Bethmann-Hollweg, and Admiral von Tirpitz. Although Haldane was an extreme Germanophile, he realized that the emperor wanted an entente with England, but at the same time "he wanted new ships"; the naval agreement sought by the English was therefore impossible.

Hitler and Goering, while giving Lord Halifax repeated assurances of their pacifism, raised the questions of Austria, of the Sudetenland, and of Danzig. Far from giving them explicit warnings against any intervention in Central Europe, Halifax observed that "from the English standpoint, it does not seem that the status quo should be maintained, in any case." With time changes might occur, particularly in matters relating to "Danzig, Austria, and

Czechoslovakia." But England wished that these changes "would come about through peaceful means."

Halifax declared himself prepared to "discuss the colonial problem." However, Hitler felt that it was too early to discuss that issue. Fundamentally this Austrian was not interested in colonies, and if he did express colonial claims it was only to exert pressure on England.

Halifax believed in the sincerity of Hitler, who explained the philosophy behind his program of claims of which, said Hitler, it would be "reasonable to undertake a settlement." The Führer gave no guarantee of his policy in Central Europe. He would be forced to take; it was best not to interfere.

Chamberlain saw Halifax's visit as a very clear success. The visit created, he thought, an atmosphere favorable to discussions with Germany on concrete questions. In reality the visit had given Hitler the assurance that the English would not fight to prevent him from satisfying his demands. The victories he had already won without a fight made him think that the western powers would not oppose his enterprises by force of arms. His determination grew firmer.

In March 1938 Lord Halifax succeeded Eden as foreign secretary. If Halifax favored a policy of "realism" and "appeasement," he did give some consideration to the reservations shown by the Foreign Office. Chamberlain now had a free hand; but the absorption of Austria would take place immediately, next would follow Czechoslovakia, and then Poland.

19

The Spanish Civil War (1936-39)

A Clash of Ideologies

For his new feats of strength, Hitler would take advantage of a major event: the Spanish Civil War, which broke out on July 17, 1936, and ended only in April 1939, after claiming a million victims.

Between the two world wars, Spain had an eventful history which ended in tragedy. In December 1923, General Primo de Rivera, who accused the parliamentary regime of leading the kingdom to ruin, took power without meeting any resistance. This represented a return to the old custom of *pronunciamentos:* the army pronounced itself against the existing regime and took power. King Alfonso XIII had thought that this rather benign dictatorship would only be a brief interruption in the constitutional history of Spain. He was accused of having violated the constitution to which he had sworn to remain faithful. Fifteen months after the dismissal of Primo de Rivera in January 1930, the monarchy itself disappeared: on April 14, 1931, Alfonso XIII left Spain. The Republic, hailed with delirious joy, was fragile. The conservative Republicans disagreed with the left-wing Republicans. After the "Red October" of 1934, which resulted in the crushing of the extreme Left, the *Frente popular* won the elections of February 1936. The clash of ideologies throughout Europe was intensified by the underground work of the Fascist and Communist internationals. Following the February victory of the *Frente popular,* the French *Front populaire* was victorious on April 26 and on May 3, giving the impression that the rise of the Left was going to be general throughout Europe. The sudden ascent of the proletariat, and above all the factory strikes carried out by optimistic crowds, caused a "great fear"—as during the French Revolution.

A major part of the bourgeoisie feared for privileges which appeared threatened by a real revolution.

Faced with hostility, Fascism and Hitlerism attempted a final reconciliation prompted by the affinities existing between them. "You want to fight Fascism," Mussolini exclaimed, "Well! Fight."

The July 1936 Uprising

Suddenly, on July 17, a rebellion erupted in the garrisons of Spanish Morocco; among the generals, General Franco quickly took charge of the insurrection. Morocco, with her legionnaires and her fierce mercenaries, marched on to conquer Spain.

The uprisings which took place all over Spain were successful in several cities, but the movement failed in Madrid and in Barcelona. The government, abandoned by its troops and its police, distributed weapons to the workers and the peasants. Battle followed battle in this "romantic" war.

The outbreak of the Spanish Civil War was totally independent of Hitler. But through the Civil War the opposition between the dictatorships, on the one hand, and the western democracies and the Soviet Union, on the other hand, rapidly crystallized. With its ups and downs, the Civil War became a part of a much grander conflict, which gave it universal significance. Several powers involved themselves, either secretly or openly. In the entire world, the Spanish war caused an intellectual mobilization divided into two camps. Opposing forces and ideologies clashed feverishly. The Fascist and Communist internationals came to grips on the bloody soil of Spain, where they rehearsed the military maneuvers of the coming Second World War.

Germany and Italy Support Franco

Germany and Italy did not want to see Bolshevism triumph in Spain, where they continually intervened. On July 30, some Italian pilots, on their way to Spanish Morocco, accidentally landed in French Morocco. Mussolini sent large forces to Spain. In March 1938, thirty-eight thousand Italians were engaged in battle; three thousand would die. The Duce sensed that his destiny was tied to Franco's victory, and, with his concern for prestige enhanced by spite, he frantically pursued the Spanish affair. Franco would receive from Italy nearly two thousand cannons and thousands of machine guns. On November 18, 1936, Germany and Italy recognized Franco's regime, and in March 1939 Franco joined the Anti-Comintern Pact.

Unlike the Italian support, the German support of the Spanish Nationalists was relatively weak. The German air force in Spain amounted to approximately four thousand men, and the rest of the German force seems never to have exceeded a few hundred men.

The camaraderie of arms between the Italian volunteers and the German aviators accelerated the Italo-German rapprochement. At the end of September 1937, Mussolini went to Berlin, where it was agreed that Germany would not obstruct Italy's ambitions in the Mediterranean.

The Spanish war could have created a dangerous split between England and France, because of their diverging sympathies. At the beginning of the conflict, the great majority of Englishmen to some extent supported Franco—the defender of order. In any case, the English were no more favorable to the Republicans than to Franco, and gladly took no interest in the political form of the Madrid government, which was, they felt, the business of the Spanish. "A civil war between democracy and Fascism?" "No," said Lord Strang, "neither less nor more than a civil war."

On August 5, 1936, the first lord of the Admiralty told Admiral Darlan, chief of staff of the French navy, that England did not want "to get involved in any way" in the Spanish war.

Nevertheless, England and, even more so, France acted as if they wanted to prevent a victory by the Nationalists, who were closely tied to Mussolini. They wondered if such a victory would not dangerously compromise the English and French interests, as well as the balance of power in the Mediterranean.

In France, after the May 1936 elections which had brought the *Front populaire* to power with a slight majority vote, the Left and the Right saw in the Spanish Civil War, through a reflection of their own fears, the threat of either Fascism or Communism. Domestic policy became more urgent than foreign policy.

Public opinion, fragmented into opposing factions, and even the government—a Popular Front government under Léon Blum—were deeply divided. Subversive agitation stirred some groups of officers. It seemed possible that the Spanish Civil War would cross the Pyrenees.

By July 18 the Spanish Republican government had asked France for arms, and above all for aircraft. On July 20 Léon Blum had shipments prepared, but on July 25, in a cabinet meeting, he cancelled them. On July 27, exports of war materiel were forbidden, but exports of civilian aircraft built by private industry were authorized.

After much hesitation, which can be explained by Radical opposition, the Paris government proposed, on August 1, 1936, a declaration of "common rules for nonintervention." To have its proposals accepted, the government sent seventeen planes to Spain on August 6, and announced on August 9 that the decision to prohibit arms exports would be reversed if a nonintervention agreement was not soon concluded. An international nonintervention committee first met in London on September 8. The control of the committee was accepted in theory by all. England and France tried, without much success, to strengthen and improve it. The nonintervention policy followed since the end of 1936 would decisively encourage rapprochement between the French and the English. It allowed the governments in Paris and London to emerge from this difficult period with more confidence and solidarity than before; never had the entente between them been stronger. They maintained the calm and self-assurance of partners aware of their own strength.

But the numerous compromises they were forced to make often gave the impression that, despite a few manifestations of firmness, England and France were united only when yielding. Their entente—often stronger in anticipation than in reality—generally limited itself to reacting against the acts and speeches of others and against the effects of government-controlled foreign presses. This disappointing nonintervention, undertaken at such a high price, thus caused a real loss of prestige.

The International Brigades

Stalin hesitated to intervene in Spain, at a time when the collectivization of land, the trials, and the "purges" were shaking his own regime. But the conflict that had erupted over Spain was obviously becoming ideological; the Soviet Union could not stay uninvolved if she wanted to remain the revolutionary pole of attraction for the world.

However, Stalin sent only small numbers of troops and little war materiel. He used foreign volunteers in battle. Starting in October 1936, volunteers from fifty-three nations enrolled in the International Brigades, of which the largest contingents were French. Ten thousand foreign volunteers died in Spain; among those who fought were the Yugoslav Tito, the Italians Longo, Nenni, and Rosselli, the Germans Ulbricht and Willy Brandt, the Frenchmen André Malraux, Billoux, Lecoeur, Rol-Tanguy, and Georges (the future Colonel Fabian).

In his memoirs Lord Strang, who directed British foreign policy from 1949 to 1958, states: "The foreigners who thought that, by taking part in the Spanish war, they were fighting for democracy and against Fascism made a pathetic mistake. The 'democratically elected' government of Spain was only a democratic facade, and even the facade barely remained in the last months of the Civil War. The real power lay with the revolutionaries, trade unionists, anarchists, and Communists, sometimes fighting each other. The fighting ran its course between two domestic factions, moved by what Arnold Toynbee has called suicidal frenzy or satanic passions. . . . What were normal Englishmen doing in this infernal brew?"

The negotiations for withdrawal of foreign volunteers began very early, but progressed slowly. The "gentlemen's agreement" made on January 2, 1937, by Italy and Great Britain was only a public declaration of good intentions. But it was followed by large dispatches of Italian contingents to Spain, and was thus a total failure.

The withdrawal of foreign volunteers was repeatedly delayed. Germany and also Italy procrastinated in order to avoid its enforcement. On March 31, Mussolini promised that there would be no further departures of volunteers for Spain. He did not keep his promise. On April 26, 1937, the horrifying bombing of the old Basque city of Guernica by planes said to be German— Berlin did not hesitate to deny that report—aroused indignation in Great Britain.

On May 29, 1937, the German battle cruiser *Deutschland* was bombed by Spanish Republican aircraft—an act of rebellion which caused about twenty deaths. On May 31, in reprisal, the port of Almería was shelled by German vessels.

On June 18 the Germans claimed that the cruiser *Leipzig* had been attacked by a submarine, but that no lives had been lost. During the summer of 1937, anti-British propaganda developed in Italy; it emphasized England's difficulties in Palestine and the decline of the British Empire. On July 27, 1937, Mussolini and Chamberlain exchanged letters; but in August the attacks on merchant ships increased. The submarines attacking these ships to prevent their arrival in Valencia or Barcelona with ammunition, oil, and food, were Italian submarines, despite Ciano's brazen denials.

The Conference of Nyon

On August 28 the French government suggested a meeting of the Mediterranean powers in Geneva. On September 5 Great Britain and France invited Italy, Germany, the USSR, Yugoslavia, Egypt, Greece, and Turkey to fight "against piracy in the Mediterranean." On September 10 nine powers met in Nyon, near Geneva. Neither Germany nor Italy was present. An agreement was reached on September 11 and signed on September 14, without Mussolini's participation. It represented the end of acts of piracy by submarines and it demonstrated Franco-British cooperation. Ciano expressed his surprise and indignation, but Mussolini decided that the lesser evil was to participate in the agreement. On September 21 Mussolini gave the assurance, and later repeated it, that there would be no more volunteers for Spain. He would violate his promise once again.

The British and the French navies were almost exclusively responsible for the execution of the Nyon agreements. From then on, the commerce of all nations in the Mediterranean would be effectively protected, and Litvinov celebrated this "step toward collective security."

Lord Strang gives a subtle but fair judgment of the Anglo-French non-intervention policy: "There was nothing heroic about it." England and France did not challenge the interventions of Germany, Italy, and the USSR. They did not want to push things too far. They only reacted to the most flagrant agreement violations, taking care not to launch a fire-ship into international relations. Most of the time, they closed their eyes, not their frontiers. In France—the territorial neighbor of Spain—the Pyrenees frontier could not be completely closed by a Popular Front government; many violations involving war materiel, arms, and even aircraft went unstopped.

However, there were limits to the tolerance of England and France. From the beginning, Italy had been warned that an attack on Spain's territorial integrity would not be allowed. "The fears so loudly proclaimed by the English interventionists, that Italy and Germany would dominate Spain to our [England's] own strategic disadvantage if Franco were not beaten, were without substance. The English government, as so often, saw further than their critics. They thought—and correctly so—that Spanish national pride would win out." Spain had not wanted Wellington any more than she had wanted Napoleon. Strang notes that in September 1939 Franco's Spain was nonbelligerent, as was Communist Russia, both more inclined toward the Nazis and the Fascists than toward the democracies, and he proposes: "Had there been a Popular Front government in 1940, in a Spain that had seen the defeat of Franco, probably Spain would have remained neutral anyway. And perhaps it was even better for England that Spain should be led by Franco, whom Hitler was more inclined not to attack, than by a leftist government which Hitler would surely have attacked." He concludes: "Franco's victory gave no lasting profit to Germany and Italy."

In 1940 Hitler would storm at Franco, who refused to act as his puppet, and denounce him as a mediocrity, endowed at most with the minor talents of an air-raid warden (*Blockwärter*) responsible for maintaining the order and enforcing the regulations of a passive defense.

During the Spanish Civil War, France did not forget the German attempt to put a Hohenzollern on the Spanish throne—the attempt which had caused the Franco-Prussian War of 1870. Léon Blum declared: "Through the lies of nonintervention, peace has been saved."

But was peace in as great danger as people thought? It did not seem then that Hitler wanted war. He was only trying to prolong the Spanish war. Mussolini, who as always remained enigmatic, intended according to General Keitel to "commit himself to the extreme limit without, however, reaching the point of a serious threat of war." During the first months of the Ethiopian conflict, Mussolini had already seen the ghost of war pass by. Neither Germany nor Italy wished to face a European war at that time, for the risks were still too great.

20

The Austrian Anschluss

How would Hitler use the method that had proved so effective?

It did not seem, wrote François-Poncet on March 9, 1936, that the answer could be doubted. The Nazis' next objective would be the conquest of Austria.

On March 16, Pius XI spoke confidentially to Ambassador Charles-Roux. "The Pope told me," said Charles-Roux, "not to doubt that Germany would make repeated drives in all the directions where she had something to regain or acquire. He listed Danzig, Memel, the Polish Corridor, Austria, and the German regions of Czechoslovakia. He told me: 'Only the chronology of these attempts cannot be foreseen. But if it is impossible to predict where Germany will begin, and in what order she will proceed, it can be expected that she will advance into each of these areas.' The Holy Father himself is inclined to think that Germany will start with Austria."

Schuschnigg in Berchtesgaden

Austria had ripened to become Hitler's chosen prey. Kurt von Schuschnigg, justice and education minister, had succeeded Dollfuss in July 1934. Prince Starhemberg, the vice-chancellor, had been expected to get the nomination, and he did not conceal his disappointment.

While Dollfuss had belonged to a peasant family from the heart of Austria, Schuschnigg came from a family of military officers. He had been born in Riva, the fortified frontier town on the Lago di Garda. He had served as a reserve officer during the war and then had practiced law in Innsbruck. His political life was tied to the Tyrol and caused him to feel coolness toward

Italy. He considered Austria as German in language and in culture, but he wanted to keep her free and Christian.

He maintained the clerical and authoritarian regime of Dollfuss, and outlawed the National Socialist Party in Austria. Hundreds of opponents filled the prisons.

Then, largely because Ambassador von Papen wanted to reach a détente even as he assisted the Nazis in Vienna, an Austro-German agreement had been concluded in July 11, 1936, to make relations between the Reich and the Austrian federal state "normal and friendly." Germany recognized the complete sovereignty of Austria; each of the two governments considered the other's internal political regime as that nation's own internal affair.

However Hitler was determined to have Austrian National Socialists enter the Vienna government, and to that end he summoned Schuschnigg to his "eagle's nest" in Berchtesgaden on February 12, 1938, only eight days after the February 4 Nazi consolidation of power in Berlin, officially called the "gathering of strength." Hitler declared himself resolved to bring to an end the so-called "Austrian question," in one way or another—*so oder so.* Accused of betraying the German cause, Schuschnigg was placed under extreme pressure; the Austrian Nazi Seyss-Inquart was appointed interior minister.

A Call for a Plebiscite

"So far, but no further!" exclaimed the Austrian chancellor in a speech on February 24. On March 9 he ordered a plebiscite for March 13, calling upon the Austrians to pronounce themselves in favor of a "free and independent" Austria.

Hitler had already been informed of the plebiscite on March 9, at ten o'clock in the morning. Furious, he ordered undersecretary Keppler, who for the last two weeks had been in charge of Austrian affairs, to leave immediately for Austria by special plane and to prevent the plebiscite. Schuschnigg had roused the indignation of Hitler's supporters, who were convinced that a free vote would not give them the majority in a country whose principal political forces were the Catholics and the Social Democrats.

Although on March 11 at two o'clock in the afternoon Schuschnigg adjourned the plebiscite, Hitler seized this opportunity to overthrow his government. After his meeting with Hitler, Schuschnigg put up a desperate effort to contain the Nazi penetration of Austria; but his effort brought about a crisis contrary to all plans, including Hitler's. Hitler suddenly decided to precipitate the *Anschluss* operations initially intended to proceed at a much slower pace. German troops were now to enter Austria on March 12.

But Hitler had not yet ordered military preparations. According to Guderian, the General Staff officers were absent on a military mission. General Halder maintained that the plan against Austria, *Fall Otto,* aimed only to oppose the restoration of the Hapsburgs, and that it had never been elaborated in detail.

What caused Hitler's sudden decision? Colonel Hossbach declared that he had attributed it, as had General Beck, to Hitler's desire to achieve a major success in foreign policy in order to distract the officer corps from the unpleasant Blomberg and Fritsch affairs.

Goering's Diplomacy; the Anschluss Proclamation

In carrying out the *Anschluss,* Goering took the initiative, politically as well as militarily. He brought to perfection the art of maneuvering by telephone. During the dramatic day of March 11, he called Seyss-Inquart and told him to resign as interior minister and to demand the resignation of Schuschnigg, who had launched a "provocation" with the plebiscite. Schuschnigg announced his resignation over the radio: "May God protect Austria!" Swastika flags rose everywhere; the Austrian Nazis had already donned their uniforms. On March 11, at dawn, German troop movements began on the frontier, and rail traffic was suspended between Germany and Austria.

Goering demanded that Seyss-Inquart be named as head of the government; president of the Republic Miklas refused that appointment, informing General Muff, the German military attaché, who then threatened to have 200,000 men invade Austria.

But Seyss-Inquart—the first of many quislings to come—formed a provisional government.

On March 11, at 8:48 P.M., with cynical offhandedness Goering ordered Seyss-Inquart and the "government formed following the resignation of Schuschnigg" to send a telegram of distress, pleading for Germany to send troops as soon as possible to save Austria from chaos and to restore order— an order not actually threatened. Miklas was forced to submit his resignation.

During the night of March 11, Seyss-Inquart, now both chancellor and president, judged it unnecessary to have further troops enter Austria, and asked that they not cross the frontier. His request was supported, that same night, by the German chargé d'affaires in Vienna, von Stein, by General Muff, and by General von Brauchitsch. Hitler was awakened; he declared that it was too late to rescind the orders given to the army to enter Austria.

Hitler was not yet planning the formal absorption of Austria into Germany;

he still thought of an informal union, placing the Austrian government under Nazi control.

On March 12, at dawn, German troops entered Austrian territory "on a friendship visit." Hitler was welcomed with delirious cheers in Linz, where he had spent most of his youth. On Sunday, March 13, in Linz, where Seyss-Inquart had joined him, he decided to proclaim the annexation of his native Austria to Germany; the *Anschluss* thus took place without a single shot. On March 14, Hitler entered Vienna.

Mussolini

The annexation of Austria in just a few hours represented a major disaster for Italy. Would she create difficulties at the last moment? Hitler did not know what the Italians would do. He had been forced to push his friend Mussolini around a little. Mussolini had not been asked what he thought.

When, at the end of November 1937, a new Italian diplomatic representative was sent to Vienna, Ciano defined his mission for him: that of a doctor who had to administer oxygen to a dying man, without letting his heir notice what was happening. "In any case," Ciano added, "the heir interests us more than the dying man."

Hitler had Prince Philip of Hesse—an ardent National Socialist and the son-in-law of King Victor Emmanuel III—deliver to Mussolini a letter announcing his decision. He accused Austria of organizing a military force hostile to Germany and of having relations with Czechoslovakia which made her "a subsidiary of Prague." Forced to act, Hitler was guaranteeing the Brenner frontier to Italy. Mussolini was determined to have that letter published to calm Italian public opinion; however, the passage about Czechoslovakia was not published.

Mussolini, who four years earlier was ready to defend Austria by arms, now deliberately sacrificed her. He accepted the whole affair in a "very friendly" manner, and to appear as a good sport he declared that the *Anschluss* had been a historical necessity. Hitler was overwhelmed with gratitude. "I will never forget this, never, whatever happens . . . The Duce can be convinced that I will stand by him whatever happens, even if the entire world is against him."

Austria in Vassalage

Despite the enthusiastic welcome many Austrians gave the *Anschluss*—Goering would later tell his judges at Nuremberg: "In Austria we were not met with rifle shots and bombs; only one thing was thrown at us, flowers"—

the annexation appeared as an act of violence. It had not been done from within, by Austria herself, but rather from without, by Germany, while hundreds of German aircraft streaked across the Austrian sky.

Austria's very name disappeared and she became the *Ostmark* (or eastern borderland) of the German Reich; she was dismembered into provinces: Carinthia, Styria, Tyrol, Salzburg, and others.

The hunt for Jews was launched; thousands of Austrians were sent to concentration camps. Schuschnigg disappeared into complete isolation for a year in the Berlin dungeon of the Gestapo headquarters. Later he was taken to concentration camps and freed only in 1945 by the Americans.

A crucial date was inscribed in history when the swastika flag was raised over Vienna on March 13, 1938. The failure of collective security became fatally apparent. Hitler's most cynical trespasses left the western democracies passive. At a crucial moment, they watched motionlessly while the annexation of Austria revealed the first glimmers of the fire that would ravage Europe and then the world.

Ribbentrop, who had just been named foreign minister, was then in London, taking leave of his diplomatic duties. The numerous telephone calls he received from Goering helped accentuate the confusion of the English leaders. Chamberlain merely confirmed the fait accompli before Commons.

As for France, she was in the middle of a cabinet crisis. Apparently avoiding his responsibilities, Chautemps had resigned on the morning of March 9. Blum succeeded him on March 13, after everything had been completed in Austria.

As German strength was growing rapidly and frighteningly, and as the western democracies were abandoning Austria, the collapse in a few hours of an independent country gave Hitler the conviction that his madness was actually a superior sense of reality. On April 10, a "free and secret" plebiscite gave a vote of 99.08 percent in favor of the *Anschluss* in Germany, and 99.75 percent in Austria.

21

Munich

The Sudeten Germans

"Death moves swiftly." A few days after the Austrian episode came Czecho-slovakia's turn. Czechoslovakia was now at the center of a major international crisis, and it soon became evident that the next disaster would be an over-whelming attack against her. Trapped on three sides by the territories of the Great Reich—Germany and Austria—as if in the grasp of "pincers," she was open to the Nazi offensive as a result of the agitation unleashed among the Germans of the Sudetenland, who until 1919 had been ruled by the Austrian branch of the Hapsburg monarchy.

Excessively optimistic, Beneš was convinced that he could always reach some arrangement with Germany. During the winter of 1936-37, he met with two Germans in Prague, Albrecht Haushofer and Count Trauttmanns-dorff, to discuss the Sudeten German minority. He asserted that Hitler had repeatedly proposed a nonaggression pact.

But after Czechoslovakia concluded a mutual assistance pact with the USSR in May 1935, she had been denounced as an advance position of the Soviets in the center of Europe, and Eden said of Beneš: "Clever, perhaps too clever, he constantly devised plans and proposals so numerous that they could not all have been good."

Hitler wanted to "digest Austria" before "resolving the Czech question"; but Hitler was a man who did not let others catch their breath. As early as March 29, only two weeks after the *Anschluss,* he ordered a study of the preparations necessary for an attack against Czechoslovakia.

Precise military plans were formulated and, to create a dramatic incident which would cause a major explosion, the Germans even thought of provoking in Czechoslovakia an anti-German demonstration in which Eisenlohr, the German minister to Prague, would be killed. Of course this dark plot would be executed without the knowledge of Eisenlohr, who was disliked by the Sudeten leaders.

France and England Confront the Sudeten Problem

The Czechoslovakian affair could not fail to have serious international repercussions.

As foreign minister in the second Blum cabinet, which lasted twenty days and which had succeeded a second Chautemps cabinet of fifty days, Paul-Boncour published on March 14 an official communiqué announcing that, in the event of aggression, "France would uphold effectively, immediately, and completely her obligations toward Czechoslovakia, resulting from a treaty known to all."

The Quai d'Orsay would have liked to confirm Franco-British solidarity. But Lord Halifax felt that the French and Czechoslovakian governments did not see the military situation as it really was, with Czechoslovakia's position greatly weakened by Germany's annexation of Austria. France had to act in Prague to bring about a solution to the Sudeten problem, which could become dangerous.

However, to impress Germany, Chamberlain declared in Commons on March 24 that if Great Britain had no obligations toward Czechoslovakia, France had such obligations that it appeared "unlikely" that Great Britain could stay out of a possible conflict. In this speech, he defined English policy with complete sincerity.

On April 10, Édouard Daladier formed a government. He gave the foreign ministry to Georges Bonnet; this represented a setback in comparison to the firm policy advocated by Paul-Boncour.

In Berlin, Ambassador Nevile Henderson saw in Hitler a pathological case, but also "a constructive genius." The worst danger, he thought, would be to exasperate this man who was "inclined to uncontrollable resentment." By April 1 Henderson already believed that autonomy for the Sudeten was necessary for a peaceful solution to the Czechoslovakian crisis. But he did not feel that the German army was ready for war. In his opinion, therefore, Hitler would not intervene in Czechoslovakia as he had in Austria, unless he was forced to do so by incidents resulting from bloodshed in the Sudetenland.

Henderson seriously underestimated the degree of premeditation Hitler had then reached. It seems that the English government shared his views.

In Prague, the minister Newton considered Czechoslovakia's position "untenable" as early as March 15: Czechoslovakia and France ought to be informed that the maintenance of a "basically unhealthy" status quo was impossible, and that Great Britain would refuse to risk war for its sake.

Henderson and Newton were harsher on Germany than on Czechoslovakia, but still they did criticize the latter. London shared their attitude. It would be a mistake to encourage France to resist Germany at the risk of a war. English leaders insistently repeated that the armaments of France and England would not suffice to prevent the destruction of Czechoslovakia if Germany attacked.

The French asserted that, if strongly emphasized, Anglo-French solidarity would be enough to preserve the peace. Chamberlain declared that "his blood boiled" at Germany's behavior, but that, if there was a war, France and England could not be assured of victory. Such a risk could not be taken before 1939. Warning Hitler would only be a bluff. Actually it would be unwise to issue an ultimatum at that time. Moreover, a promise of unconditional support to Czechoslovakia would destroy all chances for that country to reach an agreement with Germany.

The French leaders had no illusions about the weakness of their air force. General Vuillemin, the air force chief of staff, felt that the French air force would no longer exist after one week of war with Germany. It was feared that, under such conditions, Czechoslovakia could not be saved by a military move.

For four months, London had exerted diplomatic pressure on Germany and on Czechoslovakia to induce Prague to make concessions to Berlin. Henderson was aware of the seriousness of the situation; Germany was being evasive. Henderson was called to order by London because he spoke of Czechoslovakia as a "nationalities state" instead of a "national state."

The claims made by Konrad Henlein, a gymnastics teacher who was the leader of the Sudeten German party and a simple puppet in the hands of Hitler and Ribbentrop, grew progressively larger. Limited at first to a start at administrative autonomy, they had evolved by April 24 to the "eight-point" program of Karlovy-Vary, demanding an autonomous government. Prague had committed the fatal mistake of delaying by granting only one small concession at a time. The Sudeten Germans would change their goal from autonomy within Czechoslovakia to annexation with Germany, knowing, as Ribbentrop said, "that they had behind them a nation of seventy-five million people who would no longer endure seeing them oppressed by the Czechoslovakian government."

The Crisis of May 1938

There is no doubt that in May 1938 Hitler was considering military operations against Czechoslovakia. And suddenly on May 21 the international press reported movement of the German troops assembled at the Czech frontier—this report was apparently incorrect. Prague carried out a partial mobilization. Ribbentrop was wild with anger: "The Czechoslovakians are mad, they will be annihilated." Sensationalistic commentaries appeared in newspapers announcing "the retreat of Hitler," forced by international pressure to call back his troops.

Hitler had not modified his plans, but the violence he displayed in September was apparently provoked by this incident. He had been humiliated, and he was not "ready to accept the repetition of such things." On May 28 he spoke to the generals, in secrecy of course, and defined the final version of his plans for military operations against Czechoslovakia; it would be signed two days later. He declared his unalterable determination to destroy Czechoslovakia by force, and he set October 1, 1938, as the latest date for the operation.

Unrest grew among the Sudeten Germans. Two men were killed in Eger. Serious worry developed in London. Sir Eric Phipps, who had left Berlin to become ambassador to Paris, was instructed by Lord Halifax to warn the French government against "very dangerous illusions." There could not be "a European war, whose outcome would in the least be doubtful." The Prague government had to be "reasonable" in the Sudeten question.

London tried to influence Paris, where Georges Bonnet was "desperately anxious" to avoid a war. And Paris in turn reinforced the pressure exerted on Prague by the British. Henlein came twice to London, where a large degree of autonomy for the Sudetenland was desired, and stated his claims.

Except for the fanatics from the Nazi party and the young, the German people foresaw possible military operations with little enthusiasm. The idea of a plot against Hitler was considered. There were, in fact, signs of opposition from Germans who wanted to avoid a war.[1] Colonel Ewald von Kleist visited London in August. Chamberlain claimed not to attach any importance to these German opponents; he compared them to the early Jacobites of the eighteenth century, at the time when they still plotted against William III and Queen Anne in the hope of an imminent restoration of James III. There were good reasons to think that if these German generals had dared carry out their plans against Hitler, the German public would not have supported them.

1. See Maurice Baumont, *La grande conjuration contre Hitler* (Paris, 1963).

When Hitler violated the Treaty of Versailles by reestablishing the full German army without arms limitation in 1935, and by occupying the Rhineland militarily in 1936, he acted against the advice of most of his diplomats and generals. But the differences of opinion only bore on the opportunity for such undertakings and the danger involved.

Lord Runciman's Mission

The German opposition expected and advised Chamberlain to send Hitler an ultimatum. But the prime minister acted differently and assumed a leading role. Since the negotiations between the Czechs and the Sudeten Germans seemed bound to reach a dead end, he intervened personally. On July 14 he decided to propose publicly to the Prague government the nomination of an independent mediator. The Czechoslovakian government would thus be faced "with its responsibility to accept or reject this proposal." Beneš was "distressed" when he heard the proposal. Finally the Prague government invited the British government to select a person independent of all governments who, through his advice, would be able to help overcome the current difficulties.

On August 3 Lord Runciman arrived in Prague. It was obvious that Neville Chamberlain himself had taken the initiative first to send Lord Runciman and later to go to Berchtesgaden, Godesberg, and Munich in succession. France merely followed Great Britain, whose policy, opposed to any commitment to Czechoslovakia, was very clearly defined. But as the British historian Wheeler-Bennett observes, "If England led, it was because France had no leaders." Since the semirevolution of February 6, 1934, France had appeared totally indecisive and overtaken by an internal crisis whose seriousness was obvious to both Hitler and Chamberlain.

In January 1938 Chamberlain wrote that the desperate weakness of a France "incapable of having a government for more than nine months at a time" was becoming an international danger. This weakness of France brought Hitler to count absolutely on English hesitation, if serious complications were to arise.

In Hitler's eyes France appeared as a second to England, and any French decision was subordinated to her. Since 1936 Hitler had felt that the French did not want to fight. Highly placed informers had assured him of the debility of the French political system.

France was in a difficult position. Bound to Czechoslovakia by the treaty of October 15, 1925, she had lavished assurances and promises. Paul-Boncour, Georges Bonnet, Édouard Daladier, and others had solemnly expressed and renewed these commitments to Czechoslovakia. They would not keep their promises, thought Hitler; if London did not endorse them, they would be reduced to nothing.

As in the Austrian case, the British government did not want to rouse the public opinion necessary to maintain by force the abnormal position of the German minorities in the composite Czechoslovak state. Hitler was again well informed. He knew that powerful influences were working toward an entente with Germany. After the French declaration of March 14, 1938, Chamberlain simply warned Germany that if war broke out it was "unlikely" that it could be localized.

Polemics between "Hard-Liners" and "Soft-Liners"

Moreover Hitler was convinced that France would be in no position to risk war. France intended to maintain the territorial status quo but lacked the military strength which would have allowed such a policy. After the massacres of the First World War and the failure of peace, people were not eager to fight. Could France go to war with Germany? The right wing, in particular, vehemently opposed the risk which any action in favor of the Czechs would entail. Why had the Czechs not followed the example of Switzerland and made their country into a federation, allowing the Sudeten Germans to gain a genuine autonomy? It was natural for these Germans to resent being governed and judged by the Czechs. France should not get involved in this touchy affair, in a state inhabited by nine different nationalities. If Czechoslovakia had treated Austria and Hungary as equals, the situation might have been different; was France under any obligation to prevent an act of aggression which supposedly was not caused by external events but rather by internal disorder?

In an article published in *Le Temps* on April 12, the eminent legal expert Joseph Barthélemy stated: "France is not obliged to go to war in order to maintain Sudeten allegiance to Prague."

The French wanted to believe in Hitler's goodwill. On September 1, pointing out that Hitler had often assumed the role of defender of the peace, *Le Temps* stated that there was no reason to doubt his sincerity. The subtle Jean Giraudoux railed at France for living "with the obsession of war" when she was not being threatened. More subtle still, Jean Cocteau exclaimed: "Long live a disgraceful peace!" A war can always be avoided; a nation only has to grant the necessary concessions; they should have no limit.

The bitter polemics between supporters and opponents of what became "Munich" were far from being quieted down; they would continue for decades.

To justify the occupation of the Sudetenland with its German population, Hitler evoked the nationality principle, so often raised since 1848. The right of national self-determination had joined the racist doctrine, giving it a strong ideological position. Territorial concessions were unavoidable. According to the Czechoslovakian ambassador to Paris, Osusky, even Beneš was resigning himself to them.

In any case, how could France give military aid to Czechoslovakia? How could she prevent the invasion of a country whose geography made it hardly defensible? These were the arguments of the "soft-liners," the so-called "pro-Munich" faction. How could Czechoslovakia be helped? Once mobilized, France would find no means of access into Czechoslovakia and would have to be satisfied with defensive warfare along her frontier.

But the "hard-liners," who would be called the "anti-Munich" faction, asked: should France, with arms of the ready, wait for Germany to settle the fate of Czechoslovakia? After that Germany might turn and settle the fate of France. The "hard-liners" had no doubt that, united, England and France had a power that would impose respect. The greatest optimists even felt that Czechoslovakia, France, and Russia alone had a very clear superiority over Germany, who would rapidly be overcome in any conflict.

To prevent Germany from being thrown into a frightening venture, Hitler's German opponents would have eliminated him. The Siegfried line fortifications were still unfinished. As for Czechoslovakia, on September 23 she had more battle-ready divisions than Hitler could deploy against them and she was protected by her own fortifications.

The "soft-liners," who strongly opposed the "hard-liners," asked how many non-Czechs and anti-Czechs were to be found in the Czechoslovakian army. In 1941, for example, the "heroic" Yugoslav army faded away with the desertion of Pavelić's Croats, who began firing on their own Serb officers.

Outflanked everywhere, the Czech Maginot line would be totally useless. Hitler would later remark sarcastically that these fortifications were worthless, and that he would have had the engineers shot.

Lord Runciman's design was to bring "a solution" to the German minority problem. Although he was considered an independent mediator between the Czechoslovakian government and the Sudeten German party, he severely criticized the regime organized by Czechoslovakia to deal with her minorities, especially the Sudeten Germans, who were so mistrustful of the Czechs. In short, he supported the plan for dismembering the Czechoslovak Republic: the Sudeten Germans were right.

On September 7, the London *Times* advised the Czechs to surrender the Sudetenland; it was to their advantage to become "a homogeneous state."

Serious disorders broke out among the Sudeten Germans. They were no
longer satisfied to be "autonomists"; they demanded incorporation into
Germany.

Chamberlain's Trips

Since the end of August, Chamberlain had been planning a bold action,
which "would leave Halifax breathless." To save everything at the eleventh
hour, he decided to face Hitler on September 15. "The old English minister was leaving on a tiger hunt with an umbrella." During his first visit, he
listened courteously to his partner, whose intentions did not shock him
in the least: the Sudeten Germans would return to the Reich. Runciman had
already studied similar solutions. Chamberlain accepted them as the last
offers of a "businessman." He felt that "Hitler can be trusted once he has
given his word."

All that remained was to have these solutions accepted in Paris and to
impose them in Prague. The Czechs had to become resigned so that France
could be released of her "foolish promises" of military assistance, which did
not impress Hitler at all. The French government had assumed obligations
toward Czechoslovakia in circumstances very different from today's: "Germany had been disarmed, the Rhineland had been demilitarized."

Chamberlain was successful. Bearing an agreement accepted by France
and extorted from the Czechoslovakians, who had been crushed to see
France take a German ultimatum as her own, Chamberlain left for Godesberg
in the Rhineland on September 22.

The surprise came during this second trip. Hitler had not expected such
a simple settlement. He realized that his demands had not yet reached the
extreme limit, beyond which stood an absolute refusal. He added to his own
claims those of Hungary . . . and of Poland. Nothing then had been settled.
He would have to occupy the Sudeten territory immediately. When Chamberlain brought him the Czechoslovakian surrender, Hitler asked still more; he
would declare war if the Czechs did not accept all of his new demands. He
wanted his triumph to be dazzling.

The British prime minister was treated like a broker whose order was
cancelled in favor of a more lucrative deal. Hitler's violent behavior was
extremely humiliating for Chamberlain, who was deeply shocked; but his
armor of national pride probably kept him from feeling its total impact. He
did not hide "his disappointment and his astonishment" at an ultimatum
worded in the language of a conqueror who flaunts his will. Hitler agreed
to set October 1 as the date for the territorial transfer.

In Prague, where mobilization was declared, the one-eyed General Sirovy,
who incarnated unyielding resistance, formed a government of national

unity. France mobilized; soon she had over a million men under arms. The British fleet was mobilized. On September 26 and 27, President Roosevelt advocated, in two moving appeals, the convening of an international conference in which all interested nations would take part.

War now seemed inevitable. The English wondered anxiously if the French government was aware of the military consequences of these decisions.

Neville Chamberlain was committed to peace at any price. On the evening of September 27, he spoke on the radio, declaring that he refused to think that a war could break out "owing to a quarrel in a faraway country among people of whom we know nothing."

Hitler was a virtuoso in this war of nerves, which resounded with his hoarse and harsh voice. In a series of speeches displaying a crescendo of violence, his magnetic feeling for crowds was combined with admirable staging. The most vehement threats alternated with the skillful affirmation that his only wish was to bring the Sudeten Germans back into Germany. "He did not want any Czechs." He often uttered the word "peace," which was cheered with enthusiasm. His appeals to Édouard Daladier were models of their kind.

General mobilization was to be declared in Germany. On September 26, Hitler exclaimed: "I gave Chamberlain my assurance, and I renew it, that once this problem (Czechoslovakia) is solved, Germany will have no more territorial claims to make in Europe."

The Munich Conference

Chamberlain called upon Mussolini to play the role of mediator, by reviving the four-power system so dear to him. On the morning of September 28, Ciano postponed by twenty-four hours the mobilization which was to begin that afternoon. Mussolini intervened to back the idea of a conference to which Hitler would invite, on the following day, the prime ministers of Great Britain, France, and Italy, for the purpose of solemnly decreeing the execution of Czechoslovakia.

Chamberlain was in the process of reporting, before Commons, on his efforts to reach an understanding with Hitler, to whom he had suggested a third meeting anywhere in Germany to save the peace. During the session, a dispatch arrived, announcing that Hitler was inviting him, along with Mussolini and Daladier, to meet the next day in Munich. The members of Parliament sprang from their seats in enthusiasm at the news that peace might still be saved.

The breath of war had passed over Europe, spreading anxiety throughout the summer of 1938, to end in a drama filled with suspense, with an agreement: "Munich."

On September 29, at one o'clock in the afternoon, the conference began; it continued into the night. Mussolini acted as arbiter. During the night of September 29, the prime ministers of France, Great Britain, and Italy authorized Hitler to annex the territories of Czechoslovakia where Germans were in the majority. The occupation would be carried out in four steps, under international supervision. France and England guaranteed the new frontiers to be established by an international commission; these new frontiers were also to receive the guarantee of Germany and Italy, after the settlement of the Polish and Hungarian claims.

The Czechoslovakian crisis, which had subjected Europe to subtle torture for six months, finally, at the last minute, ended in peace—on September 29, 1938. But the agreement was only a retreat by the western powers, who were conscious of their weakness. They retreated only to better jump, and they would jump into an abyss.

Munich represents a profound failure in history. After the annexation of Austria and the dislocation of Czechoslovakia, the Europe of Versailles was torn to shreds. The losers of 1918, without a fight, became the victors; having lost the war, they had won the peace.

The western great powers had wanted to allow the Czech people to live in dignity, but they now sacrificed them in order to safeguard world peace. Hitler triumphed. He condescended to accept with ceremony what he had threatened to seize by force.

The joy was universal at the idea that war had been averted; the war that people wanted to avoid at any price because only twenty years had passed since the bloody trial of 1914-18, which had caused so much destruction and so many deaths.

Alone with Hitler, at one o'clock in the morning, Chamberlain suggested that they sign a declaration that he said was necessary to his parliamentary position: the German and British governments agreed to consult each other on all questions which might arise between them, in order to avoid any possible cause of divergence of opinion. Hitler signed immediately.

Did Chamberlain really believe in this paper which he brandished as he left his plane, crying: "Peace for our time"? In the car that took him into London from the airport, he sighed and said to Halifax: "All that will be past in three months." Perhaps he felt the need to show that the execution of Czechoslovakia had not been gratuitous, but that in exchange he had strengthened the peace.

Like Chamberlain, Daladier was welcomed triumphantly when he returned to Paris. Few were those who opposed the agreement, which was approved on October 5 in the Chamber by a vote of 535 to 75; the 75 who opposed the agreement included only one Socialist and one Centrist, the rest being made up of the Communist bloc raised against "Fascist hegemony." The

Senate showed no opposition. Former prime minister Pierre-Étienne Flandin sent a telegram of congratulations to the Four Powers of Munich—a gesture which generally was disapproved of, however.

England did not have the same commitments as France toward Prague. However one minister, Duff Cooper, resigned. In France three ministers who had emphatically declared themselves against Munich did not carry their condemnation to the point of resignation. A storm of criticism soon arose. People had apparently waited for Munich to become indignant; they condemned the principles of Munich, they feared its consequences, and they discovered that it was a disaster. It was a decisive failure. Once war had been avoided, they were ashamed to have given in; they felt the shamefulness of peace.

Hitler, of course, looked on the Munich agreements as a mere scrap of paper. Less than six months after signing the agreements, he occupied Prague; and even before the war broke out in September 1939, "Munich" had become a term of insult.

England and France did not take as much advantage as Hitler did of the respite for rearmament gained from the agreements of September 30, 1938. But at least by the summer of 1940 Great Britain had an air force nearly ten times greater than that of summer 1938. For her the threat of invasion had been eliminated. Lord Strang sees Munich as a disaster, but also as a tragic necessity. He even believes that, without the trial of Munich, Great Britain and her empire would not have entered the war in 1939.

The Soviets

The same debates arose between the "pro-Munich" faction and the "anti-Munich" faction, between the "soft-liners" and the "hard-liners," over a possible Soviet intervention.

On May 3 in Geneva, Litvinov declared that the USSR was determined to fulfill the Covenant obligations and, with France, to aid Czechoslovakia. The Soviet military command was ready to meet immediately with the representatives of the French and Czechoslovakian commands to examine the measures to be taken.

The exemplary firmness of the USSR would be contrasted with the criminal abandonment of Czechoslovakia by the western powers. Because of her geography, the Soviet Union did not run great risks; she was separated from Czechoslovakia by Poland, who was opposed to the crossing of her territory by the Red Army, from fear that the Soviets might remain in Poland.

Some people wondered if the British, and to a lesser degree the French, did not try to set the USSR aside rather than seek an alliance. To avoid strengthening the position of Communism was the policy at least of certain capitalist circles, if not of the cabinets themselves.

But would war in 1938, with the USSR as an ally of the eastern powers, have meant that Poland would have been in the German camp? The "hard-liners" wanted to believe that the Polish General Staff would overturn the policy of Warsaw in order to join France at the last moment. An extremely unlikely prospect.

Czechoslovakia herself wavered and refused to allow Russian aircraft to be stationed on her airfields. In 1938 the Russian air force was not a modern air force, but in August, in combat which took place around Lake Khassan, it had destroyed part of the Japanese air force. It could, therefore, be used against Hitler.

The Soviets were angered by the Munich arrangements, in which they had not been allowed to take part. During that fray they had been deliberately neglected. They wanted an international conference, such as the one advocated by Roosevelt. They had not been given a place beside the four great powers of Europe. Czechoslovakia, also a Slavic nation and an ally, was perhaps the only country likely to make them emerge from the isolation in which they had confined themselves. They had thus been insulted precisely when they were ready to meet their military commitments for the defense of their Czech ally.

Keeping her commitments was in the interest of the USSR; and geography singularly lightened the weight of these obligations, since she was separated from Czechoslovakia by Rumania and Poland. On the Rumanian side, the mountains and the lack of roads and railways limited to an extreme any possible aid which Russia might give the Czechs, other than aircraft. As for Colonel Beck's Poland, after having concluded a friendship pact with Germany in 1934, she was now claiming part of the spoils from Czechoslovakia. Beck was becoming Hitler's accomplice. The consequences of such an attitude would soon be apparent.

The Soviet Union's ambiguous diplomatic policy, which proceeded along hidden lines, took a sudden and total change of direction, falling back on Germany. Right after Munich, one of the Soviet leaders, Potemkin, announced to the French ambassador, Coulondre, that the Soviets had been left no way out except "the fourth partition of Poland."

22

The Policy of Colonel Beck

The Czechoslovakian crisis upset political and diplomatic prospects throughout Eastern Europe, and especially in Poland.

The Reactions of Poland and Czechoslovakia

Poland's relations with Czechoslovakia were very tense. Of course, the policy of Beneš toward Warsaw had not been fortunate. He had taken advantage of the victorious advance of the Red Army in 1920 to seize the Polish part of Silesia; the Teschen affair had created a breach between Poland and Czechoslovakia, and France's efforts to change the situation had been futile. Grievances which a statesman should have the art of forgetting were being revived to create in Poland a permanent tension vis-à-vis Czechoslovakia.

Polish foreign minister Zaleski had succeeded in nearly normalizing relations with Prague, but Beck, his successor, was a declared opponent of Czechoslovakia. Czechoslovakia had a strong desire to improve her relations with Germany. As there had been at the time much talk of a war between Poland and Germany, the German military men were convinced that, if such a war broke out, "Czechoslovakia would remain calm," and stay neutral. A nation where more than four million Germans lived could not possibly go to war against Germany. General von Seeckt remarked: "Czechoslovakia cannot be suspected of favoring Germany. However, she has no aggressive intentions toward us." What worried Czechoslovakia was the Austrian *Anschluss*.

In the event of a conflict in the east, Hungary was expected to neutralize any Czechoslovakian initiative hostile to Germany, because of her claims on the Slovak territories bordering on the Danube. Very close relations

247

existed between the German and Hungarian armies. The Hungarian military attaché worked regularly with the *Reichswehr* ministry, where the Hungarian army was held in high esteem. Military studies praised Hungary's attitude during the First World War, while they were not always kind toward the Austrian army. But Germany could only expect limited help from Hungary. The Hungarians themselves were kept on the alert by the Rumanians and the Yugoslavs, along a frontier lacking natural defenses. The Hungarians could only have one mission: to neutralize Czechoslovakia, which would be a significant service to the German army.

Beck was against the Czechs, but not against the Slovaks, whom he wanted to separate from the Czechs and unite to Hungary. At least the Subcarpathian Ukraine had to be taken from Czechoslovakia and united with Hungary. From outdated historical memories there emerged in Poland a strong sentimental desire for a common frontier with Hungary, for whom the Poles had feelings of friendship. The old six-hundred-mile frontier between Galicia and Hungary had become the frontier between Poland and Czechoslovakia.

Czechoslovakia of course refused any reduction in her territory, any expansion of a hostile Hungary, or the suppression of the common boundary with her ally Rumania.

The Polish defection under Colonel Beck caused a tragic wavering in the organization of a defensive front which could have been opposed to Germany. Beck demanded Teschen with rapacious brutality and took part in the dismemberment of Czechoslovakia. Not only Beck but all the Poles were ill disposed toward the Czechs, for whom they felt no sympathy. Had the Czechs not always followed a Russophile, Pan-slavic policy? Count Szembek, undersecretary at the Polish foreign ministry, overheard Neurath telling Beck: "We don't like the Czechs either."

Poland's policy greatly contributed to creating and aggravating the threat to Czechoslovakia—now exposed to Germany's designs—and therefore to her ally France. Poland's foreign minister evoked the bilateral nature of the treaties. He increased the military risks for France through a policy that could hardly have been a vital necessity for Poland.

"Watch the Czechs carefully," was one of the last instructions left in May 1935 by Pilsudski, former commander of the "Polish legions." He had opposed the dismemberment of Austria-Hungary, calling it Balkanization. In his opinion, Czechoslovakia could not survive; it was only a seasonal state. He thought that in the event of a war with Germany Czechoslovakia, with one-quarter of her population German, would not be able to fight.

Poland, on the contrary, was historically tied to Hungary, and favored

Hungarian revisionism. On February 16, 1938, Beck confided to Szembek: "What really links us to Hungary is our common attitude toward the Czechs."

Warsaw's Ultimatum to Lithuania

By June 12, 1935, Beck was already declaring to Szembek: "There are two political entities unquestionably condemned to disappear: Austria and Czechoslovakia." In March 1938, while the *Anschluss* was being carried out, Ambassador Léon Noël reminded Beck that "Austria's independence was one of the essential points of French policy." He added that an extremely thorny question was arising: Czechoslovakia, an ally of France. He was well aware of Poland's attitude toward Czechoslovakia. But "it could not be expected that Poland would be indifferent to being encircled by Germany from the south." The divergent views of the two allies—France and Poland—on the most important European problems weakened their alliance considerably.

On February 16, 1938, Beck said to Szembek: "The *Anschluss* is practically under way. The Czech problem will be next on the agenda, provided that we show ourselves ready for it." On February 23, Beck observed: "Goering has stressed that he is aware of the Polish minority and of the definite Polish interests in Czechoslovakia. He has given assurance that the Germans will do nothing in this area without previously informing us. They will not present us with any surprises." In the conflict opposing Germany and Czechoslovakia, Poland was essentially against Czechoslovakia and for Germany.

Ambassador Moltke pointed out that in Warsaw the annexation of Austria was received with absolute calm. Beck thought that the *Anschluss* would reduce German pressure on Poland, and that Austrian influence would increase in Germany at the expense of Prussian influence.

On March 18, 1938, the day following the *Anschluss,* Beck used frontier incidents as a justification for sending an ultimatum to the Lithuanians through his minister in Estonia, calling upon them to open diplomatic relations with Poland. He demanded an answer within forty-eight hours. The Vilna question had been intentionally eliminated, and Poland required, without preliminary conditions, the reestablishment of diplomatic relations.

Since Pilsudski had occupied Vilna in October 1920, a serious breach had separated the two nations, who had been historically intermingled for more than five centuries. The Lithuanian government had confiscated the great Polish estates and had broken diplomatic relations with Warsaw. A state of war without war existed between Poland and Lithuania. On September 28, 1926, Lithuania concluded a nonaggression pact with the Soviets. In spite of negotiations with Poland in March and April 1928, the relations between Lithuania and Poland remained hostile.

In March 1938 Beck obtained a resumption of diplomatic relations from Lithuania. Ambassador Moltke congratulated him on a brilliant solution of the problem, and Beck asked him to thank Ribbentrop.

France, on the contrary, had expressed the hope that Poland would not use force against Lithuania; it would be extremely unfortunate, in view of the *Anschluss.*

Szembeck related that Beck had said to Ambassador Noël, in a very cutting tone: "The French attitude toward the issue of diplomatic relations with Lithuania has always been spiteful and hostile toward Poland. During the recent crisis, France adopted a clearly pro-Lithuanian attitude. In 1919 and 1920, this attitude was dictated by the desire to spare the White Russians. Now the situation is still the same; only the color has changed." Beck had spoken "very harshly."

On July 7, 1938, he did not hesitate to tell Léon Noël: "The fate of the Czechoslovak state leaves us indifferent." During the crisis that preceded Munich, he declared that both the government and public opinion fully understood Hitler's attitude. During the Munich Conference, he congratulated himself on Poland's sincere relations with Germany, and expressed a genuine gratitude toward her.

Teschen

However Beck was displeased that Poland had not been invited to the Munich Conference; the claims of Poland and Hungary had been neglected. On October 1 he demanded, in an ultimatum sent to Prague, the evacuation of Teschen within twenty-four hours. He asked Germany if he could count on Germany's favorable attitude in the event of resistance by Czechoslovakia—"Of course," replied Weizsäcker—and if Germany would adopt a friendly attitude in the event of Soviet action against Poland. Ribbentrop declared that a Soviet intervention was out of the question.

On October 2 the Poles occupied the Teschen territory with its population of about 250,000.

Decline of the Little Entente

The Hungarians could not resolve to take strong measures. On November 22, 1938, Beck deplored the insincere, cowardly, and tortuous policy of Hungarian foreign minister Kanya and of his nation, which had been unable to take advantage of the international situation.

The Poles had always distrusted the Little Entente because of its anti-Hungarian attitude. Since the Little Entente was considered to be the work of Beneš, Beck pursued him with true hatred: "He was born to be everybody's groom." "The two B's" clashed, even after Beneš became head of state in 1935. Their policies were contradictory; one wanted to bring Russia into the western system, and the other sought a balance of power between Germany and Russia. According to what Szembek was told, "Beneš intrigues against Poland and depicts us as sabotaging all efforts to strengthen international solidarity."

An imposing diplomatic creation, the Little Entente had been formed in 1921 against Hungary, not against Germany. The three partners—Czechoslovakia, Rumania, and Yugoslavia—had committed themselves to act only when in agreement on matters involving Hungary. Poland worked at weakening Czech influence in Bucharest and in Belgrade; this was not easy because the Yugoslavs, and above all the Rumanians, distrusted the Polish-Hungarian friendship. But they were all seeking new friendships, as they felt threatened by economic vassalage or by a disguised protectorate.

Despite brilliant joint representations, the Little Entente had practically ceased to exist by 1937. It was in vain that France then proposed a mutual assistance pact in the event of German aggression. Yugoslavia was drawn by Italy, and Rumania by Poland, into divergent paths, at least in regard to Germany's attitude toward Czechoslovakia, and in spite of obligations for consultation included in the Little Entente treaty. Two of the partners had more intimate ties to an outside power than with their third associate, who remained isolated.

23

France and Eastern Europe after March 7, 1936

France after March 1936

Serious diplomats could hardly have labored under any illusion about the "rise of danger" since January 1933; after March 1936 no room was left for doubt. Men had wanted to believe that the conflict of 1914–18 had been enough for one generation to experience. But clearly they hoped in vain. The treasures of civilization would soon fall into the bloody abyss of war. For years war had reappeared in the newspapers. People were getting used to reading "communiqués": war in Ethiopia from October 1935 to May 1936, war in Spain since July 1936, war in the Far East since July 1937. The word "war" had not lost its power to terrify and its sinister ring; it spread enormous tension over Europe.

France was shaken by a social unrest, which intensified in May 1936 after the electoral victory of the Popular Front and the advent of the first Socialist government, Léon Blum's cabinet. And soon, in the name of national defense, there would be the revenge of the factory owners and the collapse of the Socialists.

Lacking national guidance, French public opinion was extremely divided politically and open to the competition of rival kinds of propaganda—Soviet, Nazi, Fascist, and Anglo-Saxon. It was unable to distinguish between matters of internal policy and the needs of foreign policy. Opposed to the totalitarian nations where public opinion was aroused, guided, inflamed, or calmed through the most modern methods, without any infiltration of contradictory foreign information, the nations where a free press welcomed all opinions and blindly accepted the propaganda of the totalitarian nations, as if this were a reciprocal gesture, were in a vulnerable position. Worse still was the fate of nations so dislocated that foreign propaganda became more influential than the official policy of their own governments. Intangible currents swept across Europe: conversations and commentaries were influenced by systems of intense propaganda; everywhere at once the diplomats and their agents in high society and in the press launched slogans and predictions.

The dictators' speeches caused commotion and clashes. In the confusion of the time, their words fostered their nations' dynamism, acquiring increasing weight.

Balance Sheet of the French Alliances

Central Europe, disturbed since 1934 by the German-Polish agreement, was still more deeply disturbed by the events of March 7, 1936. Europe saw Germany reappear more threatening than ever. In 1936 Italy abandoned her diplomatic tactics. France's authority and the true effectiveness of her entente with Great Britain were being questioned.

Since 1919 France had led a European system which united Belgium, Poland, and the Little Entene and represented the major defense of the Versailles order and the framework of European policy.

The British cared scarcely at all about this Little Entente, but still they had to accommodate themselves to it. Without ever acting against it, they did not approve of the Little Entente's mutual assistance treaties, and they deplored their consequences for Hungary, against whom the treaties were directed.

After 1936 the British acquired in Poland and in Yugoslavia an influence much greater than that of France; it gave them the superficial but natural feeling that the situation was improving. In Belgrade, they were kept informed on the 1937 Yugoslav negotiations with Italy, while the French minister to Yugoslavia was left out. In Bucharest, Titulescu had to leave the foreign ministry in 1936. Without having lost its own diplomatic system, the French faction was reduced to the role—though a powerful one—of auxiliary to the British system. The entire world, including Stalin, had great illusions about the real strength of the French armies.

France, fundamentally peace-loving, was tied to an even more peace-loving Great Britain, and united with the USSR by the mutual assistance pact of 1935—a very vague pact which had a formal nature without any definite contents. Words and formulas were substituted for action, in these treaties void of dynamic potential.

The balance sheet of the French alliances, with their liabilities and their assets, was very disappointing.

Yugoslavia and Rumania were allies without military obligations. France had a military-alliance treaty with Czechoslovakia, and another, the longest standing of all, with Poland. But what was the value of the Polish alliance? Military specialists asserted that the excellent Polish army was indeed the army of a desirable ally. Perhaps the Warsaw government interpreted their evaluation as the expression of a need, of a necessity. The loan of two billion francs obtained by the Warsaw government in September 1936 could have been considered the expression of that need.

In 1937 the most probable international danger was not a German attack on France, but aggression of an indeterminate kind against Czechoslovakia. This danger was very serious for France, because the aggression might occur in such circumstances that she would have to face it nearly isolated. Her obligations toward Czechoslovakia might become active through a policy which Poland had joined. The only link between the Franco-Polish alliance and the Franco-Czechoslovakian alliance was the League of Nations Council. French assistance to Czechoslovakia had to be granted legitimacy by a decision of the League Council verifying the aggression. But the Council might have to judge, not a clearly defined act of military aggression, but a disguised form of aggression. In that case Poland could invoke the Covenant, not openly violated. Whatever the evidence of aggression might be, Poland might not take part in a decision which could put her in the position of having to fulfill her own obligations. She might take advantage of the situation to declare her full freedom of action, and, if necessary, use that freedom against Czechoslovakia. If Poland understood her obligations toward France as limited to the event of a direct German attack on France, these obligations did not bear much weight.

Therefore France's assets were nearly nonexistent. Among liabilities were the increasing risks of the Franco-Czechoslovak alliance and the facilitating of German policy toward Czechoslovakia. Perhaps the French alliance, through which Poland gained indirect protection from the Franco-Soviet pact, was a major condition of Poland's freedom of action. Had the Franco-Polish alliance ended, the eastern dangers would have been increased for Poland, and the advantages she acquired through the Polish-German declaration of 1934 might have been greatly decreased.

When in fall 1937 Yvon Delbos, foreign minister in the first Blum cabinet and in the two Chautemps cabinets, made "a tour of France's friends," he visited Warsaw, Prague, Bucharest, and Belgrade, but not Moscow. He appeared just as the diplomatic structure built since 1921 was falling to pieces: France's friends were scattered in divergent positions. He attempted in vain to revive, reorder, and coordinate alliances or friendships; they were nearly irreconcilable. The potential for disorder resulting from this whole situation was serious for France's position in Europe.

Rumania

Rumania, worked upon by Nazi propaganda and anti-Semitism, was the ally of Poland, who was bound to the Germans by the friendship pact of 1934 and was becoming increasingly anti-Czech. Poland constantly strained to create or to strengthen in Rumania tendencies incompatible with the spirit of the Little Entente. Pilsudski and Beck were both very cool toward Rumania, but the common opposition of Warsaw and Bucharest to the Soviets demanded an alliance. For Rumania, as for the Baltic States and Poland, the enemy was Russia. After having greatly contributed to the failure in 1934 of all attempts at an eastern pact, Poland forgot about her own nonaggression pact with the Soviets and, becoming still more hostile toward Russia after the Franco-Soviet pact of 1935, attempted to lead Rumania in the same direction. The expulsion in August 1936 of Nicholas Titulescu, faithful supporter of the Little Entente and a friend of Beneš, demonstrated Bucharest's estrangement from France, despite the continued flattery of traditional declarations of friendship.

To confront obvious dangers, Rumania, who had long been unsettled by political struggles, submitted to the dictatorship of her king. In February 1938, the Orthodox patriarch Monsignor Miron Cristea formed a so-called National Union cabinet. Interior minister Armand Calinescu, a former National Peasant politician, strong, calm, and determined, had dissolved all political parties and brought the leaders of the Iron Guard to trial. In March 1939 when the patriarch died, Calinescu took over as head of the government, a position he would retain until September 1939 when he fell under the fire of the Iron Guard.

Rumania felt dangerously isolated. She had attempted in vain to reinforce the ties between Rumania, Yugoslavia, Greece, and Turkey, established since 1934 by the still existing Balkan Entente. The Axis aimed at disbanding this group, apparently linked to the French system for security in the Balkans.

Rumania was threatened by neighbors who did not hide their territorial claims, especially Hungary and Bulgaria. She feared the USSR because of Bessarabia. Finally, she knew that she was the prey to German designs.

Yugoslavia

In Belgrade the Yevtić cabinet had been in power since December 19, 1934, with Stojadinović as finance minister. Relations with the Croats were strained. Yevtić gave everyone the impression of being able neither to abandon the dictatorship nor to remain totally faithful to it. Elections in May 1935 represented the first political trial since the inauguration of the dictatorship in 1929. But since the vote was public and official pressure was intense, the results had little meaning. The relative success of the government seriously damaged Yevtić's position: 1.7 million votes for the government, 1 million for the Croat opposition, and 1 million abstentions.

A rapprochement between Yugoslavia and Italy had been taking shape since March. It was seen at this time as a success for French diplomacy and Yevtić was considered the protégé of France.

Without having assumed any military obligation toward Yugoslavia, France had invested moral capital in that country—an investment for the future! The friendship of France had roots too deep to be openly challenged. The agreement with Italy played the same role in Yugoslav policy as did the German-Polish declaration in Polish policy. The Yugoslav leaders, impressed by Mussolini's prestige, felt sanctioned by London.

On February 4, 1937, Stojadinović, who had succeeded Yevtić as prime minister in June 1935, declared: "Yugoslav policy is neither Francophile nor Germanophile nor Anglophile; it is national." His program was rather similar to that of Colonel Beck. Like the Poland of Beck, Yugoslavia made excessive use of a "realistic" policy. To demonstrate, as had Poland, that she was a great nation, Yugoslavia decided to follow an "independent" policy.

The rivalry between Italy and Yugoslavia had seemed a great threat to peace for a long time. Suddenly the long-strained relations between the two countries became cordial. Following an economic and financial agreement concluded on September 23, 1936, a friendship pact was signed in Belgrade on March 25, 1937, by Prime Minister Stojadinović and Ciano. Italy recognized the territorial integrity of the Yugoslav kingdom. The two countries gave guarantees of reciprocal neutrality, in the event of a conflict into which one of the nations would be dragged by unprovoked aggression. Economic clauses completed this agreement, which, despite assertions to the contrary, amounted to the total dissolution of the Little Entente, after months of agitation. Slyly, Stojadinović wanted to act alone. Hitler had assured him that he considered the Yugoslav frontiers as "sacred," and Ciano was considering a partition of Albania with Stojadinović.

Since the Rome-Berlin Axis strongly wished the dissolution of the Little Entente, which it considered "a weapon for France in the Danubian region," Rome and Berlin attempted to reconcile the Hungarians and the Yugoslavs. Then Hungary would renounce making good her territorial claims on Yugoslavia by force and could be oriented totally against Czechoslovakia, in order "not to dissipate political activities in all directions."

Hungary

Germany, the ardent supporter of revisionism, could count on Austria, but only with numerous reservations. It was Germany—and Hungarian foreign minister Kanya was well aware of it—who was the strongest opponent of a Hapsburg restoration.

On August 23, 1938, the Hungarian regent, Horthy, the prime minister, Imredy, and the foreign minister, Kanya, met with Hitler and Ribbentrop. They seemed little inclined to act against Czechoslovakia; they would need, they claimed, one or two more years for rearmament.

The Hungarians were striving to maintain relations of friendship and good neighborliness with Germany, without letting themselves be dragged into German ventures. They feared that the German-Czechoslovak conflict would lead to a widespread war.

Ribbentrop tried vehemently to reassure them. No one would move: not Yugoslavia, Rumania, France, or England. To have a revision of existing frontiers, it was essential to take advantage of this opportunity and to take part in the action. Stressing this point, Hitler exclaimed: "All those who want to share the meal must help with the cooking."

The Hungarians finally declared themselves ready to take part in the German action after October 1, perhaps after a delay of forty-eight hours "to see clearly Yugoslavia's intentions." Berlin felt that the Hungarians were "not reliable."

However on September 20 Hungarian delegates rushed to Berchtesgaden, just as Hitler was preparing to meet with Chamberlain in Godesberg. The Hungarians feared that the talks between Hitler and Chamberlain would lead to "a discrimination among the minorities."

Hitler told them that he intended to be "very harsh" with the Englishman. He would demand all German territories, but "it is to be feared that the Czechs may agree to anything." Military action would bring "the only satisfying solution": the best would be to destroy Czechoslovakia completely. Hungary should "immediately demand a plebiscite in the territories she claims."

Later, on January 16, 1939, Hitler accused the Magyars of having been "asleep" in September 1938 and of having been satisfied by "insignificant diplomatic proceedings," instead of forcefully stating their demands and "presenting the whole affair as a threat of wider war." It was as a result of their "extraordinary lack of seriousness" that he had been forced to negotiate with Chamberlain; "If the Hungarians had cooperated at the right time, I could have laughed in Chamberlain's face." He had been forced to be satisfied with the ethnographic solution to the Czechoslovakian problem.

Bulgaria

Bulgaria's foreign policy remained cautious, despite the marriage of King Boris to a daughter of the king of Italy. According to Hitler, Boris was reluctant to adopt a clear position. The German minister to Sofia, Bülow, who found Boris "clever, let us hope not too clever," wished that, after having followed "a policy of waiting, until now so wise," he would decide to change his course.

As for Prime Minister Georgi Kiosseivanov, "always in delicate health, fond of his comforts," Berlin felt that under him Bulgaria showed a surprising lack of dynamism in her foreign policy. She did not take a positive attitude toward revisionism, above all in the problem of southern Dobruja, "stolen away by the peace treaties." The Bulgarians hoped to obtain, at the expense of Rumania, at least partial satisfaction of their claims in Dobruja through diplomatic means. Germany did not object to settlement of that question in Bulgaria's favor. Access to the Aegean Sea was the second step in the Bulgarians' claims. They maintained that Germany would also gain from that access.

However by January 7, 1939, Germany intended to leave Bulgaria in uncertainty. And Bulgaria, always unsatisfied, knew by March 22 that without German help she would have to abandon her national aspirations.

Kiosseivanov, informed that he was accused in Berlin of following a policy too little in favor of Germany, assured the German minister that he would prefer submitting his resignation to being mistrusted so. The German minister advised him to give his foreign policy a more clearly pro-German tone.

As minister to Belgrade and as a supporter of a rapprochement with the Yugoslavs, he had concluded a pact of perpetual friendship with them in January 1937. And in July 1938 Bulgaria's neighbors had agreed to grant her equal rights, which abolished the restrictions imposed by the Treaty of Neuilly on Bulgarian land, sea, and air forces.

Bulgaria incessantly asked Germany for shipments of arms and war materiel as rearmament supplies. An agreement had been concluded on March 12, 1938. Bulgaria demanded further urgent deliveries.

On July 5, Kiosseivanov was received by Hitler, who expressed the idea that it was not in Germany's interest for Bulgaria to remain a sort of no-man's-land. She should strengthen her army. Hitler did not believe that Rumania had any aggressive intentions, with her army in such a pitiful state.

24

The German Claims on Poland

The German Initiatives of October 24, 1938

After Austria and Czechoslovakia, Hitler turned to Poland. His appetite knew no limits; his policy had taken on an irreversible momentum. Suddenly, on October 24, only three weeks after Munich, Ribbentrop proposed to Ambassador Lipski "in a very friendly manner" the return of Danzig to Germany—Poland would retain all her economic rights in Danzig—as well as an extraterritorial communications route across the Polish Corridor, which had separated the province of East Prussia from the rest of Germany since 1919. The agreement of January 1934 could be extended to twenty-five years. The Polish-German frontiers would thus be guaranteed.

On November 19 Ribbentrop renewed his proposal in another interview, still very cordial.

Hitler had thought at first that he could reach an agreement with "his friend Beck"; but on November 24 he secretly ordered preparations for the occupation of Danzig. He refrained from demanding the Polish Corridor. Pilsudski had always said: "Laying a hand on the Corridor means war." Germany was simply asking for a communications route across the Corridor. In 1935 Beck had heard suggestions about the creation of a corridor within the Corridor, with a highway contiguous to a railway, in an extraterritorial zone about thirty yards wide. Todt had precise construction plans for this *Korridorstrasse*, which would extend only about thirty miles inside Polish territory.

The Führer demanded the return to Germany of Danzig, a German city "more National Socialist than all of Germany," made a "free city" by the

259

Treaty of Versailles because it could really not be considered Polish; Danzig, whose three hundred thousand inhabitants with their "free city" seemed so few compared to the three and a half million Sudeten Germans, who in Munich had been surgically cut off from the Czechoslovak state.

At the same time, the most seductive prospects were held out before the eyes of the Poles. According to undersecretary Szembek, Goering, who had come to Poland in January 1935 on a hunting trip, observed that "great possibilities" were open to the Poles "in the direction of the Ukraine." Four years later, Ribbentrop spoke to Beck of Kiev and the shores of the Black Sea.

Proud of his initiative which had led to the agreement of January 1934, Hitler had declared to Marshal von Hindenburg that the agreement with Poland would create an atmosphere allowing for arrangements over Danzig, the Polish Corridor, and the German minorities in Poland.

In reality, Poland was far from considering territorial concessions. Despite five years of pro-German policy, she remained basically anti-German. Although Hitler claimed that the 1934 agreement had "eliminated the poison" which spoiled German-Polish relations, the wound between Poland and Germany had not healed. There was only a pretense of friendship between the two nations. Poland instinctively sensed the potential danger created since 1938 by the "distension" of Germany.

On February 24 and 25, 1939, violent anti-German demonstrations took place in Warsaw. Rocks were thrown at the German embassy. Beck quickly apologized. At the end of March, anti-German demonstrations erupted in Bromberg. Count Moltke, an excellent diplomat, took the nationalistic excesses and the struggle of the German minorities in Poland very seriously. The issue of the German minorities had been banished from the German press since 1934, but difficulties continued and the Polish authorities did not hesitate to take imprudent if not coercive measures.

Moreover the policy of friendship toward Poland met with much reluctance within Germany. The Germans of Poland wondered if they had been abandoned by the Führer. Extremely anti-Polish, they asserted that they were being submitted to an "Asiatic" treatment; their vehement complaints resounded in Berlin. In the Teschen region, just snatched from Czechoslovakia, the German minority considered the Polish yoke infinitely heavier than the Czech domination. Yet the town of Oderberg in that region had been returned to the Poles at Hitler's initiative, to demonstrate his generosity without lowering himself by bargaining unworthy of a statesman.

A joint commission for the study of minorities questions met in Berlin after Ribbentrop's visit to Warsaw in late January. It did not reach any definite arrangements.

January 5 and 6, 1939

In Poland, the reality of the political situation was hidden by the true sympathy of the Polish General Staff for the French high command, whose prestige remained very high. "Joseph Beck," wrote Weizsäcker, "was not liked by anyone." Beck himself observed that several times the French had tried to oppose him through the inspector-general of the Polish army, Smigly-Rydz, who was beginning to show some political ambitions.

By May 15, 1936, Szembek noted: "Goering very tactfully let Beck know that he doubted whether Smigly-Rydz was really a supporter of the entente with Germany."

On June 30, 1936, Smigly-Rydz warned Szembek to be on guard against the Germans. He was convinced that it was in Danzig that the conflict which would provoke a war with Germany would take place. On September 16, 1936, he said "he was always expecting a war to break out someday between us and the Germans."

On August 9, 1936, Ambassador Lipski wrote: "The larger part of the Polish military establishment has not been won to the policy of rapprochement with Germany to the degree desired by German military men."

On March 12, 1938, Szembek noted again: "In the opinion of Smigly-Rydz, we must always reckon with the expansion, the aggressiveness, and the energy of Germany, which after the absorption of Austria and Czechoslovakia can turn toward Poland. The policy of détente with Germany can be continued, although we cannot believe in it blindly."

The strictly confidential soundings undertaken by Ribbentrop spread news reports presenting German-Polish relations "in an unfavorable light." They were vigorously denied by the Poles.

Hitler thought that they would eventually accept some arrangement, whether they liked it or not.

On January 5 and 6, 1939, Beck, the object of much attention, heard Ribbentrop and Hitler state the German program. Beck claimed to be "racking his brains" to reach some arrangement over Danzig. Hitler declared his unalterable "policy of friendship" with Warsaw.

Like his ambassadors, Beck pretended to be favorably impressed by his long conversation at Berchtesgaden, although Hitler had asserted that Danzig would have to return to Germany sooner or later.

Ribbentrop's Visit to Warsaw on January 30

Invited by Beck, Ribbentrop visited the Polish minister in Warsaw at the end of January. Beck displayed optimism, but he was profoundly worried. He could not hide the fact that Germany had made precise claims. He still hoped to divert difficulties. But Ribbentrop's visit was a real disappointment. Nothing, thought Ribbentrop, could be done with the Poles. Weizsäcker observed: "How could two men as vain as Ribbentrop and Beck have possibly understood each other?"

After the German minister left Warsaw on January 30, it became known everywhere that the Danzig question was growing dangerous for German-Polish relations. On that same day in fact, Hitler was again praising before the *Reichstag* the pact concluded in 1934, "one of the reassuring factors of Europe's political life."

The tension between Berlin and Warsaw was becoming acute. However Ciano, who was staying in the Polish capital at the end of February, felt that Poland, far from being hostile to the Axis, would wait a long time with arms at the ready in order to take the victor's side in the event of a European war.

Failure of German-Polish Negotiations

The events of mid-March 1939, with the occupation of Prague and the annexation of Memel to Germany, revealed to the Poles the extent of the danger. After having wavered between anguish and hope, Europe was sliding toward catastrophe. From then on Polish-German relations were irremediably damaged.

On March 21 Ribbentrop spoke sharply to Ambassador Lipski, renewing his proposals for the return of Danzig to Germany and for a German route across the Corridor. On March 26 Lipski delivered Warsaw's refusal of Danzig as well as of the extraterritorial status of communications routes. Ribbentrop declared that the situation was becoming serious. Lipski offered counter-proposals: concession of technical facilities for transit between Germany and East Prussia.

On March 27 Ribbentrop rejected these counterproposals. He complained bitterly to the ambassador that "he could no longer understand the Polish government." Hitler's generous proposals had been rejected. The break quickly became known. In Warsaw national feeling balked at the idea of surrender, and suddenly the specter of war with Germany arose.

Hitler had thought that under great pressure Poland would yield. Exasperated by the apparent rapprochement between Warsaw and London, he ordered military preparations against Poland on April 3. On April 11 he clearly intended to go to war. But he wanted to avoid a simultaneous conflict with the western powers. He believed that the fight against Poland would remain localized "because of the internal crisis existing in France and the British reservations resulting from it."

Chamberlain's Declaration of March 31;
British Guarantees to Poland

How could a European order be established which would be different from
this Nazi law, now the "law of the jungle"? As in other decisive moments in
England's long history, the instinct of the British people told them to yield
no more but to confront the adversary. Great Britain had granted numerous
concessions to Germany, had never wanted to take sides in the conflicts of
Central and Eastern Europe, and had obstinately "preferred a dubious compromise to the direct settlement of a question if that settlement implied
the obligation to assume any responsibility whatever." Suddenly England
gave repeated "guarantees" to the nations threatened by Hitler's ambitions,
first of all to Poland, toward whom she had always been cold at heart.

Czechoslovakia had hardly disappeared from the map when Great Britain
felt the strongest worry about Rumania. It seems that at that time those
worries were not entirely justified.

To protect Rumania, Chamberlain suggested to France that they meet with
the USSR and Poland or make a common declaration with the USSR and
Poland. Since a conference seemed to involve more uncertainty and delay,
the project of a joint declaration was submitted to Moscow and Warsaw
on March 22.

The USSR refused to make a declaration against the aggressor without
Poland's participation. Beck replied that he could not satisfy the Soviet wish.

Chamberlain then suggested a reciprocal guarantee pact to Poland, in order
to force her to defend Rumania if the latter was attacked by Germany. It
was not known at that time that Ribbentrop had asked Poland on March 21
to surrender Danzig to Germany and to relinquish a passageway across the
Corridor, and that these proposals had been rejected by Beck on March 26.

Chamberlain's proposal to Poland was immediately accepted in Warsaw.
On March 31 Chamberlain publicly confirmed his offer to Poland, and the
French government joined him: "His Majesty's Government would consider
itself bound to give the Polish government all the support in its power if
Poland were clearly threatened by any action against her independence, and
if the Polish government should consider that it would be in its vital interest
to resist that assault by force."

At the beginning of April, Beck arrived in London. After a few days of
talk, the English prime minister announced to Commons that Great Britain
and Poland were willing to sign a permanent and reciprocal agreement in
order to ensure mutual assistance "in the event that the independence of one
or the other nation should be threatened."

The declaration made to the House of Commons on March 31 by Chamberlain showed a new spirit and opened a new era in international relations; after

having rejected for so long any interference in the affairs of Central and Eastern Europe as a dangerous venture, the English government was adopting a policy of guarantees and alliances. Under the terms of that declaration, Great Britain would give all possible assistance to a European state threatened in its independence.

France took the same position. On March 21 the president of the Republic, Albert Lebrun, was enthusiastically received in London.

In effect England gave the Poles the responsibility of deciding whether England should go to war in the event that the Poles believed that their vital interests were being endangered.

Liddell Hart would disapprove of Chamberlain's rash guarantee to Poland, a measure which let Warsaw control Great Britain's destiny, and which would have had a chance of stopping Hitler only if Russian cooperation had been ensured. The German-Soviet pact would practically annul the British guarantee.

25

The Occupation of Prague

Czechoslovakia after Munich

In Munich the Versailles structure collapsed, carrying down with it all the paper buttresses, all the pacts intended to support it. The crisis of September 1938 finally ended in peace, but it left behind the unfortunate Czechoslovakia, abandoned by all. The Serb Stojadinović would label her, ironically, "a sausage state made to be sliced up."

Munich, a crushing diplomatic failure, represented a heavy moral liability for the democracies. They had abandoned a small country to its powerful neighbor. "Czechoslovakia's own friends handed her to me on a platter," Hitler would later say. It is true that Great Britain was not bound to Czechoslovakia by an alliance treaty, but France had broken explicit and repeated commitments to the only ally that had always been faithful to her.

On October 14, 1938, Hitler declared to the Hungarian Daranyi that the Czechs now felt hatred for the French. On October 23 Germany's representative in Prague, Hencke, confirmed the bitterness that existed against the French.

Chvalkovsky, a pro-German diplomat, assured Germany that the Czechoslovakian government no longer had anything in common with France, and that it would follow a policy of close cooperation with its German neighbor.

Beneš had resigned as president and on October 5 had already left for England. He was replaced by Emil Hacha, an elderly judge without prestige. General Sirovy, whose reputation of being a fierce patriot served as a guarantee, signed the capitulation that cut the Sudeten German areas off from Czechoslovakia.

Called to the foreign ministry, Chvalkovsky renounced the plebiscites

265

planned at Munich. At the mercy of Germany, the Czechs gave in; all they could do now was to entrust their fate to Hitler's generosity.

Czechoslovakia was considerably reduced, having surrendered the Sudetenland to Germany—about 3,600,000 inhabitants: 2,800,000 Germans and nearly 800,000 Czechs—, Teschen to Poland, and eastern territories to Hungary. In addition autonomy had been granted to Slovakia and the Subcarpathian Ukraine. Three independently governed territories with autonomous assemblies had thus been created; there remained only a central government and a central parliament in Prague, constituting a federal state with a single president.

On October 13 in Berlin, Chvalkovsky promised Ribbentrop that Czechoslovakia would totally reverse her foreign policy. The Moscow-Prague-Paris alliance was dead and buried. Czechoslovakia asked only to be able to rely on Germany.

On October 14, Chvalkovsky renewed his assurances to Hitler, who seemed satisfied at first, as he stated in a speech in Berlin. But soon, in private conversations, Hitler no longer concealed that he was discontented that he had accepted a compromise instead of making Germany's full rights triumph. "I cannot be satisfied with the Sudeten territory."[1] Czechoslovakia continued to be a threat to Germany and he would have done better to crush her.

On October 9, only ten days after the English guarantee, Hitler's speech in Saarbrücken reduced the importance of Munich and dissipated many illusions: "We no longer need an English governess." New surprises were feared. But on October 30, 1938, Hitler delivered a rather conciliatory speech to the *Reichstag;* after the settlement of the Czech question and the Munich agreement, a lasting peace seemed assured.

On December 4, 1938, the Sudeten Germans, cut off from the Czechoslovak state by the surgery of Munich, voted to elect deputies to the *Reichstag* in Berlin. Out of 2,200,000 voters, 2,100,000 pronounced themselves in favor of the National Socialist ticket, with 26,000 against it; 99 percent approved of the annexation.

In December 1938, Chvalkovsky wished to establish an economic and customs union with Germany, to sign a military convention with her, and to appoint a minister for the remaining German minorities in the Czechoslovak state. A plan for the economic and customs union had already been established. On instructions from Ribbentrop and Hitler, the talks were stopped. Hitler felt that the Czechs were not sincere; the spirit of Beneš persisted, and the democratic regime had not been completely abandoned. Hitler wanted to wipe Czechoslovakia off the map.

1. H. Batowski, "Munich 1938, realisation des plans pangermaniques, 1918-1919," *La Pologne et les affaires occidentales,* 1966, vol. IV, no. 2.

The Franco-German Declaration of December 6, 1938

The Third Republic seemed totally powerless to maintain what remained of the Continental order established in 1919. France maintained a defensive attitude; the doctrines of the General Staff and the Maginot line showed that she was considering no war other than a defensive war.

Under all regimes, the constant concern of French diplomacy was to aim at an alliance against Germany. The Third Republic had been led to an alliance system through which France distributed guarantees to nearly all of Eastern Europe. This implied the existence of an army—not merely a defensive army, but one capable of ensuring respect for these guarantees.

But France did not have "the army suited for her policy"; unlike her navy, her army had not been sufficiently modernized, although it had the reputation of being very strong.

The fear of conflict dominated all minds. There was an obstinate desire to maintain peace, which with Hitler was no longer possible. Foreign minister Georges Bonnet was trying to find security through a transaction with Germany; for lack of a lasting entente, he wanted to gain time until the armament programs were finished in 1941–42.

French diplomacy showed a desire to "crystallize" the Munich détente through a special agreement with Germany. This was to take the form of a declaration similar to the one Chamberlain (without notifying Daladier) had had Hitler sign in Munich on September 30. The talks began on October 18 and ended a month later. On December 6, 1938, Ribbentrop came to Paris to sign a Franco-German declaration with Georges Bonnet. This was comparable to the Anglo-German declaration of September, through which the two nations committed themselves to consult one another over any difficulties that might arise between them.

The French were not displeased to receive a visit from the German foreign minister, who proclaimed the French character of Alsace-Lorraine at the precise moment when Italy was noisily airing enormous territorial claims. For the Germans, an arrangement reached in the middle of the anti-Semitic cyclone seemed to offer a serious moral advantage.

In addition, Ribbentrop believed that the declaration of December 6, 1938, would clearly confirm, after Munich, the change in French policy in Eastern Europe.

On July 6, 1939, Ribbentrop would declare to the Bulgarian prime minister Kiosseivanov that, in December 1938, he had thought that he had obtained the French foreign minister's agreement on the delimitation of their respective spheres of interest; but that in 1939 France had swerved from that line and once again increased her activities in the east.

On April 18, 1940, Ribbentrop would remind Rumanian foreign minister

Gregory Gafencu that, in signing the Franco-German declaration, he had clearly told Bonnet that Germany would in no way intervene in the French sphere of influence, and that he expected France not to intervene in the German sphere of influence.

French Diplomatic Efforts in Czechoslovakia's Favor

After the Munich agreements and the Franco-German declaration, the French government attempted to carry out a policy of détente.

The Munich agreements had guaranteed Czechoslovakia the status of an independent territory. England and France guaranteed her new frontiers, to be determined by an international commission. Italy and Germany would guarantee these new frontiers *after* the settlement of the Polish and Hungarian claims on Czechoslovakia.

The Sudeten territories were annexed to Germany; all was quickly settled. However the Czechoslovakian question remained the object of the most acute concern. France repeatedly tried to obtain from Germany the guarantee of the new frontiers. Germany was playing deaf.

On December 6 in Paris, Ribbentrop replied to Georges Bonnet that, in the question of the four-power guarantee of Czechoslovakia's new frontiers, Germany was waiting for the other minorities problems to be settled—which was not the case. A four-power guarantee could tempt Prague into returning to the old policy of Beneš. The best guarantee for Czechoslovakia consisted in the establishment of friendly relations with Germany.

The German report notes that the secretary-general of the Quai d'Orsay, Alexis Léger, seemed to attach great significance to the four-power guarantee.

Ribbentrop drew the attention of Georges Bonnet to the fact that Germany would consider a French guarantee of Czechoslovakia's frontiers to be an interference in the German sphere of influence.

On December 21, undersecretary Weizsäcker reported that Ambassador Coulondre brought up numerous times the question of the guarantee by the Munich powers, using the expression "joint guarantee."

"I replied to Coulondre that Czechoslovakia definitely belonged to the territories that have to be considered as part of Germany. Czechoslovakia's fate, I told him, is in Hitler's hands. Only a German guarantee has any meaning for Prague."

"Coulondre returned to this theme: although Czechoslovakia was completely subject to German decisions, a promise of a guarantee had been made by France and also by England."

On January 21, 1939, Chvalkovsky was received by Hitler and Ribbentrop. Hitler demanded rights for the German minorities in the Czechoslovak state and National Socialist instruction in their schools. To improve relations with Germany, he earnestly advised Chvalkovsky to undertake "a fast reduction of the size of the Czech army." Germany was ready to give her guarantee to a neutral state, and a neutral state had no need for a permanent army.

Hitler added that France did not represent the slightest danger to Germany.

On February 7 Coulondre handed a note to Ribbentrop asking for a German guarantee of Czechoslovakia. Only on March 2 did Ribbentrop answer: "According to the provisions made at Munich, that matter must wait until Czechoslovakia has settled with Warsaw and Budapest the question of Polish and Hungarian minorities."

Ribbentrop declared to the ambassador: "Germany, who respects the French sphere of interest, would consider intolerable for Franco-German relations a return to a kind of 'Beneš policy.'" In Paris, Georges Bonnet had stated that he was no longer interested in questions dealing with Eastern Europe, and any departure from that policy would be inadvisable.

Coulondre assured Ribbentrop that France would not follow a policy in the east which could disturb Germany.

On February 22, in a note to the four Munich powers, the Czechoslovakian government had raised the question of guarantees as part of a solemn commitment to Czechoslovakian neutrality. Berlin was extremely irritated; Prague should have exchanged views on that subject with Berlin alone.

On March 3 the Czechoslovakian ambassador to Berlin, Mastny, gave Weizsäcker an assurance that Prague would not renew her proceedings in the guarantee question without first approaching Germany. Weizsäcker declared that a premature guarantee would strengthen disruptive elements in Prague.

Hitler Resolves on "the Total Solution" to the Czechoslovakian Problem

Munich did not satisfy Hitler's insatiable appetite. It has been said that Czechoslovakia was a mere piece of meat between the jaws of the German wolf. If the wolf closed its jaws, Czechoslovakia would cease to exist.

Hitler expressed more and more his bitter regret at having contented himself with a partial solution: the Munich arrangement. As Ambassador Léon Noël wrote: "All the German claims led, by steps, toward infinity."

Many were the friends of National Socialism who deplored that Munich had prevented the war. After the conference, Ciano had noted: "Ribbentrop is hardly satisfied that everything has gone so smoothly," and Himmler confided his "despair" to Ciano.

Beneš himself assumed that Germany would accommodate herself to a mutilated Czechoslovakia; but Hitler did not intend to be satisfied with the Sudetenland. He declared that the fragile Czechoslovakia represented an intolerable threat to Germany. Less than two weeks after the Munich Conference, he asked General Keitel about the size of the military forces necessary to break all Czech resistance in Bohemia and Moravia. As early as October 21, he began military preparations intended to "crush at any moment what remains of Czechoslovakia." On December 17, not expecting any resistance worth mentioning, he ordered that the action be "carried out by the peacetime standing army alone, without reinforcement by mobilization," for "the world would then think that it was only a pacification action, not a war."

He had the feeling that he would be able to destroy, whenever he wished, this "rump Czechoslovakia," by raising against her the Slovaks and the Hungarians.

All groups hostile to the Czechs were secretly brought into play. The students of the Sudeten areas, invited to pursue their studies at the German university in Prague, formed a coherent body ready to play an effective role during a crisis; so did the isolated German communities which remained in the Republic, with about 250,000 Germans. Clashes occurred with the Czech police; they were exaggerated in the German press, and Berlin cried out against "Czech terrorism."

The Slovak separatists were vigorously backed by Berlin. Several Slovak politicians—deputy prime minister Durcansky, Bela Tuka, Hans Karmasin, and others—met with Goering, who promised to support them in their efforts for independence: "Without Slovakia, Czechoslovakia is still more at our mercy."

On February 12, a Slovak delegation which included Tuka and Karmasin talked with Hitler and Ribbentrop; the Slovaks declared that an association with the Czechs had become a moral and economic impossibility for the Slovaks.

At the beginning of March, serious incidents erupted. The Prague government had Bratislava occupied by police and troops. On March 10, Prague suspended Monsignor Tiso, the prime minister elected by the Slovak assembly, and replaced him with Sidor, a man loyal to Prague. On March 11 Tiso called on Germany for assistance and proclaimed a state of siege. On March 12 he left with Durcansky for Berlin, where they were received by Hitler. Tiso asked Hitler to extend his protection to Slovakia, which wished to separate from the Czechs. Hitler answered evasively that he would let the Slovaks decide about their own independence.

On March 13 the Slovak Diet unanimously resolved upon secession from Czechoslovakia and asked Hitler for his protection. Hitler agreed. A few days later a treaty was signed with Slovakia.

It is beyond doubt that the vast majority of Slovaks wanted at that time to free themselves from Prague. They were encouraged and aroused by undersecretary Keppler, sent by Hitler to Bratislava.

The Slovak secession rendered the situation unbearable for Prague. Similar tendencies were emerging in the Subcarpathian Ukraine, and Germans were rebelling in Bohemia and Moravia.

The Hitler-Hacha Meeting

On the evening of March 13, President Hacha asked Hitler for a meeting. He was told that he would be received in the evening of the following day. Accompanied by his daughter and Chvalkovsky, he was received in Berlin with the full honors due a head of state. His daughter was offered a magnificent box of chocolates by Hitler.

The meeting began on March 15 at one o'clock in the morning. Hacha expressed his respect and admiration for Hitler. He declared himself ready to place his country under Hitler's protection. He accepted the secession of the Slovaks; now that the Czechs had a closer association with the Germans, the Slovaks were closer to the Hungarians. He considered that the geographic situation required the Czechs to have close relations with Germany.

Hitler proclaimed his confidence in President Hacha, but the old "Beneš spirit" had not been eradicated. The army was still strong and full of nationalistic ideas—a complete absurdity. The Germans of Bohemia and Moravia cried out their complaints. For their protection the country had to be occupied by German troops, whom he had already ordered across the frontier. A Czech protectorate with full autonomy and all national freedoms would be incorporated into Germany. Hacha and Chvalkovsky declared that they had hoped for a friendly settlement, through which their country would maintain its sovereignty. Any Czech resistance would be senseless. But they wanted Hitler to halt the advance of his troops. It would not be necessary for German troops to disarm the Czech troops immediately. The Czech troops, progressively disbanded, would surrender their arms by themselves.

Hitler replied that it was impossible to halt the military machine already in motion. Detailed plans for the disarmament of the Czech troops should be considered with Goering, Keitel, and Ribbentrop. Keitel stressed the size of the German forces entering Czechoslovakia; Goering did not conceal the fact that, in the event of resistance, Prague would be bombed.

The talks were interrupted for a half hour. Hacha felt ill and he was given an injection by Doctor Morell, Hitler's personal physician. Chvalkovsky and Hacha telephoned Prague. Hacha announced that he had ordered the Czechs not to resist; he was ready to sign the proposed agreement.

Hitler asserted that he did not want to denationalize and Germanize the

Czech people, to whom he would grant a wide autonomy. The Czechs could only gain from coexistence with Germany. In any event, they would have more rights within Germany than the Germans had had in the Czechoslovak state.

On March 15, at four o'clock in the morning, the agreement intended to establish a protectorate over Bohemia and Moravia was signed.

Later Hacha would be blamed for his weakness. It would be claimed that if he had refused to sign and appealed to the French and English guarantees, Hitler might have been more conciliatory. It would be regretted that he had gone to Berlin personally; his trip made an intervention from the western democracies even more difficult.

The Protectorate over Bohemia and Moravia

The German troops occupied Prague in the morning of March 15. On the same day, the German government informed the French government that the two parties—Hitler and Hacha—had agreed in "expressing the conviction that calm, order, and peace must be ensured in this part of Central Europe. The president of the Czechoslovak state has declared that he has placed the fate of his people and of the Czech nation in the hands of the Führer of the German Reich with full confidence, in order to obtain a permanent peace. The Führer has accepted this declaration. German troops crossed the Czech frontier at six o'clock this morning."

The annexation of Bohemia and Moravia came five months after the conclusion of the agreements of September 29, 1938. Defying the Munich treaty, Hitler was destroying what remained of Czechoslovakia.

Hitler had said and repeated that he only wanted to bring Germans into Germany, not Czechs. His contempt for law, promises, and treaties made him appear no longer worthy of trust, a man of violence with whom it was impossible to reach any understanding.

On March 15, a proclamation to the German people asserted that the terrorism reigning in Bohemia and Moravia had made necessary the dispatch of German troops. Those troops would disarm the terrorist gangs, as well as the Czech forces protecting them, and thus would ensure the basis for a lasting settlement.

On March 16, a decree was published in Prague on the "future legal position of the Bohemian-Moravian area." It was quite different from what had been said to Hacha and Chvalkovsky the day before. Czechoslovakia had become an enormous threat to European peace; the Czechoslovak state had not succeeded in devising any reasonable means for the coexistence of the nationalities arbitrarily united under it; in the German Protectorate of Bohemia and Moravia, the Germans would be German citizens and the non-Germans would be subjects of the Protectorate and enjoy autonomy and self-administration. The rights of sovereignty of the Protectorate would be made compatible with the political, military, and economic needs of the Reich. A "protector" would be sent to Prague.

This represented the annihilation of all independence, and the Czech areas were now totally under the rule of the Third Reich.

These events aroused more surprise than admiration in Germany. While Slovakia, theoretically independent, was placed under German control with Monsignor Tiso as head of state, "the area of Bohemia and Moravia" was integrated into the Third Reich under a "protector"—Baron von Neurath, the former foreign minister of Papen, Schleicher, and Hitler. Neurath considered that "one or two generations would suffice to transform the Czech people into a historical curiosity like the Slavs of Lausitz." In twenty years the Czech language would be a simple dialect. Neurath accepted his appointment as "protector," declaring that he was making this sacrifice for Germany. He gave too much freedom to his undersecretary, a Sudeten German named Franck, who was extremely anti-Czech; but, still, Neurath did moderate certain excesses. And so in 1941 Hitler named as his successor in Prague "hangman" Heydrich.

English and French Reaction to
the Occupation of Prague

On March 15, Georges Bonnet expressed his personal feelings to Ambassador Welczeck: the German actions in Czechoslovakia were the hardest blow struck against the friends of peace in Europe. Only six months after Munich, the assurances that had been given were being ignored. The agreement for consultation reached on December 6 had not been respected. It was a deplorable disaster for the supporters of Munich. The future could only be viewed with much pessimism.

The ambassador objected that it was not a European conflict, but an intervention made necessary by the disintegration of the Czech state and accomplished with the approval of that state.

Ambassador Coulondre tried to deliver to Ribbentrop a note of protest against "the flagrant violation of the Munich agreements." After having formally refused to accept it, Weizsäcker reported its contents to Hitler. The French ambassador read to the German undersecretary the instructions he had received from Paris. After Munich, the French had believed in a beginning of Franco-German cooperation; they had signed the declaration of December 6, 1938. And now this German action against Prague!

Weizsäcker later said that he answered that Munich signified France's lack of interest in Eastern Europe. France should look to the west and to her empire, not to an area where her activity had not served the cause of peace! Germany had been forced to restore order in Czechoslovakia; the necessary action had been undertaken with the agreement of the Czech government.

Weizsäcker wanted to see the ambassador's approach as one whose purpose was merely to convey information. "Our common duty is to take steps to ensure that Franco-German relations are affected as little as possible by the events." The conversation, concluded Weizsäcker, was "sometimes heated; Coulondre remained outwardly calm."

Coulondre was called back to Paris for consultations and Henderson to London. Coulondre did not return to Berlin until five weeks later.

In England, since the "peace for our time" which followed Munich, all confidence in Chamberlain's insight had disappeared. He was on the verge of being ridiculed. So on March 18 he delivered a most energetic speech in Birmingham: "Can this be the last aggression against a small nation, or is it to be followed by others? Can this be a step along the path toward the domination of the world by force?" The policy of appeasement suddenly ended after the occupation of Prague. It was replaced by a policy of "active defense." London remained inclined to negotiate and to accept concessions, on condition that the new state of affairs not be imposed through force.

The painful concessions of Munich thus led, after less than six months, to the total destruction of Czechoslovakia. It opened people's eyes. After the remilitarization of the Rhineland, the annexation of Austria, the incorporation of the Sudeten Germans—after this string of offenses which spread exasperation and fear—the annexation of Prague demonstrated that Hitler's goal had nothing to do with justice or with the Germans' right to self-determination. Hitler aimed at supremacy throughout the world. This announced the Second World War.

After March 1939, even the supporters of appeasement understood that, with Hitler, peace was no longer possible. This man had to be contained. The British nation, united in pacifism in 1936, would be united in war in 1939. Even the average man was angered, indignant; it was time to put an end to the aggression, time to say stop!

In a haunting revival, the German wave of 1914 had formed again; it was approaching like an unleashed madness. This war erupted from the will of one man, Adolf Hitler, the prophet of National Socialism. The majority of his diplomats and his generals feared war; but his frenzied and fanatical will, his "intuitions," his tirades, had broken all resistance.

Daladier realized that the agreements of September 29, 1938, which he had proclaimed "an act of reason," had just been rent asunder.

Lord Halifax declared to Ambassador Dirksen: "The occupation of Prague has changed everything. . . . Where will Germany stop, and will she ever stop?" It was necessary to anticipate new surprises. Germany had to be stopped.

From London, where "contained anger" reigned, Dirksen sent a telegram to Berlin on March 15 saying that Georges Bonnet had told the British ambassador to Paris, Phipps, that everything or nothing had to be undertaken and that France had decided to do nothing.

The destruction of the very recent Munich compromise had led England to take sides, in one of those sudden changes of policy which mark the decisive moments in her history. This time she turned against Germany, by offering, on March 31, a guarantee of assistance to Poland, now clearly threatened. The French followed British diplomacy, traditionally very cautious in Eastern Europe; breathless, they followed the British in their "policy of a halt," which they wanted to pursue to ensure that Europe would not again be confronted with the faits accomplis that continued to succeed one another at a dizzying pace.

The Annexation of Memel

Germany forced Lithuania to cede the rights she had to Memel and its territory of 149,000 inhabitants, among them 59,000 Lithuanians. Hitler made an ostentatious visit to Memel; and on March 22 Germany occupied the city.

26

The Annexation of Albania and the British Policy of Guarantees

The Annexation of Albania

The two essential events of 1939 before September 3—for Germany the occupation of Prague in March, and for Italy the annexation of Albania in April—took place without previous notice to the partners, Italy in March and Germany in April.

Mussolini used the strength provided by German support to improve his position in the Balkans, and several English "guarantee" treaties would follow the annexation of Albania.

After the occupation of Prague, Hitler renewed his assurances to Mussolini that Germany considered the Mediterranean an Italian sea. Mussolini, in his search for a prey to "liberate," turned to Albania, which was subjected to Italian influence and where he supported the unpopular regime of King Zog, his crowned client who extended himself in gestures of friendship—Ciano had been a witness at his wedding in April 1938. But Mussolini distrusted his protégé's ambition; and he aspired to a simple annexation of the country, which would erase the humiliating memories of 1920 when "Italian troops pursued by ragged gangs" had hastily evacuated Albania.

In January 1939 Ciano had considered a partition of Albania with the ever-devoted Stojadinović, whose fall in February, combined with the German occupation of Prague, precipitated the planned operation, to the exclusive advantage of Italy. The annexation of Albania represented a "compensation" for Italy, although a very small one, while Germany "was acquiring superior importance" and was acting on her own initiative with "very little consideration" for Rome.

The conquest of Albania would be a prelude to the conquest of Greece, already being planned by Mussolini.

On April 7, 1939, Good Friday, Italy attacked Albania and quickly occupied and annexed her. Zog fled to Greece. Victor Emmanuel III, king of Italy and emperor of Ethiopia, became king of Albania.

English and French Guarantees to Greece

This brutal and cynical policy of annexation brought an immediate reaction from Chamberlain, who had once shown so much consideration for Mussolini. England considered the commitments assumed by Mussolini in January 1937, April 1938, and January 1939 to be destroyed; he had promised to respect the status quo relating to "the national sovereignty of the territories in the Mediterranean region." On April 13, 1939, Chamberlain declared that England would assist Greece and Rumania if their independence was in danger.

Traditionally Greece had followed in the British wake and King George II was a passionate Anglophile, although General Metaxas, a real dictator, felt strong sympathies for Germany. Metaxas accepted the English guarantee but rejected an alliance.

The annexation of Albania therefore brought about new Franco-British guarantee treaties. But what was involved was mainly a moral commitment, and it was unclear how it would be supported by concrete action. "Annexation, guarantee! A war of tennis volleys!" Anatole de Monzie would write.

Mussolini, furious because the Athens government had accepted such a guarantee, verbally attacked the Greek minister during a diplomatic reception. The Italian General Staff worked out plans for the occupation of Corfu and of the Ionian Islands, as well as for the invasion of mainland Greece.

Guarantees to Rumania

Rumanian diplomacy was marked by a caution which doubled after Munich, although at the beginning of 1939 Petrescu Comnenus had left Bucharest to become ambassador to Rome and had been replaced at the foreign ministry by Gregory Gafencu, a brilliant journalist, married to a French woman, whose sympathies for France were well known.

Rumania manifested a strong desire for better relations with Germany. As German minister Wilhelm Fabricius wrote on September 28, 1938, King Carol was becoming more and more aware that assistance to Rumania was receding into the background of French concerns and that good relations with Germany could protect his country, not only against the Russians, but also against the revisionist dreams of the Hungarians. "However the King does not believe that he can take the decisive step toward a rapprochement with Germany unless he receives reassurances that we will protect Rumania against the Russian threat. Today he would not yet dare to join the Anti-Comintern Pact; for he would not want, by too abrupt an about-face, to damage his relations with France and above all with England."

On September 30, Fabricius declared that the idea that Rumania ought to find her place at Germany's side was gaining ground each day. And the formula seemed worth mentioning that, if Rumania wanted to survive in her existing form, she had to maintain with Germany relations at least as good as those Germany maintained with Hungary.

The idea of a rapprochement, which was already wished for by Rumania before the Munich Conference, had become easier for Rumania and her king to realize, because Germany's relations with France and England had supposedly improved. Good relations with France, and particularly with England, would make it much easier for the king to admit a friendship with Germany—a friendship he had always desired.

Fabricius remarked that there were a great many factors favoring a rapprochement with Germany.

On October 28, George Bratianu told Fabricius of his bitter disillusionment with France, who had placed Czechoslovakia in a ridiculous position and then left her there; the idea of "everything with France" was a mistake. Maniu had also reversed his position, and he was now asking for an alignment with Berlin.

On December 13, minister Carl Clodius of the economic section of the Wilhelmstrasse noted that the belief that it was necessary to cooperate with Germany was universal in Bucharest. The growth of German power in 1938 and the fear it inspired were obvious. The collapse of France's prestige was total.

King Carol wanted to orient himself toward Germany. On November 24 he visited Hitler and assured him that Rumania wished above all to strengthen her good relations with Germany.

But on November 30, almost immediately following King Carol's visit to Hitler, Codreanu and thirteen members of the Iron Guard were shot down, supposedly because they were trying to escape. This tragic occurrence provoked violent indignation in the German press: "Our faith in Rumania's sincerity has been seriously shaken."

However the negotiations for an economic agreement that was extraordinarily advantageous for Germany were of great importance. Berlin considered that as a result of the treaty signed on December 10, 1938, Germany would participate in 45 percent of all Rumanian foreign trade during 1939.

On July 11, 1939, undersecretary Weizsäcker would note that a change in Germany's policy toward Rumania was out of the question. It was a fact that Turkey had openly gone into the enemy camp. England, France, and Turkey were trying to bring Rumania to their own side; she would not yield to their efforts.

Now was the time to bring Rumania and Hungary closer together. But how could that be done as long as Transylvania dominated everything? Budapest would never renounce Transylvania. It was even more important than Slovakia.

A German economic mission led by Doctor Clodius was in Bucharest at the time to conclude a commercial agreement, and it was believed that Germany intended to impose a real vassalage: Rumania's entire economic life would be placed under German control. It was under these conditions that the British government had decided to grant guarantees to Rumania. The British ambassador informed Daladier, who was in the Chamber, and told him that he wanted to know what attitude France would take. Daladier immediately convened the cabinet; the ministers decided unanimously to follow the British example and guarantee Rumania. "The French government considers that Rumania now represents the last obstacle to the triumph of German imperialism and of German control over the resources of Central and Eastern Europe."

Rumania, who felt much more threatened by Hungary and Bulgaria than by Germany, began a hidden mobilization. In Paris Rumania insisted upon receiving, as soon as possible, the war materiel ordered in France, and she asked for French diplomatic support in Budapest.

Germany was extremely irritated by the guarantee given to Rumania by the western powers. Gafencu confessed that the English proposal had kept him awake for nights. But he had not been able to find in it anything whatever that might disturb Rumania's relations with Germany.

He asserted that the king and the government were firmly determined not to enter into agreements which might be, even slightly, directed against Germany. The Rumanian leaders felt that they could not reject a unilateral promise of guarantee, especially since some of their neighbors had revisionist designs on Rumanian territory. Certain of Germany's good intentions, Gafencu was hoping that the German government would also make a declaration of guarantee in Rumania's favor.

Gafencu stayed in Berlin from April 18 to April 20. Ribbentrop told him that Rumania's attitude had caused unpleasant feelings in Germany. The

British guarantee made Rumania appear to be cooperating readily with "the policy of encirclement."

Gafencu renewed his assurances to Hitler that "the English declaration of guarantee cannot be described as a part of the policy of encirclement." Hitler ironically remarked on "the English mania for guarantees."

On April 30 Ribbentrop would tell the Hungarians Teleki and Czaky that acceptance by a nation of a mutual guarantee agreement with the western powers constituted an unfriendly act.

But Germany did accept the explanations of Rumania, whose economic contribution was so valuable. Rumania was constantly asking Berlin for shipments of armaments for an eventual defense against Hungary, and the German minister recommended a generous attitude.

On July 7, 1939, he noted that Rumania had remained neutral, and that she had not swerved from that policy in spite of the efforts of London and Paris. She had promised to observe faithfully her economic agreement with Germany. Under these conditions, it would be wrong to support the revisionist policy of Bulgaria against Rumania, as did the German press and especially the Italian press.

Much more serious were the problems between Hungary and Rumania, and Germany could serve as omnipotent arbiter between them.

Guarantees to Turkey

After guarantees had been granted by England and France to Greece and Rumania, England, who wanted to maintain the Mediterranean and Balkan status quo, offered an alliance treaty to Turkey, who had been deeply stirred by the annexation of Albania. Seeing a European war approach, Turkey considered vital the friendship of the Soviets; she wanted first to obtain their approval. Assistant commissar for foreign affairs Potemkin came to Ankara to give his assent on the very day that news was received of Litvinov's resignation, the signal of a radical change in Russian policy.

On May 12, England and Turkey published a joint declaration committing themselves to conclude a definitive and long-term agreement with reciprocal obligations for the sake of their national security. While awaiting the conclusion of that agreement, they were ready, in the event of an act of aggression leading to a Mediterranean war, to give each other all possible aid and assistance.

The Soviet press hailed this declaration as "a link in the chain that is the only effective protection against an attack in the Balkans."

One month later, on June 23, 1939, Turkey signed a similar declaration with France; this delay was caused by the Franco-Turkish negotiations over the ceding to Turkey of the Syrian Sanjak of Alexandretta, for which a Franco-Turkish agreement signed in July 1938 had already provided a certain autonomy, since the French had agreed on September 9, 1936, to grant Syria independence as soon as she was admitted to the League of Nations.

In moving closer to the western powers, Turkey did not doubt that she would reach an agreement with the USSR. A draft agreement was drawn up after the signing of the Turkish declaration with England and France; but before it could be signed, the stupefying news of the German-Soviet non-aggression pact of August 24, 1939 exploded.

A delegation led by Turkish foreign minister Sarajoglu left for Moscow in September; but the Soviets' proposals would have forced Turkey to break with England and France and become part of the Soviet sphere of influence. Turkey rejected these proposals and signed a tripartite pact—Anglo-French-Turkish—on October 19. War had begun, but it had not yet reached the Mediterranean area; thus Turkey was not obliged to participate in the conflict.

The hour of decision would come for Ankara when Italy entered the war in June 1940. But by then military events had emptied the 1939 treaties of their content, and Turkey would succeed in remaining uninvolved in the conflict.

27

Hungary, Yugoslavia, and Rumania after Munich

Hungary after Munich

The Munich agreements caused such a change in the situation established in 1919 that Hungary could now present her territorial claims under favorable conditions.

Kanya's resignation at the end of September 1938 marked the end of the sinuous policy to which his name had been linked since 1933. The appointment of Count Czaky as his successor was an indication that Hungary was following the Axis powers' policy. But the agreement between the Hungarians and the Germans was far from perfect, since illusions of all sorts were fostered everywhere. And thus, on October 13, 1938, the German minister to Budapest, Otto von Erdmannsdorff, drew attention to the idea developed in the French press of a Polish-Rumanian bloc which would also include Hungary.

Since Munich, the Hungarians had raised loud claims and spoken of mobilization; if they entered Czechoslovakia, however, Rumania and Yugoslavia were threatening them with an intervention by the Little Entente, which had in fact ceased to exist.

The Hungarians remained on their guard. However they impatiently awaited their hour and proclaimed their rights to Slovak territory.

The Vienna Arbitration Decision

Since the negotiations between Budapest and Prague did not bring about the ceding of those territories, Hungary called for arbitration by Germany and Italy. Hitler, irritated by the Hungarians, was at first unfavorable to the idea of an arbitration supported by Italy and quickly endorsed by Czechoslovakia.

On November 9 in Vienna, in the Belvedere Palace, Ribbentrop and Ciano pronounced the arbitration decision on the basis of the ethnicity principle. The Hungarians received territories populated by about one million inhabitants. They had hoped for more, in particular Pressburg and a common Polish-Hungarian frontier.

Hitler had temporarily diverted the Hungarians from occupying the Subcarpathian Ukraine, and they did not receive the frontier they needed if they were to be adjacent to Poland. Their criticisms exasperated Hitler. On January 16, 1939, he declared that 95 to 98 percent of their demands had been satisfied and a portion of the "territory stolen away at Trianon" had been returned to them, thanks to Germany.

As a result of the Hungarians' inaction before Munich, Hitler had been forced to resolve the Czechoslovakian problem according to ethnographic concerns. The Vienna arbitration decision had corresponded to the ethnographic solution.

Condemning her hesitant attitude during the September crisis, Hitler called on Hungary to act at the right time if she wanted to take part in the next partition.

Hungary declared herself ready to adhere to the Anti-Comintern Pact.

On December 2, 1938, the Hungarian ambassador to Berlin, General Sztojay, assured Woermann, a high Wilhelmstrasse official, that the regent considered friendship with Germany to be the foremost aim in Hungarian foreign policy; certain misunderstandings could now be regarded as resolved.

Germany and Italy urged Hungary to withdraw from the League of Nations. Hungary promised to do so by May 1939. On March 10, Weizsäcker told the Hungarian minister that he could not tolerate Czaky's hesitations over withdrawal from the League.

Continuing Problems between Hungary and Rumania

In the meantime Hungary's complaints against the Rumanians grew more acute. Hungary still wanted to achieve her territorial unity at Rumania's expense. But since Germany was about to conclude a fruitful economic agreement with Bucharest, she did not back, for the moment, the Hungarian initiatives to recover Transylvania, and she firmly opposed any step taken against Rumania.

On November 24, 1938, Hitler told King Carol that, as far as the Hungarians' revisionist ideas were concerned, he had made it clear several years ago that their desires had to remain moderate.

The king opposed Hungarian annexation of the Subcarpathian Ukraine. Hitler replied that the issue was of no importance for Germany. He had opposed Hungary's recent inclinations to occupy the Subcarpathian Ukraine by telling Hungary that the Axis powers could not ignore the arbitration decision, which had been asked from them and which they had returned. The Vienna signatures had to be respected.

At the beginning of 1939, angered because he could not be definitely assured of Budapest's policy, Hitler still refused to consider Hungary a "sure ally." However on January 5 he announced to Czaky that he was planning "a politico-territorial solution of the Czechoslovakian question," with the participation of Hungary and Poland. "All is calm and promises success, on condition, of course, of complete agreement. We have to act like a soccer team: Poland, Hungary, Germany . . . with the speed of lightning." Did Hitler include Poland only to please the Hungarians, her friends, and reassure them? Or did he still believe, as late as January 5, that his claims on Poland could be satisfied?

What is certain is that he felt free to act in the east because "his fortifications in the west stood in the way of any military interference from the western nations."

He expressed his irritation over "the ingratitude of the Hungarians"; former foreign minister Kanya was "an enemy of Germany."

On March 13, 1939, the regent, Horthy, informed Hitler that the Hungarians "would participate most enthusiastically" in the coup planned against Czechoslovakia, and he assured Hitler of "unwavering gratitude." "The arrangements have already been made: on March 16 there will be a frontier incident followed by the final blow."

The "final blow" anticipated the Magyar plans by a few days; it was to be the occupation of Prague.

Occupation of the Subcarpathian Ukraine

Confronted with the dismemberment and collapse of Czechoslovakia in March 1939, Hungary too decided to act.

In order to become once again the neighbor of Poland, to whom she was tied by old historical and social affinities, Hungary occupied the Subcarpathian Ukraine—which had proclaimed its independence—between March 11 and March 15.

After having seized the Subcarpathian Ukraine, portrayed by Czaky as "only six hundred thousand inhabitants, but three languages and three religions," Hungary seemed ready to attack Rumania. The two nations both took mobilization measures. France invited Budapest to "refrain from any military measures likely to cause concern in Rumania," and asked the Poles to support her diplomatic action.

As for Germany, she made it known on March 17 that she would not accept the role of mediator between Hungary and Rumania over the Subcarpathian Ukraine, an issue that could be resolved through a direct agreement.

Hungarian Fears

Germany also informed Budapest that the Slovak declaration of independence created a new situation. And a Slovakia placed under the protection of the Reich would shatter Hungary's hopes for territorial annexations to the north.

The Hungarians were firmly warned that they should not enter into Czechoslovakia. On March 29 they were informed that Germany did not intend to intervene in negotiations over the Hungarian-Slovak frontier.

The Magyars were extremely concerned by the Germans' crushing advance in Central Europe. For if they were seeking the support necessary for the success of their national claims, they were also proud of their independence. They balked at the idea of being absorbed into a *Mitteleuropa*.

For her own part, Germany wanted to have all revisionist ambitions contained for the moment; there had to be peace in the Balkans.

Count Teleki, who had come to power in February 1939, intended to follow the policy of the Rome-Berlin Axis, but especially of Italy, in order to establish a counterweight to German pressure; and Italy ostentatiously protected Hungary.

Teleki and Czaky, who were in Berlin between April 29 and May 2, declared that if there was a war Hungary would be on the side of the Axis. Hitler wanted an entente between Hungary and Yugoslavia, and a truce (*Burgfriede*) with Rumania.

The Hungarians constantly affirmed their goodwill, but they did not inspire confidence in Germany. The National Socialist party, dissolved and forbidden in Hungary, carried on active propaganda under the "arrow cross," which had the same significance as the swastika. Budapest expressed discontent and complained over the support given to the Hungarian National Socialists.

On May 1 Czaky told Ribbentrop that he regretted the interference of the German authorities from Vienna in Hungarian-Slovak affairs. Teleki complained that the Hlinka guards were provoking frontier incidents. Czaky asked Ribbentrop to pacify the Slovaks; sixty Hungarians had recently been arrested in Bratislava.

The confusion of a proud, decidedly chivalrous nation, overflowing with claims but sentimentally linked to Poland, appears in two letters which Teleki sent to Hitler on July 29, 1939. The first letter stated that, in the event of a conflict, Hungary would adjust her policy to that of the Axis, taking into account her complete sovereignty and her national objectives. The second specified that to "prevent any incorrect interpretation of the first letter," Hungary, "owing to moral considerations, could not undertake any military action against Poland." The Wilhelmstrasse was astonished by the "peculiar nature of these communications," and on August 10 the Hungarian foreign minister, speaking for his prime minister, asked Hitler to consider as null and void Count Teleki's two letters, in view of the "favorable progress of the negotiations being conducted with the Reich's foreign minister."

The leaders in Budapest felt that Germany's war against Poland could not be localized and would lead to a widespread, long, and difficult war. They wished to avoid a break with the western powers.

In spite of their strong revisionist desires, "95 percent of the Hungarians, from the regent to the last beggar," would look unfavorably on Germany's aggression against their friend Poland. Hungary would refuse Germany the use of her railways, which would have allowed them to attack the Poles from the rear.

Hungary's leaders had no sympathy for the National Socialist leaders, who reciprocated their feelings. Horthy considered them "brigands," unbearable and crude. Teleki saw in Hitler "a gangster" and "feared like the plague a total victory for Germany."

Yugoslavia

After Munich, Milan Stojadinović, "the leader" as he was called by those who wanted to indulge his megalomania, expressed his boundless admiration for Hitler.

The German minister to Belgrade, Viktor von Heeren, wrote that Yugoslavia had shown from the beginning a total understanding for the German claims on the Sudetenland. However she did fear the Hungarian claims on certain areas of Czechoslovakia which were not Magyar.

On January 23, 1939, Ciano suggested to Stojadinović that Yugoslavia should withdraw from the League of Nations. The prime minister avouched his lack of interest in the League; since he had taken office, he had never gone to Geneva. His wish was to leave the League gradually and without a stir. What complicated the situation was that Yugoslavia currently represented the Little Entente at the Council.

On January 23, 1939, Stojadinović told the German minister Heeren that Ciano spoke of France with "little kindness and a lot of pessimism," and he expressed his belief that the political importance of France would inevitably decrease. The anti-French feelings held by the Yugoslav minister pleased Ciano. Anything could be feared from his roguery. As in Poland, a dictatorial regime totally uncontrolled by public opinion allowed the government to deviate from traditional foreign policy.

Stojadinović had dissolved the Chamber immediately after the Munich events, which seemed to justify his realism. He won the elections; but the opposition had gained ground since 1935, and the elections showed how important an understanding with the still resolutely opposed Croats would be for the reorganization of the state.

On February 6, 1936, Prince Paul ceased to have confidence in Stojadinović, whose tendencies worried him, and he called for his resignation—Stojadinović was moving firmly toward the introduction of a Fascist regime in Belgrade. Tsvetković, the social security minister, succeeded him as prime minister and interior minister.

As a neighbor of the two Axis great powers, Yugoslavia had to systematically avoid any conflict with them. Heeren observed, on the one hand, a panicky fear of Germany and, on the other hand, sympathy for the Czech people, left to the mercy of the German giant.

Tsvetković, who was anxious to dispel any German distrust of him, asserted that he wanted closer relations with Germany. Alexander Cincar-Marković, the Yugoslav minister to Berlin, was then named foreign minister.

Although he was an Anglophile at heart, Prince Paul easily yielded to hints from Berlin and Rome.

On March 21, France asked the Yugoslav government what attitude it would take in the event of German aggression against Rumania. The Yugoslavs' reply was simply that the requests the Germans made of Rumania had never assumed the form of an ultimatum.

When on April 7, Good Friday, the Italian troops landed in Albania, the Yugoslavs accepted the fact with friendly resignation, while the Hungarians gave Rome assurances of their support.

Ribbentrop declared to the Hungarians Teleki and Czaky that Yugoslavia's attitude was clearer than that of Rumania. In the event of a European war, Cincar-Marković had promised benevolent neutrality and all means to facilitate the use of the economic resources of Yugoslavia.

But German minister Heeren felt that political stability had disappeared after the fall of Stojadinović. He observed, on March 7, 1939, that Stojadinović was the only political figure capable of maintaining a strong authoritarian regime. The Croats opposed his methods. The government now attempted to win their good graces. But at the same time it drew closer to left-wing Serb circles, who were ideologically hostile to Germany. Under these conditions, Heeren concluded, Germany must seek Croat friendship, and the German press could abandon the reserve it had maintained on that touchy question.

28

The Pact of Steel (May 22, 1939)

Military Alliance between Germany and Italy

The respective German and Italian spheres of interest had been defined by the treaty that founded the Rome-Berlin Axis on October 25, 1936: "The Mediterranean is an Italian sea; all future modifications in the Mediterranean balance must be made in favor of Italy—Germany must have freedom of action toward the east and toward the Baltic."

Hitler, who was greatly impressed by Mussolini, "the dean of dictators," had an exaggerated vision of the military importance of Fascist Italy, so proud of her air force and her fleet. But he was quite skeptical about the Italian army.

Hitler's visit to Rome in May 1938 left him with mixed emotions. He had been displeased by the remains of a medieval feudal system, whose protocol placed Mussolini behind the king. Hitler had wanted to be Mussolini's guest, not the guest of Victor Emmanuel at the Quirinal Palace.

Since Hitler's visit in May 1938, there had been talk of an alliance. In Rome in October, Ribbentrop demanded an alliance to "change the face of the world." At the beginning of 1939, Mussolini decided to accept, in principle, the German proposal, which he made his own in the face of the indignant articles published by the press, especially the British press, about his annexation of Albania. In his talks with Ribbentrop in October 1938, and with Goering in April 1939, Mussolini declared that a conflict with the democratic powers was inevitable, but that it would take place in a distant future. Following a visit by Ribbentrop to Milan on May 6 and 7, an agreement was quickly reached. Mussolini felt that the Axis should, for at least two or three years, avoid the danger of war. Ribbentrop spoke comforting words: Germany too needed four to five years of peace. Similar assurances were being given, and would be given, in the talks between the military leaders: generals Keitel and Pariani in April, and admirals Roeder and Cavignari in June. But no mention was made of such a delay in the secret protocol accompanying the treaty itself, the military alliance concluded in Berlin on May 22: "the Pact of Steel," by which Fascist Italy joined the Nazi policy of adventure.

Ambassador Attolico

Conscientious, scrupulous, well informed on German affairs although he did not speak German, of modest origins and with the demeanor of a professor, Bernardo Attolico, the Italian ambassador to Berlin, had been undersecretary-general at the League of Nations. He was aware that the international situation was becoming extremely serious. Because his adviser, Count Massimo Magistrati, was Ciano's brother-in-law, Attolico enjoyed great influence in Rome, although he was accused of trembling at the thought of war. Ribbentrop did his best to ridicule his fears.

On May 30, Mussolini wrote to Hitler that a widespread conflict must not break out before 1943 at the earliest. He needed a minimum delay of three years; it was necessary to prepare defenses for Libya, Albania, and Ethiopia. He hoped to recruit 500,000 men among the natives. He wanted to finish six large capital ships, renew his heavy artillery, transfer to the south many war factories now settled in the north, repatriate Italians residing in France, and hurry measures for economic autarchy.

On June 6, Ribbentrop assured Attolico that Hitler agreed with Mussolini's memorandum.

Italy and France

Through the formidable power of their propaganda, Hitler and Mussolini wished to reap the fruits of others' disorganization, surrender, and fear. They thought that they would succeed.

France was sinking. Mussolini grasped this downfall with disdain and considered it irremediable. He had hoped to recruit an Italian party among the French, so deep was their disunion. He had expected that this would prevent any strong action by French diplomacy. He was almost right. The disorder he had foreseen did not break out in France, and the events that took place after the end of 1937 seemed to be taking an opposite course.

Mussolini showed vindictive impatience toward France. After having emerged without incident from the Ethiopian and Spanish crises, he probably felt that with daring he would always be able to intimidate. But French opinion, so deeply divided, tended to unite before the Italo-German threat posed by the formation of the Axis.

Italy and England

Mussolini feared above all a détente or an understanding between Germany and England. Italy's position was now clearly defined; she could no longer choose an alternative. The time had passed when her good relations with the western powers could have been reestablished by the recognition of the new emperor of Ethiopia, Victor Emmanuel, and by a few assurances concerning the Mediterranean balance of power.

Mussolini now found himself associated with Germany, a power which was much stronger than Italy and which would not let him recover his freedom. He could no longer reverse his policy, as he almost did again at the League Assembly in September 1936, when he had hoped to gain League recognition of the annexation of Ethiopia. Deprived of his mobility, he had destroyed the traditional balancing policy of Italian diplomacy. Concerned over a possible revenge from the English, he had constantly maneuvered to gain a position that allowed him to take the initiative: in Spain, Libya, Palestine, and Arabia. Would not the time finally come when an isolated Great Britain would fear being at the mercy of Italian aircraft in the Mediterranean, and when Mussolini could therefore impose his own conditions? Fleeting illusion! He had humiliated the English by confronting them with the fait accompli. He had succeeded in convincing them that he was their major enemy, but without being able to inspire in them a fear extending beyond the realistic assessment of his true strength and his true resources.

Chamberlain tried to achieve a rapprochement with Rome. His "Gentlemen's Agreement" of January 1937 had not succeeded in clarifying the relations between England and Italy.

Italy was hoping that, to restore calm and peace, Chamberlain would adopt the role of petitioner. It seemed advisable for Italy to specify preconditions before reopening negotiations with London. The almost desperate anxiety displayed by the prime minister in his attempts to begin conversations with Mussolini gave the impression that England needed Mussolini. In spite of British rearmament—a program holding out some hope of power—Chamberlain took the almost spineless tone of a disarmed country fearing aggression.

Traditionally England had supported Italy. It was the League of Nations which had set Great Britain against Mussolini—stupidly. But it was still possible to reach an understanding with him, and England had to add the words "the end" to the Ethiopian episode. Had not Chamberlain himself, as chancellor of the Exchequer, given the memorable signal to end sanctions against Italy, at a banquet in the City on June 10, 1936? Could the Rome-Berlin Axis not be weakened by an Italian move toward England?

Mussolini, for his own part, did not want to remain the enemy of Great Britain; she was still powerful. But he did not wish to give the impression that he was welcoming with humility the return of a former friendship. On April 16, 1938, Chamberlain and Mussolini reached an agreement. Would Mussolini no longer stand alone with Germany? His cooperation was so valuable that Chamberlain granted him, without a war, freedom of action for an Anglo-Italian directorate over the Mediterranean, leaving France to pay for past errors.

After the ratification of the Anglo-Italian agreement, a violent demonstration was staged against France by Italian deputies on November 30, 1938. Questioned in Commons, Chamberlain declared that such incidents would not divert him in the least from the understanding achieved on his trip to Rome. He had been able, in the past, to judge the value of Mussolini's friendship: The Duce's decisive intervention in the Czechoslovakian crisis had deflected Hitler's ultimatum and had made the Munich agreement possible. England's separate agreement with Italy and the benevolent inactivity England had often shown toward the Italians in Spain tended to increase the tension between Rome and France.

Mussolini and the Near East

All around the periphery of the Mediterranean, Arab nationalism had recently won major successes. Iraq had regained her independence in 1930; Egypt in 1936, but by recognizing England's special interests. In Iraq, as in Egypt, a vociferous portion of the population looked on the English as undesirable guests. The treaty of September 1936, which was to begin the era of Syrian independence, had been concluded by France with Syria, but Paris refused to ratify it.

Palestine was plunged into turmoil. The grand mufti of Jerusalem, Hajj Amin Husseini, repeatedly threatened the "Jewish national homeland." The massive immigration of Central European Jews fleeing Nazism roused Arab anti-Semitism. In 1937 the grand mufti left Jerusalem to settle in Lebanon, and, as soon as the European war broke out, in Iraq.

The British white paper of May 17, 1939, showed the government's growing pessimism in its appraisal of the German threat, and its desire to pacify the Arabs by limiting Jewish immigration into Palestine to 75,000 for the next five years and by announcing strict restrictions on Jewish purchase of land in Palestine.

Did the white paper really prevent a more extreme Arab position? The Arabs criticized it for not limiting sufficiently Zionist opportunities.

As for the Jews, they had to be for England and against Hitler. Ben-Gurion would say: "We will fight the war as if there were no white paper, and we will fight the white paper as if there were no war."

On March 18, 1937, in Tripoli, Mussolini had had himself presented with the Sword of Islam; establishing positions of strength around an Italian Mediterranean, he worked to stir the Arabs against England. The Italian radio station in Bari broadcast propaganda messages. After the conquest of Ethiopia, the port of Assab in the southern Red Sea was fortified by the Italians, who concluded agreements for friendship and trade with Yahia, the imam of Yemen.

After the formation of the Axis, Mussolini's policy had been resolutely pro-Arab. In the Arab world, Hitler's anti-Semitism was a major advantage. Unlike Italy, Germany made no territorial claims in these areas. She declared herself opposed to the establishment of a Jewish state in Palestine, for this state would create for the Jewish world an instrument of power similar to the Vatican for Catholicism.

In September 1938, Germany appointed to Jedda her minister to Baghdad, Grobba, who in February 1939 met with Ibn Saud. Ibn Saud was considered a friend of England, but he distrusted England as much as he did Italy. He maintained good relations with the English to escape any pressure from them. He asked Germany for support and for arms. On June 17, 1939, Hitler promised him active German participation in the training of the Saudi army, and a month later granted him a six-million-mark credit for arms purchases. This delivery, accepted readily by Italy, would never take place, because when the war broke out Saudi Arabia ended diplomatic relations with Germany as early as September 11, at the imperative request of England.

29

The Soviet Reversal

Anglo-French Negotiations with the USSR

German-Soviet relations had become execrable after the rise of Hitler and grew ever worse with the Soviet entry into the League of Nations in September 1934, and especially with the vicissitudes of the Spanish Civil War.

To face a Germany which had again become as threatening as in 1914, or even more threatening than in 1914, a defensive agreement between the western powers and the USSR seemed probable; in 1939 Churchill called it "the Grand Alliance."

Tripartite negotiations were taking place in order to establish a common front against Germany, and the western powers tried—though too feebly—to obtain the Soviets' guarantee against further German advances.

The German occupation of Prague had strengthened the rapprochement between the Soviet Union and the western democracies. Chamberlain thought of a declaration by four powers: England, France, Russia, and Poland. But Beck tenaciously refused to sign a political agreement in which the Soviets appeared as a contracting party. Once provided with the British guarantee, he was less interested than ever in a rapprochement with Moscow.

In the Europe of Versailles, Poland separated Germany and the Soviet Union; she refused to allow the passage of Soviet troops across her territory. It was "a matter of principle," said Beck, and the Polish ambassador to Paris, Lukasiewicz, asked: "What would the French say if the Germans were sent to guard Alsace-Lorraine?"

Chamberlain greatly distrusted the Russians, who reciprocated the feeling. Stalin suspected Chamberlain of wanting to strengthen England's position with Germany through negotiations with Moscow, while carrying out secret exchanges of views with Germany. The extremely difficult talks with the Soviets continued, and all sorts of mutual assistance formulas were mentioned.

On April 16 London asked Moscow for a declaration of assistance, similar to the one England had just given Poland and Rumania. The Soviet Union suggested an agreement with Great Britain and France for the defense of the threatened nations, which would include all the countries bordering the USSR, among them Finland and the Baltic States. Great Britain especially, but also France, were greatly concerned to see the reappearance of Russian yearnings for the territories long ago acquired by Peter the Great, in the hope of widening Russia's access to the Baltic.

Finally the arduous agreement between the western powers and the Soviets seemed practically achieved. All sorts of nuances had been eliminated, if not actual differences of opinion. On July 24 Molotov declared that he considered the agreement concluded, and he asked that the military talks necessary to reach a definitive conclusion to a political understanding begin immediately.

The Military Missions

Following Moscow's suggestion, military missions left London and Paris, in no hurry, to negotiate the signing of a military pact. England wanted to make careful preparations.[1] The missions left on an old cargo ship chartered by the Admiralty. It had been mentioned that Lord Gort might be sent to Moscow; Chamberlain declared that his presence was necessary in London. The British delegation was led by the retired admiral R. P. Drax, whom the Russians blamed for having uttered nothing but commonplaces. The German ambassador to London wrote to his government that the English gave the impression of wanting mostly to "gain a correct assessment of the Soviet forces."

The minutes of the Moscow meetings are rather extraordinary. From the beginning, on August 12, Marshal Klement Voroshilov indicated that: "The Soviet Union is in a somewhat different situation from that of Great Britain and France. She is not in direct contact with the nations of the aggressor bloc. . . . Thus Russia can be of only secondary importance in opposing any aggression."

Great Britain, France, and the nations linked to them by treaties against the aggressor were directly bordering these aggressor states. They had to

1. On this very controversial question, see: Général Beaufre, *Le drame de 1940* (1965)–Beaufre was a member of the French mission as a captain; also the study by Colonel A. Constantini, *Négociations militaires entre la Grande-Bretagne, la France, et l'U.R.S.S., en août 1939* (Service historique de l'Armée, 1967).

make plans against possible military attacks from the aggressors. As long as the Soviet Union did not know what these plans were, it was difficult for her to submit her own plans.

In the morning of August 13, General Doumenc, the leader of the French military mission, asked his listeners to forget what they were going to hear as they were leaving the room, and then declared with much optimism that the French army was ready for combat, and that 200,000 Spanish Republicans had asked to join it. He asserted boldly that there were fortifications "along the entire frontier," and that "the Maginot line had been extended to the sea." The fortifications stretching from the Jura to the Belgian frontier were "the most modern and best reinforced possible. Between Belgium and the sea, they can be compared to the Siegfried line. It will be possible for General Gamelin to organize a powerful attack in a short time. . . . This powerful attack will prevent the transfer of enemy troops from the west to the east."

If the Germans sent their major forces toward the east, they would be forced to "leave at least forty divisions at the French frontier, and in that case General Gamelin would launch an offensive against the Germans with all his forces."

Marshal Voroshilov asked: "According to General Gamelin, at least forty German divisions will remain on the French frontier?" "Yes," General Doumenc confirmed, "at least forty divisions," and he continued: "Hitler declares that the Siegfried line is impregnable. . . . But there are no impregnable fortresses." "That is my opinion as well," Voroshilov agreed. Doumenc added: "The French have studied means of infiltrating that line. . . . In any event, General Gamelin will force the adversary to bring back his forces from the eastern front. If he does not do so, he will be crushed."

In reply to questions from Voroshilov, in the afternoon of August 13, General Doumenc showed on the map the Maginot line, which, as he had announced during the morning session, extended to the sea.

As for General Heywood, he saw everything through rose-colored glasses. He presented the British plans: "To mobilize a convoy of sixteen divisions to be ready at the first stage of war." Voroshilov asked how much time would be required after the declaration of war to bring these sixteen divisions into action. General Heywood answered: "The shortest possible time." Voroshilov pressed again: "If war broke out tomorrow, how many divisions could be sent to France and how long would it take?" Heywood replied: "In Great Britain there are now five infantry divisions and one mechanized division which are at full troop-strength . . . and which can be sent immediately. In the last war, we started with six divisions and finished with about one hundred. This time we could play a much greater part at the beginning of the war."

General Heywood spoke of a second convoy: "Nineteen divisions already exist, and the organization of thirteen more is in progress." "Thus," Voroshilov concluded, "the first convoy amounts to sixteen divisions."

On August 13, British admiral Drax thought that "if the USSR had a military treaty with the western powers, joint action by Italy and Germany would become doubtful. It also appears . . . that, if Hitler were faced with such a military treaty, he would not run the risk of war."

Before reporting on the Soviet troops, Marshal Voroshilov wished to have the Anglo-French missions answer one question: "How do the general staffs of Great Britain and of France envisage the participation of the armed forces of the Soviet Union . . . in the fight against the aggressor? Is my question thoroughly understood?" The participation of the Soviet Union in the war was only possible "on the territory of neighboring states, Poland and Rumania in particular."

On August 14, Voroshilov found the explanations of General Doumenc insufficiently clear. "Excuse my frankness, but we soldiers have to be frank. You may be certain, General, that the Fascists will never break through the front defended by the Soviet armed forces, whether we reach an understanding with you or not." General Doumenc replied: "I am very happy to hear these assurances from you, Marshal."

However, Voroshilov wanted to "obtain a clear answer to a very clear question about the joint operations of the armed forces of England, France, and the Soviet Union against their common adversary. . . . I am interested in a related aspect of my question: Do the general staffs of Great Britain and France anticipate that Soviet troops will have the right of unhindered passage over Polish territory to make direct contact with the adversary if he attacks Poland? And over Rumanian territory if the aggressor attacks Rumania?" "I believe," said General Doumenc, "that Poland and Rumania will beg you to come to their aid, Marshal." Voroshilov: "Perhaps not." Admiral Drax: "If a man is drowning in a river and another man on the bank reaches out a lifebuoy to him, will the drowning man refuse the help offered him?" Voroshilov: "If you wish to speak in parables, allow me to do the same. . . . What would happen if the lifebuoy was so far away that it could not be thrown to the drowning man? . . . The passage of our troops over Polish territory through Vilna and Galicia, and over Rumanian territory . . . is the precondition of our negotiations. . . . The Soviet military mission regrets that the British and French military missions have no precise answer to the question asked about the passage of Soviet forces through the Polish and Rumanian territories."

On August 16, Voroshilov declared: "As long as our mission has not received the reply to our question, about which the British and French missions have questioned their governments, any preliminary work is useless."

On August 17, Voroshilov repeated: "The Soviet mission feels that until we have received the reply to the questions we have asked, we must interrupt the work of our conference."

On August 21 he concluded: "The Soviet mission feels that the USSR, which has no common frontier with Germany, can come to the aid of France, Great Britain, Poland, and Rumania only on condition that her troops can cross Polish and Rumanian territories, for there is no other way for them to make contact with the aggressor's troops. Just as in the World War, when the English and American troops could not have undertaken military cooperation with the armed forces of France if they had not been able to operate on French territory, now the Soviet armed forces would also be unable to take part in military cooperation with the armed forces of France and Great Britain if they could not cross Polish and Rumanian territory. That is a military axiom."

The British and French military missions were then very politely granted their leave.

The Russians shifted all the responsibility for the failure of the conference on to Poland. On August 25 Molotov told French ambassador Naggiar that "a great nation such as the USSR could not go so far as to beg Poland to accept Russian aid which Poland did not want at any price."

Molotov Replaces Litvinov

Many diplomats thought that Chamberlain was pursuing his laborious talks with the USSR only to calm the opposition, and that he would later seek again an understanding with Germany. In a speech given on March 10, 1939, Stalin expressed his distrust of the capitalist world; the USSR "did not intend to pull chestnuts out of the fire" to help certain war inciters. Ribbentrop stated that he had brought the speech to Hitler's attention immediately, and that he had asked his authorization to make contacts in order to ascertain the real meaning of these words. Skeptical, the Führer had preferred to wait. But in his speech of April 28 to the *Reichstag,* he refrained from his usual invectives against Bolshevism and made no reference to the Soviets—a remarkable discretion noticed by others.

In the spring of 1939, rumors circulated in Berlin that Hitler was on the verge of reaching an understanding with Stalin. On August 23, Stalin would tell Ribbentrop that he had given his speech of March 10 to show clearly his desire for a rapprochement with Germany; Germany had understood.

On May 3 the Jew Litvinov, who had led foreign affairs since 1930 and was considered "very European," was replaced by the Aryan Molotov. The German leaders were very impressed by this dismissal.

Ribbentrop in Moscow

In Berlin as in Moscow, for a long time there had been talk of negotiations for a commercial agreement. After an interruption of several months, the negotiations were resumed.

The Soviet chargé d'affaires in Berlin, Georgei Astakhov, met with the German trade advisor in charge of eastern economic questions, Karl Schnurre. During their talks Schnurre determined that the undecided questions between Moscow and Berlin could be settled.

On May 20, in a very cordial atmosphere, Molotov proposed to Ambassador Schulenburg that they link political negotiations to the economic negotiations, since the two could not be separated.

The Russians having taken the first step, on May 25 Ribbentrop advised "a frank discussion" with Moscow. Talks began at the end of May. Berlin wondered if the Russians were sincere; did they not simply want to put pressure on England and France? Also, Germany had to be careful not to displease Japan, who feared that the Soviet Union might make greater use of her strength in the Far East, were she freed from strong pressure on her western frontiers.

On June 28, Molotov declared to Schulenburg that a normalizaton of Russo-German relations was "desirable and possible." The Russians did not want the resumption of negotiations with Germany to assume a sensational character, but they declared themselves ready for major political discussions.

The negotiations were held in Berlin. They led to a trade agreement on August 19, and the possibilities for a political agreement involving essentially Poland and the Baltic States were specified.

Emerging from his extreme caution, Hitler wanted to establish a solid basis of friendship with the Soviets. Ribbentrop offered to go to Moscow to set forth Hitler's views to Stalin. Extremely flattered, the Soviet government preferred less display.

The German-Soviet Pact

On August 17, Ribbentrop informed the Soviets that Germany was ready to conclude a long-term nonaggression pact with them. Hitler telegraphed Stalin that Ribbentrop could go to Moscow—for a day or two at most, owing to the international situation.

On August 21, Stalin informed Hitler that he was ready to receive Ribbentrop on August 23. He hoped that "the nonaggression pact would be the foundation for a genuine improvement in relations" between the two nations, and that it would allow them to restore mutual "peace and cooperation."

Ribbentrop arrived in Moscow on the afternoon of August 23, and on the same day a ten-year nonaggression pact was signed—the Germans had suggested twenty-five years, the Russians five.

When Ribbentrop was received by Stalin and Molotov that evening, he expressed the desire to harmonize the interests of the two nations. Stalin stated that he too wanted to reach an understanding with Germany; for years, the Germans and the Russians had "thrown buckets of manure on each other," but they could indeed be on good terms.

The conversation continued and became more specific in the most favorable way: "Respective spheres of influence were defined in the nations located between Germany and the Soviet Union. Finland, most of the Baltic States, and Bessarabia would come in the Russian zone of influence." According to Ribbentrop, Stalin declared that he had no intention of modifying the political structure of those states.

As for Poland, Ribbentrop claimed to have said that Germany would do everything to settle the Polish question peacefully, but that because of the situation the possibility of a Polish-German war had to be considered. In the event of a conflict with Poland, and "to avoid potential frictions," a line of demarcation would be established between Germany and Russia, along the Vistula, the San, and the Bug rivers.

Regarding the Baltic States, the Russians wanted to include the port city of Libau in their zone of influence. Although Ribbentrop had full powers of negotiation, he insisted on obtaining Hitler's explicit agreement. The talks were temporarily suspended so that Ribbentrop could telephone Hitler. They were resumed at ten o'clock that evening. The nonaggression pact and the secret protocol were signed before midnight.

The protocol had to be secret because it involved nations other than the contracting powers, and also because the German-Soviet agreement was contrary to the conventions signed by the USSR with Poland and France. By the 1936 treaty, Russia and France committed themselves to consult each other before concluding agreements with third parties. "The Russian national interest comes before everything else," declared Stalin. Bursting with cordiality, he expressed his admiration for Hitler, and proposed a toast: "I know how much the German nation loves her Führer; . . . I wish to drink to his health."

On the evening of August 24, Ribbentrop related to Hitler, Goering, and Weizsäcker what had happened in Moscow. He said that he had felt as though he was in the company of "old party comrades."

Weizsäcker observed that "what interested Hitler was to be able to start his campaign against Poland." He had crossed the Rubicon.

Ribbentrop, who wrote his memoirs, *From London to Moscow,* in his cell before his trial by the interallied tribunal at Nuremberg, strove to present the Third Reich's foreign policy as pacifist. He claimed that, in his opinion, the signing of the pact "would incite Great Britain to display more caution, and that as a consequence Poland would be more inclined to negotiate than before."

To the loyal believers in the religion which was National Socialism, a friendship pact with the Soviets was an incredible thing. For twenty years Hitler had incessantly used the most insulting words against the Bolsheviks. After having diffused his hatred for the Soviets throughout the world, he now sent them Ribbentrop, the man of the Anti-Comintern Pact. He diverted Stalin from the west long enough to win a war. As Rumanian foreign minister Gregory Gafencu wrote: "The Munich agreement, a default by the West, opened the door to disorder; the Moscow agreement, an eastern reply to Munich, opened to door to war."

This was, of course, one of the most cynical treaties in world history. Negotiating with both sides at once, Stalin was master of the game. He protected himself by dealing with London, and he cultivated the German advances. He had a choice between two wills of unequal strength, and the will of men is a major factor in the course of history. In dealing with Hitler, he had one certainty: immediate gains along the German borderlands.

Stalin considered war with Poland inevitable, and Polish defeat certain. Why not escape from the conflict now and wait to intervene—this time for the sake of world revolution—until the opponents had first exhausted themselves in a bloody fight? In the meantime, it would be possible to restore, at least partially, the territorial boundaries of 1914, not only to recover a large part of a Poland not long ago Russian, but to reoccupy the former Baltic provinces, those "windows on the Baltic" opened by Peter the Great. The USSR would escape from the frontiers imposed on her twenty years earlier.

And Hitler was convinced—or pretended to be—that the Russian alliance would last for a long time. In his conversations, he insisted upon the military, political, and economic advantages of the alliance. The two totalitarian nations rejected formal democracy and western capitalism, and they had much in common.

Hitler burst with happiness; never had he been so successful. Russia was making common cause with Germany against Poland. The war against Poland would be short; it would last at most a few weeks. Germany no longer had to fear the outcome of an armed conflict with the western powers; she was ready to fight them.

It has often been claimed—it was, for example, Meissner's opinion—that without this Russian insurance, which eliminated the danger of war on two fronts after the rapid invasion of Poland, the Führer would not have dared attack the Poles.

But Russia was thought to be militarily weak. It was the belief not only of the English, French, and Polish experts, but also of the German experts, of Goering and of Hitler himself. After the confused Tukhachevsky affair, so many higher officers had been liquidated—Lord Chilston, British ambassador to Moscow, asserted that the purges had struck down 65 percent of the higher officers since the spring of 1937—that the Soviet command badly needed reorganization.

On May 21, 1939, Ribbentrop told Ciano that "Russia was weak and could not be of much help to the western powers if she did take their side."

And on August 7, 1939, Goering said to the Swede Dahlerus and to three English industrialists, friends of Chamberlain, that Russia wanted to use the great powers against one another, and he ridiculed the faithful attitude assumed by the western democracies toward Stalin.

On August 11, in a talk with Carl Burckhardt, League high commissioner for Danzig, Hitler, who boasted that he would destroy Poland "in three weeks," stated that the Russian army had no offensive strength. "We have beaten the Russians everywhere we have encountered them. France and England won't give me goose bumps by threatening me with the Russian army."

With the conclusion of the Moscow pact, claimed Colonel Beck, "not much would be changed, actually."

Even if there had been no German-Soviet pact, it is not impossible that Hitler would still have attacked Poland. The crisis was too severe not to erupt. However, the agreement with "enemy number one" swept away all factors that might have hindered the aggression.

The pact stupefied the states where Hitler was admired for his unrelenting struggle against Bolshevism: Spain, Portugal, and others.

General Oshima, Japanese military attaché and later ambassador to Berlin, was very close to Ribbentrop. Undersecretary Weizsäcker had to summon Oshima at midnight to tell him that Ribbentrop had just left for Moscow. Oshima's surprise was total: "From yellow, his face turned to gray." At the beginning of 1939, he had plotted with Himmler to assassinate Stalin, in the hope of provoking the disintegration of the Soviet Union.

The Japanese cabinet would withdraw before an arrangement contrary to a secret protocol of the Anti-Comintern Pact. Already in August 1938 and May 1939 the Red Army had struck back with great force after the repeated frontier incidents initiated by the Japanese to test its strength.

Bloody fighting had stopped the Japanese from being tempted to carry their efforts any further, and on September 15, 1939, they signed an agreement with Moscow.

In Germany, many military men, including General Keitel, felt that the pact made an encirclement of Germany impossible, and that Poland would no longer want to run the risk of a now hopeless fight.

According to what Stalin said at Yalta, he had wanted above all to gain time. Beneš thought that Stalin intended to delay his entry into the war until the others had reached exhaustion; the imperialist conflict could then be transformed into a world revolution.

In August 1942, Stalin told Churchill that he had thought that Great Britain and France were not at all convinced that there would be a war in the event of an aggression against Poland, but that they hoped only to intimidate Hitler. He himself was convinced of the opposite: a war against Poland would take place. In addition, the French and English military men present at Moscow had spoken of a much smaller number of divisions than he wanted. He was convinced that, after Munich, Germany was stronger and that Hitler was bent on war.

A few days after the signing of the pact, Molotov had declared before the Supreme Soviet of the USSR, that when hostility existed between the USSR and Germany it was to the disadvantage of the two nations; Germany and the USSR were the two nations that had suffered the most from the Great War.

Churchill felt that "a deadly bomb" had been thrown at the democracies. As for Chamberlain, he saw the pact as an unpleasant surprise which would in no way prevent him from helping Poland. On August 23, he sent a letter to Hitler in which he repeated that an Anglo-German war would be the greatest of calamities.

Having hoped that England "would lose her nerve" after the Moscow pact, on August 24 Hitler replied violently: "The peaceful settlement of European problems depends above all on those who have constantly opposed a peaceful revision of the criminal Treaty of Versailles."

30

The Last Days of the Peace

France was constantly asking for the establishment of military conscription in England, where armaments expenditures had more than doubled from 1937 to 1939. On March 29, Chamberlain announced plans to double the reserve army. Although it greatly displeased British public opinion, on April 27 a call-up of all Englishmen aged twenty and twenty-one was decided on. Chamberlain declared: "We are no longer in a time of peace . . . within the meaning that can honestly be given to that word."

Liddell Hart saw the proclamation of conscription as a measure dictated by panic. And it does seem that during these tragic weeks, when blanket guarantees were distributed, British reactions were not all distinguished by self-control.

In a speech to the *Reichstag* on April 28, Hitler denounced, in a vengeful riposte, the naval pact of 1935 with Great Britain, as well as the German-Polish agreement of 1934, which he had so movingly praised in his speech of January 30, 1939.

Poland remained unmoved. Beck, whose energy had finally won him in Poland a popularity previously withheld from his tortuous policy, replied on May 5 to the German denunication of the 1934 agreement. Poland refused to lessen her sovereignty over her own territory; she did not believe in the idea of peace at any price.

Repeatedly Hitler had detailed battle plans drawn up for the destruction of the Polish army. The Germans would stage deliberate provocations, set off carefully prepared frontier incidents: corpses dressed in Polish uniforms were found on German territory. The victims came from concentration camps. Hitler remained convinced that England would not risk war because of the inadequacy of her anti-aircraft defense. The democracies definitely did not have the necessary means to fight. "A bucket of water to extinguish a global fire," said Vansittart.

England and France lived in the illusion that their combined forces would suffice to stop the German thrust. Hitler would retreat at the last moment, for unlike the German leaders of 1914 he could not possibly cling to the hope that Great Britain would remain neutral, since the English ceaselessly repeated that they would intervene.

However, having concluded the pact with the Soviets, Hitler expressed his fear that some "swine" (*Schweinhund*) might propose mediation. He wanted to launch hostilities against Poland on August 26. He was in a great hurry to begin the campaign before the rains and mud made the Polish roads impassable.

Italian Objectives

Hitler had erected a war machine against Poland without considering Italy's plans. On June 15, Attolico certified that Germany would attack Danzig sometime in mid-August. On July 26 Ribbentrop reassured the ambassador: Hitler agreed with Mussolini that they should avoid a general war. However, the Italian military attaché noted the intensity of war preparations. The Italian embassy was convinced that a German attack was imminent. On July 31, Berlin postponed a meeting to be held between Hitler and Mussolini on August 4 at the Brenner frontier.

Disturbed by the "alarmist bombardment" carried out by Attolico, Ciano wanted to know what was really happening. He asked Ribbentrop to receive him and left for Salzburg, where he met the German foreign minister alone on August 11, and accompanied by Hitler on August 12.

During a ten-hour meeting, Ribbentrop, who until then had kept Germany's bellicose plans secret, informed Ciano of Hitler's determination to settle the Polish affair at any cost. "What do you want exactly," asked Ciano, "Danzig or the Corridor?" "More than that," answered Ribbentrop, "we want war."

Hitler wanted to waste no more time; the die had been cast.

Citing the 1938 precedent with Czechoslovakia, Ribbentrop asserted that Great Britain and France would watch the execution of Poland without making a move. He would claim later that Great Britain had entered the war in September because she knew that Italy would not fight, and it is a fact that the British ambassador to Rome, Sir Percy Loraine, always assured his government that Italy would not intervene. In any case, Ribbentrop was convinced that even Franco-British intervention would not prevent a total victory for Germany.

Less cutting and more cordial with Ciano than Ribbentrop had been, Hitler remained unalterable in his decision. He had concluded an agreement with Italy for the removal of the German ethnic group from the southern Tyrol, which gave his policy a northern and eastern orientation and diverted any chance of rivalry with Italy. He needed the wood from the Polish forests—a need incomprehensible to a southern European. Mussolini and Hitler had to wage "the Great War" while they were still young. The fate of Danzig, the "Nuremberg of the north," would be settled by the end of August. Poland had to be destroyed rapidly because she had shown that, in the event of a general conflagration, she would certainly side with the western powers. It might have been better to be patient for two or three more years, but it was impossible to wait any longer.

The western powers would not intervene; if—an absurd hypothesis—they did intervene, it would be because they were determined to fight the Axis in any case, even without German aggression against Poland. But there would be no general conflict, and Germany would not have to ask Italy for help.

Ribbentrop did not even want to admit that the western powers would make common cause with Warsaw. Hitler himself was not totally certain that the war with Poland could be localized; but he earnestly hoped so. When Ciano pointed out on August 12 that the Italians believed that the Polish conflict would develop into a general war, Hitler replied: "It is over this point that opinions differ." He was personally convinced that, at the last moment, the western democracies would not dare bring about a general war.

On August 14, at a meeting of military leaders, he asserted: "The men I met in Munich are not the kind to begin another world war. England will make threats, recall her ambassador, perhaps declare a trade embargo; but she will not intervene militarily in the conflict."

Hitler and Ribbentrop invited Ciano to "take advantage of the opportunity presented by the Polish war" to settle the Italian dispute with Yugoslavia "in Croatia and Dalmatia." Mussolini was strongly tempted. On August 16 he ordered plans for the invasion of Yugoslavia and Greece; these plans were ready by the end of the month. The Italians made contact with Croat leaders who wanted independence. But on August 23 the Croatian leader Maček concluded an agreement with Belgrade which made him deputy prime minister, brought six Croat ministers into the cabinet, and gave a wide autonomy to Croatia. Aware of his military weakness, Mussolini abandoned the idea of intervening against Yugoslavia at the moment.

Mussolini had to endure Hitler's sudden decision to go to war. Extremely displeased at not having been informed sooner of the Nazi intentions toward Poland, he was conscious of a certain change that was gradually taking place among the Italian people, who were offended by Italy's subordination to Germany. At the last moment, Mussolini tried hard to prevent the attack on Poland. Carried away by his "intuitions," Hitler was now determined to destroy Poland, whatever the consequences. Ciano vainly urged him not to throw himself into a struggle, the outcome of which, while undoubtedly favorable in Poland, remained hypothetical with respect to the western powers, behind whom the United States would rise. After the fast annihilation of Poland, the chances for victory in a war with the western powers were only 50 percent, whereas in three years they would be 80 percent.

In three years, Franco's Spain would have recovered from the ravages of the Civil War and would be able to help the Axis. In three years, Germany would have built the powerful battle fleet she needed against Great Britain. In three years, the United States would no longer be led by Franklin Roosevelt; this "matador" of the Democrats and the democracies had no chance of being reelected for a third term as president if there was no war. All these arguments developed by Ciano on August 11 and 12 glided off the determination of Hitler and Ribbentrop "like water off marble," as Ciano wrote. "If even more were given to the Germans than they had asked, they would attack anyway . . . I realize how little we are worth in their eyes."

Hitler rejected a communiqué written by Mussolini himself about the Salzburg meeting, in which he mentioned "international talks to resolve the questions that endanger the existence of Europe."

As head of the government and holder of numerous ministerial portfolios, Mussolini allowed no one to slight his own actions. His son-in-law Ciano, fortified by the criticisms of King Victor Emmanuel and of such Fascists as Balbo and Emilio de Bono, suggested to Mussolini that he declare that Italy would not fight. The pact under which the alliance was concluded had made the Italians "partners, not slaves."

Mussolini hesitated. He sensed that the Italian people wished to remain neutral, that it was especially the desire of the financiers, the economists, and the generals, not to mention the Vatican. But he did not want to break the Axis. He thought that it was too late to foresake the Germans. He could not accept the fact that Italy seemed afraid of war, and that he should "watch from a window."

Finally he authorized Ciano to see Ribbentrop and "claim the rights of a partner." In the afternoon of August 21, Ciano telephoned his German colleague to relate his intention to meet him at the Brenner frontier. Ribbentrop declared that he could not reply immediately, because he was expecting an important message from Moscow. During that evening, he announced his departure for Moscow and proposed a meeting in Innsbruck. Mussolini and Ciano felt that it would be better to postpone the meeting until Ribbentrop returned from Moscow.

On August 23, Mussolini was informed by Hitler of the German-Soviet pact; he warmly congratulated Hitler. "There is no doubt," he told Ciano, "that the Germans have brought off a master stroke."

On August 25, he informed the Führer that "for the moment" Italy had to wait with her arms at the ready. Lack of oil and coal made it impossible for her to intervene. Her indefensible coastline might provide easy victories for the western allies. She had the most imperious needs for war materiel and primary materials. "At the time of our discussions, the war was planned for a date subsequent to 1942. At that time I would have been ready on land, on sea, and in the air," wrote Mussolini.

When Hitler asked about Mussolini's needs, he was sent an enormous list, "enough to kill a bull, if a bull could read," Ciano would later write. And to completely discourage the Germans, Attolico insisted that delivery had to be immediate.

Hitler did not insist; he had understood. Under the Pact of Steel, Italy was under the obligation to declare immediate mobilization, not to enter a war. On August 26 the Führer wrote to Mussolini that he understood his problems. "For the moment," Italy could not participate in the conflict. He was only asking Mussolini to keep his nonbelligerence secret as long as possible, and to take the military measures necessary to immobilize the largest possible number of French and English troops.

Hitler could not know when Mussolini would abandon Italy's nonbelligerence.

Efforts to Prevent British Intervention

On the "black day" of August 25, Hitler postponed the tragic deadline which he had set for August 26. First Mussolini declared that he would be unable to fight at the side of Germany "for the moment." And later, England signed the mutual assistance pact with Poland in London, two days after the German-Soviet pact had been concluded.

Hitler strove to separate Poland from the west in an attempt to isolate her through last-minute diplomatic maneuvers. He told Keitel that he "needed time to negotiate." In a supreme effort, he hoped to prevent British intervention.

On August 25, in the early afternoon, he sent for Ambassador Henderson and expressed his strong desire to reach an understanding with England. After the settlement of the Danzig and Corridor problems, which created a "Macedonian" situation in the east, he proposed an agreement through an offer as comprehensive as the one he had just made to the Soviet Union. Not only did he accept the British Empire, but he was also ready for "a reasonable limitation of armaments"; finally, he would agree that "the western fortifications marked the definitive western frontier of the Reich."

England must convince Poland "not to be unreasonable." "An artist by nature," he wished to devote himself to works of peace. But the existing situation could not continue; that very day five men had been killed. Henderson was to inform his government personally.

During the same afternoon of August 25, Hitler summoned Ambassador Coulondre and asked him to relate to Prime Minister Daladier his assurance that he had renounced all claims to Alsace-Lorraine. It would be painful for him to see the shedding of "the blood of two equally brave nations," but he could no longer endure the Polish massacres of Germans.

The English Proposal for Direct
German-Polish Negotiations

On the night of August 28, in reply to what Hitler had called "England's last chance," Henderson delivered the answer of the British government, which suggested that the Polish question should be settled through direct negotiations with the Poles. Since Hitler did not reject that proposal, Halifax telephoned Ciano: "It is still possible to plan for a peaceful settlement." On August 29, Mussolini advised Hitler to follow the path of the negotiations. At the last moment, the scale trembled between war and peace.

Hitler, who did not believe in the possibility of an agreement with the Poles, informed London on the evening of August 29 that he was ready to receive a Polish negotiator with full powers, who was to be in Berlin on the following day, August 30, before midnight. He would be offered fair proposals for the resolution of the Danzig and Corridor questions.

On August 30, no Polish emissary arrived. Beck still remembered the tragic visits paid Hitler by Chancellor Schuschnigg in February 1938 and by President Hacha in March 1939. He did not want to "cast a fly wantonly into that spiderweb," as it would be expressed at Nuremberg.

Late in the morning of August 30, mobilization posters appeared on the walls in Warsaw. Beck feared that the British government might express a decisive opinion on Polish affairs without consulting him. He did not want to send a Polish negotiator to Berlin to accept the German proposals. This represented an ultimatum, "the supreme attempt at blackmail."

Poland greatly overestimated her strength and believed that she could resist the German armies.

During the night of August 30, Ambassador Henderson succeeded in being received by Ribbentrop, now more disdainful and arrogant than ever and "imitating Hitler at his worst moments." Ribbentrop hurriedly read him a note concerning the German demands. It was no longer just a question of Danzig. Germany demanded a plebiscite on the Corridor, with voting rights for all the Germans who had left Poland in 1918 and for their children.

An international commission was to investigate the complaints of the minorities in Germany and Poland.

Ribbentrop refused to give Henderson a copy of this note, declaring that in any event it was "too late" for negotiations, since no Polish negotiator had come on August 30. Weizsäcker describes Ribbentrop as beaming when he left the ministry, calling Henderson "trash."

At two o'clock in the morning, Henderson saw his colleague Lipski. Rome considered the German proposals to Poland moderate, but Warsaw found them exorbitant. At the very instant they were put forward, they were declared lapsed and cancelled.

England and France vigorously urged Warsaw to begin direct conversations with Germany immediately. On August 31, pressured by the French and British ambassadors, Beck declared himself ready to begin negotiations with the German government, and he sent Ambassador Lipski to make inquiries at the Wilhelmstrasse.

On the same day, Halifax urged Ciano to intervene so that direct contact might finally be established between the Germans and the Poles. Harassed by Attolico, at eight o'clock in the evening Ribbentrop received Ambassador Lipski, who declared that Poland was ready to negotiate. Ribbentrop merely asked him if he enjoyed full powers to negotiate. Since that was not the case, he would inform the Führer of their meeting.

The German intelligence services had deciphered the telegram transmitting Beck's instructions to Lipski: "Avoid conducting official negotiations under any circumstances whatever." Goering had the English informed of the contents of this telegram, for like Mussolini he wished to avoid war; he advised Hitler against a "go for broke" gamble. Hitler answered: "Throughout my entire life, I have invariably played 'go for broke.'" Goering, marshal of the Reich, resorted to the services of a Swedish friend, the engineer Birger Dahlerus, who with great mystery constantly traveled back and forth by special plane between Hitler and Chamberlain.

Last Attempts for a Conference

On September 1 at dawn, the German army crossed the Polish frontier without a declaration of war.

On August 31, Ciano had proposed to Halifax that Danzig be offered to Hitler before any negotiations. The British declined that proposal, and Ciano then offered, for September 5, the meeting of a conference entrusted to revise the Treaty of Versailles. Lord Halifax replied that he would submit the idea to Chamberlain.

Now that the war had begun, the Italians, urged by the French, sounded

Berlin on the possibility of such a conference. The English demanded that Germany first evacuate the Polish territory already occupied. The Italians refused to present to Hitler an idea he would certainly reject, "perhaps with anger." Munich was not to be started over again. During the night, Georges Bonnet inquired whether it would not be possible to obtain at least a symbolic withdrawal of German forces from Poland. Ciano dropped that suggestion. The last glimmer of hope had been extinguished. The Poles began digging trenches, distributing gas masks, setting up antiaircraft defenses, and evacuating the children.

War

With incredible hypocrisy, Hitler contrived to have the war declared by the western powers—at least in the eyes of his countrymen. On September 1, England and France ordered general mobilization, and during the evening they informed Germany that they would fulfill the obligations they had assumed toward Poland if the German army did not withdraw from Polish territory.

On September 3 at five o'clock in the morning, the British ambassador to Berlin was told by London to request a meeting with the German foreign minister for nine o'clock that morning; he was to deliver to the minister a last note: if Germany did not declare within the next two hours that she was willing to answer the British communication of September 1, a state of war would be declared between the two countries.

Fearing a bombing of Paris, the French government wished to delay. A tumultuous House of Commons expressed its ill humor. In its lobbies, the Quai d'Orsay was accused of trying to avoid action. Chamberlain was extremely concerned; his nervousness was at a peak. Beck too thought that France was too slow in entering the war.

On September 3, at noon, the French ambassador informed the Wilhelmstrasse that the French government found itself under the obligation to fulfill, as of that very day, September 3 at 5 o'clock in the afternoon, the commitments France had undertaken toward Poland, which were well known to the German government. Thus did England, at eleven o'clock, and France, at five o'clock, go to war. They remained alone with Poland to face Germany.

Conclusion

Deceits and Failures

In September 1939, Hitler's wish was to achieve his dream of hegemony without firing a shot, and, as he told Goering, to renew the "Czech affair" with Poland, forcing her into vassalage without war. He would have been quite satisfied with a war against Warsaw. In the thick shadows of deceit, a small war, but one that would have soon been followed by a major war. And against whom? *Sekulär gesehen,* common assumptions, in the words so dear to Hitler and Ribbentrop.

The conquest and occupation of a large part of European Russia by the German army in 1917–18, from the Gulf of Finland to the Caucasus, developed for many Germans the idea of a vast area for colonization in the east. If, with a little more patience, Hitler had been able to limit his appetites somewhat and crush his adversaries "one after the other" according to his own plans, who knows if his dream of hegemony might not have succeeded? If Colonel Beck had helped him against Moscow, as he had so readily done against Prague, Hitler would have had a serious chance of overcoming the Soviet Union, who, after being attacked in June 1941, escaped disaster by a hair's breadth and thanks only to unbelievable sacrifices.

One of the principles of geopolitics—the pseudo-science so dear to Hitler (who, during his captivity in 1924, had assimilated a few of its arguments from a book by Friedrich Ratzel which he had found in his Bavarian prison) is that Germany, as natural master of the Ukraine, was master of Europe, and. thus "above everyone." By dominating Eastern Europe, Germany would have been in a good position to exercise a domination that could become universal. France's turn would undoubtedly have come before long; Hitler

312

could not long have remained insensitive to the cries of the "Germans of Alsace-Lorraine," and he would have repeated what he had said to Chamberlain about the Sudeten Germans: "I have decided to make war in order to free them."

Hitler's personal responsibility cannot be too strongly emphasized, when, through his own conceptions and initiatives, he made crucial decisions in international affairs. It is not to be doubted that he himself made these decisions. Of course, he was influenced, especially by a few intimates always at his side: "deputies" and "experts" of the party.

According to Colonel Hossbach, Hitler was planning, around 1935, the establishment of a government more accountable to the German people, and a certain "normalization" of the regime. To the misfortune of his own historical evolution and to the misfortune of Europe, he was supposedly diverted from that idea as from other moderate tendencies by the Nazi party, itself subject to conflicting internal factions which created a certain lack of discipline. In 1938, major quarrels existed among the Austrian Nazis, as well as among Henlein's Sudeten followers. In the United States, Ambassador Dieckhoff was irritated by the activities of Kuhn and his German-American *Bund,* just as Papen in Vienna had been exasperated by the intrigues of the Austrian Nazi leader Leopold. Finally, the activities of different parallel Nazi party organizations brought them into foreign policy matters and helped strengthen extremist tendencies, as did Alfred Rosenberg's "A.P.A." and Wilhelm Bohle's "A.O."

Anyone wishing to write the diplomatic history of the Hitler years, 1933–39, is faced with a superabundance of documents: "white papers" and other diplomatic publications in the colors of many European powers, transcripts, minutes, diplomatic notes, recollections, memoirs . . . One can argue endlessly over these texts, and to one text oppose another.

Before the gloomy drama being acted out, the negotiations drew a curtain of feints, excuses, and false pretenses.

The drama, stripped of the minor characters and of the scenery obscuring it, has the simplicity of an action in which a few characters clash in a conflict of wills. The strongest will remains that of a crafty being filled with demonical guile: Adolf Hitler, who plunged Europe and the world into a tragedy beyond measure.

Germany and England had then the leading roles in Europe. The real drama of the second road to war was played, from 1937 to 1939, between Hitler and Chamberlain, with Mussolini in the background, and Stalin coming on stage at the end.

The "go for broke gamble" Hitler had thrown himself into in August 1939, actively but foolishly followed by Ribbentrop, had failed. After unbelievable vicissitudes, the Second World War—far more global than the first, for never had a war been so widespread—ended in unprecedented catastrophe for Germany, engulfed totally after having occupied most of Europe, from the North Cape to Crete, from the Pyrenees to the Caucasus, and, having crossed the "quiet Don," defied insolently the "Mother of Russia," the *mamushka:* the Volga.

Since according to Tacitus "posterity gives each man his due," there are good reasons to believe that posterity will be guided by the judgment rendered on Hitler by one of his most intimate aides, Meissner, who was undersecretary for, successively, Ebert, Hindenburg, and Hitler—such dissimilar personalities that Meissner must have been "a monster of flexibility." Meissner denounces in Hitler a name soiled by blood and crime, a regime bound to the annihilation of millions of human lives, the destruction of German culture, and the debasement of Germany herself. Having grown into the most important figure of the 1930s, Hitler provoked the worst catastrophe in European history. He brought more calamities to the world than any other man of modern times.

Bibliographical Note

The books and publications consulted by the author are almost countless. For a selective bibliography, the reader may refer to my book, *La faillite de la paix, 1918-1939:* volume 1, *De Rethondes à Stresa, 1918-1935;* volume 2, *De l'affaire éthiopienne à la guerre, 1936-1939* (fifth edition, brought up to date in 1968).

As a supplement to this systematic bibliography, the reader may consult in the *Revue d'Histoire de la Deuxième Guerre mondiale*—published quarterly— the bibliography compiled in each issue by the Bibliothèque de Documentation Internationale Contemporaine, and especially chapter 2: "Situation internationale avant la guerre."

Index